HISTORY OF THE MIDDLE EAST

HISTORY OF THE MIDDLE EAST

A COMPILATION

The Arabs: A Short History
BY HEINZ HALM

The Ottoman Empire: A Short History
BY SURAIYA FAROQHI

Iran: A Short History
BY MONIKA GRONKE

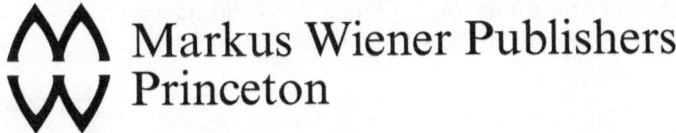
Markus Wiener Publishers
Princeton

Copyright © 2013 by Markus Wiener Publishers, Princeton, New Jersey

All rights reserved. No part of this book may be reproduced or transmitted in any form or by any means, whether electronic or mechanical—including photocopying or recording—or through any information storage or retrieval system, without permission of the copyright owners.

Cover illustration: The bazaar in Ankara; detail from a painting by J. B. Van Mour, a French artist who lived in Istanbul, 1111–50/1699–1737. Rijksmuseum, Amsterdam.

For information, write to:
Markus Wiener Publishers
231 Nassau Street, Princeton, NJ 08542
www.markuswiener.com

Library of Congress Cataloging-in-Publication Data

History of the Middle East : a compilation.
   p. cm.
Includes bibliographical references.
ISBN 978-1-55876-569-6 (hardcover : alk. paper)
ISBN 978-1-55876-570-2 (pbk. : alk. paper)
1. Middle East—History. I. Halm, Heinz, 1942- Araber. English.
  II. Faroqhi, Suraiya, 1941- Geschichte des Osmanischen Reiches.
  English. III. Gronke, Monika. Geschichte Irans. English
DS62.H675 2012
956—dc23
                    2012029581

Markus Wiener Publishers books are printed in the United States of America on acid-free paper and meet the guidelines for permanence and durability of the Committee on Production Guidelines for Book Longevity of the Council on Library Resources.

Table of Contents

The Arabs: A Short History ◆ 1

Notes on Pronunciation 3
1. Pre-Islamic Arabia 4
2. Arabia and Islam 16
3. The Arab World from 900 to 1500 CE 47
4. The Arab World from 1500 to 1800 CE 61
5. The Nineteenth Century 71
6. State Building and Independence in the
   Twentieth Century 85
7. The Beginning of the Twenty-first Century 100
Bibliography 103

The Ottoman Empire: A Short History ◆ 107

Acknowledgments 109
Pronunciation of Turkish Letters 110
Introduction 111
1. Rise and Expansion (1299–1481) 144
2. Between East and West (1481–1600) 158
3. Hard-Earned Successes and Serious Setbacks
   (ca. 1600–1774) 180
4. "The Longest Century of the Empire"
   (From Küçük Kaynarca to the End of World War I) 202

5. The Ottoman Military, World War I,
   and the End of Empire 226
In Lieu of a Conclusion: Continuities and
   New Beginnings 245
Chronology 252
Ottoman Sultans 256
Notes 258
Suggestions for Further Reading 266

Iran: A Short History ◆ 269

Introduction 271
1. The Early Islamic Period (642–1055) 276
2. Iran under the Turks and Mongols (1055–1501) 299
3. Iran in the Early Modern Period (1501–1779) 321
4. From the Qajars to the Islamic Republic
   (1779 to the Present) 338
Chronology 368
Selected Bibliography 371

THE ARABS

A SHORT HISTORY

Heinz Halm

Translated by Allison Brown
and Tom Lampert

Notes on Pronunciation

Arabic names and terms have been transliterated in a form facilitating pronunciation for English-speaking readers. The macron always denotes a long vowel. If a word has only one long vowel, this is generally also the accented syllable. The *r* indicates an *r* rolled at the tip of the tongue, and the *gh* is a glottal *g*; *k* corresponds to the English *k*, while a *q* is a throaty, dark (velar) *k* (not *qu*); *kh* is pronounced like a hard *ch* as in the German *Bach*; *th* corresponds to the voiceless English *th* in *thing*, whereas *dh* is pronounced as a voiced *th*, as in English *the*; *s* is always voiceless, and *z* is always voiced. The *h* is always an audible consonant and not used to make a long vowel (e.g., *Mahdi*).

The right half ring, ' (hamza), indicates a glottal stop, whereas a left half ring, ' ('ayn), is a voiced pharyngeal fricative that is difficult for non-Arabs to pronounce. Since it is a consonant, words such as *Ka'ba or San'ā'* have two syllables.

CHAPTER 1
Pre-Islamic Arabia

Name and Origin

Arabs call themselves *al-'Arab*, a collective term used to designate the Arab people as a whole. *Al-'Arabī* is the term for an individual member of that people. This affiliation is based first of all on the use of the Arabic language: An Arab is someone who speaks Arabic. There are approximately 280 million Arabic-speaking people in North Africa and the Middle East today, from the Atlantic Ocean to the western edge of the Iranian plateau, that is, from Morocco and Mauritania in the west to Iraq in the east, and from Syria in the north to Oman, Yemen, and Sudan in the south. This expansion of the Arab people and the Arabic language is a relatively recent historical phenomenon related to the spread of Islam beginning in the seventh century CE.

The first known use of the term Arab is found in an inscription of the Assyrian king Shalmaneser III from 853 BCE celebrating a victory of the Assyrians over the coalition of Syrian kings (including the King of Israel) at the Battle of Qarqar in Syria. According to the inscription, the Syrian coalition was supported by a contingent of a thousand camel riders of Gindibu, King of the Arabs (*Aribi*). Inscriptions of Assyrian kings from the eighth and seventh centuries BCE repeatedly mention kings and queens of the Arabs, for the most part as tributaries and auxiliary forces of the Assyrians.

The *Aribi* mentioned in Assyrian inscriptions appear to have been nomadic groups living in the Syrian Desert, in other words, on the inner margins of the Fertile Crescent (Palestine/Jordan, Syria, and Iraq). As Shalmaneser III's inscription indicates, the name *Aribi* was from the beginning tied to the use of dromedaries. As pack and riding animals but also as sources of meat and wool, these animals enabled human life in the desert steppe (*bādiya*). It is from the latter term that Arab nomads or Bedouins derive their name (*al-badawī*). Numerous Assyrian reliefs from the era of King Sennacherib (705–681 BCE) depict Arabic camel riders in battle. For the Assyrians, whose imperial claims included all of Syria, controlling the Arabs of the Syrian Desert was of great strategic importance.

There were no significant changes in the Neo-Babylonian Empire after the fall of Nineveh in 612 BCE. Nabonidus, the final king of Babylon (556–539 BCE), even continued to live for ten years in the palace he had built in the northwestern Arabian oasis of Taimā, leaving Babylon to his son Belshazzar, the crown prince. His sphere of control extended to Yathrib, which later became known as Medina. After 549 BCE, Persian kings do not appear to have ruled the Arabs directly, but rather to have sought them as allies. Herodotus reported (III, 88) that before the Persian king Cambyses conquered Egypt in 525 BCE, he obtained consent from the Arabs. Xerxes also used Arabs as archers on camelback during his campaign against Greece (480 BCE) (VII, 69; 86).

Almost all of these reports portray the *Aribi* as inhabitants of the inner periphery of the Fertile Crescent in the Syrian-Mesopotamian desert and in northern Arabia, where they initially appeared as nomadic camel herders, but also as farmers in the oases of northwestern Arabia. It is here that the name "Arab" appears for the first time (we do not know the origin of the term), and it is here as well that the (North) Arabic language—the bond that continues to unite the Arab people—has its roots.

Arabic is one of the Semitic languages, a language family named after Shem, the son of Noah, according to the Table of Nations in the Old Testament (Genesis 10) the progenitor of both the people of Israel and the Arabs. Arabic is thus closely related to the languages spoken in the Fertile Crescent during antiquity (Akkadian = Babylonian/ Assyrian, Phoenician, Canaanite, Hebrew, and Aramaic), as well as to Old South Arabian and the languages of Abyssinia (Ethiopian, Tigre, Tigrinya, and Amharic). The oldest evidence of the (North) Arabic language are brief inscriptions found at the oases extending like a chain of pearls from the south of present-day Jordan through the Ḥijāz and down to ʿAsīr. Such graffiti has been documented since the era of Assyrian rule. It was initially written in alphabets that were closely related to Old South Arabiia and that developed—like Greek and Latin—from a Phoenician prototype. The Arabic alphabet used today thus has the same roots as our Latin alphabet, even if its appearance would hardly suggest it. As this alphabet had less than thirty letters to denote spoken phonemes, it spread across the entire Middle East, replacing the much more complicated writing forms of the ancient Orient, cuneiform scripts and hieroglyphics.

Ancient South Arabia

The territory that constitutes present-day Yemen lay outside the Assyrian Empire's sphere of influence, although the kings of Sheba are occasionally mentioned in Assyrian inscriptions. With 10,000-foot mountain peaks and heavy monsoon rains, the southwest of the Arabian Peninsula is a world unto itself. The ancient landscapes here of terraced fields and stonewalled cities present a marked contrast to the rest of the peninsula. Since time immemorial, people in this area had mediated trade between the Indian Ocean and the Mediterranean. In particular, frankincense (a tree resin) extracted around Dhofār in present-day Oman was traded through the kingdoms of South Arabia to the north, where large amounts were used in temples and later in churches of the Middle East and Greece. The Incense Road led from Dhofār through several dominions that, while not producing any incense themselves, controlled and thereby profited from the trade in it: Ḥaḍramawt, and west of this Qatabān with its capital of Timna'; Sheba with its capital Mārib; and Ma'īn with its cities in al-Jawf (northeast of Ṣan'ā'). The Old Testament tells of the Queen of Sheba (almost certainly a legendary figure) who is said to have visited King Solomon in Jerusalem. Sheba and Ḥaḍramawt (*Hasarmaweth*) also appear in the Table of Nations in the Old Testament (Genesis 10).

The Kingdom of Ma'īn, which can be documented from approximately 550 to 125 BCE, extended at times into northwestern Arabia. It established a trade colony in Dedan (present-day al-'Ulā) in the fourth century BCE, and its merchants reached Egypt and Syria. At times Ma'īn fell under the rule of neighboring Sheba. Karib'il Watar, the king of Sheba from approximately 510 to 490 BCE, had his conquests immortalized in victory inscriptions. The Old South Arabic language, like modern Arabic a Semitic language, had its own written alphabet. Several thousand inscriptions provide us with insight into the culture of Sheba. Numerous large buildings such as temples have survived in the capital Mārib. However, the most important construction here was the Great Dam of Mārib, approximately 2000 feet long, which was used to dam the waters of the Wādī Adhana between two mountain ridges. A complicated system of locks and canals was used to irrigate the entire region around the capital city.

Arabia in the Hellenistic Period

Alexander the Great did not touch Arabia during his military campaign. However, Alexander's admiral Nearchus, on his return from India through Cape Musandam, did reach the northern point of what is today Oman, before leading his fleet back to Mesopotamia through the gulf. Alexander's own plans for oceanic exploration were interrupted by his early death in 323 BCE. Of Alexander's wealthy successors or Diadochi—the Seleucids in Syria/ Mesopotamia and the Ptolemaeans in Egypt—especially the latter had close ties to Arabia, as they exercised maritime control over the Red Sea. The Greeks were familiar with the southern Arabian kingdoms of Ḥaḍramawt, Qatabān, Sheba, and Ma'īn. Greek geographers mentioned their capital cities and the Chatramotitai, Kattabaneis, Sabaioi, and Minaioi peoples—the last named were the Minaeans from Ma'īn.

Most of the surviving inscriptions written in the precursors of present-day (North) Arabic were created during the Hellenistic period. This includes several thousand inscriptions, most of which are brief graffiti etched in rocks, in which travelers immortalized their presence or called for assistance from certain gods. While these inscriptions are written in alphabets derived from Old South Arabian (Sabaean), the language is clearly North Arabic and thus has been designated as proto-Arabic. The two most significant of these written forms are Lihyanic and Thamudic. Both written forms have been dated from at least the fifth century BCE up into the Common Era. Thamudic graffiti has been found throughout the entire Ḥijāz and 'Asīr, the Sinai, southern Palestine, and Transjordan.

The Nabataeans were also Arabs. Their capital city Petra was located in a rocky basin east of the Dead Sea. The first historical reports of the Nabataeans appear directly after the death of Alexander the Great. In 312 BCE, Antigonus, one of Alexander's generals, attempted to take Petra. The Nabataeans controlled the Incense Road to the east of their city. Antigonus had taken spoils of frankincense and spices in Petra, and the Roman historian Diodorus expressly noted that the Nabataeans transported frankincense and myrrh to the Mediterranean Sea. However, they also engaged in piracy on the Red Sea, which led to conflicts with the Ptolemaeans in Egypt. The Nabataeans gradually brought the entire Transjordan and southern Palestine including Gaza under their control. The Nabataean King Aretas III (in Arabic *al-Ḥāritha*, 87–62 BCE) was even able to take control of Damascus in 85 BCE. Although the Nabataeans spoke Arabic, as indicated by the names of their kings, they employed a script developed from the Aramaic alphabet for their correspondence and inscriptions. The Nabataeans' material culture was also influenced by the north, as is evident even today in the impressive Hellenistic façades of the rock tombs of Petra. The epithet of Aretas III was *Philhellenos,* or friend of Greece.

The Greeks' familiarity with Arabia during the Hellenistic period is also evident in the work of the geographer Ptolemy of Alexandria (second century BCE), which maps the entire Arabian Peninsula including the interior.

Arabs and Romans

The Roman proconsul Pompey traveled to Syria in 64 BCE in order to reorganize political relations in the Levant along Roman lines. In the preceding year, Roman troops had driven the Nabataean king Aretas III out of Damascus and occupied the city. Pompey now transformed Syria into a Roman province. In 63 BCE, Pompey himself advanced from Antioch through Damascus to Jericho and Jerusalem. He permitted the small Jewish kingdom of the Hasmoneans and the Nabataean kingdom to exist as Roman client states, content to have subjugated the Middle East to the *Pax Romana*. The subsequent Roman civil wars were often fought in Asia Minor. After Octavian (Augustus) annexed Ptolemaic Egypt in 30 BCE, Roman influence extended also to the Red Sea.

Like the Greeks before them, the Romans distinguished between *Arabia Deserta* or "Desert Arabia" and the "happy" *Arabia Felix,* Yemen. This epithet is the result of a misunderstanding of an Arabic term. For Arabs, who were "oriented" to the east, the south lay to the "right" (*al-Yaman*) and the north lay to the "left" (*al-Shām*). In contemporary Arabic these two words are still used to designate Yemen and Syria. Yemen, in other words, is actually the land "on the right side." However, "right" also means "propitious," and in this way the "land to the right" became "happy Arabia" (*Arabia eudaimon* in Greek). The name, however, could also be understood in a different sense: The luxury goods that Romans so desired came from here. According to the geographers Strabo and Pliny the Elder, *Arabia Felix* or Yemen was the Roman source for incense and myrrh, cassia and nard, silk, jewels, and pearls—that is, products not produced in Yemen itself but in southeastern Arabia or beyond the Indian Ocean and the Persian Gulf in India and China. Augustus' decision to send a military expedition into "happy Arabia" in 24–25 BCE was probably motivated above all by his desire to control trade in these goods. A Roman official, Aelius Gallus, commanded the Roman troops, ostensibly ten thousand in number. Syllaios, the minister of the Nabataean king, assumed leadership of the expedition, and the Nabataean king and the Jewish king Herod provided auxiliary forces. The troops were transported on 130 cargo ships from the Gulf of Suez to Leuke Kome (Yanbu'), and from there they made the grueling march through 'Asīr. They conquered Najrān and the cities of Ma'īn, but had to abandon the siege of Mārib after six days due to lack of water. The Roman army was forced to withdrawal with significant losses. The geographer Strabo, who was acquainted with Aelius Gallus, recorded the various stages of the march.

The enterprise was a complete disaster both militarily and politically, although there was no significant political force in Yemen at the time and city princes ruled the country. However, a new force was rising in the south of Yemen: the tribe of the Himyarites, whose capital city Zafār with the citadel Dhū Raydān (75 miles south of San'ā) now became the main city of *Arabia Felix*. Immediately after Aelius Gallus' failed campaign, old Sheba and the new Himyarites joined to form the "Kingdom of Sheba and Dhū Raydān." This new kingdom successively subsumed the smaller kingdoms of Ma'īn, Qatabān, and Hadramawt. The *Homeritae*, as the Romans called the Himyarites, ruled southern Arabia during the entire Roman imperial era. Trade relations between the two empires seem to have remained close, and the Romans never again attempted to take direct control of *Arabia Felix*.

The situation was different in northern Arabia. Here Arabs were not only the immediate neighbors of the Roman province of Syria, but they also lived in increasing numbers within the Roman Empire itself. Nomads moved between the villages on the edge of the Syrian Desert, occasionally settling permanently there or in one of the cities. Arabs trickled into the settled areas of the Fertile Crescent in the same way that Semitic-speaking peoples—the Akkadians, Aramaeans, Canaanites, and the Israelites—had done for thousands of years. Under the Seleucids, the Itureans (*Itouraioi*), who were almost certainly South Arabian, had pushed into Galilee in the second century BCE and taken control of the Beqā' plain between Lebanon and Antilebanon. Safā inscriptions, Arabic graffiti in the Safā Hills southeast of Damascus, from the first century BCE to the fourth century CE testify to the presence of Arabs there. In 70 CE, after the destruction of Jerusalem by Titus, Judea became a Roman province, and in 106 CE, Emperor Trajan also annexed the Nabataean kingdom, turning it into the Roman province Arabia. In this way, the entire western horn of the Fertile Crescent was incorporated into the Roman Empire. In the autumn of 129 CE, Emperor Hadrian visited Palmyra, Damascus, Beirut, and Petra, before spending the winter in Gerasa (Jerash in northern Jordan). Emperor Philip the Arab (244–249) was born in the Jabal al-Druze in a hamlet that he renamed Philippopolis (present-day Shahba, fifty miles southeast of Damascus), in which he built a theater and other magnificent structures.

Further northeast, the oasis city of Palmyra (*Tadmur* in Arabic), which owed its ascent as a trade city to the decline of Petra, gradually became Arabized. The rulers, who attempted to establish a vast Middle-Eastern empire between the Roman and the Parthian empires in the third century, had Arabic names: Odaenathus (*'Udhayna*), his bride Zenobia (*Zaynab*), and their son "Augustus" Vaballathus (*Wahb Allāt* = "Gift of the Goddess Allāt"). Emperor Aurelius ended the Palmyrians' imperial dreams in 272, bringing Zenobia and her son to Rome as captives.

Like Palmyra, Hatra in northern Mesopotamia also flourished in the second and third centuries as a result of its location at the border between the Roman and the Parthian empires and its function as a trade emporium. The city had a predominantly Arab population. It was not far from the Tigris (60 miles southwest of Mosul) but had never belonged to the Parthian Empire and had successfully resisted Roman legions, both those of Emperor Trajan (117 CE) and those of Septimius Severus (197 CE). Not until 240 CE were the Persians able to take the city.

Arabia between Byzantines and Persians

Two events outside of Arabia marked epochal changes for Arabs as well. In 226 CE, the Persian king Ardashir ended Parthian rule of Iran and Mesopotamia. The new ruler assumed the old title of *King of Kings*, establishing a Sassanid Neo-Persian Empire. The Parthian royal city of Ctesiphon on the Tigris (25 miles southeast of present-day Baghdad) became the residence of the new great kings. In 330 CE, the Roman Emperor Constantine established his capital city of Constantinople on the site of the old Greek city Byzantium, which became the new metropolis of the Eastern Roman Empire. As a result, the Syrian Desert and the Arabian Peninsula became an area of conflict for these two neighboring major powers of late antiquity, which clashed here in the north as well as in the south.

The Arabic Lakhmid tribe established their rule west of the lower Euphrates around 300 CE. The Lakhmid kingdom served the Persian Empire as a buffer state against the Eastern Roman Empire. The royal residence of the Lakhmids was al-Ḥīra (from the Aramaic *Herta* or "camp"; cf. Hatra), which was located south of what later became Kūfa (present-day Najaf). We know of more than twenty Lakhmid kings up to the beginning of the seventh century. The grave stelae for Imru al-Qays (died in 328), designating him as the "King of all Arabs," have been uncovered in Ḥawrān in Syria. Al-Nuʻmān I (ca. 400–418) built magnificent castles, including the fabulous al-Khawarnaq Palace near al-Ḥīra, which has survived in the legends and poems of later eras. As a vassal of the Sassanids, al-Mundhir III (ca. 505–554), a contemporary of Justinian, engaged in raids against Byzantine Syria, which brought him into the vicinity of Antioch. His son ʻAmr (554–569) is renowned as the patron of poets. At least three of the seven most important pre-Islamic Arab poets are reputed to have lived at his court. His mother was Christian and founded a monastery in al-Ḥīra. Starting in the early fifth century, there was a bishop in the city, although in all probability only the final Lakhmid king, al-Nuʻmān III (ca. 580–602), was himself a Nestorian Christian.

The Arab buffer state on the Byzantine side, in which the Banū Ghassān clan shielded the Syrian provinces from the desert, is much younger. The center of the Ghassānid kingdom was Jābiya in Jawlān (Golan), a cross between a nomadic camp and a settled city. There were also palatial buildings along the edge of the desert steppe, where the Ghassānids could receive the leaders of allied tribes. As vassals of Byzantium, they were Christians, although they belonged to the Monophysite (Jacobite) Church predominant in Syria. The Ghassānids reached the apex of their power in the sixth century. In 529, Emperor Justinian named al-Ḥārith II (ca. 529–569) *phylarchos* and gave him the title *patricius*, making him one of the highest dignitaries in the Roman Empire. Justinian prepared a magnificent reception for him in Constantinople in 563. His son al-Mundhir (*Alamundaros*) was also received at the court in 580, but the relationship subsequently deteriorated, not least because the Ghassānids refused to abandon their "heretical" Monophysite beliefs. Al-Mundhir was finally deported to Sicily and his son al-Nuʿmān was imprisoned in Constantinople. Ghassānid rule was brought to an end in 613–614, after the Sassanid king Khosrow II Parvez captured Damascus and Jerusalem. The last Ghassānid Jabala VI fought on the side of the Byzantines against the Arab Muslims in 636, but later converted to Islam.

Another battleground for the rivalry between the Byzantine and Persian Empires was Yemen. The Himyarites (*Homeritae*) had ruled over the former empire of Sheba since the third century. There was a coup around 500 CE, in which the ruling dynasty was deposed and a usurper with the epithet *Dhū Nuwās* ("he with the curl") assumed power. Dhū Nuwās was Jewish and called himself Yūsuf after the Biblical Joseph. Following the Roman destruction of Jerusalem in 70 CE, Judaism appears to have been spread by refugees and exiles along the Incense Road to the south and there also seem to have been some conversions among Arab tribes and clans. At the time of Muḥammad, three of the five Arabic tribes living in Yathrib (Medina) were Jewish. The Yemenite king Yūsuf /Dhū Nuwās is said to have to have persecuted the apparently large Christian population in his empire as retribution for Roman-Byzantine oppression of the Jews. In response, Christian Ethiopians, backed by Christian Byzantium, intervened. The negus or sovereign of Ethiopia conquered Yemen between 523 and 525, dethroned the persecutor of Christians, and established Christian Ethiopian viceroys as rulers, thus bringing an end to the Kingdom of Sheba and Himyar.

Abraha, one of these Ethiopian viceroys, is said to have built a magnificent church in Ṣanʿāʾ, almost certainly on the site of today's great mosque, the famous al-Qalīs (*ekklesia* in Greek). Another epochal date in South Arabian history occurred during his reign: the final destruction of the Great Dam of Mārib. Several dam catastrophes were reported in the fifth and sixth centuries. According to one inscription, Abraha was still able to make repairs in 542. A short time later, however, the dam appears to have burst a final time, turning the lowlands of Mārib, the heartland of Sheba, into desert. The memory of this has been preserved in sura 34 of the Qur'ān, "The Sabaean" (verses 15–17). Abraha is also mentioned in sura 105, "The Elephant": He is said to have taken part in a military campaign against Mecca, in which he served as an elephant leader. According to several accounts, the "Year of the Elephant," in which God miraculously allowed the Christian assault to fail, is also the year in which the Prophet Muḥammad was born (ca. 570).

Soon after this—the entire chronology of ancient South Arabia remains sketchy—the Yemenites rose up against Ethiopian foreign rule, calling for assistance from the Persian king. The Sassanids had already established themselves on the western side of the Persian-Arabian Gulf—numerous castles in Oman can be traced back to this time—and they did not hesitate to intervene in South Arabia, thereby bringing the entire trade along the Incense Road under their control as well. King Khosrow I Anushirvan sent an army, which drove the Ethiopians out of Yemen. The Persians installed local viceroys, who administered the southern Arabian satrapy for them. Yemen remained a Persian province for almost sixty years until the Islamic conquest.

Old Arabic Language, Poetry, and Script

Three developments in the north of the Arabian Peninsula on the inner perimeter of the Fertile Crescent during the sixth century proved constitutive for the development of the Arab world: the (North) Arabic language, the Arabic script (which emerged as part of a continuing development of the Nabataean alphabet and which appears to have been used throughout northern Arabia on the eve of Islam), and ancient Arabic poetry.

The Arabic language (al-'Arabiyya) appears to have emerged quite suddenly in the sixth century with an already highly developed form of poetry. We have no record of the formative phases that must have preceded this. Its central form was the qaṣīda (a longer ode) and it possessed over a dozen complicated quantitative meters. This rich prosody was without parallel or precursor among the Semitic languages of the Fertile Crescent. The poetry had its origins in the tribal milieu. The poet (*shāʿir*), who was believed to be inspired by spirits (*jinn*), initially functioned as a representative of his tribe and his clan, celebrating his own tribe and reviling others. Praise and censure, panegyric and satire were often the subject of the qaṣīda as well, even after its content had become more diverse. In the sixth century, the poets already appeared as self-assured individuals leading an autonomous poetic existence. The influence of poets was evident not only at the great annual markets on the Arabian Peninsula (such as in ʿUkāẓ near Mecca), where poets competed with their rivals, but also at the Lakhmid court in al-Ḥīra and the Ghassānid court in Transjordan, where the figure of the court poet and the panegyrist appeared. The poet Nābigha, for example, can be regarded as a court poet of the king of al-Ḥīra.

Poems were presented orally. The great poets of the sixth century were often surrounded by a group of reciters or *rāwī*, who ensured the dissemination of their qaṣīdas and thus of the authors' fame. Many poems of the pre-Islamic era were collected in the eighth century—several hundred complete qaṣīdas and countless fragments are extant—and were recorded in *dīwān*s (the word, taken from Persian, means "index" or "list"). Two of these collections are particularly noteworthy: the *Muʿallaqāt* (literally, "the suspended" or "hung," although the precise meaning of the title has never been clarified); and the *Ḥamāsa* ("zeal," "enthusiasm," or "courage") by Abū Tammām. The *Muʿallaqāt* is comprised of ten qaṣīdas (originally seven with three added), each from a different poet. Even today, this collection is regarded as the classic model of Arabic poetry. A rāwī from the eighth century compiled the initial seven poems that constitute the basis of the collection. Three of the odes are directed at a Lakhmid king from al-Ḥīra. The *Ḥamāsa* is an anthology of pre-Islamic poetry compiled by poet Abū Tammām in the ninth century.

Arabic is an enormously rich language. With its guttural (velar) and emphatic sounds, it possesses greater phonetic diversity than English. It also has a highly differentiated system of verb forms and an enormous vocabulary with numerous synonyms and a variety of nuanced expressions, such as for different types of deserts, physical peculiarities, age levels, and characteristics of cattle. One reason for this enormous variety might be the tendency and ability often attributed to Arabs (not without some justification) of becoming intoxicated with the melodiousness of their own language.

The Arabic script consists of twenty-eight letters, all of which are consonants. (Short vowels are not written, and long ones are only implied.) Most of these letters, however, have a different form depending on whether they appear at the beginning, middle, or end of a word, or whether they appear alone. This rich variety of letters also lends itself to ornamental decoration, which has contributed to an astonishing development of calligraphy in books as well as in epigraphy. Arabic is written in a cursive script running from right to left, although not all letters can be connected to the left. Naskh, the Arabic script primarily in use today, has rounded forms and emerged in Baghdad during the tenth century. It developed from Kufic script, an older calligraphic form with its straight lines and angles, which was named after the city of Kūfa on the Euphrates. However, in addition to a special Maghrebi script and the Nastaʿlīq calligraphy style in Iran with its slanted script (from the top right to the bottom left), there is also a variety of decorative forms of epigraphy, for example, "flowering Kūfī," whose extended letters can assume leaf and blossom-like forms. These developments, however, all occurred during the Islamic era.

CHAPTER 2
Arabia and Islam

Arabia on the Eve of Islam

There was no comprehensive political order on the Arabian Peninsula prior to the emergence of Islam. The kingdoms of ancient South Arabia were limited to the southwestern corner of the peninsula. The entire region was characterized by a tribal social order; not only the Bedouin herders were organized in tribes, subtribes, and clans, but also the sedentary urban dwellers and farmers. The population of the city of Mecca was comprised of members of the Quraysh tribe, which was in turn divided into a dozen clans, including the powerful Makhzūm and ʿAbd Shams, as well as the less influential Hāshim. The neighboring city of Ṭāʾif belonged to the Thaqīf tribe, and five Arab tribes inhabited the Yathrib oasis (later Medina). In pre-Islamic times, the tribes of the Arabian Peninsula were already organized on a genealogical basis predicated on the assumption that all tribes had descended from common ancestors. Qaḥṭān was regarded as the progenitor of the South Arabian tribes, whereas the North Arabian tribes were said to have descended from ʿAdnān. This distinction was evident in a profound antagonism between the two groups that continued to exist far into the Islamic period. Later—we do not know the precise date—the two lines were brought together in a genealogy based on the Old Testament: Qaḥṭān was equated with the Biblical Joktan, a grandson of Noah's son Shem (Genesis 10:25), whereas ʿAdnān was considered a descendant of Ishmael, the outcast son of Abraham and Hagar (Genesis 16:15). Arabs from South Arabia were regarded (or regarded themselves) as "true, pure Arabs," the *ʿāriba*, while Arabs from North Arabia were considered *mustaʿriba*, "arabized Arabs."

Although the various tribes spoke their own dialects, poets had already created a uniform high language that was evidently understood everywhere.

The annual fairs served as a means of exchange and also led to a leveling of differences. The locations of the fairs rotated throughout the entire Arabian Peninsula, and periods of a general, binding ceasefire guaranteed that they could be carried out in peace. Important meeting places were also the shrines to different gods and goddesses, such as the Ka'ba, a cube-shaped temple in Mecca dedicated to the god Hubal, and many other places of worship northeast of Mecca, which even today are sites of Islamic pilgrimages (ḥajj), of course devoid of such pagan idols.

We know of the world of the Arab gods, at least in broad outlines, through allusions in the Qur'ān and especially through *Kitāb al-Aṣnām (The Book of Idols)* by the Iraqi author Ibn al-Kalbī (737–821). According to the latter, certain tribes controlled the shrines dedicated to particular gods or goddesses, although members of other tribes were also permitted to worship them. The deities appeared as stones or as trees, whose rustling was interpreted as an oracle, and sometimes also as primitive statues of wood or stone. Certain clans were entrusted with caring for the shrines. Hubal, the main god of the Quraysh of Mecca, also appears to have been worshipped under the name *Allāh* (contracted from *al-ilāh*, "deity"). His oracle in the Ka'ba functioned through casting lots with arrows. At his side stood a "goddess," *Allāt,* whose holy district was near the city of Ṭā'if. Manāt, the goddess of fate, was embodied in a black stone on the road from Mecca to Medina, whereas al-'Uzza, the planet Venus, was worshipped in three trees in Nakhla, east of Mecca. The rituals connected with the worship of the god of the Ka'ba and the other shrines in and around Mecca also predate Islam. Stripped of their pagan contexts they were later retained by Muḥammad out of reverence to the Prophet Abraham, Hagar, and their son Ishmael, who were regarded as the shrines' monotheistic founders even in pre-Islamic times.

Pilgrimages and markets, as well as traveling minstrels, provided the first interregional connections among the tribes scattered throughout the Arabian Peninsula. Trade, which was largely concentrated along the incense road from Yemen to Syria, that is, from the Indian Ocean to the Mediterranean Sea, also connected the peninsula to the rest of the world. Although Mecca did not lie directly along this route, it was a very active trading city. The Quraysh themselves lived from trade. The annual winter and summer caravans they outfitted (sura 106:2) are mentioned in the Qur'ān and according to Islamic tradition, Muḥammad himself traveled to Syria as a young man.

Judaism and Christianity reached western Arabia in pre-Islamic times both from the north and the south. Roman-Byzantine Syria, whose eastern regions had already been Arabized in antiquity, was Christian. Yemen had been ruled by a Jewish dynasty until a Christian Abyssinian governor took over. In Najrān, there was a strong Christian community led by a bishop; in Yathrib (Medina), three of the five Arab tribes that inhabited the oasis were Jewish. Virtually nothing is known about how Judaism and Christianity spread in these regions. Contact with these two monotheistic religions, however, left very unambiguous traces in Islam. The Qur'ān is full of stories about Noah and Moses, the ancient patriarchs Abraham, Isaac, Jacob, and Joseph, King David and King Solomon, and the Prophet Jonah, although there are very few direct references to Christianity. While there does not appear to have been either a Jewish or a Christian community in Mecca, Islamic sources do tell of the ḥanīfs, a kind of monotheistic God-seekers without ties to either of the older religions, but no longer satisfied with the faded world of the ancient Arab gods. The Prophet Muḥammad, in other words, emerged in an environment that was by no means unprepared for his message.

The Prophet Muḥammad

Islam is without a doubt a constituting element of the Arab world, at least in the early Islamic period, when the notions of Arab and Muslim largely coincided. According to the Qur'ān, God often says: "These (*letters*) are proofs of this profound scripture. We have revealed it, an Arabic Qur'ān" (sura 12:1–2; see also 41:1 and 43:1). Only the Arab-speaking segment of humanity is addressed in this particular divine revelation, which in another form, by other prophets, and in other languages had already been revealed to other peoples. The Qur'ān "is a scripture that confirms, in Arabic," the mission of other prophets, such as Moses (sura 46:12). The notion that Qur'ānic revelation possessed a universal mission and validity appears to have developed only later.

Born around 570 as a member of the Hāshim clan in the Quraysh tribe in Mecca, Muḥammad was orphaned at an early age and like many

Meccans first earned his livelihood as a trader. As an associate and trustee of the wealthy widow Khadīja, he is said to have accompanied a caravan to Syria. There he carried on business, whereupon Khadīja—about fifteen years his senior—married him. After receiving his divine revelation around 610, when he was about 40 years old, he appeared as a prophet (in Arabic *nabī*, similar to the Hebrew *navi*) of a monotheistic faith that forebode a Judgment Day, thereby vehemently rejecting the ancient polytheistic religions of Arabia. In Mecca, the Prophet was able to gather only a small band of followers. The leading clans in the Quraysh tribe, which feared for their influential position and their income from the pilgrimages to the Ka'ba and other holy shrines in the environs of Mecca, were hostile to Muḥammad and his mission. They harassed his companions and even threatened him. Consequently, in 622 the Prophet and his companions made an emigration (*hijra*) to Yathrib (later al-Madīna), about 250 miles northwest of Mecca, referring to themselves as "ones who submit (to God)" (*muslimūn*) and to their faith as "submission" (*islām*) to God's will. The two non-Jewish tribes there had made an agreement with Muḥammad prior to this.

In Yathrib/Medina, the Prophet went from being a persecuted outsider to the powerful leader of an ever-growing community, whose cohesion was guaranteed by the profession of faith in the one God and loyalty to their prophet, rather than by kinship relations and occasional confederacies that existed up to then among Arab tribes. This new community (*umma*) competed with the traditional tribal order of society, although it was not yet in a position to replace it. It was open to all tribes and clans and was also considered indissoluble, as it was traced back to God himself.

During the tens years he was in Medina (622–632), Muḥammad managed to expand the Islamic *umma* virtually throughout the entire Arabian Peninsula. Numerous tribes—both sedentary and nomadic—voluntarily joined the community, which became increasingly powerful. Jews and Arab converts to Judaism living in the oasis of Khaybar in the Ḥijāz mountains agreed contractually to subordinate themselves to the *umma*, as did the Christian community in the bishopric seat of Najrān in northern Yemen. Yemen, which was ruled by the Persians, was won over, as was Muḥammad's hometown Mecca. There, the pagan aristocracy initially fought against the Prophet, with varying results, until the opposing pagan clans of the Quraysh finally decided their future was more secure in the *umma* than in opposition to it. They opened up to the Prophet and converted to Islam in 630. When Muḥammad died two years later, the entire Arabian peninsula was associated with the *umma,* that is, almost all Arabs were united in Islam. This loyalty, however, was tied to Muḥammad personally and was rescinded after his death by some tribes, where their own prophets now appeared. Muḥammad's successor Abu Bakr (632–634) was able again to subjugate the renegades through military force and end the "apostasy" (*ridda*).

The Arab-Islamic Conquests

Only two major kingdoms existed in antiquity and usually opposed each other as rivals: In the west there was the Hellenistic world with the later Roman-Byzantine empire, and in the east, the great Persian empire under the Achaemenids, Parthians, and Sassanids. The Islamic *umma* added a third actor to the political stage for the first time. A state emerged where there had previously been none. It quickly began to expand and—similar to the other two—developed into an imperial power.

During the decade in which Muḥammad led the *umma* in Medina, preliminary structures for a state had already been created: the basic features of a system of law that bound the tribes together, a class of administrators sent from Medina, and the rudiments of a system of tributes and taxes. The tribal order of society was not simply abolished as a result, but new "state" structures were superimposed on it.

The political and military elite in the new polity were exclusively Arabs. For this reason, the historian Julius Wellhausen titled his classic description of early Islamic history *The Arab Kingdom and Its Fall* (1927, German 1902). The core of the new elite were Muḥammad's original fellow sufferers and comrades in arms, the first Muslims. The first four caliphs, or "successors" (*khalīfa*), also came from their ranks: Abū Bakr (632–634), 'Umar (634–644), 'Uthmān (644–656), and 'Alī (656–661), Muḥammad's cousin and son-in-law. All four were members of the Meccan tribe of the Quraysh, who had been distinguished by their religious merit, in particular by their early profession of faith in the new religion (*sābiqa*). All four had also participated in Prophet's hijra, that is, they were "emigrants" (*muhājirūn*). In comparison, the Muslims of Medina, the "helpers" (*anṣār*), receded into the background very early on. None of them became a caliph, although they did at times raise such claims. Rather quickly, however, Mecca's old pagan elite of money and power reasserted its authority even within the Islamic *umma*, pushing out the class of religious meritocrats. The Umayya family, belonging to the Quraysh clan of the 'Abd Shams, assumed the leading role in this. Once a bitter enemy of the Prophet and his mission, they now joined the vanguard in the military expansion of the new state. The Quraysh aristocracy can be seen as one of the driving forces behind the ensuing conquests (*futūḥ*, literally "openings"). Their trade interests had already led them to Syria during the pre-Islamic era. It has been documented that a number of Meccans owned manors in eastern Syria even prior to the conquest. The Umayyad Mu'āwiya, a son of Muḥammad's former adversary Abū Sufyān, played a significant role in conquering Palestine and Syria. As a reward he was appointed governor of Damascus, a position he held for twenty years. His power base was in Syria, and from there he opposed the selection of the fourth caliph 'Alī. After 'Alī was murdered in 661, he was able to claim the title of caliph for himself and establish Damascus as the new capital.

The military expansion of the caliphate began under the second caliph, 'Umar, and quickly led to the conquest of Roman-Byzantine Palestine/Syria and Persian-Sassanid Mesopotamia (al-'Irāq). In 636, a Byzantine army was defeated at Yarmūk, a left-bank tributary of the Jordan, after which the Byzantine army abandoned Syria. Almost all of the cities of Palestine and Syria surrendered in exchange for more favorable conditions: protection of life and limb, guaranteed property, the continued existence of churches and protection of their property, and the free exercise of religion. In return, the cities paid a tribute, usually in the form of a lump sum. This was later converted into a poll tax (*jizya*) on non-Muslims. According to these treaties, non-Muslims were given the status of "wards" (*dhimmī*). Under these conditions, Damascus surrendered in 635, Jerusalem in 638, Caesarea in Palestine in 640, and Alexandria in 642, bringing all of Egypt under Arab-Islamic rule. The contractual partners of the caliph were the Christian patriarchs and bishops, who were the only remaining public authority once the Byzantine military withdrew.

The decisive battle in Mesopotamia took place against the Persian imperial army around 636 near al-Qādisiyya, west of the lower Euphrates.

Directly following this, the Arabs occupied Ctesiphon, residential city of the Great King on the left (eastern) bank of the Tigris (today Salmān Pāk, southeast of Baghdad). Arab Muslims also defeated the Persians in another battle at Nihavend in western Iran in 641 or 642, paving the way for the conquest of the Iranian highlands.

The rapid expansion of the caliphate is an astounding phenomenon that has been explained in various and at times contradictory ways. The most stubborn cliché, although long challenged by historians, is that of zealous masses setting off to conquer the world in order to spread Islam through fire and sword. However, it is difficult if not impossible to reconstruct the motives of actors at the time, as Arabic sources available to us were all compiled from oral tradition long after the events took place. The Qur'ān itself does not express any explicit missionary aims, nor do we have any evidence of a political program of conquest.

Reports about the initial conquests—which are chronologically confusing and uncertain—tell of individual bands of Bedouins who were and had always been active on the borders of the Fertile Crescent and who were encouraged to further endeavors by their momentary successes. The Arab conquests thus appear initially to have remained within the framework of a continuous process in the Fertile Crescent beginning in the third century BCE: the steady and at times wavelike expansion of Semitic-speaking Bedouins from the Syrian Desert—the Akkadians, Canaanites, and Aramaeans. Soon, however, these Arab incursions assumed a completely new dimension and quality, which is apparent in the fact that they expanded far beyond the Fertile Crescent—into Iran, Armenia, and Asia Minor, as well as into Egypt and North Africa. This development can be traced to the imperial desires of the new power center in Medina, although it appeared to have sought only gradually to coordinate the actions of independent armies at the peripheries of the Fertile Crescent. Most of the military leaders came from the Meccan Quraysh and the Medinan helpers (*anṣār*), whereas the rank and file soldiers were predominantly from Bedouin tribes associated with the *umma* who were interested above all in booty. One-fifth of the spoils were traditionally reserved for the caliph, who assumed the role of the pagan tribal sheikh. Later, after state structures had been established, the central government became the recipient and distributor of the regular tax revenues.

The conquests in Palestine and Syria were secured by quartering the individual troop divisions in the larger cities; in Mesopotamia, Egypt, and North Africa, on the other hand, military encampments were set up, which gradually developed into permanent cities: al-Basra in 635, al-Kūfa on the Euphrates in 638, al-Fusṭāṭ (Old Cairo) on the Nile in 641, and al-Qayrawān (Kairouan) in present-day Tunisia in 670. The soldiers (*muqātila*) stationed there were organized according to tribal groups, camping and fighting under their own leaders. They received payment (*'atā*) from their regional commander (*amīr*), drawn from spoils and tribute and later from the regular taxes and duties. Like the old religious meritocrats and their descendants, the warriors of the individual tribes also received fixed shares of the endowments entered in an army list or *dīwān* ("list, register" in Persian). The "warriors"—initially only Arabs and Muslims—were thus the beneficiaries of this fiscal system based on taxation of the non-Muslims. The need to subjugate an increasing number of taxpayers to finance a steadily growing Muslim army was certainly one significant motive for the expanding conquests. The capture of the Iranian highlands and central Asia was initiated from the military encampment cities of Basra and Kūfa and continued independently from there. The Maghreb and the Iberian peninsula were taken by armies from Kairouan.

The system described above emerged during the conquests and lasted as long as the conquests continued, into the seventh and eighth centuries, then becoming obsolete. This was the basis of what Julius Wellhausen referred to as the "Arab Kingdom": the imperial rule of Muslim Arabs over non-Muslim non-Arabs. Nowhere were non-Muslims compelled to convert to Islam; the guarantee of protection (*dhimma*) for non-Muslim subjects became an established part of Islamic divine law (*sharī'a*). Mass conversions, after all, would have undermined the financial basis of the dīwān system. It was only gradual change that led to the fall of the "Arab kingdom." Although the religious motive for expanding the Arab empire might be merely one of many, we should not underestimate the role that religion played as the link between the rulers and as the legitimation for their rule. It was not the conversion of the non-believers, but the rule of Muslims over them that was regarded as God's will.

The Caliphate of the Umayyads (661–750)

Caliph Muʿāwiya (661–680) was able to ensure the succession of his son Yazīd (680–683) and thus start a dynasty that would rule the Arab empire for ninety years. This marked the definitive establishment of the old aristocracy of the Quraysh in Mecca over the religious meritocracy of young Islam. This rule, however, did not remain unchallenged. In the next generation, descendants of the companions of the Prophet asserted their claims against Yazīd, which led to a bloody intra-Muslim conflict (*fitna*, "strife, trial"). Al-Ḥusayn, son of ʿAlī and grandson of the Prophet, was killed in 681 at Kerbela (Karbalāʾ) while trying to incite a rebellion in Iraq. He became the first martyr of the oppositional party of the Shiʿites. The sons of al-Zubayr, a companion of the Prophet, were able to set up a counter-caliphate in Mecca that survived until 691. There continued to be uprisings after this, especially by ʿAlid pretenders against the established caliphate.

In the meantime, the Umayyad ʿAbd al-Malik (685–705) was able to bring down the Meccan counter-caliphate and reestablish the unity of the empire. He was the most important Umayyad caliph and set in motion a number of significant reforms. Most important was the standardization of administrative language. From that point on, the language used in records and on coins was Arabic instead of Greek, which until that time had been used in the western part of the empire, and Middle Persian (Pahlavi), which had been used in the east. A standardized form of written Arabic was thereby established. The foundation inscription in the interior of the Dome of the Rock in Jerusalem, a glass mosaic frieze, is the oldest extant Arabic monumental inscription. It is at the same time the earliest material evidence of Qurʾān verses. The Dome of the Rock (*Qubbat al-ṣakhra*), which marks the site of the Prophet Muḥammad's ascension to heaven, bears the foundation date of 691. Its inscription addresses non-Muslims, especially Christians, strongly admonishing them to adopt the strict monotheism of Islam. The meaning of this oldest Islamic monumental construction is disputed. One possible motive was the desire to have something comparable to the splendid Christian Church of the Holy Sepulcher; another might have been the dynasty's wish to demonstrate its own power. ʿAbd al-Malik initiated a comprehensive construction program for the project, which was completed by his son and successor al-Walīd I (705–715): The al-Aqsa Mosque (*al-masjid al-aqṣā,* "the farthest mosque," as referred to in the Qur'ān, sura 17:1) was built along the axis of the Dome of the Rock, although it has not survived in its original form. The Umayyad Mosque, which was modeled on this, still exists in Damascus at the site of the Church of St. John, the former Jupiter temple. The buildings of the residence of the Prophet in Medina, in whose inner courtyard he was buried, were replaced by a new, magnificent mosque. The main mosque in al-Fusṭāṭ (Old Cairo) was also rebuilt. With these projects, in which Syrian-Byzantine and Coptic artists played an important role, 'Abd al-Malik and al-Walīd created the seminal examples of Islamic monumental architecture and Islamic architectural decoration.

The conquests continued under the rule of the Umayyads. Although an initial siege of Constantinople (Istanbul) failed in 674–678 and a sea operation against Constantinople in 717–718 was equally unsuccessful due to the Byzantines' use of Greek fire, broad regions in both the west and the east were conquered. In 711, an army of Arabs and Berbers led by Ṭāriq crossed the Strait of Gibraltar, the rock beside which henceforth was known as *Jabal Ṭāriq,* or "Ṭāriq's Mount," ending the rule of the Visigoths on the Iberian peninsula. At the same time Arab troops advanced into the Indus delta in present-day Pakistan. In present-day Uzbekistan, Bukhara was conquered in 710 and Samarqand in 715. While the Arabs did take the most remote Iranian city, Chach (Tashkent) in 751, this victory ultimately weakened the conquest movement. Even the incursion of a Spanish-Arab force into France, widely discussed in Europe, was brought to a halt between Tours and Poitiers by Charles Martel in 732 and appears in fact to have been nothing more than a foray for spoils, targeting the wealthy St. Martin's Abbey in Tours. In the end, France was not conquered, even though Roussillon and parts of Languedoc and Provence were temporarily subject to Arab rule. The counter-movement by Christian forces to reconquer the Iberian Peninsula (*Reconquista*) already began under Charlemagne.

The final decade of Umayyad rule was characterized for the most part by weak and short-lived caliphates as well as by internal conflicts. The last significant ruler, Hishām (724–743), one of 'Abd al-Malik's many sons, managed to hold the empire together. Central power was maintained from the Pyrenees to central Asia. The Caspian Gates, the passes at the eastern end of the Caucasian foothills, were fortified against a Turkish invasion from the northern steppes. Like his father and brother, Hishām was also a great builder. Numerous "desert castles" of the Umayyads can be traced back to him; they were used for controlling the Bedouins as well as for the agricultural development of the desert steppes and for hunting lodges. The ruins of Qasr al-Hayr al-Sharqī northeast of Palmyra clearly have the dimensions of a palace city. A wealth of stucco carvings has been preserved from Khirbat al-Mafjar in the Jordan valley, not far from Jericho, including a statue of the caliph (currently kept in the Rockefeller Museum in Jerusalem).

The Umayyads maintained their domestic rule through alternating support from northern and southern Arabian tribes. The Islamic *umma* had never been able to overcome the regional differences. The "Arab empire" ultimately fell, in part because it was unable to integrate the growing circles of people who wanted to be part of the *umma*. Islam claims to be egalitarian: All Muslims are said to be equal before God. In reality, however, not only did older tribal structures with their particular loyalty relationships remain intact, but new groups that joined the *umma* had difficulty asserting themselves over the established elites. In addition to the Meccan emigrants (*muhājirūn*), there were the Medinan "helpers" (*anṣār*), followed by the Meccans who had retained their pagan beliefs to the end and the Arab Bedouin tribes that had been won over or subjugated and then integrated into the *umma*. And finally there was a growing number of converted non-Arab Muslims, who had a client relationship with the ruling Arab elites and were there- fore called *mawālī* ("clients"). The dehgans, the Persian knightly nobility, quickly converted to Islam almost en masse, bringing their vassals and tenant farmers with them. As auxiliary military troops and as local authorities and tax collectors, they were indispensable to the Arabs and were thus allowed to retain their old privileges, although the Arab aristocracy refused to grant them equal status.

Arab tribal units in dispute with the central government over the distribution of spoils and tax revenues incited a rebellion, in alliance with the Iranian *mawālī*, which started in the most remote northeast corner of Iran in 747 and ended in 750 with the conquest of Iraq and the taking of Damascus. This opposition was also backed by Shiʻite groups, who regarded the Umayyads as parvenus and believed that the ʻAlids, the descendents of Muḥammad's cousin and brother-in-law ʻAlī, were the sole legitimate successors to the Prophet. Later Arab historiography has accused the Umayyads of lacking religious legitimacy, claiming that they debased the caliphate into a secular kingdom (*mulk*), although this is a religiously colored judgment that historians need not accept. The caliphate of the Umayyads of Damascus was one of the most splendid epochs in Arab history. Court literature and monumental architecture reached an apex and the political power of the Umayyad caliphate, which reached from southern France to the Indus, was never again achieved. The fall of the dynasty brought the dissolution of the caliphate only 120 years after the death of Muḥammad.

The 'Abbāsid Caliphate of Baghdad

With the fall of the Umayyads in 750, which is referred to as the "'Abbāsid revolution," a dynasty came to power that would occupy the caliphate for more than half a millennium, until the Mongol invasion of 1258. The 'Abbāsids were the descendants of 'Abbās, an uncle of Muḥammad, and were thus closely related to the Prophet—in contrast to the Umayyads. Muḥammad's direct blood descendants, the 'Alids, who initially supported the overthrow of the Umayyads, were again left empty-handed. Their supporters, the "party" (*Shī'a*), now became a fixed part of the opposition.

The revolutionary army that had brought down the old regime through its march from central Asia to Iraq and on to Syria and Egypt was comprised primarily of discontented Arabs. Although the new dynasty was Arab and Qurayshi, like its predecessor, the exclusivity of the "Arab empire" could never be reestablished. Persian "clients" had played a significant role in the coup, and men from their ranks began assuming important positions in the army, administration, royal court, and in spiritual life. A geographical shift, which included the establishment of a new capital, accelerated this process. The new rulers remained in Iraq and, after some consideration, decided to establish a new imperial residence and palace city near the old town of Baghdād on the west bank of the Tigris, calling it Madīnat al-Salām, the "City of Peace." Al-Manṣūr (754–775) was the second 'Abbāsid caliph. Around 758 he started building a circular grounds based on a Persian model, with a palace and mosque in the center. At the perimeter, inside the surrounding wall, there were government offices (dīwāns) and residences for officials and functionaries. The army was quartered outside the city. The Round City of Manṣūr, which has disappeared without a trace, was completed in 762. Markets soon developed at the four arterial roads leading out of the city. These grew into suburbs, so that the palace facility quickly expanded into an actual city. The caliph and his successor also built a number of castles on both banks of the Tigris in 773, which served as residences instead of the Round City. Under Caliph Hārūn al-Rashīd (786–809) and his son al-Ma'mūn (813–833), the metropolis encompassed a densely populated area of almost four square miles with an estimated population of almost one million. It was the largest and most populous city in the world at the time.

Around this time, changes became evident in the court of the Baghdad caliphs. While the Umayyads in Damascus and in their desert castles acted like powerful Arab tribal sheikhs, the ceremonies of the 'Abbāsids in Baghdad increasingly assumed the splendor of Great Kings in Middle-Eastern antiquity. Hidden away in his Round City far from the masses, the caliph had contact only with privileged people. Like the Sassanid Persian king and the Byzantine emperor, he held audiences concealed behind a curtain, his rank emphasized by his crown or diadem (tāj), a crown that hung over his head by a chain (shamsa), or other precious insignias. In addition to their first names, caliphs assumed an epithet when they were crowned, such as al-Mansūr (the Victorious), al-Rashīd (the Upright), and al-Ma'mūn (the Trustworthy). A special feature of 'Abbāsid rule was the emergence of the office of the vizier (wazīr = "helper"), who served as a kind of chief administrator, controlling and coordinating the major government ministries (dīwāns)—taxes, army, and chancellery—and directing domestic and foreign policies. Even before the office had been firmly established, the Iranian Barmakid family from the area of present-day Afghanistan—Yaḥyā ibn Khālid and his sons al-Faḍl and Ja'far—exercised almost unlimited power in Baghdad during the first seventeen years in Hārūn's reign, until the caliph forcibly removed them in 803.

The caliphate began to shrink after the 'Abbāsid Revolution. Once Islamic rule became rooted in the provinces, the differences between provincial interests and those of the central government became increasingly apparent. The extremely long distances made communication, and thus direct administrative control of the peripheries, difficult. Baghdad was no longer able to support the armies necessary to hold together the huge empire between the Pyrenees and the Indus.

Rule was regionalized according to two models. The first was the establishment of states independent of Baghdad. Arab warriors on the Pyrenean peninsula refused to recognize the new dynasty. In 756 they took in a fugitive Umayyad prince who had escaped the massacre of his family and who was able to establish himself as the "commander" (*amīr*) of al-Andalus—that is, the Islamic Iberian Peninsula—and pass on his rule to his descendants. In present-day Morocco another refugee, Idrīs, a descendant of the Prophet, was able to gain the support of the Awrāba. This Berber tribe had occupied the Roman city of Volubilis and helped Idrīs to power. Fez (Fās), founded by Idrīs in 789, was expanded in 808 by his son Idrīs II. Other Arab refugees from Andalusia and Kairouan made the city into the first Arab settlement in the midst of the Berber tribes of the western Maghreb.

The other model was practiced in Kairouan starting in 800. This Arab garrison town in present-day Tunisia was occupied in 761 by an 'Abbāsid army and made a subject of Baghdad. Caliph Hārūn al-Rashīd installed Ibn al-Aghlab, an officer in this army, as a governor and military commander (*amīr*) in 800. He founded a *de facto* independent gubernatorial dynasty, the Aghlabids (800–909). With the approval of the caliph, who remained the nominally recognized commander in chief, Ibn al-Aghlab governed over the central Maghreb and Sicily, which was conquered between 827 and 878. The emir paid the caliph an annual tribute and, as a sign of the caliph's supremacy, agreed that he be named at the invocation to close Friday sermons (*khuṭba*) and on coins (*sikka*). Similar dynasties headed by governors nominally subject to Baghdad were later established in Egypt as well as in eastern Iran and central Asia, greatly limiting the actual power of the caliphs in Baghdad. The conquests came to a halt and, despite numerous campaigns, Byzantine Asia Minor could not be conquered in the name of Islam.

Al-'Arabiyya: High Arabic Language and Literature

Baghdad bookseller Ibn al-Nadīm compiled a "catalog" (*fihrist*) in 988, indexing all the authors he knew and their works. He reported that more than one hundred shops of book scribes and booksellers could be found on a single lane of the bazaar in the capital of the caliphate and that he knew of a Baghdad bibliophile who hoarded the manuscripts of six generations of learned authors in a chest: on parchment, Egyptian papyrus, Chinese paper, and leather scrolls, all of which had been marked with the name of the author and certified. Ibn al-Nadīm listed more than six thousand book titles in his "catalog," which was by no means limited to Muslim authors. He was particularly interested in Greek philosophers.

The Islamic conquests not only expanded the horizons of the Arabs immensely, but also provided them with access to new technologies. Following a battle between Arab troops and Chinese border guards at the River Talas (in present-day Kyrgyzstan near the border to Kazakhstan) in 751, it was discovered that several paper producers were among the Chinese prisoners of war, who had been settled in Samarqand. Paper production soon became a local industry in eastern Iran and was brought to Baghdad by al-Faḍl, a Barmakid, in 794, quickly spreading westward from there. Paper was one of the prerequisites for the incredible production of Arabic literature that began in the ninth and tenth centuries. Another was the existence of the metropolis of Baghdad and the court of the caliph, which served not only as a crossroads and gathering point for influences from the four corners of the known world, but also as a place where science and literature were valued and promoted.

Arabic literature of the 'Abbāsid period developed above all from religious writings. An unprecedented amount of information, which until that time had been passed down primarily in oral form, was collected and put down in writing. During the final years of the Umayyad period, Ibn Isḥāq (died ca. 767) of Medina had already compiled the hagiography (*sīra*) of the Prophet Muḥammad. His work has survived in an abridged edition by Ibn Hishām of Basra (died ca. 830). Al-Wāqidī (747–823), a protégé of Caliph Hārūn al-Rashīd and the Barmakid Yaḥyā, collected the chronicles of Muḥammad's military expeditions and campaigns (*al-maghāzī*). His secretary Ibn Sa'd (784–845) compiled the biographies of the Prophet and his companions, as well as those of the most important personalities of subsequent generations, into what is today a nine-volume work. All of these authors were "clients," *mawālī*, that is, non-Arab Muslims. Ibn al-Kalbī of Kūfa (737–821), whose *Book of Idols* includes extensive information about ancient Arab gods and their shrines and rites, lived in Baghdad for a time under the caliph al-Mahdī (775–785).

Kitāb al-kharāj, a treatise on taxation written for Caliph Hārūn al-Rashīd by Abū Yūsuf (died in 798), a Baghdad judge, marks the beginning of Arabic legal writings. Abū Yūsuf was a student of the great Iraqi legal scholar Abū Hanīfa of Kūfa (died in 767), whose mausoleum in Baghdad remains a Sunnī pilgrimage site to the present day. The Sunnī legal schools (singular *madhhab*), which continue to exist even today, emerged from the student circles of Abū Hanīfa, the Medinan Mālik (died in 796), the Palestinian al-Shāfi'ī (767–820), who died in Egypt, and Ibn Hanbal (780–855) of Baghdad and were a prerequisite for the flourishing, extensive production of Islamic legal writings, which today fill entire libraries with their fundamental treatises, commentaries, and supercommentaries.

A short time later the traditionaries also started their collections. At first they compiled the oral traditions, usually short, anecdotal reports about the sayings and decisions of the Prophet Muhammad, which had become increasingly important in legal, theological, and political debate beginning around 700. They reviewed the sayings according to a criteria of authenticity they themselves had developed and recorded them systematically in written form. The most notable collector of these traditions, or *Hadīth* ("events"), was al-Bukhārī (810–870), a scholar of Persian descent from central Asia, who traveled to Baghdad, Mecca, and Egypt "in search of knowledge" (*fī talab al-'ilm*). The Sunnīs regard his *Sahīh* ("The Authentic"), containing 2762 hadiths, as the most important religious work after the Qur'ān. The other five Sunnī standard collections of the Prophet's traditions from this era emerged in a similar way, by means of extended travels in order to collect such materials. By and large they were written in Arabic by Iranian or central Asian men. In addition to the Qur'ān and its commentaries, it was primarily these collections of traditions and legal works that allowed classical High Arabic to spread to the remotest corners of the caliphate after having been standardized in Basra and Baghdad.

This growing interest in the history and early period of Islam helped to strengthen the sense of cohesion among Muslims, whether they were of Arab descent or not. The first recountings of historical events occurred orally in the form of individual tidings (*khabar*), which were then recorded during the 'Abbāsid period in written form in chronological collections, as was done for the sayings of the Prophet as well. The oldest preserved chronicle is one by Khalīfa ibn Khayyāt (died in 854), a Basran. The history of the Arab-Islamic conquests was compiled in Baghdad by al-Balādhurī (died in 892), a man of Persian descent. The zenith of early 'Abbāsid historiography is *Ta'rikh al-rusul wa al-muluk* (*The History of Prophets and Kings*), a chronicle of the world from creation to the author's present, written by the Iranian Ṭabarī (839–923). This mammoth, thirteen-volume work follows his travels to Syria and Egypt using older collections in Baghdad, providing most of our knowledge about early Islamic history.

In addition to these works related to Islam, the belles lettres also developed. This genre was unambiguously secular in nature and was written and read not by the religious scholars (*'ulamā'*), but by the courtiers and officials of the dīwāns, the "secretaries" (*kuttāb*). The apex of courtly poetry can be found in the poems of Abū Nuwās (died in 815), a Persian "client" at the court of Hārūn al-Rashīd and his son al-Amīn, who despite his Persian background was and continues to be celebrated by Arabs as one of their greatest poets, although his verses, which rebound in wine, women, and song, certainly have not found the approval of pious religious scholars. The most significant writer of entertaining secular prose (*adab*) which was often based on translations from Middle Persian is al-Jāḥiẓ (776–869), a member of a "client" family from Basra. His satires and *Kitāb al-bukhalā'* (published in English as both *The Book of Misers* and *Avarice and the Avaricious*), his polemics and his encyclopedias, such as *Kitāb al-ḥayawān* (*The Book of Animals*), remain peerless examples of Arab prose even today. Finally, it was during the era of Hārūn al-Rashīd and the Barmakids in Baghdad that the oldest Arabic core of *1001 Nights* was written.

This rich literary life gave rise to High Arabic, or *'Arabiyya,* as Arabic grammar is also a product of 'Abbāsid Iraq. The first important Arab grammarians and lexicographers, Sībawayh (died 786) and al-Khalīl (died 791), lived and worked in Basra. Although this interest in grammar originally arose from a religious desire to understand enigmatic passages in the Qur'ān as precisely as possible, a purely scholarly interest in the subject quickly developed as well. The Basra school, in contrast to the Kūfa school, attached great importance to standardizing the language, seeking to adapt the rules of the proper, high language, or *fusha* ("most eloquent, purest"), to the Bedouins' exemplary use of language, which was considered especially pure. Classical *'Arabiyya,* the high language, emerged between the eighth and tenth centuries in Iraq from the mutual influences of spoken language, literature, and standardized grammar. Even today it continues to unite all Arabs.

The Arab Reception of Antiquity

High Arabic, which assumed its standardized form in Baghdad and Basra, was also understood by educated classes in Samarqand and Bukhara, in Cordoba and Toledo, regardless of whether they were of Arab descent or not. 'Arabiyya offered a means of communication that was used from the Chinese border to the marches of France, facilitating a cultural exchange that the world had seen only once before, during the Hellenist age. Arabic now took the place of Greek, as Islam replaced Hellenism. Although Arabs were able to conquer neither Asia Minor nor Constantinople and Greece, three of the most important Hellenist metropolises did come under their control: Seleukeia on the Tigris, Antiocheia (Antioch), and Alexandria. Alexandria no longer had the central role in science that it had occupied well into the fifth century, but the heritage of antiquity was still very much alive throughout the eastern Mediterranean realm, and it was eagerly appropriated by Arabs. The story that the second caliph, 'Umar, destroyed the library of Alexandria is merely a legend.

According to tradition, the Caliph al-Ma'mūn (813–833) reported that Aristotle once appeared to him in a dream: "A man with light, reddish skin, a high forehead, thick eyebrows, a bald head, dark blue eyes, and handsome features was sitting at a lectern." The caliph turned to the great scholar and questioned him. Encouraged by this encounter, he then began collecting Greek manuscripts and having them translated into Arabic. This legend is a symbolic representation of an actual process that continued over several generations. Aramaic-speaking Christians—who comprised the vast majority of the caliph's subjects in the Fertile Crescent—were particularly responsible for the survival and transmission of the heritage of antiquity. Much of Greek literature had already been translated into Aramaic, and translations into Arabic were usually completed through this intermediate step. The first known translator into Arabic was a Christian, Yaḥyā (Yuḥannā) al-Bitrīq ("Patrikios"), who translated numerous medical works as well as Ptolemy's *Tetrabiblos,* purportedly commissioned by Caliph al-Manṣūr (754–775). His son, who was also named Yaḥyā, converted to Islam and was the protégé of a vizier of the caliph al-Ma'mūn. The younger Yaḥyā started translating the works of Aristotle: *On Heavens, Meteorology, History of Animals, Politics,* and the basic work on logic, the *Organon.* He also translated Plato's *Timaeus,* which investigates the nature of the physical world.

In 830, al-Ma'mūn opened his famous *Bayt al-ḥikma,* the House of Wisdom, which was not a university, as is sometimes claimed, but a library hall, whose constantly growing inventory of manuscripts was accessible to scholars. The caliph also sponsored translations into Arabic. A Syrian Christian, Yūḥannā ibn Māsawayh, was the first director of this institute. He was succeeded by Ḥunayn ibn Isḥāq (Latinized as Johannitius), son of a Christian apothecary from al-Ḥīra, the ancient capital of the Lakhmids on the Euphrates. He is said to have learned Greek in Alexandria and improved his Arabic in Basra. As a young doctor he entered into service for al-Ma'mūn and remained active under Caliph al-Mutawakkil (847–861). Ḥunayn is the most important translator of the Baghdad School. He translated from Greek primarily into his native Aramaic, and less often into Arabic. He is responsible for the Arabic translation of numerous treatises of Galen and other ancient physicians such as Hippocrates, Rufus of Ephesus, and Paul of Aegina. He also translated works of the pharmacologist Discorides, the geographer and astronomer Ptolemy, the mathematician Archimedes, and Plato and the Neoplatonists Porphyrios and Alexander of Aphrodisias. Ḥunayn died in 873, but the Baghdad school of translation continued into the tenth century, supported by caliphs, viziers, and other high-ranking officials. In 991 or 993, Shapur ibn Ardashir, the Persian vizier of Caliph al-Rāḍī, founded a House of Knowledge (*dār al-'ilm*) in the Baghdad suburb of al-Karkh. It contained a library with more than ten thousand volumes and was also open to foreign scholars staying in Baghdad.

Arab interest in Greek texts was selective. Only works of prose were translated, in particular those dealing with scientific or philosophical subjects. Literature—epics, drama, and lyric poetry—was completely absent. Most of Plato's dialogues remained untranslated as well. Aristotle, in contrast, was regarded as "the philosopher" par excellence; and everything that came after him—especially the extensive works of Plotinus and the Neoplatonists—was associated with him. The Greek words *philosophos* and *philosophia* were borrowed in Arabic as *faylasūf* and *falsafa*, as were countless terms from the fields of medicine, botany, pharmacology, and astronomy.

The significance of the Arab reception of antiquity is twofold. In the first place, it enriched and expanded intellectual life in the Islamic world. On this basis, a philosophy arose that was independent and Arabic—albeit only "Islamic" to a limited extent. Its first representative was al-Kindī (ca. 800–870), the descendant of an Arab family from Kūfa, who was a protégé of the caliphs al-Ma'mūn and al-Muʿtaṣim (833–842) and a teacher to one of the latter's sons. Kindī's system was greatly influenced by Aristotelian and Neoplatonist thought. The philosopher al-Fārābī (872–950), a Turk from Transoxania, also resided in Baghdad and later in Syria. The physician and philosopher Ibn Sīnā (Latinized as Avicenna, 980–1037) was born in Bukhara and lived and taught in many cities in Iran. His central texts, *Al-Qānūn (The Canon of Medicine)* and the philosophical *Kitāb al-Shifā' (The Book of Healing)*, came to be standard works, not only among Arabs, but soon in the Christian western world as well. The religious scholars (*ʿulamā*) of Islam always suspected that Greek philosophy was heretical, although they often employed Aristotelian logic in theological disputes. The natural sciences, on the other hand, were adopted without reservation and developed further. The "ancient sciences" (*al-ʿulūm al-qadīma*) were added to the canon of the religious—that is, Islamic—sciences as a matter of course.

The Arab reception of antiquity, however, proved to be as important for the Christian Western world as it was for the Arabs themselves. While monastery libraries did contain Latin texts, Greek literature existed at most in Latin translation. The mediating role played by the Arabs here was invaluable. Texts from antiquity translated into Arabic found their way to western Europe, above all via the Iberian peninsula. After Charlemagne took Barcelona in 801, the creation of the Spanish March (Marcia Hispănica) in Catalonia brought the Franks in close contact with the "Saracens," as Christians called Muslim Arabs. The name comes from the Greek term *Sarakenoi*, an Arab tribe on the Sinai Peninsula. Gerbert d'Aurillac, a scholar and cleric who later became Pope Silvester II (999–1003), spent three years in his youth studying in the Catalonian bishopric of Vic and in the nearby Ripoll monastery. There he used Arabic sources to develop his knowledge of mathematics and astronomy, using primarily astronomical instruments such as the astrolabe and the armillary sphere. The Christian reconquest of Toledo in 1085 by King Alphonse VI of Castile created another site where Europeans encountered Arabic literature. The circle of Archbishop Raimund I (1126–1151) was responsible for extensive translations from Arabic into Latin, performed by learned clerics from all over Europe. In addition to Michael Scot and Robert of Ketton (Robertus Ketenensis), Herman of Carinthia, also known as Herman Dalmatin, worked there as well. Peter the Venerable, the abbot of Cluny, encouraged Robert to prepare the first Latin translation of the Qur'ān, a project that was completed in 1143. While the conquest of Jerusalem during the first crusade in 1099 had sparked interest in Islam, scholarly interest independent of the church's missionary aims emerged quickly. Aside from the Qur'ān, Robert also translated Al-Khwārizmī's *Algebra* into Latin in 1145. Central among those works of antiquity that reached the Christian Western world through Islamic Spain were those dealing with mathematics and astronomy. Arab-Islamic scholars also produced independent contributions of their own, such as the astronomical tables of the Spaniard Maslama al-Majrīṭī ("of Madrid," died ca. 1007), which were rendered into Latin in 1126 by English scholar and cleric Adelard of Bath. About fourteen years later, the tables of the elder al-Battānī (Albategnius), which were based on observations made in Mesopotamia around 900, were translated by Plato of Tivoli. Gerhard of Cremona translated the *Toledan Tables*, which are based on observations by many Muslim and Jewish astronomers of Spain, including al-Zarqālī (Arzachel). Copernicus cited Albategnius and Arzachel in his major work *De revolutionibus orbium coelestium (On the Revolutions of the Heavenly Spheres)*, focusing on their corrections of Ptolemy.

The Andalusian Aristotelian Ibn Rushd (Latinized as Averroēs, 1126–1198) of Cordoba exercised perhaps the greatest influence on Western philosophy. After his extensive oeuvre was translated into Latin, it triggered a wave of Aristotelianism throughout Western Europe. It was in fact through Averroēs that the Western world was introduced to Aristotle, and even Thomas Aquinas was forced to critically address the Latin Averroism.

Arabic Numerals and the Zero

During his studies in Vic and Ripoll in Catalonia from roughly 967 to 991, Gerbert d'Aurillac, later Pope Silvester II, was one of the first Western scholars to become familiar with "Arabic" numerals and how to do arithmetic with them. The Romans, in contrast to the Greeks, had also used a numerical system, but it was poorly suited for arithmetic computation. The Arabs, on the other hand, had a much more practical and versatile tool for writing numbers, composed only of glyphs for the digits one to nine and the zero. It is the same system—except for a few graphic modifications, in particular a ninety-degree rotation—that continues to be used throughout the world today as "Arabic numerals." The Arabs themselves referred to this method of numerical computation as "Indian arithmetic," which suggests that they presumed the system originated in India. What was unique about this system was the use of decimal positions and the related use of a special sign as a placeholder, the zero—*ṣifr* in Arabic, "empty"—which corresponds to the words *cipher* or *zero*. The Sumerians and Babylonians also used a decimal place value system and eventually even developed a sign for zero, but their system was never popularized. The Indian system had probably already spread to Iran during the late Sassanid dynasty. In India itself, the astronomer Aryabhata (ca. 476) had worked with nine ciphers, and the mathematician Brahmagupta (598–665) had developed arithmetic rules that used a zero. The Iranian Muḥammad al-Khwārizmī (from Khwārizm, the inland delta of the Oxus/Amu Darya, south of the Aral Sea) is responsible for the general widespread use of the system. In 820 he wrote his fundamental work *Al-Khwarizmi on the Hindu Art of Reckoning*, which describes the basic arithmetic operations and setting up of equations. The treatise introduced the system and thus made it practicable throughout the Arab world. The work became known in the West in its Latin translation as *De numero Indorum* and in an adapted form as *Liber Algorismi de pratica arismetrice*. The Latinized form of Khwārizmī is *Algorismus*, which led to the coining of the mathematical term "algorithm." Another work by Khwārizmī was even more sig-nificant: *al-Mukhtaṣar fī ḥisāb al-jabr wal-muqābala* (*The Compendious Book on Calculation by Completion and Balancing*). *Al-gabr* or *al-jabr*—literally the "setting" of a dislocated bone—actually refers to the completion or transposition of terms from one side of an equation to the other, whereas "balancing" refers to what we normally call "reduction." When Robert of Chester (Robertus Castrensis) translated this work in 1145 under the Latin title *Liber al-gebras et almucabola* and a short time later Gerhard of Cremona prepared an improved translation entitled *De jebra et al-mucabola,* the way was paved not only for "Hindu reckoning" in the West, but also the term for it: algebra.

Arabization and Islamization

The caliphate established the framework for two related but clearly distinct processes: linguistic Arabization and religious Islamization, which did go hand in hand with one another, but occurred at different tempos and with varied success in the various countries. Neither process was ever definitively concluded.

Arabic, the language of the Qur'ān and thus of divine revelation, became the language of all religious and juristic writings. Under Caliph 'Abd al-Malik (685–705) it became the sole official language; under the 'Abbāsid caliph of Baghdad it was also established as the language of scholarship, spoken by scholars and the educated from Samarqand to Toledo and from the Caucasus to Yemen. In addition, during the conquest period the Arab army had carried their language to distant garrisons, where it initially existed in scattered linguistic enclaves, such as Old Cairo in Egypt or Kairouan in present-day Tunisia, isolated from the surrounding indigenous language environments.

On the Arabian Peninsula, the North Arabic of the Ḥijāz rapidly replaced Old South Arabic. North Arabic, which is now generally referred to simply as Arabic, is also spoken in Yemen today. Old South Arabic has survived only in small communities there: Mehri on the mainland and Soqotri on the island of Socotra in the Indian Ocean. Both of these languages have preserved the grammatical structures of Old South Arabic, but their vocabularies are now North Arabic to a great degree.

Within the Fertile Crescent, Arabic eclipsed Aramaic, which had been the local language since about 1000 BCE, spoken by all groups in the population regardless of their religious faith. It showed particular resistance to change as the language of the literature and liturgy of the Christian churches—the Syrian Jacobite as well as the Nestorian Church in the former Persian empire. Aramaic is spoken even today by Christians in Syria in the area around Ma'lūlū north of Damascus and among the "Assyrian" or "Chaldean" (Nestorian) Christians in the border triangle of Syria, Iraq, and Turkey.

Iran, on the other hand, resisted Arabization. Although there as well, Arabic was the language of Islamic literature, philosophy, and science, the Semitic language, which is starkly distinct from Indo-Germanic Middle Persian, was never adopted by the Iranian populace. Although powerful Arabic-speaking colonies were established in the aftermath of the conquest, (New) Persian nevertheless became the national language of literature beginning in the tenth cen-tury, initially for lyric and epic poetry, and soon afterward for secular prose as well. Vizier al-Bal'amī produced a Persian translation and edited version of Ṭabarī's great chronicle of the world in 963, and around 995 Ferdowsi wrote the *Shāh-nāmeh (Book of Kings)*, which became the Persian national epic. Ibn Sīnā (Avicenna) also wrote scientific prose in Persian and verse in both Arabic and Persian. In preserving its national language and traditions, Iran remained outside of the Arab world.

In Egypt, the use of Arabic was long limited to the al-Fusṭāṭ (Old Cairo) military camp and a number of garrisons such as Alexandria or Aswān, whereas in rural regions the old languages of the pharaohs were spoken in their most modern form, Coptic (Arabic *qifṭī* or *qubṭī,* meaning "Egyptian"), and maintained as the language of literature and liturgy of the Coptic church. Because Arabic, rather than Greek, was introduced as the official, administrative language and was the only language the authorities permitted, it soon became the spoken language as well, especially among the educated classes. Today Egypt is an Arab country; Coptic is used only in church liturgy and is no longer understood even by Christians.

Libya and the Maghreb comprised the Latin, western part of the Roman Empire. Latin was the language of the urban populace and the Catholic Church. Large segments of the population, peasants and Bedouins alike, however, spoke those languages referred to jointly as "Berber"—literally, "barbarous." There had been a steady decline in the number of Roman cities in North Africa since the third century, causing the Latin-speaking urban population to diminish. Consequently, the Arabs encountered only moderately urbanized landscapes when they conquered the region at the end of the seventh century. Here, too, al-Qayrawān (Kairouan), the military settlement from the period of conquest, and smaller urban garrisons were the locus of Arabization. While the military was continually supplemented and reinforced with advancing troops, the rural population remained Berber and retained their own languages. The first major immigration of entire Bedouin clans and tribes did not occur before 1050, when the government in Cairo took the tribal branches of the Hilāl, Sulaym, and Ma'qil, who had become nomadic in Upper Egypt east of the Nile, relocated them across the river, and unleashed them on the apostate Maghreb. In 1052 the Bedouin armies defeated the emir of Kairouan at Jabal Haydarān in southern Tunisia and, as a contemporary chronicler noted, inundated the entire country "like a swarm of locusts." This marked the beginning of an unremitting flow of immigrant Arab Bedouins into the Maghreb, as the various tribes and clans followed their relatives from the Sinai and the Arabian Peninsula. The actual extent of Bedouin devastation in the former Roman Africa, Numidia, and Mauritania is disputed among scholars. While the immigrating Arab tribes destroyed neither cities nor roads and bridges, their advance resulted in the unambiguous displacement of Berber nomads, especially the Zenāta tribe, from Algeria's high plateau, which became grazing areas for Arab Bedouins. The Berbers were forced into the mountains, where they continue to live today as farmers and semi-nomads. Whereas only remnants of Berber-speaking peoples can still be found in Libya and Tunisia, the Kabyles (from Arabic *qabīla*, "tribe") in Algeria make up thirty percent of the population. The westernmost region of present-day Morocco was the least Arabized; here the Berber-speaking population survived primarily in the high mountains of the Atlas range and the Rif, where they comprise about forty percent of the population today. The Bedouin invasion reached as far south as Mauritania. The Arabic dialects of the Maghreb are those of the immigrant Bedouins.

The Iberian Peninsula remained largely Latin-speaking, even under Islamic rule. Only a segment of the immigrants were Arabs; over the course of the centuries, Berbers made up a much larger proportion. Nevertheless, *al-Andalus*, as the entire peninsula was called (presumably a Visigothic word), was part of the Arab world. The southern half of the peninsula was most strongly influenced by the foreign religion, culture, and language, due in part to the Christian *Reconquista* advancing from the north. Whereas

Barcelona returned to Christian rule as early as 801, Toledo in 1085, and Zaragoza in 1118, Cordoba remained Islamic until 1236, Sevilla until 1248, and Granada until 1492. The linguistic influence on Spanish (Castilian) can be recognized even today in the numerous borrowings from Arabic. While the rivers in the north have retained their ancient names: Ebro, Duero/Douro, and Tajo/Tejo, those in the south have Arabic roots, as is evident in their compounding with the word *al-wādī:* Guadalupe, Guadiana, Guadalete, Guadalquivir (*al-Wādi al-kabīr,* "the great river").

Sicily (*Siqilliya*) was part of the Arab world for a much shorter length of time. The Tunisian Aghlabids' conquest of the Byzantine island lasted from 827 to 878. Palermo (*Bālarm*), the seat of the Arab emir, was called *al-Madīna* ("the city"); Taormia became *al-Muʿizziyya*. Numerous locations have retained their old Arabic names, such as Marsala (*Marsā ʿAlī*) and Caltabellotta (*Qalʿat al-ballūṭ,* "fortress of the oak"). Even the Arabic name for Mount Etna, *al-Jebel* ("the mountain"), has been incorporated into the local name for the mountain, Mongibello. Linguistically the island appears to have been largely Arabized. In any case, Greek disappeared entirely when the island was re-Christianized and then completely Latinized following the Norman conquest (1060–1091).

The process of religious Islamization should be distinguished from that of linguistic Arabization. Although the two were parallel developments, there are important distinctions between them.

In Iran and Iraq, the Zoroastrian "state church" of the Sassanids perished with the fall of the Persian empire. The fire temples were destroyed or fell into ruin. This development was probably the result of the rapid conversion to Islam by the dehgans, the Persian knightly nobility. When almost the entire aristocracy converted en masse to the new religion, the rest of the populace followed. It is certainly significant that—in contrast to the Christian churches—the priestly hierarchy here simply ceased to exist. The "magicians" (*majūs*), as the Arabs referred to the Zoroastrians, were able to enjoy the status of *dhimmīs,* since they were monotheists and considered "People of the Book," as were Christians and Jews. A large portion of Zoroastrian scripture was not codified until the early Islamic period, especially under the ʿAbbāsid caliphs. All of this, however, did not prevent the almost complete disappearance of Zoroastrianism. Only small communities have survived to the present, primarily in central and eastern Iran. There is also a Parsi (i.e., Persian) minority on the Indian subcontinent.

In contrast, the Nestorian church, which was officially recognized in the Persian empire, continued under caliphate rule. The primate of the church, the Catholicos, established his seat in the newly founded city of Baghdad, playing an important role at the court of the caliph as the officially recognized head of his church. Remnants of the Nestorian church, which calls itself the "Assyrian" or "Chaldean" church, are present today especially in northern Iraq and across the borders to Turkey and Iran. There are numerous Christian churches in Mosul on the Tigris, which is the seat of both a Jacobite bishop, or maphrian, and the Chaldean (Nestorian) metropolitan. The Jews, who had been residents of the country since the Babylonian captivity (597 or 586 BCE), were of course also "People of the Book." The Babylonian Talmud originated here. During the Sassanid dynasty the seat of the Jewish exilarch or "head of the exile" (Arabic *Ra's al-jālūt*), from the lineage of David, was in Ctesiphon. The exilarch later resided in Baghdad, where—like the Nestorian Catholicos—he was an esteemed member of the caliph's court.

In contrast, followers of the religion founded by Mani (215–277), which started in Iraq, were persecuted and systematically murdered by Muslims. The Manichaeans were dualists and therefore were regarded with suspicion by the strictly monotheistic Muslims. The severe persecution by the 'Abbāsid caliphs between 780 and 795 destroyed Manichaeism. The seat of their leader—originally in Babylon—was moved in the late tenth century to Samarqand, where many Manichaeans had immigrated. Manichaeans are known to have still been living in central Asia into the fourteenth century, where their trail disappears. Numerous Gnostic sects and groups that were often simply referred to collectively as Manichaeans suffered a similar fate in Iraq. Only a small Baptist sect of the Mandaeans has survived in the marshy regions of southern Iraq.

As former provinces of the Roman-Byzantine empire, Syria, Lebanon, Palestine, and the Emirate of Transjordan—always referred to by Arabs as a single country, *al-Shām*—were Christian lands with Jewish and Samaritan minorities. They long retained this status even under the Muslim Arab rule, and to the present have maintained both the Monophysite Syrian ("Jacobite") and the Greek Orthodox ("Melkite") churches with their patriarchs, metropolitans, and bishops, and numerous churches and monasteries.

The Church of the Holy Sepulcher in Jerusalem was always in Christian hands—except for a short interim between 1009 and 1020 under the Fāṭimid caliph al-Ḥākim. The Maronite church of Lebanon, named after the Syrian monk Maron (ca. 400), did not become independent until the eighth century under Islamic rule. A Uniate church, the Maronites are today the largest Christian group in Lebanon with their own patriarch.

In Egypt, the Arab-Islamic conquest ended the predominance of the Greek-Orthodox (Melkite) church, thereby alleviating the indigenous Monophysite Coptic (that is, Egyptian) church from extreme hardship. From then on the Coptic patriarchs of Alexandria led the Christians not only of Egypt, but also of Nubia, Sudan, and Ethiopia (Abyssinia). The new Arab metropolis of al-Fusṭāṭ (Old Cairo) became a bishop's seat. Egypt's population remained largely Christian, probably into the fourteenth or fifteenth century. Though the precise point in time cannot be determined, the scales began to tip as a result of a steady influx of Muslims—soldiers, officials, and Bedouins—and the attractiveness of Islam as the prevailing religion and the religion of the rulers. There was also occasional gentle pressure from above, especially on Coptic officials, who had dominated tax administration for centuries. Today the Coptic segment of the Egyptian population is estimated at about ten percent.

Christianity in the Maghreb—in contrast to Egypt and the Middle East—disappeared entirely, along with the Latin language. The Roman Catholic church offered less resistance, perhaps in part due to the gradual dwindling of Roman cities since late antiquity. The city of Thamugadis (Timgad) in present-day Algeria was already destroyed by Berbers in 485. The last bishop of Sitifis (Sétif) was mentioned in 525; the last one of Cuicul (Djemila), in 553. All of this happened long before the Islamic conquest, which perhaps merely continued, or even accelerated, a process that had been going on for centuries. In the late tenth century there were still forty-seven bishoprics in the Maghreb, fourteen of them in the southern part of present-day Tunisia. In 1095, however, Pope Leo IX lamented in a letter to the bishop of Carthage that "in all of Africa" only five bishoprics were still occupied. A short time later the Catholic church as an organization must have vanished entirely from the Maghreb, although St. Louis IX, King of France, did encounter a few Christians in Carthage on his crusade in 1270.

Al-Andalus, the Iberian peninsula, is a special case insofar as the Christian *Reconquista* started here immediately after the Islamic conquest. As a result, Islamic influence on the peninsula was gradually forced southward and in the thirteenth century limited to present-day Andalusia. The situation of the non-Muslim minority was no different here than in North Africa and the Middle East. Islam was the prevailing religion; Christians and Jews enjoyed the protected status of *dhimmīs*. There is no evidence that the atmosphere here was particularly tolerant or liberal in comparison to Asia Minor and the Middle East. The "Alhambra Islam" frequently invoked by present-day authors is more utopian fantasy than historical reality. Nevertheless, minorities here were not treated more harshly than they were elsewhere. There were Jewish and Christian viziers and high-ranking officials here, as well as non-Muslim scholars.

The *Reconquista* had different consequences in the regions of Spain and Portugal that returned to Christian rule. In the eastern kingdom of Aragón the nobility was more tolerant with its new Muslim subjects, well aware of the economic repercussions their expulsion or extermination would bring. In contrast, the influence of the church and the orders of knighthood—the most important supporters of the conquest movement—prevailed in Castile, where policies of complete re-Christianization through forced baptism or expulsion were enacted. When Granada was conquered in 1492 by the "Catholic Kings" Ferdinand and Isabella, this policy was implemented throughout all of Spain under the influence of Cardinal Cisnero. There were revolts by Arabs and Berbers of Andalusia who were forced to convert but secretly remained faithful to Islam. This led to the decrees of 1609 to 1614 by which King Philipp III expelled all of the "Moriscos" from the peninsula. With them—almost 300,000 people—Islam and Arab influence disappeared entirely from the Iberian peninsula. Aside from Sicily, this was the most significant loss the Arab world was forced to accept.

The Mamluks

In the ninth century, an innovation developed in Baghdad under the 'Abbāsids that had enormous military, social, and political consequences for the Islamic world: the emergence of the military caste of the Mamluks.

The Arabic word *mamluk* is a passive participle of the verb "to own." A Mamluk therefore is someone owned by someone else, a slave. The word came into use for a new kind of soldier. This phenomena is specific to the Islamic world and exerted a decisive influence there far into the modern era. When Napoleon landed in Egypt in 1798, he was confronted by an army of Mamluks.

It was Caliph al-Muʿtaṣim (833–842), a son of Hārūn al-Rashīd, who in 815 was the first to purchase Turkish slaves from central Asia when he was a prince. He gave them military training and used them as soldiers in his guard. In 832 he already had a core group of 4000 slave soldiers; after acceding to the throne he continued to buy slaves on a grand scale. They came from the nomadic Turkish tribes of central Asia, that is, from present-day Uzbekistan, Turkmenistan, and Kazakhstan, and were sold primarily at the market in Samarqand, where they were purchased by agents of the caliph. The young men, removed from their families and homeland, developed a personal loyalty to their new owner. Unlike the Arab soldiers, who had previously comprised the armies of Islam, they had no tribal ties. The new troops, however, proved to be such an impediment in the metropolis of Baghdad and so onerous to citizens that in 836 the caliph established Sāmarrā, a new residence on the Tigris about seventy-five miles northwest of Baghdad, for himself and his new army. The next seven successors also resided there, expanding the Turkish army and the city, whose ruins extend today about thirty miles along the banks of the Tigris, making it one of the world's largest archaeological sites.

The new army soon developed a dynamic of its own. The soldiers imported as slaves were set free after a certain period of time and were then able to rise to the ranks of officers and generals or obtain positions in offices at court or become provincial governors. Al-Muʿtaṣim ensured that soldiers were supplied with Turkish slaves as wives, so that the troops increased in number not only through purchases but through births as well. In Sāmarrā itself the army must have ultimately comprised about 20,000 men.

The disadvantages of this system, inherent to all praetorian guards, soon became apparent: The first generation of liberated slaves attained high offices and distinctions and began acting as kingmakers. They installed and deposed caliphs at will, even murdering them on occasion. When the ʿAbbāsid caliphate threatened to sink into anarchy, Caliph al-Muʿtamid decided to move the court back to Baghdad in 892.

This new type of military continued to prevail, although it was never used exclusively. There were always units of free mercenaries as well from all over the world: Kurds, Iranian Daylamites from the southern shores of the Caspian Sea, Berbers or Arab Bedouins as light auxiliary troops. The Mamluk type of soldier, however, dominated not only the military, but also the political world—not only in Sāmarrā and Baghdad, but in Syria and Egypt too. Soon the kingmakers became kings themselves. In many countries, including Afghanistan and India, former slaves and their descendants assumed power and founded Mamluk sultanates. The most important of these was the Egyptian sultanate, which will be discussed below. In Spain and North Africa, the soldier slaves were not of Turkish, but of eastern European descent and were sweepingly referred to as "Slavs" (ṣaqāliba, sing. ṣaqlabī). They were brought primarily from across the Adriatic Sea.

The emergence of the Mamluks is significant primarily because for centuries they provided the Arab world with military and political elites who were of non-Arab origin and who, even if they adopted the Arabic language, retained an awareness of their foreign traditions. In the last millennium up to the present day, it has been more an exception than the rule that reigning houses in the Arab world were of Arab descent.

CHAPTER 3

The Arab World from 900 to 1500 CE

The year 909 CE marks an epochal year in the history of Islam. A caliphate was established in Tunisian Kairouan in that year that for the first time could challenge and rival the 'Abbāsid caliphate in Baghdad on a long-term basis. The Fāṭimid dynasty, which claimed (albeit disputedly) to be direct descendants of Muḥammad's daughter Fāṭima and Caliph 'Alī, was able with the support of the Berbers to assume control of present-day Algeria. In 910, 'Abdallāh al-Mahdī, who had previously campaigned for himself in the underground, appeared openly in the city of Kairouan and assumed the title of caliph. His caliphate (909–934) was the first of an extremely successful dynasty that challenged not only the religious and political claims of the 'Abbāsids in Baghdad to be Muḥammad's heirs; the Fāṭimids' Shi'ite Isma'īlī sect of Islam also offered a religious alternative to the ruling Sunnīs. In 929, the Umayyad emir of Cordoba 'Abd al-Raḥmān III (912–961) also assumed the title of caliph. This meant that three "successors"—two Sunnīs and one Shi'ite—each claimed the exclusive heritage of the Prophet Muḥammad. The disintegration of the caliphate, which had in fact been long in the making, was now officially sealed.

Iraq

Mesopotamia, the land of the Tigris (*Dijla*) and the Euphrates (*al-Furāt*) rivers, consisted of two different landscapes for Arabs: the actual *al-'Irāq*—the name probably means "low lands" or "flat country"—in the southeast; and *al-Jazīra*, the "island," in the northwest between the middle reaches of the two rivers. The military camps of al-Baṣra and al-Kūfa, which had been established by Arabs, and the caliphate capital of Baghdad were located in

Iraq. After the founding of Baghdad, Seleucia-Ctesiphon (*al-Madā'in* or "the cities" in Arabic), the ancient royal city of the Parthians and the Persians, diminished increasingly in significance. Babylon had already disappeared as a city even before the Islamic conquest. The metropolis of the north was Mosul (*al-Mawṣil*) on the Tigris, across from the ancient ruins of Nineveh.

As the seat of the 'Abbāsid caliph, the metropolis of Baghdad long remained the center of the Islamic world. After the turmoil in Sāmarrā and the emergence of the western caliphate, however, the political significance of the caliphs in Baghdad increasingly declined. While the 'Abbāsid caliph in Baghdad continued to rule without interruption until the Mongol invasion in 1258, only isolated representatives of this dynasty actually governed themselves and then only as a kind of Iraqi territorial prince. The Baghdad caliphate was repeatedly subject to the tutelage of military "patrons," who usurped political power and—equipped with formal legitimation from the caliphs—exercised the real power for them. The focus of such rule lay primarily in Iran. Iraq was often little more than a western province of Iran.

The first patrons of this kind were the Būyids (932– 1055), a widely branched Iranian condottiere family that established a series of dominions (Shiraz, Isfahan, Hamadan, Kerman) in western Iran and also seized power in Baghdad in 934. For 110 years, Būyids administered a protectorate over the caliphates, formally as commanders-in-chief (*amīr al-umarā'*) of the army, but in reality as sovereign rulers. They did not even eschew assuming the ancient Persian title of great king or emperor (*Shāhānshāh*, "king of kings"), which is completely antithetical to Islam. While the caliph had always been a Sunnī, the Būyids were Shi'ites and vigorously promoted members of this faith. A large portion of the Shi'a religious writings arose under their aegis. The burial places of their imams, which had been pilgrimage sites for Shi'ites for centuries, were expanded into magnificent shrines and received elaborate endowments: the grave of 'Alī in al-Najaf near Kūfa; the grave of the third imam (the Prophet's grandson al-Ḥusayn) near Karbalā'; the double grave of the seventh and ninth imams in al-Kāẓimiya in the north of Baghdad as well as the graves of the tenth and eleventh imams in Sāmarrā; and the site at which the twelfth imam is supposed to have disappeared into "occultation" and from which he is expected to return.

The Būyids were overthrown by the Seljuqs, a Turkish dynasty that had forayed into Iran as the leaders of a wandering tribe of Turkish nomads from Central Asia. In 1038, their leader Toghril Beg had himself proclaimed sultan in eastern Iran, transforming the word *sulṭān*, which actually means "ruler," into a title. As the protector of Sunnī Islam, he compelled the Baghdad caliphs to officially recognize him and then appeared in Baghdad in 1055 with his followers to accept this recognition. The capital of the "Great Seljuq" Empire, however, was Isfahan in Iran, while Baghdad was left to the powerless caliphs.

With the Seljuq dynasty, Turks or Turkmen appeared for the first time in the Islamic world not as imported military slaves, but as larger tribal groups. A steady flow of Turkish tribes now moved westward through northern Iran. In 1071, the Turks succeeded where Arabs had continually failed: After defeating the Byzantine Emperor Romanus IV Diogenes at Manzikert (present-day Malazgirt north of Lake Van), the Seljuqs overran what had been Greco-Christian Asia Minor.

Although Baghdad lost its political significance under the Seljuqs, it remained a cultural center with enormous appeal and influence, particularly after the Seljuq vizier Niẓām al-Mulk (1065–1092), an Iranian, established a madrasa, a legal, theological institution of higher education based on Iranian precursors, and appointed the famous Sunnī theologian and mystic al-Ghazālī (1058–1111) as the institution's first professor. A large number of similar institutions quickly arose in Baghdad. The Mustanṣiriyya, founded by Caliph al-Mustanṣir in 1233, is today Baghdad's best-maintained monument from the pre-Mongol era. The work by the Sunnī jurist and preacher al-Khaṭīb al-Baghdādī (1002–1071) offers an excellent example of intellectual life in the caliphate capital during this period. His *Chronicle of Baghdad* (*Ta'rīkh Baghdād*)—actually a lexicon of scholars—comprises fourteen volumes with entries on no less than 7,831 people active in the intellectual life of the city.

Even after the gradual disintegration of the Seljuq empire, Baghdad remained a strategic object in particular for eastern rulers, even if individual caliphs such as al-Nāṣir (1180–1225) were occasionally able to exercise their own rule on a regionally limited basis. The invasion of the Mongols, however, brought all of this to an end. In 1235, Hulagu Khan, grandson of Genghis Khan and brother of the Mongolian Great Khan Mongke, was ordered to subjugate the caliphate. When Caliph al-Musta'ṣim (1242–1258) refused to comply with official demands to support the Mongols with an army, the Mongols overran Iran from the Oxus (Amu Darya) and attacked Iraq. In January 1258, the Mongols were outside Baghdad. The caliph, his vizier, and the Nestorian Catholicos—Hulagu's mother was Christian—attempted in vain to negotiate. On February 10, the Mongols forced their way into the city and began to burn, murder, and plunder. The caliph and many of his dignitaries and family members were strangled. Thus the caliphate, the succession of the Prophet Muḥammad, came to an end. Although the Catholicos and numerous mosques and madrasas were spared, the city itself did not recover from this blow until the nineteenth century. Iraq was incorporated into the Mongol Empire. Mongol rulers in Iran, the Il-Khan and their successors, quickly converted to Islam, but they resided in Iran and adopted Iranian Islamic culture. In Iraq, they were always regarded as foreign occupiers.

Syria/Palestine

Arabs commonly treat the territories of present-day Syria, Lebanon, Jordan, Israel, and Palestine as a unity they call *Bilād al-Shām*, the land to the left or land of the north, in contrast to Yemen, the land to the right or to the south. In political terms, however, this territory was divided into small cantons by its mountains and had never formed a unified whole, even under Islam. When regionalized political rule was established in the ninth century, the southern part—Palestine, Transjordan, and southern Syria including Damascus—was tied to the respective emirs ruling in Egypt, whereas northern Syria with its emerging metropolis of Aleppo (*Ḥalab* in Arabic) constituted an emirate onto itself under the dynasties of Bedouin origin, the Ḥamdānids (945–1004) and the Mirdasids (1023–1079). The Islamic emirate of Aleppo usually paid tribute to the Christian Emperor in Byzantium, although sometimes it was ruled as a joint Byzantine-Egyptian condominium, functioning as a buffer state between the Christian and the Islamic worlds. During this era, three Arab Bedouin groups exerted the decisive political pressure on the western horn of the Fertile Crescent. From the Transjordan, the Tayyi pressed across the Jordan River into Palestine in pursuit of grazing land, booty, and the recognition of their Sheiks as provincial governors; in the center, the Kalb pushed the Palmyrenes out of the oasis of Damascus; in the north, the Kilāb moved into Aleppo, which they ultimately also ruled as Mirdasid emirs.

This division of the region appeared to become firmly established when Turkish Seljuqs invaded Asia Minor from Iraq in 1071, expanding their rule into northern Syria, while the south remained under control of the Fāṭimids in Cairo. The first Crusade, however, altered this in a completely unforeseen manner. In June 1098, Crusaders conquered Seljuq Antioch (Antakya). On July 15, 1099, they took Fāṭimid-controlled Jerusalem and engaged in a terrible massacre of the Muslim population. Four western, Roman Catholic states were established: the county of Edessa with its epicenter east of the Euphrates; the Norman Principality of Antioch; the county of Tripoli under the Count of Toulouse at the foot of Mount Lebanon; and the Kingdom of Jerusalem—the most important of the four— with its alternating Lotharingian (later Lorraine) and French ruling houses.

The foreign rule of the "Franks" (*al-ifranj*), which lasted almost a century, met with no unified resistance from the Muslim side. Ibn al-Athīr (1160–1233), a historian from Mosul, complained bitterly about the disunity of the Muslims in his world chronicle *al-Kāmil fī al-ta'rīkh* (The Complete History). However, neither the Fāṭimid caliphs in Egypt nor the caliphs in Baghdad and their Seljuq protectors were in fact capable of preventing the transformation of Palestine, Lebanon, and large parts of Syria into Christian feudal domains.

Resistance was organized only when the emir of Mosul, Zengi (1127–1146), son of a Turkish Mamluk, was able to destroy the first of the four Crusader states by taking Edessa in 1144. His son and successor Nūr al-Dīn ("Light of Religion," 1146–1174) established his residence in Aleppo and successfully continued the war against the Crusaders. In 1154, he was able to occupy Damascus, where a Seljuq emir ruled, without a fight. Then he attempted to bring Egypt under his military control, in rivalry with King Amalric I of Jerusalem. His success marked the end of Crusader rule. Yūsuf ibn Ayyūb, whose epithet was *Ṣalāḥ al-Dīn* ("Righteousness of the Faith," *Saladinus* in Latin), was a Kurdish military leader under Nūr al-Dīn. He assumed power in Cairo in 1171 with the aid of the Syrian army, bringing down the Fāṭimid caliphate. After Nūr ad-Dīn's death in 1174, Saladin, as he was known in the West, proclaimed his independence from

Aleppo and began to expand his power from Egypt to Transjordan, Syria, and northern Mesopotamia, and on to Mecca and Medina and Yemen. In a letter to Baghdad, Saladin justified his actions against the Muslim rulers there by pointing to the necessity of uniting Muslims in a just war or *jihād* against the infidels. The caliph provided him with a diploma of investiture for Egypt and Nubia, Arabia, Palestine/Syria, and the entire Maghreb, thereby legitimating Saladin's military conquests. After 1177, the new sultan adopted the title "Restorer of the Empire of the Commander of the Faithful" (that is, of the Baghdad caliph). The three remaining Crusader states were surrounded for the first time by a united Islamic empire, which would soon crush them. On July 4, 1187, Saladin's army defeated the Crusaders led by King Guy de Lusignan at Hattin (*Ḥiṭṭīn*) near the Sea of Galilee. Within a few months, Saladin had conquered almost all of Palestine. Jerusalem capitulated on October 2, 1187. After this, Syria/Palestine was united politically with Egypt.

Egypt

After the Arab-Islamic conquest in 641–42, Egypt became a province of the caliphate. Its emirs resided in the Arab military camp of al-Fusṭāṭ (or Fusṭāṭ Miṣr) in the south of what later became Cairo. The land was ruled by hereditary dynasties for two brief periods of time. The Turk Aḥmad ibn Ṭūlūn (868–884) from Sāmarrā was the first governor of the Tulunid dynasty, which ruled until 905. The Ibn Tulun mosque, which he erected next to his palace complex, still exists today. The Ikhshīdids ruled Egypt from 935 to 969. Their first governor, Muḥammad al-Ikhshīd, had also been a Turkish general.

However, Egypt did not become the center of a truly independent empire until 969, when after a series of failed harvests, epidemics, and other catastrophes the notables of al-Fusṭāṭ decided to transfer rule to the Shi'ite Fāṭimid caliph of North Africa, the fourth Fāṭimid ruler al-Mu'izz (955–975), who sent an army of Berbers and "Slavs" led by the freedman Jawhar. The army marched into Egypt in 969 and immediately began building a new capital city north of al-Fusṭāṭ, which the caliph entered from Tunisia in June 973. The new palace city was named "The Victorious of Mu'izz" (*al-Qāhira al-Mu'izziyya*). Under the rule of the Egyptian

Fāṭimids (969–1171), Cairo (*Qāhira*), with its new Friday mosque the Al-Azhar (The Brilliant), became one of the largest metropolises of the Arab world, soon to rival Baghdad in size and importance. The fall of the 'Abbāsid caliphs in Baghdad remained the declared goal of the Shi'ite counter-caliphs in Cairo. Egypt's Muslim population—which was still a minority in comparison to Coptic Christians—remained Sunnī even under the Shi'ite dynasty.

Control over the holy sites of Mecca and Medina, with the attendant responsibility for protecting the annual pilgrimage (*hajj*), fell to the Egyptian Fāṭimids almost automatically. In contrast, they were forced to fight a hard battle for control of Palestine/Syria and even then were able to assert control only temporarily, particularly in Aleppo. Thanks to a rebellious Turkish general, Friday prayers for the caliph in Cairo were held in Baghdad for an entire year, 1059, before the Seljuqs were able to re-occupy the city. The Shi'ites were never able to restore this kind of unity to the caliphate. In the west, Cairo ruled at least nominally over what is today Libya and Tunisia and large parts of Algeria (where the Zīrid Berbers ruled the Maghreb for Cairo as a kind of viceroy), as well as over Sicily, whose emirs regularly had themselves reaffirmed in Cairo. Due to its control of the Red Sea and Yemen, Egypt became the hub of world trade at the time between the Indian Ocean and the Mediterranean. Immense wealth flowed into the country from this, as well as from surplus agricultural production, high-quality textiles, and the export of alum, a mineral in great demand, also in Europe, for tanning leather and which was mined as a state monopoly. Under the Fāṭimids, Italian maritime trading cities became active in the Levant—first Amalfi and Pisa, and later Venice and Genoa. This trade reached its apex during the Crusades.

The loss of the Maghreb in 1044 when the Zīrids established their independence did not weigh all too heavily against these Fāṭimid successes. The dynasty, however, did experience a serious internal crisis during the era of the Crusades. It lost not only its Syrian-Palestinian provinces, but was also occupied a number of times by armies of the King of Jerusalem, becoming a protectorate of the Cru- saders. However, the fall of the Fāṭimids and Saladin's reestablishment of Sunnī orthodoxy in 1171, along with his subsequent unification of Cairo, Damascus, and Aleppo proved to be prerequisites for a resumed, even greater expansion of Egyptian power.

Saladin's victory over the Crusaders at Hattin in 1187 brought almost all of Palestine, including Jerusalem and the Syrian coast, under Muslim control again. The Franks led by King Richard the Lionheart of England and King Philip II (Philip Augustus) of France did retake Acre in 1191, and Emperor Friedrich II was even able to negotiate a restitution of Jerusalem from the Egyptian Sultan in 1229 without a struggle, so that only the Temple Mount with the Dome of the Rock and the al-Aqṣā Mosque remained in the hands of the Muslims. This intermezzo, however, lasted only until 1240.

The Saladin dynasty, the Ayyūbids (named after Saladin's father, Ayyūb = Job), was a dynastic ruling alliance. All the princes of the original Kurdish family were given provinces and ruled in continually changing constellations from Yemen to northern Mesopotamia. Cairo and Damascus remained the centers of Ayyūbid rule.

Sultan al-Ṣāliḥ Ayyūb (1240–1249), a great nephew of Saladin, reinforced the Mamluk troops in Cairo through extensive purchases of Turkish war slaves, establishing the Baḥrī (River) Regiment, which was named after their barracks on Roda Island in the Nile. This elite troop took advantage of French King Louis IX's crusade against Cairo in 1249 to remove the Ayyūbid dynasty. One of the Mamluk officers, the Turk Aybak, proclaimed himself Sultan and established Mamluk rule over Egypt, Palestine/Syria, and the holy shrines, which lasted until 1517. The Turkish Mamluks enjoyed several spectacular successes, which legitimated their usurped rule and bolstered their reputation as champions of Sunnī Islam. On September 3, 1260, at the "Spring of Goliath" ('Ain Jālūt) near Nazareth, they defeated the Mongols, whose vanguard had already pushed through up to Gaza. In 1261, the important Mamluk Sultan Baybars (1260–1277) named an 'Abbāsid prince, who had fled from the Mongols, "caliph" in Cairo. However, like his successors prior to 1517, this caliph had no real power and had only to "install" the respective Mamluk sultan. Baybars, who sought to complete Saladin's work, was also able to conquer the castles of the Ismāʿīlī assassin sects along the Syrian border between the Crusaders and the Muslims. In almost annual campaigns, the already diminished territory of the Crusaders was continually reduced further. Baybars re-conquered Caesarea, Ashkelon, Jaffa, Haifa, and Antioch. Under Sultan Qalāwūn, the city of Tripoli in Lebanon fell in 1289. In May 1291, his son al-Ashraf

Khalīl was able to take Acre, the final base of the Crusaders on the Levant coast.

The rule of the Mamluks in Cairo (1250–1571) was one of the most remarkable and successful examples of state building in the Arab world. The Malmuk military aristo-cracy was, as Jerusalem historian David Ayalon writes, a "one-generation aristocracy": Only Mamluks brought in from outside—initially of Turkish and beginning in the fourteenth century of Circassian descent—could ascend the military hierarchy and ultimately become sultan. Their children were forced, in principle, to take up civil professions. Many of them became scholars, who produced the abundant religious and secular literature we have about the Mamluk era. Despite the non-Arab origins of this elite, Egypt remained an Arab country, and it was almost cer-tainly during the Mamluk period that Muslims for the first time constituted a majority of the population. This era still today has an influence on the city of Cairo. While work on the citadel began under Saladin, the majority of the mosques, madrasas, and mausoleums in the city can be traced back to endowments by Mamluk sultans and officers. Even after the Ottomans conquered Egypt, the Mamluk military aristocracy continued to lead the country.

The Maghreb and al-Andalus

No independent state developed in premodern times in what is today Libya. The two urbanized regions there in antiquity—the five cities of the Greek Pentapolis with its main city of Cyrene (Cyrenaica) and the three cities of the Roman Tripolis, Oea, Sabratha, and Leptis Magna—were separated by a great distance. While the former was administered primarily by Egypt under the name of al-Barqa, the latter lay within Kairouan's sphere of influence.

Under Arab rule, the former Roman provinces of Africa and Numidia were combined to form the region of Ifrīqiya, which encompassed not only Tripoli and present-day Tunisia but all of northeastern Algeria as well, including Constantine, Bône, and Bougie. The Arab city of al-Qayrawān (Kairouan), originally a fortified military camp, replaced the abandoned city of Carthage as the urban focus of the region, becoming a significant center for religion and the arts and sciences. Under the Aghlabid dynasty

(800–909), which was nominally subject to Baghdad, Kairouan acquired a metropolitan character. The mosque of Emir Ziyādat Allāh I (817–838), which was completed in 836 and still exists today, became a model of architecture and architectural decoration for the entire region. The palaces and parks in Raqqāda (six miles south of Kairouan) have been uncovered by contemporary archeologists in extensive excavations.

The Aghlabids were driven out of Algeria by a Berber army in 909. A year later, the Fāṭimid ʿAbdallāh al-Mahdī proclaimed himself caliph in Kairouan. This Ismāʿīlī-Shiʿite dynasty brought the Maghreb ("the West" in Arabic) into open conflict with the Sunnī caliphate of the ʿAbbāsids in Baghdad. A new palace city, al-Mahdiyya, was built on the coast of a rocky peninsula, and another palace, al-Manṣūriyya (directly south of Kairouan), was erected later. After the peaceful assumption of power in Egypt in 969, the fourth Fāṭimid caliph al-Muʿizz settled in the newly founded city of Cairo in 973, leaving the Maghreb to his viceroy, the Zīrid Berber prince from Algeria, who moved into the abandoned Fāṭimid palaces.

When the Zīrids renounced their allegiance to Cairo in 1044 and returned to Sunnī Islam, recognizing the distant Baghdad caliph, it triggered an emigration westward by Arabic Bedouin tribes between 1050 and 1052, marking the beginning of the Arabization of southern Tunisia and the central Algerian steppe.

In Arabic, Morocco is called *al-Maghrib al-Aqṣā*, "the farthest west." Six successive Muslim dynasties have ruled Morocco up to the present. These dynasties have consistently drawn their power from indigenous Berber tribes, even if they themselves have for the most part been Arabs from the Middle East and Asia Minor. The model for this form of rule, which is typical for Morocco, was established by a political refugee, Idrīs, who was a direct descendant of Muḥammad's grandson al-Ḥasan. Idrīs established his rule around the old Roman city of Volubilis in 789, supported by the Awrāba, a Berber tribe. Idrīs's mausoleum in nearby Moulay Idriss remains a kind of national shrine for Moroccans even today. His son Idrīs II (793–828) expanded the city of Fez (*Fās*), which had been founded by his father, into a metropolitan center of Arab rule. The Kairouan (al-Qarawiyyīn) Mosque in Fez became the country's religious and intellectual center.

Following the fragmentation of Idrīsid rule into a dozen local entities, the Tunisian Fāṭimids and the respective rulers in al-Andalus battled over control of Morocco. The country was then unified by Ibn Yāsīn, a pious man who had founded a monastery-like Islamic fortress or ribāṭ in southern Morocco. Warriors of the Sanhāja, a Berber people from the western Sahara whose men wore blue veils, gathered around Ibn Yāsīn and formed the militia of the "Ribat people" (*murābiṭūn*, in the Spanish derivative *Almorávides*), which was quickly able to conquer all of Morocco and the coast up into the area around Algiers. In 1062, their secular prince Yūsuf ibn Tāshfīn (1061–1106) founded Marrakech (Marrākush, in Spanish *Marruecos*, from which the current name Morocco is derived) as his capital, which, in contrast to Arab-influenced Fez, was a city of Berber-African character.

Yūsuf ibn Tāshfīn crossed the Strait of Gibraltar with an Almoravid army in 1086 to intervene in al-Andalus. The caliphate of Cordoba had ceased to exist in 1031, and the Islamic sphere of power there had splintered into more than a dozen regional "party kingdoms" (in Arabic, *mulūk al-ṭawā'if*; in Spanish, *Reyes de Taifas*) in Malaga and Sevilla, Cordoba, Valencia, Toledo, and Zaragoza, and others. This period of numerous small courts was very rich in cultural terms. Poetry, science, and the arts blossomed. The al-Ja'fariyya Palace (in Spanish, *Aljafería*) near Zaragoza testifies even today to the magnificence of the *ṭā'ifa* princes. They were unable, however, to resist to the rising Christian *Reconquista*. The intervention of the Almoravids unified the dwindled al-Andalus once more under the Berber dynasty of Morocco. The advance of King Alfonso VI from León and Castile in 1085, however, led to the definitive loss of Toledo.

The Almoravids were strict Sunnīs. The reform movement of Ibn Tūmart (Berber for Ibn 'Umar), the Berber holy man from the High Atlas, opposed the Almoravids' dogmatic and legally ossified understanding of Islam and probably their customs as well, which were unfamiliar to Arabs, such as men rather than women wearing veils. Ibn Tūmart was able to win over the Masmūda farmers from the high mountains, who called themselves "The Monotheists" (*al-muwaḥḥidūn*; in the Spanish derivative *Almohades*), and came down from the High Atlas to topple Almoravid rule. When Ibn Tūmart—who was revered as the Mahdī ("The Rightly Guided One") sent from God—died in 1130, one of his students, 'Abd al-Mu'min (1130–1163), assumed leadership of the religious movement (regarded as heterodox by Sunnīs) and called himself caliph, successor, to the Mahdī Ibn Tūmart. This was the first time a non-Arab ruler assumed this sacred title, which until this time had been reserved for members of the Quraysh tribe from Mecca. After 1145, the Almohads subjugated all of al-Andalus that remained Muslim and defeated King Alfonso VIII of Castile at Alarcos (west of today's Cuidad Real) on July 18, 1196. It was the last important Muslim military victory against the Christian Spaniards. The entire Maghreb up to Tunis and Tripoli also came under Almohad rule; in particular the Bedouin Hilāl tribe was subject to this centralized rule.

The Almohad court was influenced by the culture of Cordoba. Especially the architecture of the epoch testifies to the predominant influence that the so-called "Moorish" art of Andalusia had on Morocco and Algeria. The great mosques of the Almohads, the Mosque of Tinmal in memory of Mahdī Ibn Tūmart in the High Atlas (1153), the Great Mosque of Tlemcen in Algeria (1136), the Kutubiyya (Booksellers') Mosque in Marrakech (around 1150–1196), the enormous mosque of Rabat including its unfinished minaret, the Ḥassān Tower (around 1190), the Great Mosque of Sevilla with its minaret, which today serves as a bell tower for the cathedral (1195; in Spanish, *la Giralda*, "the weathervane"), and the Torre de Oro (Tower of Gold) (1220) on the Guadalquivir River in Sevilla were all products of the Almohad epoch.

The court of the second Almohad caliph Abū Yaʻqūb Yūsuf (1163–1184) became a center of scholarship and literature. He sponsored the astronomer, physician, and writer Ibn Ṭufayl (ca. 1100–1185) from Cadix, whose *Ḥayy ibn Yaqẓān* (Alive, Son of Awake) was the most important philosophical romance of Arabic literature: the story of a young man who grows up alone on a deserted island and who must develop his insights and capacities solely through his own intellect and reason. Translated into Hebrew as well as Latin (under the author's name Abubacer), the novel continued to be influential into the modern era in Europe. Ibn Ṭufayl drew young intellectuals from al-Andalus into his circle, including the jurist and Aristotelian philosopher Ibn Rushd (Averroës), who was born in Cordoba in 1126 and became a protégé of Caliph Abū Yaʻqūb Yūsuf. Ibn Rushd served the Caliph as a judge in Sevilla, Cordoba, and Marrakech (1183), where he then succeeded Ibn Ṭufayl as court physician. Under Caliph Abū Yūsuf Yaʻqūb (1184–1199), Ibn Rushd fell out of favor in 1195, and all of his philosophical writings were burned. However, after being banished for a brief period of time, he was rehabilitated and allowed to return to Marrakech, where he died in 1198. Ibn al-'Arabī (1165–1240), the most important Arab mystic, also struggled with the intolerance of Almohad religious scholars. Born in Murcia, Ibn al-'Arabī left the Almohad Empire in 1204, finding refuge in Damascus after an extended journey.

The Almohads abandoned their heterodox religious doctrine voluntarily. In 1230, Caliph Idrīs al-Ma'mūn personally renounced the Almohad doctrine on the pulpit (minbar) of Marrakech cursed the Mahdī Ibn Tūmart, and proclaimed the return to Sunnī Islam. Even before the Almohads were defeated at Las Navas de Tolosa by a coalition of Christian kings from northern Spain, their decline was imminent. The cities of southern Spain now fell to the Christians in rapid succession, including Cordoba in 1236 and Sevilla in 1248.

Up to the end of the fifteenth century, three Muslim states determined the fate of the Maghreb and Andalusia. From Tunis, the dynasty of the Ḥafṣids—founded by the Almohad governor Abū Ḥafṣ, a student of the Mahdī Ibn Tūmart—ruled all of Ifrīqiya, that is, Tunis and eastern Algeria, between 1228 and 1574. The Banū Merīn (Merinids), a nomadic Zenāta Berber clan, came to power in Morocco and western Algeria. In 1216, they advanced from the Sahara to Morocco, occupying Marrakech in 1269. Like their predecessors, Merinid rulers were the heirs of Moorish culture and the art of Andalusia. They also adopted the eastern institution of the madrasa, the legal, theological institution of higher education. The magnificence of Moorish architectural decoration, which had arisen in Cordoba, reappeared in the madrasas of the Merinid in Fez, Marrakech, and Meknes. The Merinids, however, no longer intervened in al-Andalus. Only the Nasrid dynasty in Granada (1230–1492), which attempted to maneuver between Moroccan rulers and Christian powers, remained Islamic. In 1492, the palace of the Nasrids, the Alhambra (al-Ḥamrā = "the Red"), fell into the hands of the "Catholic Kings" Isabella of Castile and Ferdinand V of Aragon. It is not wholly fortuitous that the fall of Granada was contemporaneous with Columbus's mission and the discovery of the new world and thus with one of the dates marking the dawn of the modern era.

The historian Ibn Khaldūn (1332–1406) developed a theory about the rise and fall of Muslim empires based on the vicissitudes of Moroccan-

Andalusian dynasties. Ibn Khaldūn was the scion of an old Arab family, which was originally from Ḥaḍramawt but had already settled in Sevilla in the eighth century, and later in Ceuta and Tunis, where Ibn Khaldūn was then born. The scholar led a checkered life, traveling to numerous minor courts in North Africa and then to Granada, before he ended up in Cairo, where he served in a number of positions as a judge, although he was also jailed repeatedly during this time. He began his historical work on the Berbers with an extensive "prolegomena" (*Muqaddima*) investigating the laws of historical events. According to the work, clan solidarity (*'aṣabiyya*) of tribal associations makes up the powerful driving force for the development and expansion of political power, and the inevitable weakening of such solidarity in urban settings ultimately leads to dynastic decline. Ibn Khaldūn is often considered the "first sociologist," and in fact his highly original work, which comprises three volumes in modern book form, is unparalleled in medieval literature.

CHAPTER 4

The Arab World from 1500 to 1800 CE

There is a widespread perception that in the early modern era and even in the late Middle Ages the Arab world—and the Islamic world as a whole—experienced a developmental rupture that is best described by terms such as "stagnation" or "decline." Muslims, according to this argument, failed to undergo particular developments that were fundamental for the history of Europe—the Reformation, the French Revolution, and the industrial revolution—and for this reason have remained "backward." This failure supposedly left Muslims both defenseless against European colonial intervention and unprepared for modernity (to which they are said to react with uncertainty and violence even today). A variety of different factors are mentioned as possible or ostensible causes for this "decline and stagnation," including the ossification of religious doctrines in Sunnī Islam during the late Middle Ages, the European discovery of the Americas and of sea routes to India with the accompanying shift in the world trade routes, and the lack of communal self-administration and self-reliance in Middle Eastern cities.

In a series of recent studies, historians have demonstrated that at least the thesis of general economic decline needs to be modified. In the sixteenth century, the Ottoman Empire possessed an expanding and tautly organized central state, which had abolished numerous borders and thus established an economic region and trade routes that it was quite capable of securing. Coffee trade across the Red Sea, which resulted in an economic boom especially for Egypt, compensated for the shift of the spice trade to routes around the Cape of Good Hope, which were controlled by Europeans. Silk production in the Levant also remained competitive for quite some time.

Nevertheless, it is indisputable that the age of discovery ushered in an epoch of unparalleled European global dominance. Almost the entire Islamic world gradually came under the political, military, or economic control of European nations. This fate, however, was not limited to the Islamic world. It also occurred in the Indian subcontinent, Southeast and East Asia, as well as in North and South America. It is therefore hardly possible to hold Islam responsible for this development. What instead requires explanation is the precise, unprecedented dynamic that allowed Europeans to subjugate the rest of the world. There is as yet no convincing and generally accepted account of this.

The Crusades can be regarded as a prelude to this development. They represent the first attempt by western Europe to resolve internal demographic, social, and economic problems through measures taken beyond its own borders. It is certainly no coincidence that ascendant trade municipalities such as Pisa, Venice, and Genoa, with their dynamic bourgeois merchant elite, were both the driving force and the benefactors of the "armed pilgrimages" to the Holy Land. The age of discovery also marked the beginning of the expansion of European interventions in North Africa and Asia. The Portuguese occupied Ceuta as early as 1415 and Tangiers in 1471. After taking Granada in 1492, Spain also sought to control the North African coast across the Strait of Gibraltar. However, the aspiring Ottoman Empire proved to be a worthy opponent for the Spanish monarchy.

The Fertile Crescent under Ottoman Rule

By the beginning of the fourteenth century, the small Turkish principality of the Ottoman (*'Uthmān*) clan in northwestern Asia Minor had rapidly developed into an important territorial state. In 1357, the Ottomans were able to establish a foothold on the Balkan Peninsula, crowning their conquests with the capture of Byzantine Constantinople in 1453. While all of this took place outside of the Arab world, Arabs were directly confronted with the new empire in the early sixteenth century. Sultan Selim I brought down the Mamluk dynasty in Syria and Egypt. After the victory over the Mamluks at Marj Dābiq north of Aleppo in August 1516, the sultan occupied all of Syria and Palestine and then, in 1517, Egypt too. The Sharif of Mecca immediately sent him the key to the Ka'ba.

Under Selim's successor Suleyman I (the "Magnificent") (1520–1566),

Iraq was also incorporated into the Ottoman Empire. In 1534–35, Azerbaijan with its capital city of Tabriz and northern Iraq with Baghdad were occupied, and in 1546, the south with Basra as well. In 1552, the Ottoman army expanded into the eastern coast of Arabia, where the province of (Sanjak) al-Ḥasā (around Hofūf) was established. The Ottomans were able to assert their maritime predominance through two naval bases, one in Basra on the Persian Gulf and the other in Suez (*Suways*) on the Red Sea. Ottoman Turkish rule over the Arab countries of the Fertile Crescent continued for the next four centuries until the empire finally collapsed during the First World War.

Turkish rule certainly had some positives aspects. The urban economy prospered, particularly in the trade center Aleppo. Damascus and above all Baghdad flourished again, after having endured numerous campaigns from Iran following the Mongol invasion. Centralized power in Istanbul, which remained unbroken in the sixteenth century, was maintained through strong governors (pashas), tax collectors, judges, and foreign garrison troops recruited in part from the Balkans. The unified legal system, codified under Sultan Sūleyman—whom the Turks called the "Legislator" (*Qānūnī*)—and a tightly organized and highly efficient cadastral registration and tax assessment system were introduced everywhere. At the beginning of the seventeenth century, however, the reins began to loosen. The united elite, which as merchants and landowners had traditionally dominated economic and religious-intellectual life, began to (successfully) demand participation in political life. In Iraq, the governor Hasan Pasha (1704–1723) established his own de facto independence through his private army of Georgian and Circassian Mamluks, bequeathing his power to his son Ahmad Pasha (1723–1747). After this, outright Mamluk rule in Baghdad and Basra was established, which was tolerated and recognized by Istanbul and would continue until 1831. A similar situation developed in Mosul. In Syria, the local al-ʿAẓm family played a comparable role from 1725 to 1807 as local governors recognized by the central government. Their palace in Damascus still testifies today to their wealth and magnificence. The pasha of Sidon, Ahmad al-Jazzār (1775–1804), whose fortress in Acre even Napoleon Bonaparte was unable to capture, ruled in a similarly independent manner.

The loosening of central power in the Ottoman Empire in favor of local and regional princes, however, did not automatically signify economic decline. While the empire itself was thrown into a serious crisis, the semi-autonomous provinces of the Arab world were able to thrive economically. As always, the Bedouins remained a disruptive factor, pushing repeatedly into settled territories in Syria/Transjordan as well as in western Iraq.

The Arabian Peninsula

In 1516-17, the Turkish Ottomans conquered Syria, Palestine, and Egypt, which meant that the Ḥijāz along with the cities of Mecca and Medina were also subject to the Sultan of Constantinople. In 1517, the Sharif of Mecca sent the key to the Ka'ba to Sultan Selim I and in return was confirmed in his office. From this point on, the Ottoman Sultan bore the title "The Custodian of the Two Holy Shrines" (*khādim al-ḥaramayn*), a title given to Egyptian Mamluk sultans prior to this (and used today by the king of Saudi Arabia). The sultan was now responsible for the support and care of the holy sites of Islam as well as for the organization and protection of the annual pilgrimage, the hajj, with pilgrim caravans from Damascus and Cairo.

Given its variety of starkly differing geographies, Yemen was not exactly predestined for political unity. Separate minor dynasties had been established in 'Aden, on the plains of Tihāma at the Red Sea, and in the metropolis of the highlands Ṣan'ā'. The most permanent force in Yemen was the Zaydī-Shi'ite imamate of northern Yemen with its center in Ṣa'da, which had been established in the ninth century and remained intact until 1962—the longest-standing dynasty of the Islamic world. Its territory, however, did change over time. The Zaydīs repeatedly occupied Ṣan'ā', only to lose it and then reoccupy it again. In 1538, the Ottomans began to subjugate Yemen as well. They occupied Ṣan'ā' in 1546, compelling the imam to recognize the suzerainty of the sultan in 1552. Over time, however, the Ottomans were unable to sustain their rule, especially after European colonial powers appeared in the Indian Ocean and in the Red Sea—at first the Portuguese, then the Dutch and English. The Turks withdrew from Yemen in 1635.

Oman (*'Umān*) is separated from the rest of the Arabian Peninsula by deserts that long ensured its isolation. Since time immemorial, its coastal residents have been seafarers, who used the monsoons to reach the coasts of East Africa and India, making their living from maritime trade. In the sixteenth century, the Portuguese took control of the ports of Qalhāt and Masqaṭ (Muscat) in Oman as well as port of Hormuz (1514) on the Iranian side of the gulf. Oman remained part of the Portuguese colonial empire for a century and a half. In 1650, local Ya'rubīs were able to retake Masqaṭ. The succeeding Āl Bū Sa'īd dynasty (beginning in 1741) was able to expand its power to the island of Zanzibar off the African coast, giving rise to a remarkable double empire across the Indian Ocean.

In the eighteenth century, a form of political rule was established in the interior of the Arabian Peninsula that has continued, albeit with interruptions, to today: Wahhābism, the religious revival movement that led to the establishment of the Āl Sa'ūd monarchy (in Arabic, Āl = family; not to be confused with the article *al-*). The wandering preacher Muḥammad ibn 'Abd al-Wahhāb (1703–1792) sought to reestablish a pure and strict Islam true to its original form by opposing blasphemous "innovations" such as saint veneration, the worship of graves, and the mysticism of the dervish orders. Only the Quran and sayings of the Prophet were supposed to guide Muslims. Support from the tribal leader Muḥammad ibn Sa'ūd (died in 1765) ensured the dissemination of Ibn 'Abd al-Wahhāb's teachings in the oases and among the tribes of central Arabia. As a result, Ibn Sa'ūd's son 'Abd al-'Azīz (1765–1803) was able to establish a powerful desert empire. The religious furor of the Wahhābīs was directed against the Sunnīs in Mecca and Medina, as well as against the Shi'ites in Iraqi Najaf and Karbalā'. The imam shrines of the Sh'ites were destroyed in 1802 by Wahhābīs armies, who also took Medina in 1804 and destroyed the al-Baqī' cemetery, where numerous companions of the Prophet and several Shi'ite imams had been buried. However, they did not dare to touch the Prophet Muḥammad's grave, although they did close it off to visitors. The Ottomans were unable to take direct action against these desert warriors. In a series of campaigns from 1811 to 1818, their Egyptian viceroy Muḥammad 'Alī destroyed this first Saudi kingdom, and in 1815, Ottoman rule over the holy shrines was restored.

Egypt

The Ottomans conquered Egypt in 1517, transforming it into a province of the Turkish empire. New foreign elites appeared in Cairo, headed by the Turkish governor (*wālī*) who had the rank of a pasha and was accompanied by an army made up of the many nationalities within the Ottoman Empire. Especially the infantry of the Janissary corps (in Turkish, *Yeni Ķeri*, "new troops") – comprised of Christian children from the Balkans forced into military service—were an increasingly important power factor. Egyptian Mamluks, however, were also employed in a new regiment.

The ties between the Egyptian province and central government in Constantinople were initially very close. However, the reins loosened over the course of time, as was also the case in Syria and Iraq. Access to power opened up again for local elites, as the foreign army was gradually "Egyptianized." In the seventeenth century, a Mamluk faction, the Faqāriyya, was able to rule Egypt for thirty years, limiting the power of the wali. In 1660, a rival faction, the Qāsimiyya, ousted the Faqāriyya. Something approaching a civil war ensued, in which the two sides crippled and almost annihilated each other, opening the way again for foreign intervention. The Janissary corps regiment was now able to control the country for an extended period of time and to defy the governor until the eighteenth century, when rivalry between Mamluk factions arose again. After 1760, Malmluk beys ruled the country, ultimately in a kind of duumvirate between rivals Ibrāhīm Bey and Murād Bey (whom Napoleon Bonaparte encountered upon landing in Alexandria in 1789).

A number of factors (such as the aforementioned coffee trade) testify to Egypt's prosperity during the time: Cairo's population doubled (from approximately 150,000 inhabitants in 1500 to about 300,000 in 1700); the city limits were extended; and a great variety of monumental buildings were erected during this era—mosques, schools, baths, caravanserais (*khān*), and mausoleums. Of the many educational institutions in Egypt, the Al-Azhar Mosque in Cairo became the most distinguished in the late seventeenth century. Its elected leader, the *Shaykh al-Azhar*, came to be recognized as the foremost legal and religious authority, not only in Egypt, but throughout the Sunnī world.

The Maghreb

During the early modern era, the western Mediterranean served as the stage for antagonisms between the Christian maritime powers of Spain and Portugal on the one hand and the Ottoman Empire on the other. Through the use of its fleet, the Ottoman Empire attempted to gain control of the lands at the eastern and western ends of the Mediterranean by assuming the role of the protector of Muslims on the Iberian Peninsula (albeit without success) and in North Africa.

After taking Ceuta in 1415, the Portuguese continued their maritime expansion along the Atlantic coastline, occupying a series of bases on the Moroccan coast after 1458. The Spanish emerged as a naval power in the Mediterranean. The port cities of the North African coast became centers for a privateer war—understood as a *jihād*—against the Christian countries north of the Mediterranean. Booty and ransom were the economic motivations for these "Barbary pirates" of the Maghreb as well as for their Christian counterparts. After a raid by Moroccan corsairs on the Spanish cities of Alicante, Elche, and Malaga in 1505, the Spanish occupied all of the important ports of the Maghreb coast from 1505 to 1511: Marsā l-kabīr (Mersel-Kēbir), Oran, Mostagānem, Tenes, Cherchell, an island off the coast of Algiers, Bougie, and Tripoli. In response, the Ottoman sultans encouraged and supported the corsairs by sending ships. Four brothers from the island of Lesbos (including the legendary Khayr al-Dīn, also known as Barbarossa) emerged as the leaders of this maritime enterprise against the Christians from 1504 to 1510. After 1516, Algiers (in Arabic, al-Jazā'ir, "the Islands") developed into a virtual corsair state under Khayr al-Dīn, tolerated by the Hafsid sultans of Tunis and supported by the Ottomans. Sultan Selim promoted the corsair to *beylerbey* (Turkish "bey of beys" for the Arabic *amīr al-umarā'*, "leader of leaders") with the rank of a pasha and provided him with troops and artillery. In 1534, he was able to occupy Tunis in the name of the Ottoman sultan. This success led to the intervention of Christian powers—Charles V sent his fleet to Algiers and Tunis in 1535 and Mahdia (al-Mahdiyya) was occupied from 1550 to 1554. In 1571, a Christian coalition of the Holy Roman Empire, the Papacy, and the Republic of Venice defeated the Ottoman fleet by Lepanto (Nafpaktos) near the entrance to the Gulf of Corinth, and in 1573, Don Juan de Austria took Tunis. Both were bitter setbacks for the sultan, but the Spanish were still unable to assume permanent control of the North African coast. In 1574, Sinan Pasha occupied Tunis from Tripoli. Spain decided to abandon the fight. In 1581, King Philip II agreed to an armistice with the Sublime Porte, ending the century-long power struggle and ceding North Africa to the Muslims.

The indirect Ottoman rule established in Tunis and Algiers led to curious polities. The Turkish army and fleet jointly ruled these two "regencies": Officers and captains sat together in the ruling councils (dīwān). In Tunis in 1591, a revolt of forty local officers with the Turkish title of *dey* ("uncle") removed the weak pasha from office. The deys placed one of their own in command, who then appointed the commander of the fleet (*qabtān* = "captain") and the bey, that is, the military officer responsible for collecting taxes from the local tribes of the interior. Throughout the entire seventeenth century, Tunisia was governed by deys, although the actual power gradually shifted to beys, who commanded their own troops. In 1705, there was a putsch by the agha (commander) of the *sipāhī*, the elite mounted force within the Ottoman cavalry divisions: Ḥusayn ibn ʻAlī appointed himself bey and did away with the office of the dey. After 1710, the Husseinite dynasty ruled in Tunis as beys and struggled to transform the former corsair enclave into a modern state.

In Tripoli as well, local militia officers removed the pasha from power in 1603. A similar development also occurred in Algiers: Janissary officers (aghas), who dominated the divan, initially governed alongside the weak pasha. In 1659, the pasha's prerogatives were reduced to a merely honorary title with the Janissary officers rotating in a two-month cycle. After a military revolt in 1671, the deys elected by the militia headed the provincial government, which the Porte recognized as a sovereign state in 1711.

Morocco was the only country of the Maghreb that was able to avoid both Spanish and Ottoman rule, thanks to an Arab family from the south, from Sūs in the backcountry of Agadir. The Banū Saʻd were descendants of the Maʻqil Bedouins, who had immigrated to the Maghreb in the eleventh century. They formed an alliance with a marabout, a local spiritual leader, and in 1511 began to engage in a jihād against the Portuguese (who had occupied Agadir in 1505), subsequently expanding their power to the North over the High Atlas. In 1524, they captured Marrakech, where Saʻdi graves in the magnificent mausoleum still testify to their power. They were able to take Agadir from the Portuguese in 1541, occupy Fez in 1549, and conquer corsair-ruled Tlemcen (*Tilimsān*) in western Algeria in 1550. An invasion by the Portuguese was thwarted in the Battle of the Three Kings in 1578, which took place at al-Qasr al-Kabīr (*Alcazarquivir* in Spanish). King Sebastian was defeated and killed in the fighting, as were the Moroccan pretender al-Mutawakkil and the Saʻdi sultan ʻAbd al-Malik.

The Saʻdi dynasty disintegrated after attempting a massive expansion into the Niger region. The Alawites, the dynasty that continues to rule Morocco today, was able to achieve the renewed unification of the country. As their name implies, they are descendents of ʻAlī and Fāṭima, the daughter of the Prophet Muḥammad, and thus Sharifs (the Arabic plural is *shurafā*ʼ; in French, *chorfa*). Their progenitor was a descendant of the Prophet from the al-Ḥasan line who had immigrated to the Maghreb from Yanbuʻ on the Red Sea and settled in Rissani (Risānī) in the Tafilalt oasis at the eastern foot of the High Atlas in the early thirteenth century. The Alawite Sharifs ruled the Tafilalt oasis beginning in 1636, and proceeded to conquer the rest of the country from there. After taking Fez in 1666, Moulay (Mūlāy) al-Rashīd assumed the title of sultan. His brother Moulay (Mūlāy) Ismāʻīl (1672–1727) succeeded him to the throne at age twenty-six and was the most significant ruler of the dynasty. He built Meknes (Miknās) into the new capital city and into a garrison for his powerful army, which consisted in part of sub-Saharan Africans, freed slaves, and Christian renegades. Moulay Ismāʻīl drove first the Spanish out of al-Maʻmūra and al-ʻArāʼish (Larache) and, after a five-year siege, the English out of Tangiers, which they had taken from the Spanish in 1622. The sultan was in fact able to subjugate almost all of Morocco, namely, that part of the country required to pay taxes to the central government (the "government lands," *bilād al-makhzan*), including the tribes on the High Atlas and the edge of the desert. In addition, the sultan was able to modernize the army and, like contemporary European countries, sought to institute a kind of mercantile economic policy that would stimulate and direct trade and the economy through directives from above. In doing this, his most important partners were the French King Louis XIV and his minister Jean Baptiste Colbert. The fact that after Moulay Ismāʻīl's death his powerful state was again subject to riots and revolts demonstrates the actual lack of inner cohesion in the largely rural country, which was splintered into Berber and Arab tribal territories.

The "Moriscos," who had been driven out of Spain, contributed significantly to the economic prosperity of the Maghreb in the seventeenth century. In 1563, King Philipp II issued a ban prohibiting Moriscos (who had been forced to convert to Christianity but were in large part still secretly faithful to Islam) from possessing weapons without special authorization; and in 1566 he issued an edict banning Arab clothing and the veil as well as religious ablutions, ordering the surrender of all Arabic books and the exclusive use of the Castilian language within three years. Rioting ensued, particularly in Andalusia, between 1568 and 1571, which was quashed by force. Although many Muslims hoped the Ottoman fleet would intervene, it did not. Between 1609 and 1614, edicts were issued under Philipp III, authorizing the dispossession and expulsion of the Moriscos. While approximately 25,000 former Muslims remained in the country as Catholics, about 275,000 people left the Iberian Peninsula, seeking refuge in the various cities of the Maghreb. This influx brought life to North African cities, not only economically but also culturally. The Moriscos' contributions to art, architecture, and folklore are still recognizable in North Africa today.

CHAPTER 5
The Nineteenth Century

The Mashriq

During the nineteenth century almost the entire eastern (*al-Mashriq*) part of the Arab world—the Fertile Crescent, Egypt, and segments of the Arabian Peninsula—remained part of the Ottoman Empire, even though various autonomous regions sporadically appeared. The Arab countries were therefore subject to decisions made in Constantinople and increasingly to those in other European metropolises as well. They were greatly affected by the crises of the Ottoman Empire, which had to accept significant territorial losses in the Balkans and north of the Black Sea. Just as consequential were the sultans' reform efforts starting in 1792 and the growing political, military, and economic influence of the major European powers.

A summary of all the developments of the Ottoman Empire would exceed the scope of this book; only the milestones of its development can be mentioned here: army reform based on the European model by Selim III (1789–1807) and the violent eradication of the Janissary corps (1826); Gülhane's reform edict of 1839, the *Hatt-i Sherīf* ("noble edict"), declared in response to pressure from Europe, which for the first time made Muslims and non-Muslims equal before the law; the "reorganization" (*tanẓīmāt*) of the legal and educational systems based on a new reform edict, the *Hatt-i Humayun* ("imperial edict") of 1856; the creation of a civil code, the *Mejelle* ("code," 1870–1876), which applied to the entire Ottoman Empire and continued to be effective after the collapse of the empire; and the introduction of a constitution in 1876 and the convening of the first Ottoman parliament in 1877, which, however, was suspended after only two short sessions in 1878 by the autocratic sultan 'Abdul Ḥamīd II (1876–1909).

Prior to the First World War, a consensus existed among the major powers of England, France, Austria, and Prussia/Germany not to contest the territories of the Ottoman Empire, which in particular was intended to prevent Russia from gaining control of Constantinople and the Balkans. Greek independence in 1829 was the only exception. The European powers even helped the Ottoman government, the Sublime Porte (*Bāb-i ālī*), in securing its rule over the Arab countries, preventing in particular the emergence of a major Egyptian kingdom. In return the Ottomans opened their empire to the trade interests of the major powers, which led the Porte to become increasingly dependent on the Europeans. This development culminated in the Anglo-Ottoman trade agreement of 1838, the empire's bankruptcy in 1875, and the establishment of an international debt administration (*Administration de la dette publique ottomane*) in Constantinople in 1881.

Iraq. Mesopotamia, which was largely rural, remained to a great extent a domain of Arab nomads, the Bedouins, into the nineteenth century. In the few urban centers, local dynasties were established, which were then tolerated by the Porte: in the north the Jalālī emirs in Mosul; in the south the Mamluks of Georgian descent in Baghdad, who also controlled the port city of Basra. Nevertheless, the Porte removed the local rulers in 1831 through a military intervention and reinstated the direct administration of Iraq. One of the most significant governors and modernizers was Midhat Pasha (1869–1872), Grand Vizier (1872), and Minister of Justice, and the father of the constitution of 1876, who later became governor of Damascus (1878–1880).

The cities along the Euphrates, al-Najaf and Kerbelā (Karbalā), had special status. The two holy Shi'ite shrines, the tombs of 'Alī and his son al-Ḥusayn, had attracted numerous Shi'ite clerics and scholars from Iran in the eighteenth century and developed into centers of Shi'ite jurisprudence and theology. Because the Shi'ites in the two cities remained largely to themselves, the Sunnī Ottomans didn't intervene, but when the Ottoman administration started forcing the nomadic Bedouins of southern Iraq to settle, the Shi'ite clerics found fertile missionizing ground among the tribes that had been only superficially Islamized. Within only a few decades, all of southern Iraq became Shi'ite, and the shrines found a loyal and generous clientele among the tribal sheikhs cum landed gentry. A tight symbiosis, often reinforced through marriage, developed between the clergy of the two shrines and the rural population of southern Iraq, which has continued to today.

Syria. The history of Greater Syria (*bilād al-Shām*) started in the nineteenth century with Napoleon's failed advance from Egypt, which was stopped by Ahmad Pasha al-Jazzār's defense of Acre. The Porte maintained its Syrian provinces and was even able to push back the local forces to the benefit of the central government. In Damascus the supremacy of the al-'Azm family ended in 1808. Although Greater Syria came under the control of the Egyptian pasha Muḥammad 'Alī in 1831, he was forced to abandon his conquests in 1840 due to pressure from England and Austria, which had come to the aid of the Ottoman Empire.

Lebanon assumed an exceptional position, having been a refuge for religious minorities since time immemorial. The Maronites controlled the north of the mountainous region; this Christian community was a Uniate church and had maintained close ties to western Christianity and France since the Crusades. Under their emir Bashīr II al-Shihābī (1788–1840), the Maronites established the foundations for their centuries-long dominance in the mountains of Lebanon, especially at the expense of the Druze settling in the southern parts of the mountains, a splinter group that had broken off from the Shi'ite Isma'īlīs. Maronite attempts to expand to the south had already resulted in heavy fighting between the two Arab groups several times in the nineteenth century (1841–45, 1860). In response to pressure from France, an autonomous province of Mount Lebanon was established in 1861, albeit without the port cities. With France's protection it continued to exist until the end of the Ottoman Empire. The Arab Christian population (Maronites, Greek-Catholic or Uniate, and Greek-Orthodox) outnumbered the Muslim minorities (Druzes, Sunnīs, and Shi'ites). After the First World War, Mount Lebanon became the nucleus of the Republic of Lebanon, which the Allies wanted to maintain as a Christian state and a European sphere of influence.

Arabia. The invasion of Iraqi Kerbelā in 1802 by the Wahhābīs under the leadership of the Sa'ūd family, as well as the conquests of Medina in 1804 and Mecca in 1806 directly affected the interests of the Ottoman Empire and led the sultan to take the title of "Custodian of the Two Holy Shrines." Egypt's pasha, Muḥammad 'Alī, was ordered to challenge the Wahhābīs. After expanding his army he was able to retake Mecca and Medina in 1811–13, and in 1818 he even succeeded in capturing and leveling Dir'iyya in central Arabia, the stronghold of the Wahhābīs and the Saʿūd family. Emir ʿAbdallāh ibn Saʿūd was deported to Constantinople and executed there. Egyptian-Ottoman control of central Arabia, however, could not be maintained in the long term and the Saʿūd family was able to reestablish its control only a few years later, albeit on a local scale. The Ottomans used this opportunity once again to consolidate their rule in the Ḥijāz and along the coast of Red Sea. In 1872, Yemen too was returned to Ottoman control.

The Ottomans were forced to accept the fact that the British had established themselves throughout the Arabian Peninsula. In 1839 the East India Company took control of Aden, an important station along the route to India and a base at the entrance to the Red Sea, although its ultimate significance only became evident after the Suez Canal was built. The tribes of the hinterlands became tied to Britain through treaties. A similar development took place on the Arabian gulf coast starting in the 1820s. The conclusion of a permanent truce in 1853 transformed the "Pirate Coast" into the Trucial States, a British protectorate (since 1971, the United Arab Emirates). Of particular significance was the 1899 Anglo-Kuwaiti agreement between Britain and Sheikh Mubarak. The Porte considered Kuwait the end station of a Baghdad railway that had been in planning since 1888, which was to connect the capital, Constantinople, with the Persian Gulf. Because the railroad was being built by an Ottoman-German consortium, the British feared the German Empire could use this to gain influence at the gulf, so it strengthened its ties with the sheikh family of Āl Sabāḥ in 1899 through a treaty of protection that de facto released the city-state from the Ottoman Empire. This step would have repercussions in 1990–91 in the Kuwait conflict.

Egypt. During the first half of the nineteenth century, Egypt was certainly the most important Arab country. Although the significance of the landing of Napoleon's army in 1798 was greatly exaggerated with respect to the Islamic world in general, for Egypt itself it represented a major turning point. The French army, which was modern as in terms of both structure and weaponry, defeated the Mamluks at the pyramids. For the first time, the Egyptians were confronted with an efficient administration, modern jurisprudence, and modern scientific methods and instruments. Shock and admiration of this innovation are reflected in the diary and chronicle of the Cairo intellectual and scholar, al-Jabartī (1753–1825).

After the British and the Ottomans had forced the French to retreat in 1802, the Porte again appointed pashas as governors in Cairo. A violent coup in 1805 installed Muḥammad ʿAlī, an Arnaut (Albanian) from Macedonia, as pasha. His reign (1805–1848) is considered one of the most notable epochs in Egyptian history. After he had three hundred Mamluks massacred in the citadel of Cairo in 1811, he began building up a modern army and initiated a series of reforms that transformed Egypt for a time into a major power of the eastern Mediterranean and the Red Sea. He brought European technicians, consultants, and instructors to the country, especially from France, and sent students to Paris. Most importantly, Muḥammad ʿAlī revolutionized Egypt's agriculture. Cultivation methods were improved, irrigation was expanded, and cultivable land was increased. Production focusing on exports (wheat, rice, sugar cane) was promoted and, finally, starting in 1821 a cotton monoculture was created, which for a short time brought in rich yields, but also made the economy prone to crises. The state also tried to achieve a monopoly, not only in the area of agriculture, but also in manufacturing and the beginnings of industrial production and in trade.

Through this centrally planned and forcibly imposed economic policy, Muḥammad ʿAlī created the basis for a huge army, which grew to over 150,000 soldiers and served as a means of imperial expansion aimed at obtaining raw materials. After defeating the Wahhābīs in Arabia, the Egyptians conquered Sudan in 1820–23, which remained aligned with Egypt until the end of the century. From 1822 to 1827 the Egyptian fleet and army, in agreement with the Porte, intervened in the Greek war of independence. The pasha's goal was to control Cyprus, Crete, and the Peloponnese (Morea), but his fleet was annihilated in 1827 in the Bay of Navarino by the allied fleets of the British, French, and Russians. By invading Syria and Asia Minor in 1831 he started pursuing his own power politics at the expense of the Ottoman Empire. The Egyptians were able to take Greater Syria and Cilicia (with Adana and Tarsus) in 1831–1840. England and Austria, acting in their own self-interest, came to the assistance of the Porte, forcing the Egyptians to abandon their conquests (except for Sudan). England wanted to prevent the emergence of a major Arabic power that might obstruct its trade interests and could threaten its ties to India.

Muḥammad 'Alī's Egypt is often compared with Japan during the era of Emperor Meiji (1868–1912), who attempted a similar experiment in forceful modernization and emancipation from European influence, and succeeded. Egypt under Muḥammad 'Alī was indeed the leading Arab country economically, technologically, and militarily. The fact that it failed here was certainly primarily due to European—especially British—intervention, although the structural weaknesses of the country, which were covered over by the forcibly imposed economic prosperity, certainly also played a significant role.

To some extent as compensation for the shattering of his plans to become a great power, Muḥammad 'Alī was assured the succession of his sons and grandsons, who were confirmed as pashas by the Porte. His son Sa'īd ruled from 1854 to 1863, followed by his grandson Ismā'īl, who reigned from 1863 to 1879 and received the title of khedive (Persian *chadīv* = viceroy) from the sultan in 1867. The Suez Canal was planned during the reign of Sa'īd and built from 1859 to 1869. It was a project that led within two decades to the ruin of the Egyptian state finances and the country's loss of independence. In contrast to Muḥammad 'Alī, who had prevented any and all foreign intervention, his successors opened Egypt up to all European influences and especially to European capital, since they hoped Egypt would thus catch up with the major European powers and allowed to enter their ranks, as reformers of the Ottoman Empire in Constantinople also hoped at the time. In fact, however, Egypt fell prey to foreign trade and money interests. An international pack of financiers, investors, and speculators exploited the opening of the country and sought their profits in a new El Dorado of the Middle East. Sa'īd Pasha's most egregious error was to let himself be talked into acquiring forty-four percent of the Suez Canal stocks, which threw him deeply into debt. In order to cover his short-term financial obligations he had to take out a long-term government bond on a London bank, for which he mortgaged the tax revenue of the provinces of the Nile delta. Because the debts could not be paid off, they accumulated astronomically under his successor Ismā'īl. On top of that came Ismā'īl's ambitious plans to modernize the country and his attempts to create an Egyptian imperium on the upper Nile and in equatorial Africa, in Eritrea and Abyssinia. More and more long-term government bonds had to be purchased, with growing concessions. The revenue earned by the recently built Egyptian railroad was mortgaged, as was the income of the private domains of the khedives. The astronomical level of the national debt ultimately led to the country's financial ruin in 1876 and the forced appointment of French and English financial controllers (dual control), who were responsible for monitoring all of Egypt's financial affairs. In 1876, the state debt administration came under foreign control with the establishment of the *Caisse de la dette publique*. The same thing happened five years later in Constantinople. A new, so-called "European" government was formed in Egypt in 1878, as an Englishman ran the financial department and a Frenchman became Minister for Public Works.

Now the resistance of the khedives and local officers and notables was aroused, but the European powers forced the Ottoman sultan to depose Ismāʿīl and to name his son Tawfīq (1879–92) as his successor. In early 1882 the opposition, led by Aḥmad ʿUrābī and supported by Egypt's large landowners and businesspeople, succeeded in taking power for a short time in Cairo and temporarily forcing out the foreign Mamluk, Turco-Circassian elite. However, as early as September of that year British troops occupied the country.

The Maghreb

The fates of the three North African regencies that formally belonged to the Ottoman Empire (Tripoli, Tunis, and Algiers) took a similar course, though with considerable chronological delays. In the phase of dīwān rule, the council (*dīwān*) of officers of the Ottoman fleet and army governed the port city and its environs. This period was followed in all three by the establishment of a dynasty that developed from the dīwān and which over the course of the nineteenth century came under economic and military pressure from Europe and were ultimately forced to give way to direct colonial rule.

This development was first concluded in Algiers. There, the French took advantage of an incident to intervene in 1827. The dey of Algiers is reputed to have hit the French consul with a flyswatter. After a lengthy blockade of the port, French troops occupied Algiers in June-July 1830 and forced the dey, Husayn, to step down. The Bourbon king Charles X was still reigning when the coup occurred, but even the constitutional monarchy of Louis Philippe, the "Citizen King," and, after 1871, the Third Republic continued to control the country under pressure from the military. In the face of vehement resistance, Constantine was taken in 1837, but the Tuat oases in the southwestern corner could not be occupied until 1900.

The dynasty of the beys in Tunis solidified its rule by abolishing the Janissary corps at the beginning of the century, similar to Muḥammad ʿAlī in Egypt. The Mamluk officers of Circassian descent continued to comprise the military and political elite. Tax reform and even the brief experiment with a constitution (*dustūr*) and a parliament (1861–64)—albeit a powerless one—were supposed to modernize the country and relieve the pressure from Europe. But like the situation in Egypt, the policy of purchasing government bonds in Europe led to a growing national debt starting in 1863, and in 1869 a financial commission was appointed to look after the interests of the European creditor nations of France, Italy, and Britain, thereby undermining the state authority. The era of Khayr al-Dīn Pasha (1869–1879), an Abkhas from the Caucasus who sought to modernize the country in the style of the Ottoman tanẓīmāt reforms, instead led to an even greater influx of foreign capital into the country. The situation rapidly worsened and, ultimately, the French occupied Tunisia in 1881 in order to forestall the colonial ambitions of a recently united Italy. Under their protectorate—the bey remained in office—the country now opened to European settlers, especially the French, but also Italians, who immediately started acquiring estates and engaging in agriculture and viticulture in grand style.

In Tripoli the dynasty of the Qaramanli pashas (starting in 1720) had already been eliminated by the Ottomans in 1825, who turned the semiautonomous regency back into a directly administered province. This move was an attempt to counter Egypt's independence efforts under Muḥammad ʿAlī and the French conquest of Algeria. As a result, European influence remained very weak in Tripoli. Not until the Italian conquest of Libya in 1911–12 did it become part of North Africa's colonial framework.

In Morocco, too, direct colonial rule was not established until the early twentieth century. The sultans of the ʿAlawid dynasty in fact had control only over the Atlantic coastal plain with the four royal cities of Fez, Meknes, Rabat, and Marrakech, and over a territory that often fluctuated in size and in which the central government was able to levy taxes with the help of loyal tribes. This area was called the *makhzan* (literally "warehouse, magazine") and its size varied according to the momentary political constellation. Powerful regional princes (*qā'id*, "leader") and monastery-like centers (*zāwiya*, "corner, hermitage") run by religious orders (*ṭarīqa*, plural *ṭuruq*) exercised power in certain regions that proved difficult if not impossible for a centralized authority to control. France and Spain agreed in 1904 to divide up the country into spheres of interest. The German Empire had similar ambitions, but these were quashed at the Algeciras Conference in 1906. When in March 1912 the French set up their protectorate covering most of the country, Morocco was divided. The north became a Spanish protectorate and the port city of Tangier obtained international status.

Strategies against European Intervention: Europeanization, Islamic Renewal, Nationalism

Local elites in the Middle East and North Africa clearly recognized the pressures exerted by the European powers starting in the nineteenth century and correctly assessed the ensuing dangers. There was no scarcity of attempts to resist the growing foreign control. Reforms in the Ottoman Empire, in the largely autonomous Egypt, and in Tunisia sought to institute a forced modernization, or even Europeanization. They hoped in this way to catch up to Europe, which was becoming increasingly powerful—economically, politically, and militarily—and to be accepted into the community of nations as equal partners. This failed to occur due to the Europeans' own interests, which put greater value on opening markets for their own industries than on allowing potential competition to emerge.

The policies pursued by both the Ottoman and the Egyptian governments to open up to Europe nevertheless had positive effects as well. In the Fertile Crescent and in Egypt, the amount of productive agricultural land increased considerably; in Iraq, the increase was even tenfold, as a result of settling the Bedouins. The construction of the first Aswān High Dam on the Nile in 1902 made agriculture independent of the fluctuating peaks in the annual flooding of the Nile. Telegraph networks and railroad lines made vast areas accessible—just a few examples should suffice here: the Baghdad railroad line (1888–1940) and the Ḥijāz line (1900–1908), which connected Damascus and Medina and was intended to continue on to

Yemen via Mecca. Steamship navigation connected waterways, which was particularly significant on the Tigris and the Euphrates; the construction of the Suez Canal eliminated the need for maritime trade routes around the Cape of Good Hope. Turkish and Arabic print media emerged. The flip side was that opening up to foreign capital, which largely financed these improvements in infrastructure, came at the expense of local trade, crafts, and agriculture.

European investors and entrepreneurs were not the only beneficiaries of the increased agricultural land area and intensified cultivation; local elites profited as well. A new class of local wealthy bourgeoisie and large landowners developed in the nineteenth century in the agrarian countries of the Middle East. Prior to the upheavals in the 1950s the notables came from these social classes and held political sway. In addition to these groups, who remained attached to the cultural and religious customs of their native roots, an elite developed in all of these countries which was oriented toward Europe and distanced themselves rigorously from the popular masses and their traditional ways of life, especially in the rural areas. This division of society, which of course also includes intermediate stages, has remained characteristic of Middle Eastern societies to today.

Europeanization was opposed especially by those segments of the population that viewed themselves as victims of the process, including the urban middle classes, the farmers, and the Bedouins. Countering the powerful foreign influences with something of their own meant returning to established traditions, especially Islam. Since the foreigners were perceived primarily as Christians, their own self-definition as Muslims was an obvious connecting link. In numerous places, charismatic religious leaders organized resistance, which was open to everyone who saw their status threatened by the rapid social changes.

Armed resistance first formed in places where the colonial power was immediately evident in the form of military troops. Thus the French in western Algeria encountered the resistance from the irregular militias around 'Abd al-Qādir, son of a sheikh of the mystical Qādiriyya order, who in 1832 called himself the "Sultan of the Arabs." The French had recognized him in a number of agreements and treaties as the leader of a partly independent west Algerian state, but when he started to constantly expand his sphere of power and declared *jihād* against all non-believers, the French opposed him with military strength from 1840 to 1847, ultimately forcing his surrender. He spent the rest of his life writing mystical works in exile in Damascus (1883).

The revolt of the Mahdī in Sudan was similarly rooted in the traditions of the mystical orders (*ṭuruq*). The forty-year-old sheikh Muḥammad Aḥmad claimed in 1881 to be "The Rightly Guided One" (*al-mahdī*), the savior and redeemer of Islam sent by God and anticipated by all Muslims. He vowed to expel the non-believers, referring to the British, whose General Charles Gordon had led a merciless regiment from the Sudanese capital of Kharṭūm (Khartoum), expanding Egypt's sphere of power—in reality Britain's—as far as equatorial Africa from 1874 to 1879 in the name of the khedive. The Anglo-Egyptian Convention of 1877 played a significant role in the rise of the Mahdī. The convention abolished slavery in Sudan, which was a powerful blow to the slave traders and holders there. Corresponding to his title, the Mahdī appeared as the renewer of Islam. His supporters called themselves *anṣār*, or helpers, based on the model of the Prophet Muḥammad's supporters in Medina. In the province of Kordofan, an Islamic state headed by the Mahdī emerged. Gordon, who in 1884 was redispatched by London, was killed in January 1885 when the Mahdī's soldiers stormed Kharṭūm. But the Mahdī also died the same year. The regime of his successor (*khalīfa*) was weakened by famine and internal strife, which allowed the British to regain control of Sudan in 1898. The family of the Mahdī continues to be involved in Sudanese politics even today.

In Libya, it was the Sanūsiyya (Sanusi) Order that took up the struggle against the Italian invaders in 1911. Founded in 1843 by the mystical sheikh Muḥammad al-Sanūsī (1787–1859), the strictly puritanical order, which—similar to the Arab Wahhābīs—recognized only the Qur'ān and the Sunna as foundations of Islam and frowned upon music and dance, established a number of religious centers (*zāwiya*) and was thus able to expand his influence and economic power from the Sirte and Cyrenaica (East Libya) all the way to central Africa, up to Lake Chad and the Wadai mountains. From its center in the Kufra oases (as of 1895), the order controlled the tribes and peasant inhabitants of a vast area. The Sanusi order tenaciously resisted the French in the Sahara and, starting in 1911, the Italians in Libya. Their resistance remained unbroken into the First World War and the Italians were forced to recognize their state. Libya's royal house developed after the Second World War from the dynasty of the order sheikhs.

Such religiously inspired resistance movements remained limited to certain regions and, with the exception of the Sanusis and the Arab Wahhābīs, were suppressed by the colonial powers' superior military strength. Towards the end of the nineteenth century, however, pan-Islamic ideas also emerged. Their most important advocate was the enigmatic agitator Jamāl al-Dīn al-Afghānī (ca. 1839–1897). He tried to hide his Iranian, Shi'ite family background behind supposedly Afghani—that is, Sunnī—origins. At the court of the king of Afghanistan, in Cairo and then Istanbul and then back to Cairo (1871–1879), in India, London, and Paris, in Russia, Iraq, and Iran, and finally back to Istanbul, he tirelessly spoke out as a teacher, author, and journalist for a strong, modern Islam that would unite the Muslim peoples in their struggle against the Europeans. He shied away neither from conspiring against Muslim monarchs who were submissive toward Europeans, nor from harshly criticizing the backwardness of the traditional Islamic scholars, the *'ulamā'*. Afghānī inspired an entire generation of Islamic modernists around the turn of the century. His most notable student was the Egyptian Muḥammad 'Abduh (1849–1905). The Islamic legal scholar, who was also a journalist, succeeded in winning the support of the khedive 'Abbās II in 1892 to reform the revered Azhar University, which then introduced modern subjects. In 1899 he became Grand Mufti (chief religious jurist) of Egypt. His Islamic modernism is open to various interpretations. It is invoked today by liberal as well as by Islamist ideologues. *Al-Nahḍa*, the "rebirth" or "renaissance," is the collective term for the movements of the late nineteenth century that proclaimed the revival of an Arabic and an Islamic identity.

Discussion on the future role of Islam in Middle Eastern society also raised the question of the function of the caliphate. The Turkish sultans only began using the title of successor (*khalīfa*) to the Prophet Muḥammad in the eighteenth century. They adopted the title so they could appear before the Russian czar as the patron of his Muslim subjects, since the czar claimed the role of protecting the orthodox Christians in the Balkans. Although the Ottomans were neither members of the Quraysh tribe nor even Arabs at all, they were recognized in Arab countries as the legitimate leaders of the Sunnī *umma*. As the only Muslim state that was still halfway intact, the Ottoman Empire was the obvious political frame of reference for the Sunnī Muslims. At most a kind of Turco-Arabic dual monarchy was considered as a possibility, similar to the Austro-Hungarian Empire—an idea advocated by the secret society of the *Qaḥṭāniyya* (named after the legendary progenitor of the Arabs), founded in 1909 by Syrian officers in Constantinople.

The mood began to change after a coup brought the Young Turks to power in Constantinople in 1908. Their regime pursued a course of forced Turkization of the empire. The Turkish language was to take precedence in the army, administration, judiciary, and school instruction; and Arabic was to be repressed. Even the sanctified Arabic call to prayer was to be replaced by a Turkish formula. This Turkish nationalism provoked an Arab nationalism. The idea of the Arab countries' seceding from the Ottoman Empire was raised and the establishment of an Arab caliphate was discussed as well. In 1901 the Syrian 'Abd ar-Rahmān al-Kawākibī (1849–1903) published a book in Cairo entitled *Umm al-qurā* (The Mother of All Cities)—referring to Mecca—in which he called for the reestablishment of an Arab caliphate. When in 1924 the Turkish national assembly in Ankara declared the caliphate of the Ottoman sultan abolished, scholar and journalist Muḥammad Rashīd Riḍā of Syria (1865–1935) called for the reestablishment of the office of the caliph in his treatise *al-Khilāfa aw al-imāma al-'uẓma* (The Caliphate or the Great Imamate). As a follower of Muḥammad 'Abduh he had immigrated in 1897 to Egypt, where he founded the influential monthly *al-Manār* (The Lighthouse, 1899–1940). Rashīd Riḍā proposed that the holders of the office should be determined by the leading scholars of the entire Islamic world: the scholars of the Azhar in Cairo, the Fatih and Süleymaniye mosques in Istanbul, the Zaytūna Mosque in Tunis, and the religious academy in Deoband, in northern India. One of the most promising candidates for the office was the Sharif of Mecca, al-Ḥusayn ibn 'Alī (ca. 1853–1931), who had been appointed in 1909 by the Young Turks as "Custodian of the Two Holy Shrines." As a descendant of al-Ḥasan, grandson of the Prophet, he was a member of the Quraysh tribe and the Hāshim clan and therefore also legitimated through religious tradition.

Aside from such pan-Islamic ideas that were rooted in al-Afghānī's agitation, a secular Arab nationalism also became apparent. The question of the existence of an "Arab nation" was posed for the first time in the early twentieth century. In 1869 the Ottoman tanzīmāt reformers proclaimed an "Ottoman" nationality, which included all the countless nationalities of the empire, but the artificial construction was disavowed after 1908 as a result of the Young Turks' crass policies of Turkification and disappeared with the collapse of the empire. Arab nationalisms—at first in plural form—broke new ground. Patriotic clubs and secret societies emerged in major cities such as Damascus and Constantinople, where the future shape of an Arab state was discussed. The framework of considerations remained at first limited to Greater Syria and Mesopotamia as the nucleus and the Arabian peninsula—entirely or in part—as an accessory. Egypt, under British control, remained out of reach. There the notion of an "Egyptian nation" had grown in the nineteenth century; with the territorial isolation of the Nile valley and its five-thousand-year history—first brought into public consciousness by Napoleon's expedition—this was certainly not lacking in historical roots. The Maghreb, however, did not even enter the field of vision at first. There was not yet any talk of a pan-Arab nationalism. A secular Arab nationalism, based on the Arabic language and Arab history and culture, without emphasis on the Muslim religion, appeared attractive especially for the Christian minorities. It is striking that numerous representatives of Arab-nationalist ideologies were Christians.

CHAPTER 6
State Building and Independence in the Twentieth Century

The First World War and the Mandatory Period

The decision of the Young Turk regime to enter the First World War on the side of the Central Powers sealed the fate of the Ottoman Empire. In response, the Allies abandoned the policy of supporting the "sick man of Europe" and began planning the partition of the empire. In their correspondence from July 1915 to March 1916, the British High Commissioner in Egypt Sir Henry McMahon promised the Sharif of Mecca Ḥusayn ibn 'Alī the crown of an Arabian kingdom in return for fighting against the Turks. From the outset, however, there were disagreements about the borders of this kingdom. According to the Arab position, the northern border was to run about thirty to forty miles north of the current Syrian-Turkish border and include Cilicia with Adana, Tarsus, and the port of Alexandretta (Iskenderun). The British, however, were adamant that predominantly non-Muslim areas such as Mount Lebanon should not be part of the future Arab kingdom. This was to apply for Palestine as well, where, as British Foreign Secretary Arthur Balfour declared on November 2, 1917, "a national home for the Jewish people" was to be established. However, on May 16, 1916, British diplomat Sir Mark Sykes and French Consul General in Beirut François Georges-Picot had already secretly determined their countries' future spheres of influence in the Fertile Crescent.

In the meantime, Sharif Ḥusayn ibn 'Alī and his sons Fayṣal and 'Abdallāh had taken up arms against the Turks in the summer of 1916. On October 29, Husayn ibn 'Alī assumed the title "King of the Arabs." The British and the French, however, only wanted to recognize him as "King of the

Ḥijāz." British Colonel T. E. Lawrence ("Lawrence of Arabia") coordinated attacks on the most important Turkish supply line, the Ḥijāz Railway, and on the Turkish stronghold of al-'Aqaba, which ended with Husayn triumphantly entering Damascus on October 1, 1918.

The end of the First World War and the Paris peace negotiations raised Arab elites' hopes for imminent independence, in particular since U.S. President Woodrow Wilson had tied the United States' entry into the war with the establishment of the "right to self-determination." As a result, British and French plans to partition the territory could not take place openly. The newly founded League of Nations legitimated their intervention only in the form of preliminary "mandates," which were in fact supposed to prepare those countries for independence.

The Syrian National Congress convened in June 1919 and proclaimed the country's independence on March 7, 1920. The French, however, were not prepared to concede this without a fight. In July 1920, the French defeated the troops of the Sharif's son Fayṣal and in September secured statehood for Lebanon, that is, the Christian—Maronite-dominated Mount Lebanon, which was expanded to encompass coastal cities, including Beirut, thereby cementing the partition of Lebanon and Syria.

In 1920, Shi'ite clerics in Iraq called for a revolt against the British, who had taken power in the country three years earlier. The uprising was quashed in 1921. The British installed Faisal—son of the "King of the Ḥijāz"—as king, while Fayṣal's brother 'Abdallāh had to content himself with the title "Emir of Transjordan." Jordan became formally independent in 1923, but remained under British mandate. Instead of the hoped-for "Kingdom of the Arabs," the Hashemites were given only three limited territories, two of which remained under British influence. Despite its formal independence, Iraq in particular remained closely tied to British interests through the Anglo-Iraqi treaty of October 1922. The British also retained direct control of Palestine, where the Balfour Declaration—to create a "home for the Jewish people"—was supposed to be implemented. As indicated in a statement by Colonial Minister Winston Churchill, the British were apparently considering a binational state dominated by non-Muslims similar to Maronite-Druze Lebanon. Jewish immigration to Palestine meanwhile continued. In July 1922, the mandate of the League of Nations came into force.

The Hashemites were also the losers on the Arabian Peninsula against the Saudis (Āl Sa'ūd) of Najd. In 1902, the young 'Abd al-'Azīz "Ibn Sa'ūd" recaptured Riyadh, thereby initiating the gradual reestablishment of a Saudi-Wahhābī kingdom. He occupied al-Ḥasā, the eastern province of the Ottoman Empire on the Persian Gulf, in 1912, and conquered 'Asīr, the mountainous landscape south of Mecca, in 1920. Although al-'Azīz was initially forced to recognize Ottoman suzerainty and content himself with the title of provincial governor in 1914, the titles he assumed illustrate his inexorable rise. In 1915 he declared himself "Emir of Najd," and in 1921, "Sultan of Najd and Its Dependencies." His political power was based on the military settlements he had established in 1913, which were comprised of Bedouin tribes he had settled and won over to Wahhabism and that formed a secret religious fraternal organization known as *al-Ikhwān* or "the Brotherhood," which he used in battle whenever necessary. After the Turkish National Assembly in Ankara declared the caliphate of the Ottoman sultan abolished in March 1924, a conflict emerged with the Sharif of Mecca Ḥusayn ibn 'Alī. The Sharif assumed the title of caliph, in response to which Ibn Sa'ūd sent his Ikhwān to Mecca, which he entered in December 1924. On January 8, 1926, Ibn Sa'ūd had himself declared "King of the Ḥijāz and Sultan of Najd." The British recognized Ibn Sa'ūd's independence in 1927, and his state was officially named "The Kingdom of Saudi Arabia" in 1932.

Zaghlūl Pasha (Sa'd Zaghlūl), a graduate of Azhar University and a lawyer by profession, led the struggle for independence in Egypt. He was the leader of a delegation (*wafd*) to London that sought unsuccessfully to negotiate the abrogation of protectorate status. The delegation also traveled to the Paris Peace Conference but there as well efforts remained fruitless. Zaghlūl's arrest and exile triggered rioting in Egypt that ultimately led the British to end the protectorate status, which was officially abolished in 1922. Egypt became a constitutional monarchy in 1923. Khedive Ismā'īl's son was crowned King Fu'ād I, but the British retained military control over the country. Until his death in 1927, Sa'd Zaghlūl, head of the Wafd party and briefly Prime Minister, sought to limit the king's autocracy. In 1936, an Anglo-Egyptian treaty regulated the rights of the former protectorate power and continued to allow British troops to be stationed at the Suez Canal.

The Salafiyya and the Muslim Brotherhood

Like its rival the *Wafd* party, the Muslim Brotherhood (*al-Ikhwān al-muslimūn*) in Egypt opposed the royal court and its politics. The brotherhood was founded in 1928 by Ḥasan al-Bannā (1906–1949), a primary school teacher who had belonged to various religious associations before establishing the brotherhood. With Bannā as "Supreme Guide" (*al-murshid al-'āmm*), the Muslim Brotherhood was organized according to a strict discipline. Modeled on mystic Sufi orders of the past, it developed into a modern mass movement with about half a million members in Egypt after the Second World War and numerous offshoots in the mandate territories. The goal of the organization was a total "Islamic order" (*al-niẓām al-islāmī*), that is, a political, social, and economic order based exclusively on the Qur'ān and the Sunna. The details of this order remained vague, as al-Bannā's missives and journal contributions were rather abstract, as were the principles established at a general conference held in Cairo in 1939. While the basic precept was undisputed, namely, that the traditional Islamic legal order of the Sharī'a should be reintroduced, it remained unclear what form this uncodified—and in principle uncodifiable—order should take.

The Muslim Brotherhood is the oldest and most successful of the various modern organizations that force Islam into an ideological corset and a self-sufficient organizational form for the purpose of achieving political and, above all, social aims and that can be designated as "Islamism"—as it is a modern ideology—in distinction to traditional Islam. The Muslim Brotherhood was the heir to those intellectuals who founded the Salafiyya movement around the turn of the century, an ideology that propagated an idealized conception of an original Islam, the golden era of "the pious predecessors" (*al-salaf al-ṣāliḥ*)—that is, the Prophet Muhammad, his first four successors, and their companions—as a model for the present. In particular the publicist Rashīd Riḍā can be seen as a pioneer of this idea. Islam as a total system regulating all domains of life "is at once a religion and a state order" (*al-Islām dīn wa-dawla*). While this ideological postulate largely ignores the facts of Islamic history, it has nevertheless proved extremely effective as a slogan: "Islam is the solution" (*al-Islām huwa al-ḥall*) to all political and social problems. Like the founders of the Muslim Brotherhood, the supporters of the movement have largely been members of the middle class and farmers, groups on whose behalf the organization has intervened when the state lacked either the will or the means. The brotherhood seeks to provide food and education as well as a technical infrastructure for the rapidly growing and barely urbanized populace in larger cities. After a member of the Muslim Brotherhood assassinated Egyptian prime minister Nuqrāshī Pasha in 1948, the movement was banned and went underground. Ḥasan al-Bannā was killed by the political police in 1949.

The Palestine Question

The British Balfour Declaration, which affirmed "the establishment in Palestine of a national home for the Jewish people," remained unfulfilled even a number of years after the First World War. Many Arabs were alarmed by increased Jewish immigration. Between 1932 and 1935, the Jewish population in Palestine rose from seventeen to twenty-seven percent. There had already been repeated riots and clashes in the 1920s. The polemic became increasingly heated and assumed religious tones. In 1933, Rashīd Riḍā declared that anyone who sold land to the British or to Jews was a traitor to Islam, and in 1935, the Mufti of Jerusalem Amīn al-Ḥusaynī issued a *fatwa* or legal pronouncement, which, in a free interpretation of Qur'an 33:72, designated Palestine as the "possession (*amāna*)" divinely entrusted to Muslims. The Nazi persecution of Jews and the global depression contributed to increasing Jewish immigration and an intensification of the conflict. Militant groups formed. The first revolt of Palestinian Arabs against the British mandate began in 1936 and ended when the Second World War started in 1939. In 1937, the British Peel Commission presented a partition plan that sought to limit the future Jewish state to Galilee and the coastal area down to south of Tel Aviv with Jerusalem and the port of Jaffa remaining part of the mandate territory. There were Arab conferences on Palestine in 1931 and 1937 addressing the future of the country, but neither was able to achieve any palpable success.

The Second World War and the Establishment of the Arab League

Many Arabs sympathized with the Axis powers during the Second World War. This was due in part to the enmity Arabs felt toward Great Britain and France as colonial powers as well as to concerns about continued Jewish immigration to Palestine. Fascist organizations arose sporadically, and anti-Semitic currents—in fact foreign to traditional Islam—also became evident. The British curbed Jewish immigration in 1939, and in May 1941 Foreign Secretary Anthony Eden even declared his support for future Arab unity. However, de Gaulle's government in exile granted independence to Lebanon in 1943 and to Syria in 1945, thus sealing the permanence of their partition. For the duration of the war, France and England retained their control of Arab countries.

The impending Allied victory raised the possibility of independence for the remaining Arab countries as well as issues of Arab unity, especially that of Palestine's place in the Arab world. For this reason, increased preparations for liberation were made even during the war. After preparatory negotiations in Alexandria in 1944, Egypt, Transjordan, Lebanon, Syria, Iraq, and Saudi Arabia, all of which were already formally independent, approved the Pact of the League of Arab States in Cairo on March 22, 1945. (North) Yemen joined on May 5, and the charter came into force on May 11. The goal of the pact was to promote economic, cultural, and social cooperation among Arab countries. It obligated all members to a foreign policy that did not contravene the interests of other member states and that affirmed the right of Arabs to Palestine.

Membership in the Arab League

Year	Members	Year	Members
1945	Egypt, Jordan, Lebanon, Syria, Iraq, Yemen, Saudi Arabia	1971	Bahrain, Qatar, United Arab Emirates, Oman
1953	Libya	1973	Mauritania
1956	Sudan	1974	Somalia
1958	Tunisia, Morocco	1976	Palestine (represented by the PLO)
1961	Kuwait		
1962	Algeria	1977	Djibouti
1967	South Yemen	1993	Comoros

The Founding of Israel and the First Middle East War

In 1947, the United Nations presented a partition plan for the future of Palestine. Arab states, however, refused to recognize this plan and voted against it at the UN General Assembly. Consequently, Great Britain announced that at midnight on May 15, 1948, it was abandoning its mandate for Palestine. In Tel Aviv on May 14, 1948, David Ben-Gurion proclaimed the state of Israel. Troops from member states of the Arab League responded by advancing on the following night. This intervention by Arab allies, who were poorly organized both militarily and politically, ended in a debacle. When a ceasefire was declared on January 7, 1949, Israel had made territorial gains considerably beyond the UN partition plan. The ceasefire line, which in Jerusalem ran directly west of the city wall in the old city, remained the de facto border between the Jewish state and its Arab neighbors for almost twenty years. The West Bank with East Jerusalem went to Jordan, while the Gaza Strip went to Egypt.

The catastrophe (*al-nakba*) was enormous. Flight and expulsion (about sixty percent of the 1.4 million Arab residents of the former mandate territory emigrated), dispossession, and the destruction of more than four hundred Arab villages by Jewish settlers laid the foundation for a conflict that continues even today and to which no end is in sight. There is no political development, no conflict in the Middle East that is not in some way affected by the Palestine conflict.

Ba'th Party and Nasserism

The major ideologies of the nineteenth and twentieth centuries—liberalism, socialism, communism, and fascism—all had their supporters in the Arab world as well. Following the Second World War, Arab nationalism, which had previously assumed a more regional form ("Egypt for Egyptians"), took on pan-Arab tones. The establishment of the Arab League indicated the direction of future developments. People spoke of a single "Arab nation," defined in particular through a common language, history, and culture, and no longer through Islam. It was above all Christian authors from Syria and Lebanon who laid the theoretical foundations for secular Arab nationalism (Pan-Arabism). This is evident, for example, in the fact that in

1940 two Syrian teachers, the Christian Michel 'Aflaq and the Muslim Ṣalāḥ al-Dīn al-Bīṭār, founded the *Ba'th* ("resurrection" or "renaissance"), a socialist party opposing the power of the wealthy bourgeoisie and large landowners. It did not take long before additional leftist nationalist groups merged with the party. The declared goals of the Ba'th were Arab "unity, freedom, and socialism." The party was oriented around a secular nationalist ideology, in which Islam was regarded as merely one part of a common cultural Arab heritage.

While the Maghreb states initially remained under French rule, there was a series of revolutions in the eastern part of the Arab world directed against the ruling elite: the land-owning class (which had arisen in the nineteenth century), the wealthy bourgeoisie, and the established dynasties. These revolutions were triggered above all by unresolved social problems, as well as by the failure of old elites with regard to the Palestine issue and their collaboration with the former colonial powers (which continued to exert influence in the area). Leaders of the revolutionary movements were frequently officers, who themselves came from the middle classes and found support there.

A series of military coups began in Syria in 1949, resulting in successive military dictatorships. However, the actual decade of revolts occurred between 1952 and 1962. It was during this period that the remaining Arab countries obtained their independence. In Egypt, the "Free Officers," including Gamāl 'Abd al-Nāṣir (Nasser, 1918–1970), brought down the regime of King Fārūq (1936–1952) in 1952. In Syria, after the parliamentary system was reinstituted in 1954, the Ba'th had their first great election vic-tory. The party was the driving force behind the experimental unification with Egypt (see page 158). In the same year, a long guerrilla war against the French began in Algeria. By 1962, approximately 20,000 French and 1,000,000 Algerians had lost their lives in the conflict. The Algerian independence struggle mobilized people far beyond Algeria and the Arab world. It came to be seen as the paradigm for liberation movements throughout the Third World. The "Independence" party (*Istiqlāl*) was founded in Morocco in 1944. The popular Sultan Muḥammad V (1927–1958) led the national movement. The French exiled him to Madagascar in 1953, but due to the rioting in the country they were forced to bring him back, and granted Morocco full independence on March 2, 1956. On that same day, Habib Bourguiba (*Bū Ruqaiba*), a lawyer, assumed leadership of the New Constitutional Party (Neo-Destour) in Tunisia. In Iraq, King ʿAbdallāh was deposed and murdered in a putsch by Colonel Qassim (*al-Qāsim*). In Yemen, there was a coup by the army against the Zaydī imam al-Badr in 1962; the proclamation of a republic led to a civil war that lasted eight years. Last to fall was the monarchy in Libya. Here young officers, led by Colonel Muʿammar al-Qaddafi (born in 1942), deposed King Idrīs from the dynasty of the Sanusi sheikhs in 1969. In the same year, the military led by Colonel Jaʿfar Numayrī assumed power in Sudan.

During Nasser's presidency (1954–1970), Egypt assumed the leading political role in the Arab world. Nasser was successful in a number of actions that greatly enhanced his prestige, even far beyond Egypt's borders. The first of these was his treaty with the British in 1954 regarding the definitive withdrawal of their troops. The nationalization of the Suez Canal in July 1956 did lead to the final military intervention by France and Great Britain in alliance with Israel in October and November of that year, but this was brought to a halt by the two superpowers, the United States and the Soviet Union. On February 1, 1958, Nasser announced that the Syrian Baʿth Party had agreed to a union between Egypt and Syria as the "United Arab Republic" (UAR), which Yemen—at the time still governed by the imam—formally entered. This union was supposed to be the seed of a united Arab nation. A joint National Assembly was formed in 1960. Only a year later, however, the Syrians, who felt dominated by the Egyptians, withdrew from the union following a rightist coup. When revolutionary officers in Yemen brought down the imam in 1962 and proclaimed a republic, Nasser took their side and supported the revolutionaries in the subsequent civil war from 1962 to 1969, especially with his air force.

The United States sought to contain the Soviet Union and keep it out of the Indian Ocean and away from Middle Eastern oil reserves by means of the Baghdad Pact of 1955 (between Turkey, Iraq, Iran, and Pakistan), the Middle East Treaty Organization orchestrated by Britain and the United States. Nasser initially attempted to lead the Non-Aligned Movement, but then increasingly sought support from the Eastern bloc, which helped to finance the enormous new Aswan High Dam. Iraq, Syria, Libya, Algeria, Somalia, and South Yemen (which became independent in 1967) all relied on support from the Soviet Union and on intimate economic, military, and political cooperation with the Eastern bloc.

The Six-Day War (June 1967)

Nasser's star began to wane when he overestimated his own power and engaged in a war with Israel to liberate all of Palestine. Palestinian exiles in Kuwait—including Yasir Arafat (1929-2004)—founded the Fataḥ Organization (*al-Fatḥ*, "the victory") in 1959. In January 1965, the organization called for an armed struggle against Israel. The Syrian Ba'th party's support of the Fataḥ Organization led Nasser to worry about his reputation as leader of the Arab nation; although inadequately armed he took the reins of a movement that threatened to slip out of his control. He provoked a war by occupying the Sinai Peninsula and demanding the withdrawal of UN troops. Like the war of 1948–1949, the Six-Day War (June 5–10, 1967) ended in a military disaster for the Arab side. Israel took not only East Jerusalem (the old city), which had been in Jordanian control, but also the entire West Bank and the Gaza Strip, where a Jewish settlement policy was introduced that has subsequently been supported or tolerated by all Israeli governments.

This defeat marked the demise of Nasserism, the failure of an ideology of nationalist, pan-Arabist, and socialist ideas. Nasser's death in 1970 bolstered Islamic movements and groups throughout the world.

The Sadat Era (1970–1981): The October War, the Infitāḥ, and the Oil Crisis

In 1971, Egyptians approved the new liberal constitution (which nonetheless granted the president extensive powers) presented by Nasser's successor Anwar al-Sadat (al-Sādāt). In October 1973, Sadat sent troops across the Suez Canal in a surprise attack, though the victory was quickly neutralized by the United States' intervention. Nevertheless, Egypt regained the Sinai, and the Suez Canal was opened again in 1975. Sadat paid for this partial success by turning to the West politically, ending Egypt's socialist experiment, and liberalizing the economy, in short, by "opening" (*infitāḥ*) the country to Western capital. In 1977, Sadat made a surprise trip to Israel, prayed in the al-Aqṣā Mosque, and spoke before the Knesset. On March 26, 1979, Egypt became the first Arab country reach a peace agreement with Israel at the U.S. Camp David, which included the recognition of their shared border. A "rejectionist front" formed by other Arab countries opposed the peace agreement, and Egypt's membership in the Arab League was suspended from 1979 to 1989.

One consequence of the October War of 1973—known as the Yom Kippur War in Israel and the Ramaḍān War among Arabs—was the so-called oil price revolution. The founding of the Organization of Petroleum Exporting Countries (OPEC) in 1960 marked an attempt to counterbalance the power of multinational oil companies. The oil embargo of 1973-74, which was agreed to in Vienna as a political weapon, led to unparalleled price increases: The cost of a barrel of oil increased tenfold. This led to an unprecedented flow of capital into the oil exporting countries, particularly Saudi Arabia. The oil embargo was not successful in terms of foreign policy, as consumer nations were able to turn to their own resources to reduce consumption and to develop alternative energy sources. In terms of domestic politics, this influx of capital did more to cement existing political structures than to change them. Saudi Arabia, as a distributor of petrodollars, was now able to exercise a certain hegemony over the other Arab countries, especially those without oil reserves and those bordering on Israel. The Saudis used their influence to strengthen Islamist movements, first and foremost the Muslim Brotherhood, as well as regional tribal leaders, for example in (North) Yemen and South Yemen, thereby weakening leftist revolutionary movements and parties.

The Islamic revolution in Iran in 1978–79 toppled the pro-American regime of the Shah and led to the establishment of the Islamic Republic of Iran under Āyatollāh Khomeinī. It also fueled the hopes of Arab Islamists that similar coups would be possible in their own countries. On November 20, 1979, a group of approximately five hundred Saudi sectarians proclaiming the return of the awaited Mahdi occupied Islam's most sacred shrine, the Masjid al-Ḥarām mosque with the Ka'ba in Mecca. Authorities were able to overpower them only after a two-week siege. The murder of Sadat during a parade in Cairo on October 6, 1981, was also the work of militant Islamists from Upper Egypt. Between 1983 and 1985, Sudanese dictator Colonel Numayrī, who was supported by the Muslim Brotherhood, experimented with implementing Islamic law, introducing penal and tax codes based on the Sharī'a.

The Lebanese Civil War (1975–1990) and the Iran-Iraq War (1980–1988)

For the regimes of most Arab countries, the 1970s, 1980s, and 1990s proved to be a period of unprecedented stability. In July 1968, the Iraqi Ba'th party led by General Aḥmad Ḥasan al-Bakr ousted President 'Ārif in a bloodless coup and assumed control of the country for the next thirty-five years. Colonel Qaddafi came to power in Libya in 1969 after bringing down the monarchy and continues to rule the country even today. In 1970, then Syrian minister of defense Ḥāfiẓ al-Asad participated in a coup and established a Ba'thist regime, which his son Bashar has continued after Asad's death in 2000. The assassination of leading politicians did not affect this stability. In Egypt the transition from Sadat to President Ḥusnī Mubārak (born in 1928) in 1981 brought no fundamental political changes. The murder of King Faisal in 1975 shook the Saudi monarchy as little as did the transition from his successor Khālid to King Fahd in 1982. The Hashemite king Hussain ruled Jordan from 1952 to 1999, King Ḥasan II ruled in Morocco from 1961 to 1999, and Sultan Qābūs has governed Oman since 1970. The FLN (*Front de libération nationale*), which led Algeria's war for independence against France and came to power after independence was achieved in 1962, has also successfully cemented its power. Habib Bourguiba, who had ruled Tunisia after independence in 1956, was removed in 1987 by the former prime minister General Zīn El-'Ābidīne Ben 'Alī (born in 1936), a change of power that also took place within the ruling elite.

This stability was attained almost universally by the cementing of existing power relations and the rigorous use of police and secret service. In Syria, President al-Asad violently suppressed the opposition of the Muslim Brotherhood. More than 10,000 people are said to have died in the bombing of the city of Ḥamāh. The governments of Egypt, Jordan, and Morocco have, in contrast, attempted to integrate the Islamist opposition through concessions and limited, controlled government participation.

Despite their nationalist, pan-Arabist ideology, the Ba'th regimes in Syria and Iraq had only narrow regional power bases. Ḥāfiz al-Asad was supported especially by the Alawites, a small Shi'ite religious community in the Syrian coastal range (not to be confused with the Alevis in Turkey).

Many Alawite men have made a career in the Syrian military, particularly in the air force. Saddam Hussein (born in 1937), who took control of the Iraqi Ba'th party in 1979, ruled the country with the help of the Tikrīt clan, a circle loyal to him with its roots in and around Tikrīt, Saddam's native city on the Tigris. This regional and narrowly limited power base and a political agenda organized primarily around securing its own rule have made both Ba'th regimes completely incapable of effectively representing pan-Arab interests and have also brought them into open rivalry with each other more than once.

Lebanon, in contrast, has been unstable. An unwritten "national pact" has existed here since independence in 1943, regulating the separation of power in the legislative and executive branches according to precisely balanced percentages of the different religious groups. It gave Christians, especially the Maronites, political advantage over Druzes, Shi'ites, and Sunnīs. However, consensus on this proportionality disintegrated in the 1970s as a result of demographic displacements caused primarily by the influx of Palestinians, as well as growth in the Shi'ite population in southern Lebanon. As the government had lost virtually all control over the south of the country, fighters of the Palestinian Liberation Organization (PLO), founded in 1964 in response to the defeat in the Six-Day War, were able to settle here among the primarily Shi'ite population after being driven out of the West Bank, establishing training camps and engaging in attacks on villages on the Israeli side of the border.

Open civil war erupted in Lebanon in 1975. The PLO was the spearhead for the Muslim minorities here, who sought to break the Christian dominance that had been firmly established since the nineteenth century. The Syrian military intervened on the side of the Muslims, an action that the Arab League then legitimated through a retrospective mandate in the summer of 1976. After the Islamic Revolution in Iran in 1979, the Shi'ites in southern Lebanon became increasingly radicalized. Their militant organization Hezbollah (*Hizbu'llāh*, "party of God") joined in the struggle against Israel. This led to a military intervention by Israel in 1982–83, which ended with the occupation of Beirut, a renewed but brief invigoration of Christian forces, and the expulsion of the PLO from southern Lebanon. PLO leader Yasir Arafat went into exile in Tunisia. The general exhaustion of the embattled militias prepared the way for negotiations, which led to a peace plan under the aegis of the Arab League in Ṭā'if, Saudi Arabia in the fall of 1989. The plan was supposed to end the civil war and establish a new political basis in the country. At the end of 1990, the Ṭā'if Agreement was enforced by Syrian troops and written into the constitution.

After the Islamic Revolution led to a regime change in Iran in 1979, Iraqi president Saddam Hussein believed that he could now assert Iraq's old claims to the mouth of the Shatt al-'Arab (the confluence of the Tigris and Euphrates rivers) and to the Iranian border province of Khūzestān, an area rich in oil with a predominantly Arab population. For the United States and its Western allies, Saddam's war against the new Iranian regime offered a welcome opportunity to retaliate against an enemy that had subverted an important pillar of American alliance building in the Middle East, and they provided the Iraqis with support. This war in the Persian Gulf region lasted eight years (1980– 1988) and ended in a stalemate. Initially pushed back by Iranian troops, the Iraqis were subsequently able to regain territory. When the Iranian leader Khomeinī was forced to accept a ceasefire, the prewar borders at Shatt al-'Arab were reestablished.

The 1990s: The First Intifāḍa and the Gulf War

Mikhail Gorbachev's policy of perestroika beginning in 1986 and the collapse of the Soviet Union in 1990 marked the dissolution of antagonisms between the Soviet Union and the United States. The Cold War had allowed the Arab states to seek support from one superpower or the other according to their needs. The United States was now the sole superpower that Arab governments had to come to terms with.

The end of the opposition between East and West also rendered Palestine superfluous as a substitute battleground for the superpowers. It was now possible for the United States and the Soviet Union to work together for a solution to the conflict in the West Bank and the Gaza Strip. There had been strikes and heavy rioting in these areas in late 1987. This first *Intifāḍa* ("uprising") continued throughout 1988 and 1989. The central committee of the PLO, which was still in exile in Tunis, declared Yasir Arafat president of an "Independent State of Palestine." Israel took part in top-secret talks with the PLO in Oslo, and official negotiations were held under the aegis of the United States and the Soviet Union in Madrid in October

1991. These negotiations were facilitated by the election of the Labor Party in Israel and the formation of Yitzhak Rabin's government in the summer of 1992. A limited autonomy on the basis of the formula "Land for Peace" was ultimately negotiated on August 19, 1993. Initially for Gaza and Jericho, it was supposed to be gradually expanded. Israel and the PLO agreed to recognize each other. The agreement, which was signed in Washington in the presence of President Bill Clinton on September 13, 1993, appeared finally to provide the foundation for lasting peace in the Middle East. Arafat, Prime Minister Rabin, and Foreign Minister Shimon Peres were awarded the Nobel Peace Prize in 1994.

In the meantime, however, U.S. involvement in the Middle East had acquired a new dimension when, in August 1990, Saddam Hussein occupied Kuwait and claimed its oil reserves as compensation for his expenditures in the Iran-Iraq War. The independent country of Kuwait, a member state of the United Nations, was proclaimed a province that had historically belonged to Iraq. Saddam hoped that in alliance with Syria and Yemen he could break Saudi Arabia's hegemony and gain access to oil reserves along the Persian Gulf. However, if Saddam had thought that the United States would tacitly support or tolerate this move, he was grievously mistaken. Supported by a United Nations resolution, the United States forged an alliance of twenty-eight nations, including most Arab countries, even Syria. Only Libya, Jordan, and the PLO sided with Iraq. After the ultimatum expired in January 1991, American and allied troops defeated the Iraqi army in the fourteen-day operation called Desert Storm, which was launched from Saudi territory. Coalition forces, however, neither advanced to Baghdad nor toppled the Ba'th regime. Saddam Hussein was even able to violently suppress a Shi'ite uprising in the south of the country in 1991 and to retaliate with mass executions without any reaction by the victors. The economic sanctions imposed by the United Nations seriously damaged the economic infrastructure of the country and hit the civilian population the hardest. The victors also erected no-fly zones north of the 36th parallel and south of the 33rd parallel in order to protect the Kurds and the Shi'ites from further reprisals. Iraq's constant obstruction of UN weapon inspectors, who were supposed to prevent Iraqi production of nuclear, biological, and chemical weapons, soon brought Saddam Hussein into renewed conflict with the United States.

CHAPTER 7
The Beginning of the Twenty-first Century

The Second Intifāḍa

In the summer of 2000, talks between the PLO and the Israeli government of Ehud Barak resumed under the aegis of the United States, nourishing hopes for a final peace in the Israel-Palestine conflict. But Camp David II was an utter failure, especially—although details were never officially made public—regarding the issues of the fixing of the border, the problematic right of return for displaced Palestinians, and the question of Jerusalem. The Arab enclaves in East Jerusalem would have remained separated from the Palestinian state and interspersed with Jewish settlements. On the Ḥaram al-Sharīf—the Temple Mount of the Jews—the Palestinians would have had owned the al-Aqṣā Mosque and the Dome of the Rock, but not the ground on which they stood. Yasir Arafat rejected Barak's offer as unacceptable for the Palestinians. Then the provocative appearance on the Temple Mount by Ariel Sharon, then right-wing leader of the opposition, on September 28, 2000, triggered the Second Intifāḍa, which led to an extraordinary escalation of the conflict, with a series of suicide attacks by the radical Islamist Palestinian organizations *al-Jihād al-islāmi* and *Ḥamās* ("enthusiasm, zeal"; actually an acronym for Islamic Resistance Movement) and military reprisals by Israel, during which 'Arafāt was temporarily besieged in his headquarters in Ramallāh. The "road map" proposed in 2003 by U.S. president George W. Bush in cooperation with the United Nations, the European Union, and Russia, which was intended to lead to a final peace, was quickly removed from the negotiating table. Even though the Jewish settlements in the Gaza Strip have been removed, the resolution of the conflict seems more distant than ever. The electoral victory of the radical Islamist Ḥamās in the Palestinian territories and the Israeli army's attack on the positions of the Hezbollah militias (Shi'ites supported by Iran) in southern Lebanon in the summer of 2006 dangerously intensified the situation.

The Iraq War

The attacks on the World Trade Center and the Pentagon on September 11, 2001, by nineteen terrorists of Arab descent led to a provisional reorientation of U.S. Middle East policies, the ultimate effects of which remain to be seen. A second military intervention in Iraq was part of considerations by the U.S. government from the very beginning. Various justifications were offered for attacking Saddam Hussein's Ba'th regime: Saddam's alleged production of weapons of mass destruction; support for the terrorist organization Al-Qā'ida ("the basis") of Usāma bin Lādin, which was responsible for the attacks of September 11; and regime change in Iraq to start the process of democratization in the entire region. Only the last of these carries any real weight. The U.S. government evidently planned to restructure the entire region. The attack by U.S. and British units, this time from bases in Kuwait, started on March 20, 2003, and toppled Saddam Hussein's regime with the capture of Baghdad on April 9. Saddam himself managed to escape, but was apprehended on December 13. Many senior officials were arrested or turned themselves in. Civil authority was initially placed under American civilian administration, which was responsible for the country's reconstruction. The armies of the victors, meanwhile reinforced by Poland and other allies, remained in the country.

Whether or not Iraq can be pacified is largely dependent on the position of the Shi'ite population, which makes up about sixty-five percent of the total Iraqi population. If the autonomous Kurds are not included in these statistics, then the Shi'ites comprise seventy-five percent of the Arab population, compared to twenty-five percent Arab Sunnīs. Even in the capital of Baghdad, which lies within the so-called Sunnī Triangle, the Shi'ites have probably long since become a majority of the population. The influx of refugees from the south following the Iran-Iraq War of 1980–88 have transformed the suburbs of al-Kāẓimiyya in the north, with its Shi'ite shrine, and the former Saddam City in the east (now named Sadr City, *Madīnat al-Ṣadr,* after a Shi'ite Āyatollāh murdered at the behest of Saddam), with their two to three million residents, into Shi'ite strongholds.

These could play a significant role in a conflict for power in the future Iraq. Although Āyatollāh as-Sīstānī, leading cleric of the Shi'ite university complex in Najaf, supports nonviolent resistance in the time-honored quietist tradition of senior Shi'ite clergy—in contrast to the young Muqtadā aṣ-Ṣadr, who organizes armed militias in Sadr City—the Shi'ites oppose foreign occupation forces in general, which coincides with the Sunnī opposition. A national resistance in which Arab identity carries more weight than religious affiliation is starting to form. Any order imposed on the people from the outside without their approval would remain unstable. But no matter how the experiment ends, the occupation and subjugation of a major Arab country by the United States has opened up a completely new chapter in the history of the Arabs.

The Arab countries between the Atlantic and the Tigris are today considered part of the "crisis belt," which extends even farther to include Iran, Afghanistan, and the Indian subcontinent, all the way to southeast Asia. The centers of conflict in this part of the world are indeed numerous. Violent coups, wars, and civil wars have followed one after another since the end of the Second World War. The perpetual conflict around Palestine seems far from resolution. Again and again, oil reserves in several Arab countries provide grounds for foreign powers to intervene politically or militarily in pursuit of their own interests. And let us not forget that for a period of time the entire Arab world, with the exception of central Arabia, was subject to more or less direct European colonial rule; that is a trauma that still has enormous aftereffects today and continues to feed anti-Western attitudes. Especially the foundation of Israel, a state of European emigrants, is viewed within this context as a source of outrage as long as the Palestinians are not allowed to have their own country. On top of this are the immense demographic and economic problems and the unresolved questions of the future political order. The models of the dictatorial or patrimonial regimes and the traditional monarchies that have prevailed until now are competing with the ideas of democratic constitutions and with drafts for Islamist state and social systems, as favored by the Muslim Brotherhood. The Arab countries have meanwhile become fully integrated into the framework of the global economy and world politics. Their internal policies will have to adapt to that. The momentous upheavals that began with the "Arab Spring" of 2010 and 2011 certainly represent the beginnings of such an adaptation.

Bibliography

General Works

Jonathan P. Berkey, *The Formation of Islam: Religion and Society in the Near East, 600-1800* (Cambridge: Cambridge Univ. Press, 2003).
Michael Cook, general ed., *The New Cambridge History of Islam*, 6 vols. (Cambridge: Cambridge Univ. Press, 2010).
Ulrich Haarman and Heinz Halm, eds., *Geschichte der arabischen Welt*, 4th revised and expanded edition (Munich: C. H. Beck, 2001).
Albert Hourani, *A History of the Arab Peoples* (New York: Warner Books, 1992).
Bernard Lewis, *The Arabs in History*, 6th ed. (Oxford and New York: Oxford Univ. Press, 1993 [first ed.: London and New York: Hutchinson's University Library, 1950]).

Pre-Islamic Arabia

G. W. Bowersock, *Roman Arabia* (Cambridge, Mass.: Harvard Univ. Press, 1983).
Robert G. Hoyland, *Arabia and the Arabs from the Bronze Age to the Coming of Islam* (London and New York: Routledge, 2001).
Jan Retsö, *The Arabs in Antiquity: Their History from the Assyrians to the Umayyads* (London and New York: Routledge Curzon, 2003).

The Beginnings of Islam

Hartmut Bobzin, *Mohammed*, 3rd ed. (Munich: C. H. Beck, 2006 [2000]).
_____. *Der Koran* (Munich: C. H. Beck, 1999).
Michael Cook, *Muhammad* (Oxford: Oxford Univ. Press, 1983).
_____. *The Koran: A Very Short Introduction* (Oxford: Oxford Univ. Press, 2000).
Patricia Crone. *Slaves on Horses: The Evolution of the Islamic Polity* (Cambridge: Cambridge Univ. Press, 1980).
_____. *The Meccan Trade and the Rise of Islam* (Princeton: Princeton Univ. Press, 1987).
Fred McGraw Donner, *The Early Islamic Conquests* (Princeton: Princeton Univ. Press, 1981).
G. R. Hawting, *The First Dynasty of Islam*, 2nd ed. (London; New York: Routledge, 2000).
Hugh Kennedy, *The Early 'Abbāsid Caliphate: A Political History* (Totowa, NJ: Barnes and Noble, 1981).
_____. *The Prophet and the Age of the Caliphates: The Islamic Near East from the Sixth to the Eleventh Century* (Harlow: Longman, 2004 [1986]).
Rudi Paret, *Mohammed und der Koran* (Stuttgart: W. Kohlhammer, 1957) (reprinted numerous times).
_____. *Der Koran* (Stuttgart: W. Kohlhammer Verlag, 1999).

Montgomery Watt, *Muhammad at Mecca* (Oxford: Clarendon Press, 1953).
_____. *Muhammad at Medina* (Oxford: Clarendon Press, 1956).
Julius Wellhausen, *The Arab Kingdom and Its Fall*, trans. Margaret Graham Weir (Beirut: Khayats, 1963 [first English ed.: Calcutta: Univ. of Calcutta, 1927]).

'Arabiyya

Johann Fück, *Arabiya: Untersuchungen zur arabisch Sprach- und Stilgeschichte* (Berlin: Akademischer Verlag, 1950).
Hamilton A. R. Gibb, *Arabic Literature: An Introduction* (Oxford and New York: Oxford Univ. Press, 1962).
Wolfhart Heinrichs, *Neues Handbuch der Literaturwissenschaft,* vol. 5: *Orientalisches Mittelalter* (Wiebelsheim: Aula Verlag, 1990).
Charles Pellat, *The Life and Works of Jāḥiẓ*, translation of selected texts, trans. D. M. Hawke (London: Routledge & K. Paul, 1969).

Arab Reception of Antiquity

Ahmad Dallal, *Islam, Science, and the Challenge of History* (New Haven: Yale Univ. Press, 2010).
Dimitri Gutas, *Greek Thought, Arabic Culture: The Graeco-Arabic Translation Movement in Baghdad and Early 'Abbāsid Society (2nd-4th, 8th-10th centuries)* (London and New York: Routledge, 1981).
Franz Rosenthal, *The Classical Heritage in Islam*, trans. E. and J. Marmorstein (Berkeley: Univ. of California Press, 1975).
George Saliba, *Islamic Science and the Making of the European Renaissance* (Cambridge, Mass.: MIT Press, 2007).
Gotthard Strohmaier, *Von Demokrit bis Dante. Die Bewahrung antiken Erbes in der arabischen Kultur* (Hildesheim, Zurich, and New York: Georg Olms, 1996) (Olms Studien 43).
Juan Vernet, *La cultura hispanoárabe en Oriente y Occidente* (Barcelona: Ariel Historia, 1978).

The Mamluks

David Ayalon, *The Mamluk Military Society* (London: Variorum Reprints, 1979).
Daniel Pipes, *Slaves Soldiers and Islam: The Genesis of a Military System* (New Haven: Yale Univ. Press, 1981).

Tenth to Fifteenth Centuries

Mark R. Cohen, *Under Crescent and Cross: The Jews in the Middle Ages*, 2nd ed. (Princeton: Princeton Univ. Press, 2008 [1994]).
Francesco Gabrieli, *Arab Historians of the Crusades*, selected and trans. from Ara-

bic sources by Francesco Gabrieli; trans. from Italian by E. J. Costello (Berkeley: Univ. of Calif. Press, 1969). [Original title: *Storici Arabi delle Crociate*]

Sidney H. Griffith, *The Church in the Shadow of the Mosque: Christians and Muslims in the World of Islam* (Princeton: Princeton Univ. Press, 2008).

S. D. Goitein, *Jews and Arabs: Their Contacts through the Ages*, 3rd ed. (New York: Schocken Books, 1974 [1955]).

Gustav E. von Grunebaum, *Medieval Islam: A Study in Cultural Orientation*, 2nd ed. (Chicago: Univ. of Chicago Press, 1966 [1946]).

Heinz Halm, *The Empire of the Mahdi: The Rise of the Fāṭimids*, trans. Michael Bonner (Leiden and New York: E.J. Brill, 1996).

_____. *Die Kalifen von Kairo: Die Fatimiden in Ägypten 973-1074* (Munich: C. H. Beck, 2003).

Joel Kraemer, *Humanism in the Renaissance of Islam: The Cultural Revival during the Buyid Age*, 2nd ed. (Leiden and New York: Brill, 1996).

Maurice Lombard, *The Golden Age of Islam*, trans. Joan Spencer, new preface by Jane Hathaway (Princeton: Markus Wiener Publishers, 2004).

Macolm C. Lyons and D.E.P. Jackson, *Saladin – The Politics of Holy War* (Cambridge and New York: Cambridge Univ. Press, 1982).

Hans Eberhard Mayer, *The Crusades*, trans. John Gillingham (Oxford and New York: Oxford Univ. Press, 1972 [1965]).

Adam Mez, *The Renaissance of Islam*, trans. Salahuddin Khuda Bukhsh and D. S. Margoliouth (New York: AMS Press, 1975 [1st English ed., London: Luzac & Co., 1937]).

From 1500 to 1800

Jane Hathaway (with contributions by Karl K. Barbir), *The Arab Lands under Ottoman Rule, 1516-1800* (New York: Pearson Longman, 2008).

Abraham Marcus, *The Middle East on the Eve of Modernity* (New York: Columbia Univ. Press, 1989).

The Nineteenth Century

Khaled Fahmy, *All the Pasha's Men* (Cambridge: Cambridge Univ. Press, 1997).

Albert Hourani, *Arabic Thought in the Liberal Age 1798-1939* (Cambridge and New York: Cambridge Univ. Press, 1962 [reprinted numerous times]).

Josef Matuz, *Das Osmanische Reich. Grundlinien seiner Geschichte* (Darmstadt: Wissenschaftliche Buchgesellschaft, 1985).

P. J. Vatikiotis, *The History of Egypt from Muhammad Ali to Sadat* (Baltimore: John Hopkins Univ. Press, 1969).

M. E. Yapp, *The Making of the Modern Near East, 1792-1923* (New York: Longman, 1996).

The Twentieth Century

Henner Fürtig, *Kleine Geschichte des Irak* (Munich: C. H. Beck, 2003).
Toby Craig Jones, *Desert Kingdom: How Oil and Water Forged Modern Saudi Arabia* (Cambridge, Mass.: Harvard Univ. Press, 2010).
Gudrun Krämer, *A History of Palestine: From the Ottoman Conquest to the Founding of the State of Israel*, trans. Graham Harman (Princeton: Princeton Univ. Press, 2008).
Reinhard Schulze, *Geschichte der islamischen Welt im 20. Jahrhundert* (Munich: C. H. Beck, 1994).
M. E. Yapp, *The Near East since the First World War: A History to 1995* (New York: Longman, 1996).

THE OTTOMAN EMPIRE

A SHORT HISTORY

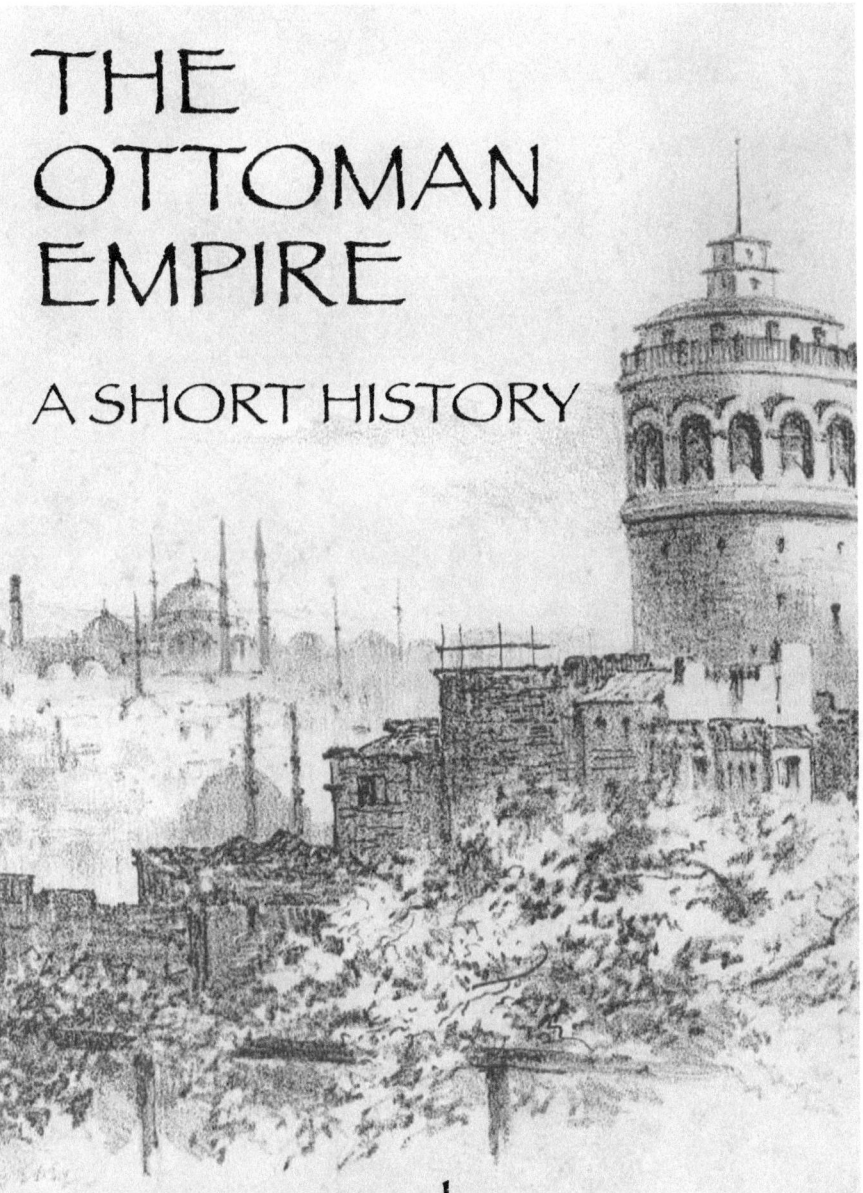

Suraiya Faroqhi
Translated by Shelley Frisch

Acknowledgments

Every book is a product of many people: as a first step after writing, the manuscript is read by the author's colleagues, who suggest changes and, most important, provide encouragement. I am especially grateful to Machiel Kiel, who upon reading the first German version of this text said that it was easy to criticize—but very difficult to provide a satisfactory account of Ottoman history in a small book. In the meantime, several reviews have appeared, and in spite of occasional dismay, I have benefited from them when producing the English version: more than a third of the present volume has been newly written. As for the translation, I am greatly indebted to Shelley Frisch. Furthermore, several synthetic works have appeared since 2000, and I have had the opportunity to learn a great deal, especially from Caroline Finkel's fine study.[1]

Other "food for thought" has come from my students in Munich and Istanbul, without whose questions and curiosities this text would never have been produced. In Munich, Yavuz Köse made it possible for me to write in spite of the bureaucratic distractions inherent in today's university systems; and the same thing must be said about Elektra Kostopoulou and Sinan Çetin in the History Department of Bilgi University in Istanbul. At a later stage of preparation, I had much help, particularly from Bill Blair, whose searching questions made me look into certain issues that I would otherwise have neglected. To all these people, and to my publisher, Markus Wiener, my heartfelt thanks. Of course, I am responsible for the many defects that doubtless remain.

Pronunciation of Turkish Letters

(From Geoffrey Lewis, *Turkish Grammar* [Oxford: Oxford University Press, 1967], p. 1)

a	as in 'but'
c	as in 'jam'
ç	as in 'child'
e	as the first vowel in 'elder'
ğ	almost inaudible, between vowels
ı	as the 'a' in 'serial'
i	as in 'sit'
j	as in French 'jeune'
ö	as the first vowel in French 'jeune'
ş	sh
ü	as the 'u' in French

Introduction

After a long eclipse, empires are back in force as a topic of discussion, and a number of scholarly projects have been dedicated to the Roman, Chinese, Moghul, Spanish, Russian, and British empires both in their formal and informal versions—to say nothing of other varieties closer to home. The Ottoman Empire forms part of this select but still sizeable group of polities that claimed to govern if not the whole world, then at least a major part of it; and it now is receiving a certain amount of attention on the part of historians interested in comparative studies on empires and other topics. This inclusion of Ottoman history into a broader context in which it traditionally played no role is quite novel, and at least in part due to the large amount of archival documentation that has become accessible in recent years. The present book is meant to give an idea of why a student interested in the present-day Middle East, urbanism, global labor migration, or the history of women and the family might find research on the Ottomans to be of value.

Before we begin our discussion of the Empire's political, economic, social, and cultural history, it therefore makes sense to introduce the results of certain major studies that recently have enriched our field; they have for the most part been published during the last ten years or in some cases are even still in the dissertation stage. In the present introduction, we will begin with a discussion of the three hundred years that separate the conquest of Constantinople in 1453 (from now on: Istanbul) from the military, political, and economic crisis of the late 18th century. This period is called "modern" in Turkish historiography and corresponds to what is called "early modern" in the English-speaking world. These three hundred years will be the focus of attention here, as I believe that 19th- and 20th-century developments cannot be understood without taking the preceding period into account. Afterwards, we will turn to a crop of new studies that deal with the "transition years" between the 1760s and the mid-19th-century restructuring of the Ottoman administration known as the Tanzimat. From there, we will proceed to some of the research that has been done on the Empire's final years. To round off the discussion, we will present a few major recent syntheses.

Legitimizing the Empire: Conquests and Instability in the Borderlands

How the Ottoman elites viewed their position in the world and legitimized the rule of the sultans has become a significant focus of scholarly attention. In the eyes of authors close to the sultans' court who wrote on these matters, the lands that made up the Empire possessed a special value. Praising their extent and qualities formed part of the legitimizing stance that sultans and their chroniclers broadcast to friend and foe. Already in the 16th century, the possession of Istanbul was regarded as a reason for assuming that God had endowed the sultans with a special grace; and when an Ottoman ambassador visited the Shah of Iran in the early 1720s, he also felt a need to emphasize the beauty of the sultan's capital in order to make the rival ruler aware of Ottoman glory.

In addition, the Ottoman elite saw itself as privileged in the sense that it claimed to govern the most important Sunni Muslim polity, which was at least in principle continually expanding. Delineating the borders of the empire was therefore problematic. While Istanbul, and during earlier centuries Bursa and Edirne (Adrianople), were the clearly defined centers, even in the later 1600s the northern and Mediterranean frontiers were still being extended, albeit at the expense of secondary European powers such as Venice and Poland. Well into the eighteenth century, the sultans thus regarded it as an important element of their role as legitimate rulers that they extended—and should be viewed as extending—the borders of the Muslim world. Of course, imperial propaganda did not exclude pragmatism: for the most part the Ottoman elite were well aware of what was possible at any given time and took a practical approach when war and peace were at issue.

Ottoman expansion in Europe was a key feature when it came to legitimizing the sultan because this small continent was ruled and inhabited by "infidels." Throughout the 14th, 15th and early 16th centuries, the Ottoman armies advanced at a rapid pace: Balkan polities of the period were small and relatively unstable, and the few coalitions patched together by western European rulers to "roll back" the sultans' armies were all resounding failures. After the death of Süleyman the Magnificent (r. 1520–66), however, gains at the expense of the Habsburgs slowed down, and in the Long War of 1593–1606 were limited to a few fortresses. After all, even if we consider only the Vienna-based branch and leave out the mighty Spanish Habsburgs, the successors of Ferdinand I (1503–64) ruled an empire that could compete with that of the Ottomans. Unlike the princes of southeastern Europe, the Habsburgs were well entrenched in a large territory encompassing today's Austria, the Czech Republic, Slovakia, and a strip of Hungary, to say nothing of possessions farther west, for instance in Alsace. Moreover, while the title of Holy Roman Emperor did not convey a great deal of power, the Habsburgs of Vienna held this honor on a quasi-hereditary basis, and in wars against the Ottomans, they could raise troops from a variety of German princes on account of their imperial status. These factors all had a role to play in halting the advance of the sultans' armies and, in 1683, bringing about what was from the Ottoman viewpoint the disaster of the second campaign against Vienna.

As they developed during the 16th and 17th centuries, Ottoman-Habsburg relations meant that both sides regarded their borders as inherently unstable. Within extensive zones, frontier skirmishes were routine. Certainly the notion of delineated borders, defined by means of natural or man-made markers and agreed upon with some neighboring ruler, was known to sultans and viziers long before the Treaty of Karlowitz (1699), in which Mustafa II (r. 1695–1703) had to recognize the loss of Hungary. There were some treaties with the kings of Poland that even in the 1400s determined concrete borders; but as, according to Islamic law, the sultans could only conclude short- and medium-term agreements with non-Muslim rulers, these borders did not imply permanency: they were called into question come the next war.

Yet the sultans did conclude treaties that prescribed lengthy periods of peace even with their Habsburg opponents, twenty years being normal in the 1600s. What is more, the sultans typically abided by the agreements they concluded. This fact did not go unnoticed at the Iranian court: in the early 18th century an Ottoman envoy to the shah was made uncomfortable by a pointed reference to the recent Treaty of Passarowitz (1718), with the length of its duration a particular embarrassment. Once more work has been done on the poorly documented relations of the sultans with other Islamic rulers, we will be able to say more about the manner in which Ottoman claims to preeminence among Muslim empires were received abroad. At present this remains an open question.

Unstable borders were not limited to neighboring Christian polities. From our perspective, both the Ottomans and the Safawids who governed Iran between about 1500 and 1722 were Muslim rulers; but the two sovereigns concerned did not see each other in that light at all. On the contrary: while competing for territory in Iraq, Azerbaijan, and the Caucasus, neither side regarded its opponent simply as a political rival. Presumably encouraged by their respective rulers, Sunnite religious cum legal scholars in Istanbul and their Shiite counterparts in Isfahan did their level best to exacerbate the conflicts between the two varieties of Islam, proclaiming "the others" to be heretics who did not deserve to be recognized as Muslims. This aggressive stance explains how Ottoman sultans could so easily legitimize their campaigns in western Iran, which were numerous.

When waging wars against the Safawids, and not just in confrontations with Christian rulers, the Ottoman sultans thus asserted that they were constantly expanding the sphere of Sunni right belief and thereby of Islam. Tabriz was conquered several times, even though the Ottomans were never able to hold on to the city for more than a few months or years. Campaigns in the Caucasus, which in the 1500s and 1600s was also mainly an Iranian sphere of influence, were defended with the same argument. Furthermore, these wars produced material benefits in the form of numerous Georgian slaves, but that was not a matter that Ottoman chroniclers discussed in any detail.[1]

The northern borders presented further complications. From the late 1400s, the Black Sea was an Ottoman lake, as the Genoese had been driven out of their trading posts and the khans of the Crimea obliged to recognize Ottoman suzerainty. However, the latter remained semi-independent rulers; moreover, they were Sunnites. Thus in the Ottoman view they could engage in wars of their own against the "infidel" tsars, but more importantly, the Tatars were expected to supply advance forces for Ottoman campaigns in central Europe.

In the north, for a long time there was no fixed border: in these lands the Tatars conducted major raids that supplied the slave markets of Istanbul and Aleppo, and fought battles against Cossack freebooters whose raids in the early 17th century extended to the southern shores of the Black Sea. Sometimes these confrontations led to outright warfare against the Polish kings as rulers of the Ukraine and the Russian tsars, for in one way or another, the Cossacks had pledged allegiance to either one of these rulers. At least this was true most of the time; for in 1648 and again in 1668 a group of Cossacks instead decided to recognize the sultan as their overlord. A long spate of warfare in 1681 was concluded by an agreement with the Russian tsar that a broad swath of territory would remain empty and neither side would establish any settlements therein. In the 18th century, when the Tsars and their subjects were progressing southwards, the Ottomans accepted the great rivers that empty into the Black Sea as the borders with the Russian realm and concentrated on defending a set of major fortresses, currently the subject of archeological studies. However, as time went by and the sultans lost territory, the borders were moved to rivers lying farther to the west (Bug, Dnjestr, Prut). As for the Tatar domains, in 1783 they were annexed by the Tsarina Catherine II; and the last khan fled to Ottoman territory, where he was soon killed.

Last but not least, there were the southern borders. They are not well documented and consequently have attracted few researchers. Central Africa was of interest to the Ottomans only very intermittently, but there were some interactions with Kanem and Bornu in the late 16th century. As for the southern border of Egypt, Ottoman garrisons followed the Nile and established an outpost near the First Cataract. Excavations have brought to light earthenware pots filled with documents issued by local qadis, mainly in Arabic but also in Ottoman Turkish; a few soldiers came from faraway Hungary and Sofia.[2] Yet farther to the east, close to the Red Sea and the Indian Ocean, in the 16th and 17th centuries there was a province of Habeş (Abyssinia) that consisted of a strip of coastal land, the interior remaining under its own Christian king. The sultans' central administration at one point considered this territory important enough to attach to it the port of Jiddah on the Arabian Peninsula: thus access to the holy city of Mecca by sea was to be controlled ultimately by the governor of Habeş.[3]

However, Ottoman chroniclers have mostly ignored this remote outpost of the Empire, and as a result we do not know much about the circumstances under which the sultans' governors first established their rule in this province, and later withdrew from it. Somewhat more information, however, is available on the Ottoman presence in Yemen. The first conquest (1538) was soon reversed by local forces. But in 1568-71 another campaign, conducted by the Grand Vizier Sinan Paşa, who had also added Tunis to the sultans' realm, resulted in a renewed Ottoman domination that lasted slightly over half a century. However, it is unlikely that the governors residing in San'a and the tax collectors stationed in the Red Sea and Indian Ocean ports ever exercised a great deal of control over the mountainous hinterland. Yet the dues collected from Indian Ocean traders arriving in Yemen did give the administration access to quantities of pepper, which was in demand in the Ottoman lands just as much as in contemporary Europe. Moreover, the popularity of coffee, hitherto an Abyssinian and Yemenite specialty, rapidly increased throughout the sultans' territories in the second half of the 16th century—presumably the most enduring consequence of the Ottoman presence in these lands.

While the interior of the Arabian Peninsula remained outside the sultans' control, in the 16th century the Ottomans did establish a province on the eastern coast that they called al-Hasa or more often Lahsa. From here, trade links were formed to southern Iraq, where after the conquest of Baghdad by Sultan Süleyman in 1534 the Ottomans had placed a janissary garrison in the port city of Basra and formed a set of new provinces. However, holding on to Basra proved difficult, as the area was separated from Baghdad by a broad strip of marshland, whose inhabitants were never completely subdued. Even so, the garrison of Basra was supplied by river transport from remote Bire/Birecik on the Euphrates; but in the 17th century, the city came to be governed by a local dynasty that only nominally acknowledged the Ottoman sultans as their overlords.

In many cases, the Ottomans on the southern borders of their empire were confronted with Muslim rulers; and this fact made it more difficult to legitimize conquest. Quite often, these regions were too poor to support even the garrisons sent out to retain them in the sultans' orbit. Pragmatically speaking these "outposts of empire" were worth conquering and keeping because the soldiers stationed there could protect the resources of the inland provinces. Such postings seem to have been unpopular not only among soldiers in the sultans' service but also among their commanders.

Given this situation, legitimizing discourses included the protection that the Ottoman sultans accorded to Mecca and Medina, which in the 16th century were under threat from Portuguese attacks. This stance was of special importance in the case of Yemen and other parts of the Arabian Peninsula, where Ottoman documents highlighted, in addition to Portuguese "unbelievers," the threat of Safawid "heretics" and their spies. As the Zaydi Imam of Yemen was a Shiite, his rule presumably appeared illegitimate. In Abyssinia, the Ottomans supported a Muslim candidate to the throne against his Christian rival; religious considerations apart, a Christian monarch could count on Portuguese support.

In the southern as in the northern borderlands between 1450 and 1650, the Ottomans did not encounter solidly constituted polities like the Habsburg and Safawid Empires. None of the principalities that they confronted in these regions could have resisted the sultan's armies for very long if they had not been protected by two factors. On the one hand, the distances involved were enormous and routes of communication passed through seas and rivers that were unsafe for navigation, or else through deserts. As a result, Ottoman campaigns in the northern as in the southern frontier regions were extremely costly. On the other hand, these borderlands were, in the eyes of the Ottoman central administration, simply not valuable enough to justify spending enormous sums of money on armies and garrisons. Once the conquest was officially regarded as complete, the governors of the southern borderlands normally operated on minimal budgets, and as a result, local forces soon were given a chance to reassert themselves.

Lords of Two Seas?

Maritime borders were another source of instability, and in the Ottoman case, such borders were both numerous and lengthy. Yet among his many titles, Sultan Süleyman the Magnificent styled himself "lord of the Mediterranean and the Black Sea." In the south, the Indian Ocean was the limit, at least while the struggle with the Portuguese was going on during the first half of the 16th century, and in an attenuated form, as long as the Ottomans controlled Yemen, until 1636. After that, the ocean was rarely an official concern except insofar as Indian traders and pilgrims to Mecca arrived by that route. Yet Ottoman records concerning these people were usually put together not in Istanbul but in Cairo. We may thus say that the Indian Ocean was downgraded to a provincial concern. In the north, the Black Sea was surrounded by Ottoman territories, but control was less than perfect; for as we have seen, in the early 17th century the constant attacks of Cossack pirates from the no man's land between the great rivers made it necessary to fortify coastal towns in northern Anatolia and even guard the approaches to Istanbul.

In Ottoman eyes, the most important maritime border was doubtless the Mediterranean. Why this sea should have been a border at all is worth some discussion; for by the late 1500s only the northwestern quarter of the lands bordering this great inland sea was not occupied by Ottoman provinces. Spain, France, and the Italian principalities jostled for possession of a rather limited strip of coastland. However this non-Ottoman shore happened to be the richest in terms of rainfall, a precondition for agriculture and thereby for manufacture and trade. As a result, the sultans' navy, in spite of its impressive successes, was not able to bottle up its Spanish and other opponents in their ports, or even to conquer Malta, an island that controlled the passage between the eastern and western sections of the Mediterranean (siege in 1565). Maritime borders thus remained permeable. Perhaps for this reason they were mostly ignored when it came to agreements with foreign sovereigns; whatever border arrangements were concluded concerned the Eurasian land mass.

Instability in the realm of maritime affairs further increased in the

1600s and 1700s, when the rulers of Algiers, Tunis, and Tripoli, while continuing to recognize the paramount position of the sultan, insisted on concluding their own treaties with foreign rulers. These claims to at least a limited sovereignty had serious practical consequences. Any arrangements providing for the protection of foreign ships which the sultans might have concluded were not honored by the captains of Algiers, Tunis, and Tripoli unless they had been confirmed by their own provincial councils. Some European governments were pragmatic about such matters and concluded multiple agreements. But others were not and threatened to cause diplomatic problems if their ships were robbed in spite of having signed treaties with the sultan. Viewed from a different angle, Ottoman rulers were concerned about the possible erosion of their sovereignty over provinces that could only be controlled by a navy whose access was limited to a few months during the summer season. They therefore put pressure on the administrations of the North African provinces, usually with at most moderate success.

In spite of these difficulties, the Ottoman Empire, like its Roman predecessor, depended on the political control of maritime routes. Grains from the coastal regions of today's Bulgaria and Romania, purchased by officially recognized merchants under the tightest possible state control, fed the army, the navy, the court with its many servitors, and above all Istanbul, probably the largest city in Europe, at least in the 1500s. From north of the Black Sea there arrived clarified butter, while the coastlands adjacent to the Aegean Sea produced grapes, an important sweetener in an age when sugar was scarce and expensive. Therefore, it was only in the mid-17th century, when central control was no longer as absolute as it had been a hundred years earlier, that Izmir, previously just a large village adjacent to a landing scale, developed into a major international port.

The Core Provinces

When discussing an empire it makes sense to differentiate between core and border provinces; and members of the Ottoman elite also recognized this distinction. Since today's Turkey consists of Anatolia, the eastern section of Thrace, and Istanbul, a city of at least ten million straddling two continents, people often assume that these were the core regions of the Ottoman Empire as well. Yet this is not entirely true: the rule of the sultans expanded in southeastern Europe far more rapidly than in Anatolia. In 1521 Sultan Süleyman stood poised to invade Hungary, having taken the border fortress of Belgrade, in today's Serbia. Yet in the east-central parts of Anatolia, Ottoman rule during those very same years was not very secure, as the adherents of a certain local dynasty started a major rebellion in favor of their previous rulers.

We should therefore view the Ottoman Empire as spreading out from a center that included Bursa, Edirne, Salonika, and Istanbul as the major cities. After 1517, the Fertile Crescent became another basis of Ottoman power. Well into the 19th century, the Empire's core encompassed the regions to the west and east of the Aegean Sea as well as the provinces that make up today's Syria, Lebanon, Israel, and Palestine. Egypt had been a core province until the mid-1700s, but had lost that position well before Muhammad Ali Pasha established his vice-regal domain in the early 19th century. Creating a new core region in Anatolia thus was a 19th- and early 20th-century effort; and supplying Istanbul from this landlocked region became possible only after a certain number of railroads had been built.

Fostering Loyalty in Predominantly Christian Regions

How was this far-flung polity held together? Even though the sultans had achieved their position by conquest, it would be a mistake to assume that the empire was only maintained by military power. Ottoman forces in the inland provinces usually were quite small, garrisons numbering a few thousand men or, in smaller towns, no more than a few hundred. Moreover, the citadels of the interior were often allowed to decay; a 17th-century Ottoman traveler, when accounting for a decrepit fortification, might explain this situation by the simple statement that this or that town was far away from the frontiers. Heavily fortified places, by contrast, were typical of border zones such as eastern Anatolia and above all Hungary, where battles in the open field were rare; typically Ottoman and Habsburg military men fought for control of these fortresses. But border regions were not densely settled; therefore such concentrations of military power could not do "double duty" in securing the rule of the sultans.

This state of affairs is noteworthy especially if we keep in mind that large sections of the Balkan Peninsula remained Christian. King Philip II of Spain (r. 1556–98) knew what he was doing when, during the wars of his Vienna-based cousins with the sultans (1593–1606), he refused various suggestions to provoke uprisings in southeastern Europe. Religious concerns figured prominently among the reasons why most Balkan subjects of the sultans were not at all enthusiastic about coming under Habsburg domination; for both the Spanish and the Austrian branches of this dynasty were strongly committed to the Counterreformation, and thus made it state policy to enforce Catholic conformity among their subjects. As the majority of Balkan Christians were Orthodox, and in Hungary and Transylvania Protestants of varying denominations were also quite numerous, we can explain why except under special circumstances, they were unlikely to prefer the Habsburg option. There were some exceptions, however, especially the commitment of Kosovo Serbs to the imperial cause during the 1680s and 1690s; in the end these people migrated to the Habsburg territories, where they found employment in the border militia.

The loyalties of Balkan subjects became more problematic once the 18th-century tsars of Russia, staunch promoters of Orthodoxy, developed territorial ambitions in the Balkans. But even then, the numerous incursions of Russian troops did not, for the most part, spark local anti-Ottoman rebellions. The one exception was the Peloponnesus in 1770, where Ottoman rule had previously been reestablished after a Venetian interlude and the new arrangements had resulted in a certain degree of local disaffection. Presumably Russian serfdom was a major deterrent: for while from the peasants' viewpoint Ottoman rule had its drawbacks, at least villagers were considered freemen and could often obtain legal redress from local qadis, or else by petitioning the sultan himself. Russian wartime taxation must also have contributed to the lack of enthusiasm among Balkan subjects of the sultans. It was mainly in crisis situations, such as during the Russo-Ottoman war of 1768–74, when unpaid soldiers ravaged the countryside of present-day Bulgaria that people who had been bankrupted by these attacks threw in their lot with the armies of the tsar: no taxation without protection.

On the positive side, Ottoman policy with respect to the Orthodox Church contributed materially to the stabilization of the regime. In all probability, the Ottoman government developed a certain partiality for this church in preference to other varieties of Christianity, if only because the spiritual heads of Orthodoxy were domiciled on the sultans' territory. For a long time it was assumed that the "millet system" which granted the recognized religious communities a considerable degree of judicial autonomy, was instituted in its entirety by Mehmed the Conqueror (r. 1451-81). Many scholars today question this view. Arrangements in this early period were probably more ad hoc and much less formalized than they were to become in the 19th century; and the millets should rather be regarded as work in progress. In the 16th and 17th centuries judicial autonomy was in no way absolute: in spite of repeated condemnations by their men of religion, many Christians and Jews preferred to bring their disputes before the qadis.

But even so, the Orthodox Church had already become an integral part of the Ottoman tax-collecting machine by the 1500s: appointments to ecclesiastical dignities needed to be paid for, and bishops, metropolitans, and patriarchs recouped these payments to the Ottoman exchequer from their believers. As a result, these churchmen could be sure that the sultans would support them in case, for instance, members of their churches deserted them in favor of other denominations. Such support was forthcoming when in the 1700s and early 1800s Gregorian Armenians or Arab Christians of Aleppo decided to become Catholics—not that political pressures always sufficed to retain people within their established churches. But at the same time, the Orthodox Church which did not require elaborate training for most of its priests remained reasonably close to the faithful. This double involvement on the part of the church, with both ordinary believers and the sultans' governing apparatus, must have facilitated the integration of Orthodox believers within the Ottoman polity.

INTRODUCTION

Integrating Local Elites

In provinces with Muslim and Christian majorities, establishing the Ottoman order meant integrating local elites. Only in exceptional cases such as Cyprus or Crete, where the Venetians and their close adherents either were killed in the fighting or else left the country, was this issue not of major importance; and even on these two islands, the Ottomans dealt with the Orthodox Church as a kind of local elite.

In the 15th and early 16th centuries a pattern emerged concerning the integration of Muslim territories: the sultans might at the beginning allow a member of the original princely family that had rallied to the Ottoman cause to govern as a kind of viceroy; or else they might chose their first governors from among this same dynasty.[4] At a later stage, descendants of such potentates still might be appointed as governors; but now they were sent to places far away from their fathers' or grandfathers' zones of influence, which by this time were governed as "regular" Ottoman provinces.

However, to this rule there were many exceptions; and after 1550 the pattern lost most of its validity. Now new conquests might be centrally governed from the outset, as happened in Cyprus and Crete, as well as in Podolia during the short-lived Ottoman annexation of the 1670s and 1680s. On the other hand, beginning in the late 1500s, provinces that had originally been closely controlled by the central administration, such as Tunis and Egypt, were dominated by local military men and sea captains who the authorities in Istanbul tolerated as long as they sent a certain amount of tribute and recruited some soldiers for the sultan's campaigns.

The most remarkable exception to the standardized process of centralization observed in earlier ages is surely that of the provinces which today make up Syria, Lebanon, Israel, and Palestine. These regions had all been part of the Mamluk sultanate. After 1516 the Ottoman government discontinued the importation of the military slaves, for whom the whole system had been named, and thus instituted a wholly new type of administration in the region. Yet while governors were appointed from Istanbul, the central authorities did not uproot the local gentry, whose fortified houses in some parts of the area continued to dominate the countryside. On the contrary, these people were incorporated into the sub-provincial administration, particularly where the protection of the Damascus pilgrimage caravan to Mecca was concerned. Only in the 1630s, after serious local uprisings had been suppressed, was there an attempt to eliminate these grandees from the provincial administration.[5] Centralization thus came rather late in the day.

Central Rule Mediated through Provincial Notables

If in the province of Damascus and its neighbors, Ottoman ambitions to rule directly were rather short-lived, this tendency towards decentralization was part of an empire-wide trend. From the 17th century onwards governors increasingly were expected to finance their own military forces, and this meant either farming local taxes or else cooperating with established tax farmers. After 1695 it became possible to acquire tax farms on a lifetime basis, and whoever held such major farms had a good chance of governing the province, even if his official title was more modest. Often the governor was in office only for a short period or for the most part absent on campaigns, so that real power was exercised by the receivers of taxes that he appointed. In addition, recruiting the armed bands that a governor was expected to bring to the sultans' campaigns cost money; and this money had to be raised by the people who had the bad luck to live in the relevant province. Such demands were typically for lump sums; and distributing the total levy over villages and taxpayers might be a source of power. By demanding less from one village and making its neighbors make up the deficit, a small-scale tax collector could acquire clients and thereby develop a local power base.

In areas that were visited by foreign merchants, such notables could moreover expand their power base by selling the goods that they had collected as taxes. Or else notables used their contacts with foreign merchants to mediate business deals for the peasants: while the mediators profited in terms of money and social power, the sellers, at least in some cases, got better prices than they would have received on their own. Such commercial arrangements meant that an intermediate stratum imposed itself between the government in Istanbul and the provincial population.

Some notables of this type were able to increase their power to the point of becoming magnates, who in the 18th and 19th centuries came to govern their territories with very limited interference from Istanbul. When, however, the central administration considered such a personage to have become a major threat, it was common practice to entice his rivals in the same or neighboring provinces to attack him. The victim then was deposed, executed, and his possessions confiscated; soon after, these items were sold to claimants for the vacant position that might include members of the dead man's family. As a result, in some provinces there emerged dynasties that held on to power for a couple of decades.

Particularly in the Arab provinces, these families or "politically active households," established by military men, might demonstrate their ascendancy by sumptuous public construction. Mosques were part of this program, and Mosul and Baghdad benefited from the attempts of local rulers to redistribute wealth and leave their imprint on the cityscape; in some regions new combinations of charitable endowments were created. These developments have greatly interested art historians, who currently show considerable interest in the findings of "regular" Ottoman historians. Palaces also might assert the power of the local dynasty, as happened in Damascus but also, and quite dramatically, in the eastern Anatolian town of Doğu Beyazit, close to the Iranian border.

In spite of their obvious power, the number of magnates aspiring to independent royalty remained quite limited. It has been suggested that lifetime tax farms contributed substantially toward securing their loyalty to the sultan; for these revenue sources surely would be jeopardized once the Ottoman Empire was no longer available to legitimize the extraction of taxes.[6] Furthermore in many cases there were several lifetime tax farmers who claimed revenue from the same region. If one of the competitors were to set up a petty principality, the others were likely to lose their claims; and this situation explains why the central government found it so easy to mobilize magnates or notables against one another.

Decentralization or power-sharing with local notables thus probably had a stabilizing function in the 18th-century Ottoman Empire, as these power brokers were kept in dependence to the sultan. While once widespread, claims that these developments necessarily represented a "decline" are today viewed with skepticism. After all, while decentralization began in the late 16th century, the Ottoman Empire held together reasonably well for about two hundred years more, not a bad performance as empires go. In the same vein, scholars today do not consider these assorted magnates to be proto-nationalists, as was common among historians of the Arab world some forty years ago. Ethnically, these provincial power-brokers usually had nothing in common with the populations that they taxed and controlled; and in those cases in which we can make out a cultural orientation, these personages identified themselves as Ottoman gentlemen and not as representatives of local populations. Whether they negotiated on behalf of the latter, securing tax and other benefits, and thus acted as a kind of informal representative, or alternatively exploited the taxpayers of their province without giving much in return, depended on circumstance; it is impossible to give a universally valid answer to this question.

Peace, Foreign Trade, and the Capitulations

Economic historians have long since concluded that the Ottoman Empire possessed a reasonably strong commercial base, largely due to the size of the domestic market. Moreover, caravan routes to Asia continued to be important well into the early 1800s, and were not marginalized by oceanic trade in the 17th century as had long been assumed. Throughout the 16th and 17th centuries, merchants subject to the sultans, both Muslim and non-Muslim, traded with Iran and India to the east and Venice, Holland, England, and France to the west. Venice was a magnet, being the only Christian city routinely visited by Muslim traders. By the 1700s the Habsburg domains also gained importance as trading partners; this area was mainly frequented by Orthodox merchants who sold yarn to textile manufacturers and leather to saddlers and shoemakers. Even the Leipzig fairs were frequented by sizeable numbers of Ottoman subjects. Thus official emphasis on the expansion of the realm of Islam did not imply that peaceful relations with "unbelievers" were considered impossible or that Ottoman Muslims were officially discouraged from trading with outsiders to the realm.

In this domain as in so many others, pragmatism was dominant: Mehmed the Conqueror (r. 1451–81), for instance, hoped to reroute the international spice trade through Istanbul, his newly conquered capital, an enterprise for which he would have needed the cooperation of Venetian, Genoese, and other foreign traders from non-Muslim countries. In the late 16th and early 17th centuries as well, the Ottoman administration was very conscious of the fact that protecting traders meant that the exchequer would benefit from customs revenues. When discussing this issue with foreign rulers like the hereditary princes of Mecca, known as the Sharifs, but also with the Doge of Venice, the officials of the sultan liked to point out that if a ruler did not protect traders, they would stop coming, and that could only be harmful to princely finances. Privileges to Muslims at the expense of non-Muslim competitors were not at issue in these exchanges.

Trade could be properly conducted only in times of peace; when the sultan was at war with a given ruler, his/her subjects normally left the realm, although commerce was often continued through local intermediaries, or else through neutrals. Revenue aside, the support of trade might yield political benefits; and as the sultans' servitors often viewed commerce in this light, they were willing to provide privileges to the subjects of foreign potentates—known in European parlance as capitulations.[7] These grants allowed traders and other sojourners subject to a given ruler, who was the actual grantee, a degree of immunity from Ottoman taxation and administrative rulings. Sovereigns whose subjects benefited in this manner were not necessarily part of Christendom. In the 16th century as in the 18th, Armenian merchants subject to the Shah of Iran, known as the Acem tüccarı, enjoyed similar privileges, and when they wished to submit complaints to the sultan's administration, they did so through the mediation of their consul, called the şehbender.

The Challenges of French and British Traders

While in the 16th and 17th centuries capitulations in Ottoman law were regarded as unilateral grants of the sultans that these rulers could abrogate at will, by the later 1700s these concessions were to turn into serious limitations of Ottoman sovereignty. From a long-term perspective, this change was connected to the defeats of the 1680s and 1690s, when for the first time the sultans made political concessions to Louis XIV of France in return for diplomatic support against the Habsburgs.

Special exemptions from Ottoman administrative interventions were granted not only to ambassadors and consuls, but also to their servitors, including the interpreters through whom the sultans' government needed to be approached. One of the major abuses of capitulations-based privilege was due to this convention, namely the issuing of certificates as "interpreters" to non-Muslim merchants in large numbers. Often these people did not even reside in the towns where they were supposedly employed or were ignorant of the relevant languages. European consuls and ambassadors, while often recognizing that the practice was a serious abuse, employed these pseudo-interpreters because a large crowd of clients raised the prestige of the diplomat in question; in many cases, moreover, the interpreter candidates paid good money for the privilege of being employed. From the non-Muslim merchants' perspective—as we have come to appreciate in recent years—the investment made sense, especially in the second half of the 18th century, when the pressing needs of the exchequer sometimes resulted in confiscations on flimsy pretexts or even without any legally acceptable reason. People who could claim the protection of a foreign state typically were immune from such exactions.

Seeking the protection of foreign embassies or consuls was not a strategy open to Muslim merchants; the privileged position of Christian and Jewish protégés, who in time might even become subjects of the state protecting them, must therefore have given rise to many complaints about unfair treatment. While Selim III (r. 1789–1807) and Mahmud II (r. 1808–39) issued privileges to woo both Muslim and non-Muslim merchants away from foreign protection, the numbers of people so favored were quite limited. Moreover, for some traders and artisans, enjoying "foreign protection" was more than just a business advantage: it became part of their self-image.[8] Thus the entire issue should be regarded as part and parcel of the crisis that the Empire suffered in the late 18th century.

INTRODUCTION

Confronting the Tsars

While the Ottoman socio-political system worked reasonably well until the 1760s, after that difficulties came thick and fast. War was the major problem. A recent work has stressed the military disadvantages of the long period of relative peace between 1718 and 1768. For as a result, the changes in the conduct of battle that took place in Europe during the War of the Austrian Succession and the Seven Years' War were not incorporated by the Ottomans until it was already too late. However, this relative withdrawal from armed confrontation is but one aspect of a more complex problem: for the Empire desperately needed peace in order to recuperate from the destructive wars of 1683–1718; and the relative peacefulness of the mid-18th century had even made a moderate expansion of manufacturing possible. Yet without some economic growth, there is no telling whether the Empire would have held up during the crises that followed; Ottoman policy-makers were thus caught between the devil and the deep blue sea.

Even more seriously perhaps, the Russian Empire was much better endowed with all the resources needed for warfare than the Ottomans. Enormous forests provided wood for shipbuilding in much larger quantities than were available in the semi-arid zones where the sultans' territories were mostly situated. Metals were also quite abundant, and after the peasants subject to the tsars had expanded southward into the fertile "black earth" lands, grain was also cultivated in significant quantities. Once these resources could be mobilized, due to the political rearrangements enforced by emperors/empresses such as Peter I (1672–1725) and Catherine II (1729–96), it became very difficult for the Ottomans to regain the initiative. Still, recent research has also stressed the fact that Russian serf-soldiers were poorly fed and supplied in comparison to their Ottoman counterparts, although as a result, the baggage trains supplying the sultans' armies during 18th-century campaigns were large and costly.[9]

These competitive disadvantages were probably understood in Istanbul only at a late date because the early efforts of Tsar Peter to build up a navy had not been very successful, nor had been his military campaigns against the Ottomans on land. The entrance of a Russian naval squadron into the Mediterranean was thus quite unprecedented, and so was the virtual annihilation of the Ottoman fleet near Çeşme in 1770. Moreover, between the Treaty of Küçük Kaynarca in 1774 and outright Russian annexation nine years later, the Crimea was lost to the Ottoman Empire, an event all the more traumatic as now a Muslim population was involved. These losses must have led to a legitimization crisis as well; but remarkably enough, none of the sultans lost his throne because of the defeats of the 1770s and 1780s.

Throughout the 19th century the Russian tsars remained the Ottomans' principal opponents. Much of the fighting for territory took place in Moldavia and Walachia, in today's terms Moldova and Rumania, respectively. Once Serbs and Bulgarians had gained a degree of local autonomy, the tsars patronized these polities. Many political figures in the Russian Empire hoped for an ultimate partition of Ottoman territory in which they would gain Istanbul; these projects were first formulated by Catherine II, who named one of her grandsons Constantine in anticipation.

Reshaping the Empire: New Perspectives on the Reforms of the 19th Century

Given the bitter experience of the wars against Russia, Selim III attempted to replace the janissaries, whose military value by now was highly questionable, with troops trained according to a "new model" (*Nizamı cedid*). The attempt misfired: the sultan was deposed and ultimately killed. New studies of the sultan's policies and their ramifications are currently underway; one of them concerns the attitude of the Ottoman notables as a group during those crisis years, and another investigates the actual rebellion that brought down Sultan Selim in 1807. In addition, there are two projects that focus on the Tatar khanate, with considerable emphasis on its later years, whose results will hopefully be published soon. As we can therefore expect a rather extensive re-thinking of our previous assumptions, which to a considerable degree are based on studies undertaken thirty or forty years ago, it is only prudent to avoid any sweeping claims.

Much work is also being done on the Tanzimat, the major administrative refashioning that in the middle of the 19th century was supposed to make the Empire competitive in a rapidly changing world, where ever more sophisticated technologies were available to European governments and wars could no longer be won without them. While older studies have generally dwelt on the inefficiency of the old structures and their relative imperviousness to reform from above, our perspectives have changed quite dramatically during the last few years.[10] In the context of "multiple modernities," historians have concluded that the route to modernization as followed by England and France was not the only one possible. Japan, imperial Russia, and China all undertook significant socio-political measures that can be described as "modernization." The Ottoman Empire also launched its own variety: beginning with the restructuring of the military, sultans and viziers then proceeded to revamp the bureaucracy, the legal framework within which the administrative apparatus was expected to function, and last but not least, education.[11]

As refashioning the military so as to make it once again capable of winning wars was the major motivating factor, many of the newer studies focus on this issue. The plans of Sultan Mahmud II and the grand viziers of the mid-1800s were inspired by the example of Mehmed Ali/Muhammad Ali Pasha, governor and later viceroy of Egypt. The latter had built an army that not only reconquered the holy cities of Mecca and Medina for the sultan, but when it came to armed conflict with the sultan, also defeated whatever forces Mahmud II could mobilize against him. Recent research has made us aware of the tremendous sacrifices that this policy demanded from the population of Egypt.

In conformity with the model instituted by its rebellious governor, the Ottoman central administration began the search for recruits that were to serve in the army for long years and, after having gone through the relevant drills, fight battles in the European style. Non-Muslims were considered undesirable except in certain technical capacities, and the recruitment of Muslim Turks was disproportionate; apparently it was heavy enough to result in a lower-than-average rate of population growth. By contrast, certain Albanian clans that in previous generations had served as irregulars in the Ottoman army in exchange for tax exemptions were now given to understand that their services were no longer required and that they would have to provide taxes and recruits like everyone else. Refusal to conform was deemed a sign of "savageness" and merited serious coercion. It might thus happen that while trying to cement loyalties, the late Ottoman state created disaffection where none had existed before.[12]

Revamping the bureaucracy and establishing a police service presented further challenges. These enterprises were also part of the state formation project, which is how today's historians interpret the Tanzimat. Historians now highlight the concrete activities of officials "in the field," for instance the activities of reforming governors such as Midhat Paşa (1822-83). Reform meant that the literary skills that had previously characterized an accomplished scribe were no longer much in demand. To speak with Carter Findley, post-Tanzimat officials no longer saw themselves as craftsmen producing correctly worded and calligraphically exquisite documents, but as people committed to implementing particular policies.[13]

Studies of bureaucratic reform include internal matters such as recruitment, hierarchical structures, promotion patterns, and sociability. Formal training of future administrators in a special school known as the Mülkiye was instituted, and examinations began to play a role in determining the placement of officials. Ministries were formed and recruited specialized personnel: in the mid-19th century one of the main routes to high office was service in the translation chamber, where young officials learned French and diplomatic skills, which they honed while serving as junior secretaries in the Ottoman embassy in Paris. But at the same time, it remained possible to make a successful bureaucratic career by establishing old-style patronage relations, sometimes cemented by membership in a dervish order. The government's lack of money was a major impediment to reform: with salaries low and frequently in arrears, it was impossible for many officials to subsist if they did not take fees that might shade off into bribes. Urban policemen often were caught between the conflicting expectations of their superiors and the townspeople they were supposed to control; due to the combination of low pay and exposure to socio-political pressures, this service found it especially difficult to attract literate and well-informed persons.[14] As access to the personnel files of the Hamidian period has now become possible, it seems that studies of the police apparatus are on the verge of "taking off."[15]

The new bureaucracy operated according to new laws, often adapted from European models. What adaptations were deemed necessary and how the changes were received by different sectors of the population is currently a topic of study. In addition, scholars concern themselves with the spread of private property, especially but not exclusively land. Projects of this kind have become possible because of the grand series of registers through which, in the 1840s, the government attempted to gain an overview of the taxable resources of its realm. They are now available to investigators, although it will take time before we can properly understand the considerations that prompted officials to selectively record information and taxpayers to provide the necessary data, doubtless also on a selective basis. However, it already has become clear that at least in the more accessible and commercialized districts, for instance on the Aegean coast of Anatolia, the difficulties involved in such data collection were not fundamentally different from those experienced by people in charge of comparable projects in the more remote provinces of France.

Information gathering was a crucial part of early 19th-century modernization. Some of these projects were connected with repression: in the early 1800s attempts were made to survey the population of Istanbul house by house, so as to weed out the jobless and those whose occupations were officially were deemed "unnecessary," and send them back to their provinces of origin. Apparently Sultan Selim III aimed to reduce the number of mouths to feed in the capital and perhaps also get rid of people who might take to the streets in support of janissary claims. These surveys, unparalleled in earlier times, are now being studied by urban historians.[16] In the 1830s an attempt was made to count the male population in many provinces of the Empire, in order to locate men who might be drafted into the army. Not surprisingly, this aim became widely known, and many potential draftees fled. Moreover, in the 1840s the government employed a large number of well-paid informers to report what was being said about matters of public concern, both in public and in private. Unlike in later cases of this type, the people thus reported were not to be punished; the aim was merely to survey "public opinion."[17] These projects all indicate that governments of the day were conscious of the value of information. During the last few years historians have shown that within the limits of available technology, pre-Tanzimat governments were in the business of data collection.

As we have seen, bureaucrats in the new ministries, as well as military officers, had to be educated in schools, and here the strategy adopted by the Ottoman elite rather resembled the practices found in many European countries. Arrangements were made for professional education while the preparation of the students for these programs was usually insufficient; professional schools therefore tended to institute their own preparatory courses. A sequence of schools from which students needed to graduate before they could tackle the next stage was instituted quite late; and at the lower levels, skills and information quite often took second place to the inculcation of piety and loyalty to the sultan. Given the small number of civilian high schools, certain Muslim families sent their children to missionary schools in spite of repeated official prohibitions. At the level of higher education too, civilian professions remained a poor relation to the technical expertise that could be acquired in the military; the University of Istanbul only began to function regularly in 1900. As a result non-Muslims and latter also Muslims who could afford it quite often arranged for their sons to study abroad. Given this state of affairs, a good general education was a major piece of "cultural capital;" and when in the early 20th century quite a few younger members of the elite concluded that the Ottoman Empire was unlikely to last much longer, they often used their educations to make careers for themselves in newly developing branches such as university teaching, communications, publishing, and entertainment.

The Last Decades of the Ottoman Empire in Current Historiography

In Ottoman studies, the years from 1840 to 1922 are currently being investigated with great intensity; this is due at least in part to the enormous mass of documentation that has recently become available. The archives in Istanbul are now accessible for the Hamidian period, including the documentation originally stored in the Yıldız palace, from which sultan Abdülhamid II (r. 1876-1909) ran his government. These archives have yielded material for a number of semi-official document publications.

Political considerations play a major role as well. Among the Turkish public there is an enormous demand for the commemoration of the battle of Çanakkale/Gallipoli (1915), a concern shared in certain circles in Britain, Australia, and New Zealand as well. For a non-specialist, it is often impossible to say where historical research ends; and the cultivation of memory takes over. Viewed from a broader perspective, the emergence of nationalism in the Balkans and afterwards in Syria and in the Turkish provinces, the Armenian disaster, the history of Muslim refugees from the Balkans and the Caucasus, and the fates of the victims of the Greco-Turkish population exchange have all motivated scholars to delve into the archives. Some of them write in order to defend a political position; attempts at a more or less detached survey of actions and attitudes are few and far between. At present, a consensus is nowhere in sight.

In the long run work in the Russian archives will probably change our perceptions of the "great game" between the British and Russian governments in various regions of Asia, including certain Ottoman territories, just as research in the Japanese archives has allowed a more realistic evaluation of Meiji policies towards the Ottomans than had been possible from published sources alone. For the present, imperialism and the "Eastern Question" have mainly been studied on the basis of British archives and materials from western and central Europe. The accessibility of the Public Record Office in London must have motivated many historians to focus on the materials found there. Yet other factors play a role as well: while imperialism has a strong economic dimension, the Ottoman archives apparently do not contain a lot of material from which statistics relevant to production, investment, and trade can be compiled. Also located in Istanbul, the archives of the Banque Ottomane, a foreign-owned bank that played a central role in the financial dependence of the last Ottoman decades, have now been catalogued and studied by a few researchers; but they remain difficult to access.

As for monographs, as we have already seen, considerable work has been done on the bureaucracy and the educational system. Documents in the central archives are helpful because they reflect Ottoman attitudes in negotiations with foreign powers and companies. This emphasis probably explains why in the last few years we have seen a crop of new studies on railway construction, an issue that acquires a new dimension when Ottoman concerns can be taken into account. Institutions and cultural history are also being brought to the fore: the city administrations, founded for the most part during the last quarter of the 19th century, are a favorite topic, especially since in recent years, municipalities have been active in promoting a sense that "our town is our home." Istanbul has attracted the most attention, but we also have detailed work on Salonika and certain towns in Syria and Palestine, as well as North Africa. These monographs are especially interesting because in city administrations, career bureaucrats almost always needed to work together with ad hoc committees of local notables who, given the notorious lack of money in the state's coffers, provided the financing for certain projects. Accordingly, they also demanded to be heard when it came to establishing priorities; and in many places these personages might themselves take the initiative when it came to public works. As a corollary, the emerging *beaux quartiers* of many Ottoman towns were notoriously better supplied with even basic utilities than the poorer parts, a problem that continues to the present day in certain places. Work on urban renewal, post-Tanzimat style, thus implies studying the interface of officialdom and at least the upper levels of urban society.[18]

As for the laboring classes and their places of work, studies of factories have been undertaken by historians working in Bulgaria; for it was here that proto-industrial weaving of woolen cloth was first moved into factories when dependable orders came in from the reorganized Ottoman army. However, other factories that produced partly for state needs and partly for the market were soon established in and around Istanbul, and some of the documents produced in these institutions have recently become accessible. From these sources it has emerged that only some of the workers were hired on the "regular" labor market; others were boys serving in the factories after they had been sentenced to reform school. Yet others were young non-Muslims who in the 19th century were not being drafted into the army, but instead were sometimes called up to do their military service in state factories.[19] Draftees also played a major role in the coal mines of Zonguldak in northern Anatolia: some were villagers who, in the manner that had been customary since the 16th century, were made to spend a number of months every year servicing the mines and extracting minerals. Others were workmen who had been transformed into soldiers during wartime. All these people suffered badly from accidents and diseases that often could have been avoided through more investment and better education.[20]

But most Ottoman industrial production took place not in factories or mines but in small enterprises: for it has been shown that the ever-increasing importation of foreign products after 1815 did not result in the disappearance of local manufacturers. The latter often remained in business by self-exploitation and the exploitation of apprentices and family members, practices which have been well described by the term "labor squeezing."[21] In order to stay competitive, such enterprises typically sold their products at prices that made capital accumulation and investment all but impossible. These observations and interpretations are highly important; but even so, the history of Ottoman workers is still in its beginnings.

In terms of cultural history, we can study the changing face of Ottoman towns and cities, because in the second half of the 19th century a growing number of people developed an interest in drawing or painting cityscapes. Even more dramatic was the increasing interest in photography; and there survive large accumulations of official and unofficial photos showing the larger cities of the Empire and "tourist centers" such as Jerusalem. Photographs of people at their workplaces in schools, hospitals, construction sites, and factories also survive in substantial numbers. Of course, photographs need to be studied just as critically as written sources: thus it has emerged that as foreign tourists demanded certain kinds of pictures as souvenirs, studios often made them up. "Picturesque" street artisans or languid Ottoman ladies thus might be impersonated by people whom the photographers could mobilize for that purpose. In a different vein, recent studies have taught us that the photo albums which Sultan Abdülhamid sent to foreign governments were intended to convey a political message: the Ottoman Empire was now possessed of all the accoutrements of modernity.

Therefore, by implication, there was no reason for any outsiders to intervene in the process of Ottoman modernization. Whether this discourse was appreciated at the receiving end is yet a different topic of study. Photographs thus imply statements, and it is the historian's job to tease out what their authors wanted to say.

Printing, publishing, and the book trade in Istanbul and the Empire's major cities have attracted interest for a long time already, and the same can be said of the theater. However, recent studies concern more specific issues such as the role of women in communications: a specialized institution known as the Kadın Eserleri Kütüphanesi (Library of Women's Works) attempts to bring together all works written and published by Ottoman and Turkish women, and its collections provide a starting point for research in this field. Another recent interest is censorship, a practice that emerged together with the new means of communication in the mid-19th century.[22] Newspapers and periodicals were affected, but most dramatic was the physical destruction of a prominent literary theater whose plays had displeased Sultan Abdülhamid. When the latter's absolutism was at its height, it therefore became virtually impossible to bring out original theatrical works in Turkish.

For the period after the fall of Sultan Abdülhamid, when the Committee of Union and Progress (Ittihad ve terakki) first impacted the government "from without" and after 1913 directly ruled the Empire, sources in the Ottoman archives are accessible only to a limited extent. Researchers therefore rely on foreign archives and libraries, or else on published material, which is of interest especially for the months immediately following the revolution of 1908, when for a short time, censorship was abolished. We possess significant monographs on the ideology of the Committee members and on their behavior while in opposition. A recent study has attempted to show that Sultan Abdülhamid was forced to turn himself into a constitutional monarch not merely by a military coup d'état, as had previously been assumed, but by tax strikes and other manifestations of public discontent that were serious enough to be called an authentic revolution. Other work concerns the increasing incorporation of women into the labor force due to the loss of male workers during World War I: here the government took a hand to remedy, at least minimally, the appalling poverty of soldiers' wives.[23]

Work has also been done on the war economy. In the years preceding the First World War, the losses of territory in the Balkans and elsewhere had sparked powerful nationalist reactions among the Turkish population. As a result, the political elites came to the conclusion that they could no longer trust non-Muslim businessmen and should try to create a Muslim bourgeoisie through state aid. But as "regular" accumulation through commerce, agriculture, and industry seemed too slow, there was a strong inclination to confiscate and redistribute property. As for the "battle against speculation and hoarding" during World War I, while largely ineffective as far as consumers were concerned, it provided plenty of opportunities to impose harsh penalties upon non-Muslim businessmen—a classical case of "primitive accumulation" in the Marxian sense; petty Muslim traders suffered as well. Moreover, the war fought in Anatolia and the Armenian deportation provided further occasion for confiscation. The resources thus made available were redistributed to favored businessmen. As the principal specialist on the Committee's war financing has concluded, adherents of "Union and Progress" stood a good chance of making their fortunes, while those without such affiliation were likely to lose out.[24]

Ottomans and Japanese in a World Dominated by Imperialism

How did all this compare to the experience of other modernizing countries outside of North America and western and central Europe? As we have seen, Ottoman restructuring was undertaken in order to secure the continued existence of the Empire, and throughout the world there were other polities in a comparable situation. Japan was a prime example of such defensive modernization that greatly impressed the Ottoman reading public of the late 19th and early 20th centuries. It is therefore rather interesting to review the comparative research that has been undertaken on this issue.

Without major structural changes, once Admiral Perry's American ships had enforced the opening of Japanese ports and unequal treaties had been concluded with Western powers, the danger of becoming yet another European/American colony was clear to the political elite in

Tokyo. Getting rid of these treaties as soon as feasible therefore became a major aim. Furthermore, by the late 1800s asserting Great Power status by concluding unequal treaties of their own became part of the Japanese elite's agenda where the Ottomans were concerned. Profuse expressions of friendship and reference to a common "Asian background" notwithstanding, the Japanese tended to view the late Ottoman Empire as a polity akin to Qing/Manchu China, which in 1895 had been forced to sign an unequal treaty with Japan. However, in spite of their political weakness, the successive governments of the sultans were able to rebuff this demand, and diplomatic relations were established only with the Republic of Turkey in 1924, when unequal treaties no longer were part of the agenda.[25]

Japanese society began its modernization process with significant advantages that included widespread literacy even in rural areas, agriculture open to commercially oriented modernization, a high level of urbanization, and an upper class of former military men who were able and willing to re-launch themselves as entrepreneurs. In the educational sector, Japan's head start was particularly striking: in 1868, when the Japanese population totaled 35 million, male literacy stood at 40 percent and total literacy at twenty; as a result, the Japanese elite had a much easier time convincing the dominant male section of the population of the need for profound change. Moreover, the Meiji reforms rapidly raised literacy rates for the population as a whole: in 1923 the Japanese rate already stood at close to 80 percent.

As for the Ottoman route to modernity, it is worth discussing the differences from the Japanese experience. Literacy and secular education were limited to relatively small groups, mainly connected to the armed forces. Moreover, late Ottoman campaigns to teach the three basic skills of reading, writing, and arithmetic were of limited impact: in 1923, when the Turkish Republic was founded, the total literacy rate was about 15 percent of a population of 15 million. To further complicate matters, while in Japan most centers of population and trade were easily accessible by sea, the long overland routes of the Ottoman domain made communications costly and difficult. Commercial agriculture therefore was viable only in certain areas.

Cities in late Tokugawa Japan thrived commercially. What is more, the capital generated in them was locally owned: after all, the long isolation and political pacification of the country since the early 17th century had been propitious to the accumulation of capital. By contrast, in the Ottoman realm, the political setup had made the accumulation of productive capital in the hands of tax-paying subjects relatively difficult even in the 16th century, to say nothing of less prosperous times. Moreover, the many wars of the 18th and 19th centuries had resulted in the loss of much productive capacity previously established in the Balkans; and the onerous conditions under which the mid-19th-century Ottoman government borrowed money from European lenders to finance the modernization of army and communications further contributed to budgetary deficits. By 1875 bankruptcy was the result; and due to financial tutelage by a consortium of European lenders, the governments of Abdülhamid and the Young Turks had only limited access to the taxes collected in their territory. None of this had happened in Japan.

A further complication arose from the fact that by the mid-19th century much of the accumulated capital available in the Ottoman realm belonged to non-Muslim merchants, who increasingly were caught up in the nationalist currents of the times. No parallel to this situation existed in Japan, where non-Japanese groups lived on the margins, both socially and territorially; they certainly had no access to "foreign protection" and were not prime accumulators of capital. Given these major differences, the expectation that the Ottomans should have been able to duplicate the Japanese performance hardly seems realistic.

Recent Attempts at Synthesis and Inter-Field Collaboration

In the 1960s, 1970s, and early 1980s many Ottoman historians felt that the right time for synthesis had not yet arrived. In my view at the time this hesitation made sense, for archival work tended to focus on limited questions, and it was often far from clear what conclusions should be drawn from the research. Apart from the efforts of Ismail Hakkı Uzunçarşılı, in this period only Halil Inalcik and the couple Stanford and Ezel K. Shaw attempted to provide overviews over long time spans.

It soon became clear that specialization by period and/or subject was becoming widespread in the Ottomanist field as elsewhere, and collaboration thus became a prime necessity.[26] While a scholar such as Fuat Köprülü (1890-1966) had combined work on Ottoman literature and history, to later generations these two fields had become quite distinct and could only be adequately treated by a dialog between specialists. In response to this situation, in the late 1980s and in the course of the 1990s several collaborative works were published in France, Turkey, and England.[27] While these works were intended for advanced students and researchers, Justin McCarthy courageously attempted a one-volume presentation, notable for its emphasis on environmental factors.[28]

However, with the "opening up" of Ottoman history to the wider world during the last ten years or so, we observe what may be described as a two-pronged development. On the one hand, syntheses both by groups of scholars and by individuals continue to appear: presently in course of publication is the four-volume *Cambridge History of Turkey* that in reality encompasses mainly the Ottoman Empire. Given the centrality of warfare to the life of early modern states, the monumental work by Virginia Aksan on Ottoman wars is an investigation into the state structures that mobilized the subjects' resources, fed the ever-expanding soldiery, and recruited military men; this work can just as well be read as a history of Ottoman state-society relations in the 1700s and 1800s. In addition, there is the massive yet highly readable one-volume history by Caroline Finkel, a unique example of a best-selling work based on an intimate knowledge particularly of Ottoman chronicles.[29]

The second route of communication between Ottoman historians and their colleagues in neighboring fields consists of collaborative work documented in edited volumes. Typically, a historian of the Roman world, China, or most frequently early modern Europe will organize a project on some broad and encompassing theme: my own experience in this sector includes collaborative studies of artisans' migrations, cotton production, narratives written in the first person, festivities, periodization in history, eighteenth-century urban culture, and others, to say nothing of the recently popular projects to study the operation of empires. While in the past Ottoman historians were rarely invited to participate in such ventures, this tendency is now changing, even though perhaps an invitation extended to a "token Ottomanist" can be viewed as the proverbial swallow that does not mean the beginning of summer. However, the scarcity of funding for the humanities and social sciences in many European countries has induced quite a few historians concerned with this region to network outside of their own fields, and practitioners of Ottoman history have benefited as a consequence.

To Conclude

After a lengthy stay in a kind of limbo where a few specialists concentrated on more or less arcane research, Ottoman history during the last ten to fifteen years has been gathering pace and coming out into the open. New sources have been made available not only in the archives but also in libraries. While until the 1990s most narrative sources were accessible only in manuscripts or else in unsatisfactory editions usually dating from the 19th century, many Ottoman chronicles and embassy reports are now available in critical editions, or at least in renditions of the texts accompanied by introductions providing some information on the author and the conditions under which he wrote his work. As an example, we may mention the ten-volume edition of the travelogue of the 17th-century writer Evliya Çelebi, without whose account writing the social history of that period of Ottoman history would be very difficult indeed: after twelve years as a work in progress, the edition is now complete, as the tenth and final volume appeared at the end of 2007.[30]

Certainly the level of sophistication with which we treat our sources often still leaves much to be desired. As this rapid overview has shown, the gaps in our research are numerous; and many works that we write today will presumably make our successors smile as they are found to be impossibly naïve. But it is exciting to see that our discipline is going somewhere—may the good work continue . . .

CHAPTER 1
Rise and Expansion (1299-1481)

The Beginnings of the Ottoman Polity

The oldest information concerning an Ottoman small principality takes us back to the first quarter of the 14th century. At first this was only one of the numerous small polities that filled the power vacuum that had arisen when the empire of the Anatolian Seljuks had dissolved in the second half of the 13th century and the Mongolian sovereigns in Iran were retreating from their Anatolian possessions in the first half of the 14th century. The most important competitors of the expanding Ottomans included the princes of Eretna, whose center was in Sivas, and the far longer-lived central Anatolian polity founded by the Karaman dynasty. The Aydın and Menteşe families who ruled in southwest Anatolia were also serious competitors, at least for a time.

The chronological succession of the first Ottoman conquests is not easy to determine. The early Ottoman chronicles, most of which were written towards the end of the 15th century, long after the events in question, are generally vague on chronology. Late medieval accounts penned in the various principalities of the Balkan Peninsula were not much better on this score. For this reason, today's standard works contain a variety of dates even for some key events, such as the conquest of Edirne. The first very important city the Ottomans seized under their founding sultan, Osman I (1299–1326), was Bursa. Iznik, which in the mid-thirteenth century had been home to Byzantine rulers in exile, followed in 1337. Until the conquest of Edirne (circa 1361), Bursa remained the Ottoman capital. But even when the sultans were living in Edirne for the most part, they continued to build their imposing mosques in Bursa (where they are still preserved) until the conquest of

Constantinople/Istanbul in 1453. When an earthquake destroyed the walls of the city of Gelibolu in 1352, Sultan Orhan (1326–1362) was able to enter the city easily and conquer his first important harbor site.

In 1355, the death of Stefan Dušan initiated the decline of the Serbian Empire. From 1363–1365, a series of Ottoman military campaigns in Thrace and present-day southern Bulgaria culminated in the conquest of Plovdiv (earlier: Philippopolis, Filibe). One of the last Crusades was organized by French, Burgundian, Hungarian, and other European rulers to support Constantinople, besieged by Bayezid I (1389–1402). This Crusade, whose commanders also had more far-reaching ambitions, ended with the utter defeat of the European knights (Nicopolis/Niğbolu, 1396). The result was a consolidation of the Ottoman conquests in Europe. Although the invasion of Timur (often written in the Latinized form Tamerlane, from Timur Lenk, "Timur the Lame") led to the complete, albeit temporary, collapse of Ottoman rule in Asia Minor, none of the Balkan princes were able to cast off Ottoman rule over his former territory permanently during these years, when the sons of the deposed Bayezid were competing for the throne.

Timur did not remain in Anatolia for long. After the 1403 conquest of Izmir, which was still controlled by Crusaders, he returned to Central Asia, where he died in 1405. After a long Interregnum, Mehmed I was established as the Ottoman sole ruler (1413–1421). But there was further expansion as early as the 1420s, beginning in Anatolia. In 1425, Izmir and the southwestern principalities of Teke and Menteşe were reconquered. Salonika, long the second-largest city in the Byzantine Empire, followed in 1430. In 1439 the Serbian state ceased to exist. At that time the Kingdom of Hungary, which had occupied the fortress city of Belgrade for quite some time, was the major adversary of the Ottomans in southeastern Europe.

The Age of Mehmed the Conqueror

Under these circumstances the Byzantine "empire" was little more than an enclave in Ottoman territory. Only Constantinople remained after several failed sieges (there was a blockade from 1394 on) because its strong walls and location were conducive to an effective defense. But when the young sultan Mehmed II ascended to the Ottoman throne in 1451, he immediately began building the fortress of Rumelihisarı, still extant today, to prevent the passage of enemy ships through the Bosporus. He also used artillery to bombard the walls of Constantinople, which had not been reinforced to withstand it. After a brief siege, the city fell into Ottoman hands in May 1453.

All in all, the reign of Mehmed II was a time of rapid Ottoman expansion. In the North, the principality of the Crimean Tatars, one of the remnants of Mongolian rule in what is Russia and the Ukraine today, became a dependent principality in 1475. The Genoese colonies on the Black Sea were at first tributary to the sultan, and outright military conquest soon followed; the Genoese colony of Caffa became the Ottoman provincial capital of Kefe. The small principality ruled by the Komnenos dynasty, which claimed the title of Empire of Trebizond, was conquered in 1461 and soon Islamicized by means of resettlement and conversion of local people. In Anatolia, the Karamanoğulları principality was defeated and incorporated into the Ottoman state between 1469 and 1474. As a result, the Ottomans expanded into central Anatolia and Mehmed the Conqueror's empire now bordered on the territories that had long been subordinate to the Mamluk sultanate of Syria and Egypt.

In southeastern Europe, the Peloponnesus was conquered from the Franks and Byzantines and henceforth became the Ottoman province of Mora (1460–1464). Venice also suffered serious losses (Euboa/ Negroponte became Ottoman in 1470) after the Ottoman vanguard of Mehmed II reached the easternmost part of northern Italy in 1478. Mehmed II had a fortress built in Elbasan, Albania; after the death of the Albanian Prince George Kastriota/Skanderbeg in 1468, all of Albania was under the firm control of the Ottomans. Groups of Albanians who could not come to terms with this state of affairs migrated to southern Italy. But in 1480 the Italian fortress town of namely Otranto was also conquered by an Ottoman military contingent. This event was probably intended as a first step toward the conquest of Italy, but when Mehmed II died the following year, his son Bayezid II (1481–1512) set different priorities, and the Ottomans retreated from Otranto.

At the Border

The Ottoman state was situated at the edge of the Islamic world, and could thus command resources not available to most of its competitors in the struggle for predominance in Anatolia. One example was the opportunity to expand into southeastern Europe (in Ottoman terminology: Rumeli, often Latinized as Rumelia), not only to the territories of the Byzantine Empire, but soon to the Bulgarian, Serbian, and Albanian principalities as well. With Rumelia as a base, Mehmed I and his successors rapidly reconstituted the Ottoman state after Bayezid's defeat under the walls of Ankara in 1402. Without Ottoman possessions in the Balkans this strategy would have been far more difficult, if not impossible.

During the 14th century, Byzantium experienced one succession struggle after another, and both reigning Byzantine emperors and pretenders were quite willing to bring in allies from neighboring polities. From the Byzantine point of view, Muslim neighbors appeared to be less dangerous than the knights, princes, and traders from Catholic Europe, often known as "Franks" or "Latins," who remained in the area even after their short-lived domination of Constantinople (1204–1261) had come to an end. After the Byzantine reconquest of the city, Venetians and Genoese continued to control Mediterranean trade, while parts of the Peloponnesus and numerous Aegean islands still were ruled by "Frankish" dynasties. In 1347, John Kantakuzenos, who had already married one of his daughters to the Ottoman sultan Orhan, made himself the Byzantine emperor after a successful rebellion. Additional Byzantine-Ottoman alliances followed; and these events enabled the Ottoman sultans to create a durable base on the European side of the Sea of Marmara.

One of the major political and ideological advantages arising from the border location of the fledgling Ottoman principality was the attraction it held for many young warriors of Anatolia to participate in military and marauding expeditions in the lands of the "infidels." These warriors, known as *gazis*, were in some instances subjects of neighboring Anatolian principalities; in other words, the Ottoman sultans were able to gain military resources at the expense of their Muslim neighbors. Just like the Christian Crusaders, many Islamic religious warriors easily reconciled their wish to spread the true religion with the prospect of land and spoils.

It is important to keep in mind that in the 14th century, Anatolia was inhabited by numerous nomadic tribes whose quest for pasturelands made them willing to cross over to the Balkan Peninsula. Once these nomads had settled in Rumelia, their tribal structure was soon replaced by a purely military one. We know very little about the processes involved in this momentous changeover. But the militarization of the Rumelian nomads may indicate that although the Ottoman sultans promoted the immigration of Muslim subjects into the Balkan provinces, they also sought to control the newcomers. Faced with the great number of Anatolian principalities founded by nomadic tribes, the sultans must have sought guarantees against future revolts and the creation of independent polities by immigrant tribesmen.

There is little available source material concerning the land acquisition of Turkish nomads in the Balkans. This scarcity of documentation has led to heated debates about population density in the Balkans before the beginning of the Ottoman conquest and the loss in population resulting from the wars that accompanied it. We cannot determine the extent to which the plague epidemics of the late 14th century decimated the population quite independently of war casualties. In any case, roving armies were an ideal vehicle to spread the plague. Historians in the Balkan states sometimes assume that there was a very large resident population before the Ottoman conquest, but this assessment tends to reflect nationalist interests more than anything else. Turkish historians, by contrast, as well as many Ottomanists the world over, put the numbers far lower. However, the sources allow for nothing but educated guesses.

Army and Administration

The Ottomans' rapid conquests were possible only because they had developed an efficient military structure. Warfare in the 14th and 15th centuries was conducted primarily on horseback and with swords, lances, and sabers. Ottoman horsemen were financed by so-called *timars*, allocations from mostly rural taxes, distributed by the sultans' financial administration. The holder of a *timar* was obliged to appear mounted for military campaigns, and if his *timar* was large enough, to bring along an appropriate number of armed men. He had to pay for horses and weapons himself.

At first glance the *timar* would appear to resemble the medieval European fief, and the two institutions do have several common characteristics. In both cases the taxes came from village populations that managed their family farms independently; the "home farm" of the *timar* holder, who held this supplementary resource until well into the 16th century, never had more than a secondary role. Also, both social systems had a relatively small amount of cash in circulation, but the *timars* did not function within a barter economy. Even in the 15th century—there are no sources available for earlier periods—*timar* holders could maintain themselves only when there was a market nearby where they could stock up on horses and weapons. There is no record of craftsmen serving on a rural estate in the Ottoman Empire, as there were in several periods and places in European history.

There were other significant differences between the *timar* and the European-style fief. Ottoman law had no equivalent of a *commendatio*, in which an individual placed himself under the protection of an overlord and pledged his loyalty to him, nor was there a hierarchical pyramid with a highest feudal lord in command of less powerful feudatories, who in turn served as feudal lords of less powerful underlings, and so forth. Apart from slaves, all working people were direct subjects of the sultan (*reaya*), but they were clearly subordinate to the privileged imperial administrators (*askeri*), which included both judges (*kadıs*) and *timar* holders.

While in many parts of medieval Europe feudatories judged their subordinate peasants and thus might be both party and judge, courts presided over by *timar* holders were unknown in the Ottoman Empire; in certain cases even slaves addressed the *kadı*. *Timar* holders furthermore rarely had a chance to put down roots and turn into local aristocrats, as was often the case with officials that medieval Europeen kings sent into the countryside: after all, *timar* holders were transferred from one region to another too frequently. Thus the centralized Ottoman state of the 15th and 16th centuries wielded far more power over its "feudal" cavalrymen than the pre-absolutist European kingdoms over their dukes, counts, and knights.

Recruited originally from the fifth of all war prisoners that the sultan was entitled to after every military campaign, the janissaries (Ottoman *yeniçeri*, new army) were by far the best known foot soldiers. Later, when this source of recruitment no longer sufficed, a large percentage of janissaries consisted of forcibly recruited sons of Christian peasants who were already subjects of the sultan. The secondary literature refers to this form of recruitment as "levy of boys" (*devşirme*). This same procedure was also used to select future high-level administrators. In this case, the boys were given a thorough education in the school of pages situated in the sultans' palace. As for the future soldiers, they were sent to Anatolia to serve local peasants, and there they were expected to convert to Islam and learn the Turkish language. At some point they were sent to the capital, where they were known as "novice boys" (Turkish: *acemi oğlan*) and waited for a place to free up in the ranks of the janissaries.

Until the mid-16th century, janissaries officially were not allowed to marry during their active service. They were entitled to do so only when as mature men, they had been discharged from the service of the sultan. Of course it is difficult to determine how far this regulation was complied with in practice. Moreover, any member of the janissaries or *timar* holder was a privileged servitor of the sultan. This meant not only immunity from taxation, but in the case of the janissaries also the right to be judged only by one's own commanding officer. Particularly in provincial towns a janissary often commanded great respect.

Janissaries and other office-holders of the sultan were so dependent on him that their condition bore a resemblance to slavery. In this regard, the levy of boys was in line with the medieval Near Eastern tradition of using slaves or former slaves of the ruler for military functions. The loyalty of foreign-born soldiers to their sultan, who had made possible their often substantial social ascent, was, from the perspective of the rulers, the chief attraction of this institution. For the strict exegetes of religious law, janissaries posed a problem, because these men were of course not foreign, but subjects of the sultan. On the other hand, no one who lived in an Islamic state could be enslaved, no matter what his religion, unless he was a non-Muslim and had tried to throw off Ottoman rule. But no one claimed that the conscripts or their families had done any such thing. One way around the difficulty was the argument that janissaries and other servants of the sultan were not slaves, but only appointed to serve the sultan. Even so, in the 16th century, at least in Egypt, free Ottoman subjects were known to refuse to take orders from an office-holder of the sultan whom they regarded as a mere slave.

Moreover, the Ottoman state maintained irregular troops whose job it was to spread terror and confusion as vanguard *akıncı* (raiders). Some of these units, known as *martolos,* were made up of Christians. The nomads of the Balkan Peninsula did their military service in shifts; while a limited number of men actively participated in any given campaign, the remaining members of their unit, called an *ocak*, were in charge of supplies. Peasant soldiers (*müsellem*) were another 15th-century group to serve the army without cash payment. They were rewarded for their service with tax exemptions on their farms in Anatolian villages.

At least since the time of Mehmed II the Ottoman units from the provinces were usually commanded by men who had completed their course of study at the palace school and had been sent to the provinces as military commanders and then as governors. As governors also served in the army, they were often away from the places they had been assigned to and which supplied the taxes needed to finance their activities. In the highest ranks of the administration and the military were the viziers, who convened on a regular basis. This imperial council (*divan-ı humayun*) supported the ruler in running the empire, and it issued orders in his name.

In battle the early sultans employed strategies which allowed them to continually best European feudal armies. There was just one commander in chief—in the period from 1300 to 1481 it was generally the sultan himself. Subordinate commanding officers were famous for the discipline with which they stuck to a fixed battle plan. European armies, by contrast, were mostly a conglomerate of independent forces, and it often happened that at the first sign of trouble, the mutually exclusive interests of the allies made the battle formation fall apart; the defeat at Nicopolis in 1396 is only one example among many. Moreover, European military leaders seem to have been tricked each and every time by the same Ottoman ruse. The Europeans would follow a relatively small group of Ottoman soldiers supposedly on the run, only to find, to their great surprise, that they had ended up in a trap where they were confronted with a well-organized main army commanded by the sultan. As a result the Ottoman armies of the 15th century had a reputation for virtual invincibility.

The Islam of the Early Ottomans

Most Turks who arrived in the Balkans were already Muslims. The Gagauz people, who still reside in Romania today, were an exception. These people appear to have immigrated in the 13th century, that is, in the pre-Ottoman epoch, and became Orthodox Christians. Of course, when considering nomadic groups or even members of the court of Sultans Osman or Orhan, we should not overestimate their knowledge of or compliance with Islamic customs. Thus the Moroccan world traveler Ibn Battuta (1304–1368/69 or 1377)[1] was received by Orhan's wife when he visited the royal residence, since the sultan himself was away at the time. In later centuries, a gesture of this sort would have been unthinkable. As far as the religion of the nomads is concerned, the origins of their numerous practices of non-Islamic origin are still disputed. Some experts emphasize the role of shamanism, while others focus on nature cults. In the folk Islam of rural Anatolia, rock formations and ancient trees were often associated with the miracles of saints.

While the urban high Islam of the legal and religious scholars (*ulema*) left no room for practices of this kind, some dervish communities were quite flexible. It can be assumed that the early Ottoman sultans had a friendly relationship with these somewhat heterodox sheikhs. Fifteenth-century chronicles report that a sheikh named Edebali prophesied that Sultan Osman I, after whom the dynasty was named, would rule the entire world, and the holy man gave his daughter to the prince in marriage. Edebali, in turn, seems to have been one of the rather large numbers of sheikhs who were heavily involved in a revolt of nomads, which was crushed in 1240 with a great deal of bloodshed by the current Seljuk sultan, with the aid of Frankish mercenaries. One of these mercenaries reported his adventures to the Dominican Simon of St. Quentin; his report is one of the few sources for this revolt that has come down to us. Another sheikh from the same milieu, whose followers would play a major role in Ottoman history, was Hacı Bektaş, who had escaped Seljuk persecution by fleeing to a remote central Anatolian village. It would appear that since the mid-14th century this sheikh, about whose life on earth hardly anything is known, was regarded as the patron of the most famous Ottoman corps, the janissaries. His legendary *Vita*, dating at least in part to the late 1400s or early 1500s, is one of the important documents of Anatolian cultural history.

Dervishes also had an important role in the Turkish settlement of Rumelia and the Islamization of the local population. It often happened that a religious leader known as *Baba* (father) would settle in a sparsely populated area and gather followers. After his death, his grave was venerated by the local residents, who hoped that his intercession would yield good harvests, heal illnesses, and ensure ample offspring. Donations enabled the dervishes to construct sometimes quite elaborate lodges. In Anatolia these institutions often dated back to earlier Muslim rulers, and the Ottoman sultans generally respected them and sometimes even increased the endowments. In Ottoman times dervish lodges were obliged to shelter travelers overnight so that official aid was likely to safeguard travel routes. Several Ottoman sultans apparently intended to advance the Islamization of Christian peasants and heterodox nomads by supporting dervishes who were willing to promote Sunnite right belief.

The Ottoman sultans also lent their support to urban high Islam, most notably by constructing mosques and schools (*medrese*) to teach Islamic law and theology and to train future scholars of jurisprudence and theology (*ulema*). Since Islam has no priests, it fell to these specialists to guide believers in the proper practice of their religion. Since it was assumed that God would not allow the entire community of Muslims to be misled, once the *ulema* had reached a consensus, their decisions were binding for all believers. Mosques and *medrese*s were often combined to form larger complexes (*külliye*) with guest houses for traveling dervishes, soup kitchens, and schools for young children. Generally the donors, who were often sultans, princes, and princesses, arranged to be buried near these buildings. The foundation administrators were responsible for paying salaries to the relevant employees, including the legal and religious experts who taught in the *medreses*. Exceptional scholars in this still quite rustic society soon aroused the interest of the sultans. Sheikh Bedreddin, who was both a mystic and a scholar of law, acted as an army judge for Prince Musa, one of the sons of Bayezid I who lost out in the struggle for succession. After a later unsuccessful revolt that his grandson and apologist claimed had never happened, the sheikh was hanged in Serres at the order of Mehmed I in 1417.

A New City, a New Polity

The transformation of Istanbul into an Ottoman city, with a strong Muslim presence, was one of the priorities that Sultan Mehmed the Conqueror seems to have set for himself. First the Hagia Sophia (Aya Sofya), now converted into a mosque, served as the religious center of the city. A *medrese* was added on so that theology, jurisprudence, and other subjects could be taught. In 1463 Mehmed II also began building a large complex that consisted of a mosque, sixteen *medreses*, a special school for Koran recitation, and other institutions. The buildings were located on the site of the Church of the Holy Apostles, which had been torn down for this purpose. In choosing a location for his royal residence, Mehmed II appears to have hesitated between Istanbul and Edirne, and he had large palace complexes built in both cities: the Eski Saray in Istanbul, the current site of the Suleiman Mosque and the central building of the University of Istanbul, and the Topkapı Palace, which still exists today. The palace in Edirne was blown up by an Ottoman general during the Balkan War of 1877, but until the early 18th century, it was used extensively by many sultans, especially during the hunting season.

Trade was an important complement to courtly life and Islamic high culture. In the late Byzantine era, the tiny city of Galata, with its mostly Genoese merchants, had become the economic center of the region; Mehmed II relocated it to the southern shore of the Golden Horn, where two covered bazaars (called *bedesten*) were set up on a hill, and formed the centerpiece of the present-day Grand Bazaar. Valuable wares were traded here, and Mehmed II's Grand Vizier Mahmud Paşa built a mosque nearby.

The lack of people was a major problem. Many had fled before the siege, and during the three-day rampage of the soldiery just after the conquest there were further losses. Now a time limit was set within which the refugees could benefit from amnesty and retake possession of their homes. To promote immigration from the old Ottoman provinces, new residents were promised home ownership, a pledge that was later retracted. Certain provinces had to send specified numbers of new settlers to Istanbul. These people (*sürgün*) were not allowed to leave the city to which they had been assigned, although otherwise they retained the rights of freemen. While quite a few of these immigrants were Christians, there were enough Muslims among them to give the city an Islamic character. Evidently courtiers were encouraged or perhaps even ordered to establish mosques in Istanbul that soon became the nuclei for new town quarters.

These new regulations transformed the lives of many Ottoman subjects. They were especially burdensome for those *sürgün* who had been sent to Istanbul against their will. The first recorded documentation of dissatisfaction with the policies of Mehmed II dates to his successor, Bayezid II (1481–1512). In the opponents' perspective, the old capital of the Roman emperors was a cursed place at which even King Solomon had fallen victim to the temptations of polytheism; despite its universal reputation for sanctity even the Aya Sofya was considered unable to dispel this curse.

Changes in the relationship of the sultan to his subjects also made for dissatisfaction. Peasants were obliged to pay higher taxes for the campaigns and conquests of Sultan Mehmed II; there is no record of their feelings on this subject. We have more information about the ways in which upper-class Anatolian families forfeited their privileged positions: until the time of Mehmed II, some members of the Anatolian aristocracies had held important positions in the Ottoman administration, but Mehmed II made it much harder for them to do so. The sultan preferred to fill high-level posts with men who had been trained in the school of pages at the palace and whose dependency on his person strongly resembled slavery. This way, the ruler could have office-holders executed without appealing to a court, and take over their assets after their deaths. The growing distance between the sultan and his court was also reflected in the fact that the first known regulation of court protocol, establishing a strict hierarchy of the dignitaries concerned, stems from the time of Mehmed the Conqueror. Over time, this text was revised and in the 16th century made even stricter.

Boys who had come to Istanbul either as prisoners of war or by way of the levy of boys and seemed especially talented were accepted into the school of pages. These young people were placed in a strict hierarchy, with those highest up rendering personal services to the ruler as pages. During the reign of Mehmed II, the sultan did not reside in the harem, as was common from the second half of the 16th century onwards, but in the third court of the palace surrounded by his pages. When a young man had finished his schooling, the palace arranged for him to be married, often to a woman who had been raised in the harem of the sultan. Beginning with the reign of Mehmed II, those who proved their abilities as military officers and adminstrators in the provinces could count on being brought back to the capital and appointed to high public office; the most sucessful might even become grand viziers.

Mehmed II introduced a new rule that brought about drastic changes in courtly life. He mandated that after a sultan had acceded to the throne, he should have his brothers murdered to avoid long civil wars. This practice lasted until the beginning of the 17th century. At this time there was no regulation comparable to primogeniture; in principle at least all sons of a ruling sultan were equally entitled to the succession; however, as most sultans did not live very long by our standards the eldest son might well be the only adult and thus have an advantage over his younger brothers. To prepare for their position, princes were sent to the provinces, typically accompanied by their mother and a mentor known as a *lala*. As soon as they were old enough, they began courting allies who would later support them as candidates for the throne. Anyone who could win over the janissaries to his side normally had the best chance. As a result, the battle for succession to the throne was not only institutionalized, but carried to an extreme; in order to survive, all princes had to do everything in their power to become the next sultan. If the ruler reached a relatively advanced age, the battle for succession took place during his lifetime and sometimes with his participation.

Contemporaries such as Aşıkpaşazade, a chronicler descended from an old dervish family in Central Anatolia, were evidently wary of these developments and of the courtly culture that accompanied it. Aşıkpaşazade's chronicle, which he wrote during the second half of the 15th century when he was an old man, by contrast emphasized the simple life and the accessibility of the early Ottoman sultans.

Towards the end of his reign, Mehmed II made yet another attempt to weaken the power base of the established Anatolian families, many of whose members received a portion of their income from pious foundations instituted by their forebears. These foundations served a religious and charitable purpose, and were managed by trustees, who often were descended from the family of the donor and had a certain amount of leeway in administering the assets. From the perspective of the donors, this procedure had the advantage of circumventing the prescriptions of the Islamic law of inheritance, which provides for a distribution among many beneficiaries. As we have already seen, several of these pious foundations stemmed from pre-Ottoman times, but were confirmed after the Ottoman conquest.

Mehmed II now took a step that came into clear conflict with Islamic law governing pious foundations. In his later years he confiscated numerous institutions that he had previously approved, and changed the legal status of their property into *timars*. Apart from the effects upon the donor families, Mehmed II's policies must have hurt many ordinary subjects as well, since travelers, students, and pilgrims were the usual beneficiaries of pious foundations. When Mehmed II died in 1481, his son and successor Bayezid II was embroiled in a fierce battle for succession with his brother Cem and quickly reversed this policy.

CHAPTER 2
Between East and West (1481-1600)

Consolidation under Bayezid II

Under Bayezid II, the Ottoman Empire experienced a phase of consolidation, despite several wars with Venice, Poland, and the Mamluk sultans. Ottoman control of the Black Sea coasts was made complete by the conquest of the port towns of Akkerman (Belgorod-Dnestrovskij/ Ukraine) and Kilia (Kilija/ Ukraine). In the 16th century, the Black Sea, now a purely Ottoman lake, was off limits to foreign ships, and its coastal areas served only to provide the rapidly growing capital of Istanbul with food and other necessities. Moreover, Montenegro came under Ottoman sovereignty, although this addition cannot have been very significant, considering the poverty and remoteness of the area.

From an economic point of view, the more significant development was the immigration of Spanish and later Portuguese Jews, which began in 1492 with their expulsion from Spain by Ferdinand and Isabella. Those who came directly from Spain had to leave behind their assets and could bring along only their business contacts. Many so-called Marranos, baptized Jews who secretly retained their religion, also had to flee from the Inquisition in the 16th century; but as Christians moving to a Christian land, they could salvage substantial portions of their assets. Typically these people thus reached the Ottoman domains in several stages. The new immigrants were settled in Istanbul, where the Greek-speaking Jews had been brought together under Mehmed II, and in Salonika. In the latter city the Spanish Jews made the manufacture of woolen cloth into a regional industry; the cloth was milled outside the city. The state assigned them the manufacture of fabric for the janissaries' uniforms. Additionally, around 1493, the immigrants established the first functioning printing press in the Ottoman Empire.

The Ottoman Sultans in the Near East (1481–1600)

The long war between Bayezid II and the Mamluk sultans (1484–1491) brought no decisive gains. In the place of Uzun Hasan, the prince of the Ak-koyunlu Turkmen defeated by Mehmed II, a youthful sheikh of the Safaviyeh Sufi order established himself as Shah Ismail I in 1500. Shah Ismail conquered Baghdad in 1504. In the vicinity of the eastern Anatolian town of Erzincan, the Ottoman sultanate now had a border in common with this new and ambitious ruler. Even more threatening was the attraction that the newly established polity held for the politically and militarily marginalized nomads of Anatolia. In 1511 followers of Shah Ismail rebelled against Ottoman rule deep in southwestern Anatolia and enjoyed some initial success. The crisis of the Empire was aggravated by the succession struggle between the sons of Bayezid II in 1512; in the course of these disputes, Prince Selim forced his father to abdicate, killed his brothers, and acceded to the Ottoman throne as Selim I (1512–1520).

The eight-year reign of Selim I brought rapid expansion, although this time it was in the Middle East rather than in the Balkans. After an extremely bloody suppression of the Anatolian followers of Shah Ismail, Selim defeated him in 1514 at Çaldıran and advanced as far as western Iran. Even so, the janissaries refused to follow the sultan on a campaign farther east.

The Ottoman takeover of the Mamluk state only took slightly over a year; in 1516 the campaign began with the conquest of the city of Diyarbekir in southeastern Anatolia, and in the same year the Mamluk ruler Kansuh al-Ghuri fell in the battle at Marj Dabik. His successor Tumanbay tried to refuse Selim I access to Cairo; but after the lost Battle of Raydaniyya the last Mamluk sultan was hanged in front of a gate to his capital in 1517. The Sharif of Mecca offered his submission, and Selim I showed his appreciation by allocating important Egyptian resources to support the population of the Hijaz, thus indirectly underwriting the Muslim pilgrimage to Mecca. Now the power of the

Ottoman sultan extended into the southern Red Sea, except that control over Yemen remained limited, and Ottoman rule in this territory was essentially confined to the cities until its collapse in the 1630s.

Selim I's conquests created an altogether new type of empire. Now the Ottoman realm was no longer limited to the Balkans and Anatolia and thus situated at the edge of the Islamic world. On the contrary, it now comprised the old heartlands, including the cities of Cairo, Aleppo, and Damascus. The Ottoman conquest marked a turning point in the way Syria was ruled; henceforth these provinces were no longer administered from Cairo, but rather from Istanbul. Even so, local families from Mamluk times, often resident in fortified houses at the edge of the desert, remained prominent. As for Egypt, the Mamluks continued to play a role in provincial government. It remained relatively common until the early 19th century to import young military slaves, who after training and emancipation formed a kind of local aristocracy that collected taxes in town and country. While Mamluk recruitment had been going on for centuries, there was a significant difference between the pre-Ottoman and the Ottoman epochs: after 1517 the ruler no longer emerged from among the Mamluks, and the latter had to function within an Ottoman framework, determined by the central government.

After 1517, Cairo sank to the level of a provincial city, but recent research has shown that in the 16th and 17th centuries a great deal of money was earned there and spent on magnificent urban palaces, commercial centers, and shopping streets. In addition, trade with India was blossoming, and the import of spices, dyes, and printed cotton fabrics enabled some merchants to amass considerable wealth. Coffee, originating from Abyssinia and Yemen, became popular in the mid-16th century, first in Egypt and then in Istanbul and Anatolia. The trade in coffee was also profitable, although during the 17th century this beverage was prohibited several times.[1] Coffee and spice traders could make quite a lot of money, because they dealt in goods that were not everyday or military necessities, and were therefore exempt from the strict state supervision governing the grain merchants and butchers of Istanbul. Also, these Cairo merchants proved that at least in Egypt, money could be earned and passed down to the next generation without the intervention of the central government. In the Ottoman heartlands such opportunities were far more limited. It is therefore important not to lump together developments in the various Ottoman provinces.

In the course of the 16th century, the sultan expanded his power along the North African coast west of Cairo as well. Hayreddin Barbarossa, a corsair from the island of Midilli (Lesbos) established his power base in present-day Algeria; he later submitted to the authority of Selim I's successor Suleiman the Magnificent and was appointed governor of the new province. In 1534 he advanced to commander-in-chief of the Ottoman fleet and soon thereafter conquered Tunis, which, due to the immigration of Spanish Muslims, became an important center of trade and industry. A long campaign by Suleiman the Magnificent in 1533-1536 resulted in both a brief occupation of Tabriz and the incorporation of Iraq into the Ottoman Empire, including the key cities of Mosul, Baghdad, and Basra.

Expansion in Europe during the 16th Century

Suleiman the Magnificent's accession to the throne in 1520 brought a renewed expansion westward. In 1521, the Ottomans captured Belgrade, which had been besieged unsuccessfully by Mehmed the Conqueror, and in 1526 the Battle of Mohács ended with the defeat of the Hungarian army and the death of King Lajos II. Suleiman first appointed a local nobleman named John Zapolya as king, in accordance with standard practice following Ottoman conquests, which often involved a transitional period of local rule before direct government was introduced. But Zapolya died soon thereafter, and the Habsburg King Ferdinand I asserted claims to his inheritance and appeared with an army in Hungary. A long Ottoman-Habsburg war ensued. After Sultan Suleiman's conquest of important fortresses (Pécs, Sikós, Gran), the greater portion of Hungary became an Ottoman province between 1541 and 1547, with the capital in the old royal city of Buda. Transylvania remained a separate principality under Ottoman suzerainty but was ruled by local princes, while a narrow strip of western Hungary came under Habsburg rule. In the course of this war, Vienna was besieged in 1529. Contrary to the initial expectations at the sultan's court, the

Ottoman sphere of influence had more or less attained its maximal westward expansion by the mid-1500s, and Hungary became a border area for one and a half centuries.

In the Mediterranean region, the Ottoman Empire expanded significantly when it conquered the island of Cyprus in 1571; even the victory of Lepanto by the united Spanish and Venetian fleets in 1573 did little to reverse Ottoman progress. This island, valuable because of its cotton and sugar plantations, had belonged to the Venetian colonial empire since the beginning of the 16th century. The Ottoman administration lost no time in bringing in settlers from Anatolia, primarily poor peasants and members of the religious sect of the Kızılbaş (known as "redheads" because of their preferred head covering), which the Sunnis considered heretical.[2] As townsmen and villagers in southern Anatolia could designate those people from amongst their midst that were to be sent off to populate the island, in the early stages of Ottoman domination Cyprus seems to have functioned as a place where outcasts were banished.

The Expansion of Diplomatic Relations

Even after the death of Selim I (1520) and Shah Ismail (1524), war was frequent between Iran and the Ottoman Empire throughout the 16th century. But in the peaceful intervals there were political relations as well. An ongoing point of discussion was the desire of Shiite pilgrims to visit not only Mecca and Medina, but also the graves of the descendants of the Prophet Muhammad, most of which were in Iraq. However, Ottoman authorities feared that these pilgrimages provided opportunities for espionage. There was only limited contact with the other great empire of the Islamic world, namely that of the Mughal dynasty, which had ruled northern India since 1526. This contact focused primarily on the holy cities of Mecca and Medina, which were also visited by numerous Indian pilgrims.

Suleiman the Magnificent found a European ally in Francis I, king of France, who, following his defeat in the battle of Pavia in 1525, could return to his throne only after paying a hefty ransom to his opponent, the Habsburg Emperor Charles V. Accordingly, the alliance between king and sultan had an anti-Habsburg thrust and in 1543, an Ottoman-French fleet captured Nice from the Duke of Savoy, then an ally of the emperor. French ambassadors appeared in Istanbul, the first permanently accredited legation after the Venetian. Until the late 18th century, Ottoman-French alliances were revived periodically whenever it seemed advantageous in facing their common enemy, the Habsburgs.

At the very end of the 16th century, English merchants began to do business on Ottoman territory, and sought to oust their Venetian competitors from their traditional waterways, even resorting to piracy in the process. There had been relations between Sultan Murad III (r. 1574–1595) and Queen Elizabeth I since 1580. The Ottomans were especially interested in English tin, used in the manufacture of armaments. English deep-sea vessels that the sultans hoped to "charter" when required may have played a role in the Ottoman interest in this remote kingdom as well. The basis for this relationship, cemented at one point by correspondence between Queen Elizabeth I and Murad's consort Safiye Sultan, was unquestionably the battle against the Habsburgs. The defeat of the Spanish Armada in 1588 made it clear that the war against the English Queen required significant resources on the part of King Philip II of Spain that thus could not be used against the Ottomans. The English also capitalized on the motive of a broad common front against Catholicism.

The status of envoys in residence and of merchants was regulated by so-called *ahidname*, which European historiography calls "capitulations." For the most part, they were privileges granted unilaterally by a sultan to the subjects of a ruler with whom he was on friendly terms, intended to improve relations with actual or potential adversaries of the Habsburg Empire. The capitulations were valid only during the lifetime of the sultan who had issued them, and had to be submitted to the successor for reconfirmation. These privileges set the amount of customs duties that the subjects of the ruler in question needed to pay. By the end of the 16th century, the Venetians, the French, and the English had been granted these capitulations. In the 18th, 19th, and early 20th centuries, when the balance of power had been reversed to the Ottomans' disadvantage, these capitulations became a real impediment to Ottoman policymaking. But Suleiman the Magnificent and later

Murad III, who had granted concessions to the English, could not foresee this consequence.

Ottoman Policy in the Indian Ocean Region (1500–1600)

To understand the extraordinarily successful campaign against the Mamluk Empire, which added a new territorial dimension to the Ottoman realm in 1516–1517, it is useful to consider Portuguese expansion and Indian Ocean trade in the Late Middle Ages. New developments included circumnavigation of the Cape of Good Hope in 1488, the Portuguese arrival on the western coast of India in 1498, and the Portuguese occupation of the island of Ormus in the Persian Gulf in 1515. In the course of the 15th century, the Egyptian sultans had tried to compensate for losses in tax revenues caused by the plague epidemics of the time. One such method was to declare the passage of goods from southern Asia a state monopoly; from then on, Venetian and Genoese traders had to buy the goods they wished to export from representatives of the sultan. After the Portuguese had opened up the Cape route to the Indian Ocean, the attempt on the part of their king to monopolize the spice trade for his own benefit resulted in a direct confrontation with the sultans of Egypt and Syria.

The situation was aggravated by the fact that in the course of the Late Middle Ages, pilgrims and long-term residents of Mecca and Medina had become dependent on Egypt for their grain supply. As a consequence, Portuguese incursions into the Red Sea posed a direct threat to an undisturbed pilgrimage. However, the Egyptian rulers lacked a navy. Despite the conflicts of interest in eastern Anatolia, the Mamluk sultan Kansuh al-Ghuri therefore formed an alliance with the Ottomans, who supported him with their fleet in the Red Sea. The collaboration between these unequal partners left much to be desired, however, and Kansuh al-Ghuri's support of Shah Ismail soon supplied a pretext for an attack on the Mamluk realm (1516–1517). It can be assumed that the Ottomans also intended to take control of the lucrative trade in the Red Sea region. Unfortunately, this early "economic policy" of the Ottoman sultans is not well documented.

In any case, the Ottoman rulers tried to exert their influence on the west coast of India as well. In 1538, a large Ottoman fleet appeared before the harbor city of Diu, but there was no confrontation with the Portuguese. In 1552, an Ottoman fleet under the leadership of Piri Reis attempted to conquer the island of Ormus, at that time a Portuguese possession. Piri Reis was an established cartographer and experienced navigator remembered today as the designer of a map of America surviving only in fragments, which is based on work by Columbus that is no longer extant. The operation ended with the loss of the entire fleet; a junior commander named Seydi Ali Reis attempted in vain to rescue some of the ships and wrote a report about the perilous operation he had conducted.[3] No major campaign in the Indian Ocean was organized after this disaster. Still, the Ottomans supplied firearms and artillerymen to various princes who were fighting against the Portuguese in South Asia.

It did not take the Venetians long to realize that the Ottomans were the up-and-coming power in the Red Sea region, and that future spice trading would depend on their goodwill, a consideration which explains why Venice acted cautiously after having lost several bases in the eastern Mediterranean to Mehmed II and Bayezid II. Moreover, Venetian and Ottoman merchants both wished to revitalize the spice trade through the Red Sea. The sultan himself was keenly interested because expanding trade would bring in increased tax revenues. Both sides therefore stood to benefit from the Portuguese failure to monopolize the spice trade via the Indian Ocean and the Cape route. The traditional trade route retained its full significance until the end of the 16th century.

Courtly and Imperial Culture: Architecture and the Fine Arts

As we can see from the building complexes that are still standing today, such as the sultans' mosques in Bursa and Edirne, there was an Ottoman monumental style in architecture as early as the 14th and 15th centuries. In the early 1400s Persian artisans were employed in the decoration of a Bursa mosque. Even so, Mehmed the Conqueror's efforts to develop Istanbul and Edirne into dazzling capitals represented the beginning of a new epoch. The Topkapı Palace includes buildings constructed entirely according to Iranian models, such as Çinili Köşk, which houses a ceramics museum today. On the other hand, the towers of Orta Kapu ('middle gate') and the grand loggia overlooking the sea apparently owe something to Italian models. This eclectic style was evidently intended to highlight Mehmed II's conquests and the fact that his reign was conceived as a world power. The reuse of ancient columns in the court of the mosque of Mehmed II also apparently signified the sultan's status as successor to the Byzantine emperor. Mehmed II seems to have regarded these columns as precious and kept a close eye on the way they were used.

While the eclectic style of Mehmed the Conqueror was abandoned by his successor in favor of a uniformly Ottoman architectural tradition, the appreciation of ancient columns and other workpieces could also be observed in the mid-16th century. A similar frame of mind probably explains certain legends about the Hagia Sophia. This corpus of tales derives only in part from Byzantine and Arab models and also includes innovations from about 1500. Even though these legends at one point in time apparently served to transmit protests against the new-fangled style of the sultan's government, they still contained a rich collection of stories about the famous building that continued to be popular even when the protest against Mehmed the Conqueror's innovations had died down.

The tradition that every sultan build a large mosque complex, including schools and other buildings, usually located in the capital of Istanbul, was followed by nearly all rulers into the early 17th century. In accordance with this tradition, Suleiman the Magnificent, during his long reign, had buildings constructed in the names of family members and in this way allowed them to take part in shaping the face of the capital. In nearly all cases, the same architect was employed, namely Sinan (ca. 1490–1588), head of the corps of the sultan's architects. Sinan also recorded the first Ottoman memoirs by an artist; he dictated the story of his life to one of his friends when he was quite old. These reminiscences indicate that the architect came from a small town near Kayseri and joined the janissary corps through the levy of boys. He must, then, have come from a Christian family, but we know nothing about his Christian name or his ethnicity. In the area in which he grew up, there were Greeks, Armenians, and a Turkophone group of Christians of uncertain origin, the Karamanlıs. In later years Sinan, nicknamed "the old one" on account of his long life, kept in touch with several of his relatives and established a foundation in his homeland, as a provincial native who had attained prominence often did. Sinan's relationship to his patron Sultan Suleiman seems to have been tempestuous at times, but eventually he was granted the high honor of placing his own little mausoleum in the wall of Suleiman's complex. For this reason, Sinan cannot have considered himself as an "anonymous artisan," and his contemporaries did not regard him as such.

Another specifically courtly art cultivated in Istanbul palace circles during the 16th century was miniature painting. Ottoman patrons probably encountered miniatures when they began to acquire books from the Timurid courts of central Asia. However, Ottoman miniature painting was distinguished by the important role accorded to the depiction of historical events, as evident in the illustration of the *Süleyman-name*, which records the official biography of Suleiman the Magnificent in a series of miniatures. Great importance was attached to realistic detail. Artists also used cartography to depict the capital of Istanbul.

Clients outside the court occasionally commissioned goblets, pots, and plates in highly decorated faience, but the design of buildings with large-scale ornamentation of this kind was essentially reserved for sultans and their courtiers. This art was initially an import from the domain of the Timurids, but in the 16th century, Ottoman faience artists developed their own style, characterized by the introduction of red (a previously unknown color) and by the depiction of large flower arrangements with tulips, hyacinths, narcissuses, and peonies on a white background. This art blossomed during the entire 16th century, and its decline after 1600 may be associated with the large-scale import of Chinese porcelain.

The Ottoman State and Its History

The first comprehensive chronicles in the Ottoman language were written in the second half of the 15th century to commemorate the deeds of rulers, so it is no wonder that many chroniclers held high public office at some point in their careers. These chronicles were organized according to the years of a sultan's reign, in much the same way that centuries are the organizational principle of today's history books. Campaigns were the focus of these chronicles, and costly architectural monuments were considered a sign of a ruler's stature.

Another important genre was the treatises of political advice known as "Mirrors for Princes." This genre had a long tradition in the pre-Islamic and Islamic Near East. But beginning in about the mid-1500s, these texts, which could be addressed to sultans or viziers, served as an arena for various groups within the state administration to debate their differences. For example, Lütfi Paşa, a former grand vizier of Suleiman the Magnificent, wrote a "vizier book" (*Asafname*). To put this book's advice in the proper perspective, it is interesting to note that Lütfi Paşa had lost his office because he had been abusive to his wife, who was the sultan's sister; she had reproached him severely for the cruel punishment of another woman.

But the most famous of these books of advice for the leaders of the Ottoman government is without a doubt the text written by Mustafa Ali from Gallipoli (1541–1600). Ali was a well-educated and extremely experienced man who was unable to realize his "dream career" and never got over this disappointment even though he was appointed to prestigious offices that carried substantial responsibility. However his frustration seems to have spurred his productivity. He wrote a major historical treatise, which was evidently intended mainly for his own reading pleasure and perhaps for a few close friends. Only a small portion of this work has been seriously analyzed to date, but available studies include a perceptive and highly critical biography of Sultan Murad III, whom Ali reproaches for being irresponsible and gullible. In Ali's eyes these failings were especially serious because in Anatolia and Rumelia, Islamic high culture was still a "delicate flower" that needed to acclimatize, and it was incumbent on the ruler to foster this culture. Ali's commentary on the turmoil resulting from the 1595 murder of the many sons of Murad III in Istanbul, many of whom were still children, is especially striking. Ali contends that since the sultan could have predicted what would happen to his descendants after his death, he should not have produced so many children in the first place.⁴

In the 15th century, several chronicles were written in the language of educated contemporaries. However, by about 1500, an artificial language emerged that essentially retained the Turkish syntax, but introduced words and word formations of Arabic and Persian origin. Depending on the situation, this language could be made more Arabic or more Iranian; the Ottoman educated class had a choice of various "pitches." In addition to this courtly mode of expression, there were writings for people who did not speak the elevated form of the language but were literate nonetheless; the prime examples are the aforementioned saints' lives.

Ottoman Sultans as Defenders of Sunni Islam

Courtly art was certainly conceived as a legitimation for the ruler, presenting the sultan to the members of his court as a patron of art and literature and, first and foremost, as a victor in the battle against infidels and Shiites. Parallels were constructed between these two adversaries: Ebusuud Efendi, the highest legal scholar of Suleiman the Magnificent, even thought that the Shiites of Iran should not be regarded as Muslims, and other men of religion followed in his wake. This role of the sultan as a defender of Sunnite "right belief" was made visible to a wider audience by decorating the Süleymaniye with inscriptions that identified the building as a triumph over the Shiite enemy. A panegyrist of the early 1600s also praised the mosque of Sultan Ahmed I, inaugurated in 1617, in this manner.

Non-Ottoman observers were also targeted by this propaganda for the ruler. As we have seen, once Hijas had become part of the Ottoman Empire, the sultans took over the protection of the pilgrims to Mecca. As a result, soldiers had to be made available to accompany the pilgrim caravans through the desert. Even more costly was the fact that from at least the 12th century onwards, the Bedouins of the Syrian, Egyptian, and Arab deserts had to be paid with money and goods to grant pilgrims free passage. Moreover, in the first half of the 16th century, an expensive plan for urban development in Mecca and Medina was undertaken and continued through the 1500s and early 1600s. All these projects were regarded as urgent, in part because the Mughal rulers of northern India were sponsoring the pilgrimage from their own territory and went to great lengths to court the Sharifs of Mecca. The large sums of money that were spent to support the pilgrimage were clearly aimed at making the presence of the Ottoman sultan in this remote territory manifest to Indian and other foreign pilgrims.

In this context it is also important to observe Suleiman the Magnificent and his successors' interest in Sunni pilgrims from central Asia. Political conflicts often prevented these people from taking the shortest route via Iran, so the pilgrimage took many years, entailing a detour through Istanbul. When the first conflicts with the Russian tsars occurred in the mid-16th century, the sultans also aimed at keeping access to Mecca open to central Asian pilgrims.

Even more significant were the changes in the education and duties of legal and religious scholars (*ulema*). The training of these professionals, who were of central importance to every Islamic society, had been regarded as a major concern by Ottoman sultans ever since the time of Mehmed II and before; this type of education continued to be fostered by Suleiman the Magnificent as well. Legal and religious scholars were integrated into Ottoman officialdom and promoted according to fixed standards, a state of affairs which had not existed in earlier eras. In the Islamic empires of the Middle Ages neither the sphere of activity nor the training of many *ulema* had been limited to a single state. Since the relevant disciplines were taught and practiced in Arabic, a well-traveled man like Ibn Battuta, who was from Morocco, could easily serve as *kadı* in northern India.

In the early 15th century, outstanding Ottoman scholars still belonged to this network, but beginning in the second half of the century, the training of *ulema*, who were preparing for a supraregional career within the empire, began to take place in Istanbul, Bursa, and Edirne. After 1516-17 the result was a marginalization of scholars from places like Damascus and Cairo. From the 16th century on, to qualify for a position as *kadı*, the candidate had to have completed a precisely defined career path, both as a teacher and as a judge. The highest positions required teaching experience, normally a post at the high schools of the Süleymaniye. By this point, the number of qualified candidates greatly exceeded the number of open slots; short terms of office therefore alternated with long periods of joblessness. Also, family connections and the support of the sultan were often crucial, especially for the highest positions of military judge (*kadıasker*) and top legal authority (*şeyhülislam*).

Ottoman judges applied two kinds of law, namely religious law (*şeriat*) and sultanic law (*kanun*), based on the ruler's decrees. Moreover, locally enforced practices (*örf*), especially in matters pertaining to tax collection, could become Ottoman law. In principle, sultanic law was supposed only to fill in the gaps in religious law, but in practice new legal arguments were rather common. Ottoman law was based on the assumption that all land used as forests, fields, and meadows belonged to the sultan; only houses and gardens were the private property of the subjects. The peasants were hereditary leaseholders and the holders of *timar*s only managers and tax collectors; they did not own the villages that were allocated to them.

One significant feature of Ottoman law was the statute of limitations of fifteen years, after which no claims could be made. This statute had been in effect from the 16th century onwards and possibly even earlier. The officially sanctioned circumvention of the Islamic ban on charging interest, in which many pious foundations took part starting in the late 15th century, and the rationales provided for this circumvention should also be regarded as a facet of sultanic law.

As time went on, the influence of religious law became more and more pervasive; all Ottoman judges were familiar with this law, which formed part of their training: "secular" law schools did not exist until the 19th century. In consequence the *şeriat* acquired a central significance not just in religious but also in civil life. Nonetheless, the broad authority of the sultan in legislation, and the related ability to create new laws, was a distinguishing feature of the Ottoman state.

Muslims and Non-Muslims

Selim I's conquests had made the Ottoman polity into an empire with a pronounced Muslim majority, and the term "non-Muslim minorities" can be applied beginning with his reign. The largest minority group was

Greek Orthodox. Members of this group, who might or might not speak Greek as their first language, lived in the Balkans, on the island of Cyprus, and in the Syrian provinces. Egypt was home to the Coptic minority, while in the mountains of eastern Anatolia, some cities in Asia Minor, and the capital of Istanbul there were groups of Gregorian Armenians. The Ottoman Empire had a very limited number of Catholic subjects, on the Aegean islands and in Dalmatia, Bosnia, and Hungary. Only in Hungary and Transylvania were there Protestant (i.e., Calvinist) groups of any significant size.

Among the Jews, the established (Romaniotic) groups played only a minor role in comparison with the new immigrants who came from Spain and Portugal, and sometimes from Italy. There was also an Ashkenazi influx from Central and Eastern Europe; the linguistic and cultural differences were thus quite significant. But by the 16th century, there was clear evidence of assimilation to the Ottoman milieu, including Jewish songs sung to Ottoman tunes. Spanish immigrants used Spanish written in the Hebrew alphabet (*ladino*) in addition to Hebrew, the language of worship.

Scholars long assumed that the institution of *millet*s, religious communities of non-Muslims regulated by bishops, priests, and rabbis, had been introduced as far back as the 15th or 16th century. This assumption is now being questioned. Religious communities, most notably the Orthodox Church, existed right from the beginning and were recognized by the Ottoman sultans. But in the 16th and 17th centuries, the authority of spiritual leaders over their communities often seems to have been quite limited. Research on the early history of the immigrant Jews in particular has shed light on these internal conflicts.

Non-Muslims of any religion paid a poll tax called a *cizye*. Until the end of the 17th century, this tax was sometimes levied on an entire village as a collective payment, but in principle every able-bodied man was required to pay *cizye*. Taxes were on a sliding scale to reflect individual wealth.

Non-Muslims were disadvantaged in the legal arena; for example, they could not testify against Muslims in court. In business this was a serious problem, which many tried to circumvent by registering their transactions with a *kadı* and thereby creating a paper trail. Rules concerning clothing and items of personal use were supposed to make it clear to even a casual passer-by who was a Muslim and who was a Christian or a Jew. The use of the color green was reserved for Muslims, and so were certain kinds of footwear. In addition, non-Muslims were not supposed to ride unless they were traveling, and bearing arms was a Muslim privilege. All these prohibitions were enforced with greater or lesser energy depending on time and place. It was also illegal for non-Muslims to build houses that were higher than those of their Muslim neighbors; sometimes, even long after an Ottoman conquest, a church was confiscated from its community and transformed into a mosque. In order to gather a sufficient number of worshipers in the vicinity of a given Muslim house of prayer, non-Muslims who lived nearby might even be forced to sell their houses and move away. But the practical reality was often more accommodating than the word of the law and the orders of the sultan. Although officials frowned on Muslims and non-Muslims living side by side, they did so for centuries in several Anatolian cities.

Involuntary conversions to Islam were rare, in stark contrast to the situation in the European states of that era, in which the threat of expulsions and even executions enforced religious conformity. Even some slaves were able to resist the pressure to change their religion. Still, the majority of the slaves, as well as the young men who were drafted into the service of the sultan by the levy of boys, had little choice in this matter. Some people who were considered troublemakers for the Ottoman administration were faced with a choice between severe punishment and conversion to Islam.

The overwhelming majority of all conversions appear to have been voluntary, however. There were several motivating factors: first of all, the unending religious disputes between the Greek Orthodox, Catholics, and Protestants were so repulsive to many people in southeastern Europe that they were no longer inclined to believe in a divine mission of the Christian churches. For less contemplative people, there were of course more "secular" reasons. Apart from getting rid of the *cizye*, conversion to Islam opened up possibilities for social advancement, for example in the service of a governor. Some people may simply have preferred to live as "first-class" rather than as "second-class" subjects.

Sometimes there were also conversions of entire villages or families, whose reasons can no longer be reconstructed because of a lack of source material. But the significance of the *cizye* as a source of revenue must have kept Ottoman provincial governors and *kadıs* from enforcing the conversion of the "infidels" too vigorously.

Earning a Living: Agriculture and Crafts

The peasants formed the backbone of the tax-paying subject population; if it had been up to the privileged servitors of the sultan, the whole lot of them would have had to remain in this position. In order to leave the village, a peasant needed permission from his *timar* holder—at least in theory. In practice, an exodus to the city, or perhaps to a province with lower taxes, and joining a mercenary troop were certainly viable alternatives. Soldiers who distinguished themselves in a border region stood to be awarded a *timar*. But the status of these men remained uncertain as long as people still recalled their humble beginnings.

The basis of the village organization was the family farm, which was passed down from father to son and managed independently. As a rule—though there were certainly exceptions—a farm was not divided among the heirs, but managed jointly by them. The *timar* holders cannot have contributed much to the day-to-day operations, since they were often absent. But as some taxes were demanded in kind farmers must often have been prevented from varying the composition of their crops. Conflicts arose about the delivery of tax grains and also about services that farmers owed to the local representatives of the sultan, especially in wartime.

Areas with a high agricultural productivity were more the exception than the rule. In both the Balkans and Anatolia, a good portion of the land was mountainous, so the option of using the more effective heavy plow remained quite limited. In most areas farmers had to stick with the light *aratrum*, which only scratched the surface of the earth but did not turn it over. The potentially fertile coastal plains were swampy and barely usable in the summer because of the danger of malaria. On the Anatolian highlands there was a constant water shortage, which necessitated an annual rotation system with fallow land and posed an additional threat to the harvests, not very plentiful even under the best circumstances. In some places the yield amounted to no more than four times the seeds sown. The decades around 1600, in which there were many crop failures in Italy as well, were especially drought-prone. Rivers suitable for navigation were few, and this fact must have made it especially difficult to ensure an adequate food supply even when crop failures were limited to small areas.

In the course of the 16th century, rural population increased substantially, in line with trends throughout the Mediterranean. In territories that were conveniently situated, this increase in population seems to have fostered relatively labor-intensive specialized cultivation; one example would be the silk growing that began about 1600 in the region around Bursa. At the coasts, raisins, grape syrup, lemon juice, and pomegranates were produced for wealthy customers in the capital, although the lion's share of the profits probably flowed into the pockets of merchants and shipping agents. In response to the denser population structure a sizable number of nomads settled down.

In the villages, the major portion of the goods harvested and produced were most likely used for home consumption, for bartering with neighbors, as seeds for future harvests, and for taxes. In any case, we have no information about the paths these products took except when they left the village. We have already seen that a certain number of markets were indispensable for the functioning of the *timar*s. But there are indications that in the second half of the 16th century, at least in the coastal Anatolian provinces, the number of markets rose appreciably. Commerce now also took place on summer pastures, where farmers and nomads got together every year, resulting in a growing market orientation. A significant volume of trade also was conducted at country fairs that in the Balkans often were held at the feastdays of the patron saints of the local churches. In the second half of the 16th century, some of these fairs seem to have been visited by so many merchants that they attracted investments by Ottoman viziers. These kinds of gatherings also encouraged the exchange of goods between regions.

Artisan producers were usually organized in guilds. The masters attempted to limit access to their craft as best they could, and claimed that in doing so they were defending consumer interest in high quality goods. When quarrels arose between guild masters, the market supervisor or the *kadı* could be brought in. Cases of this kind were generally decided according to traditional practice, which was normally set down in writing only when disputes were resolved. In cases in which neither religious law nor orders from the sultan provided guidelines, the Ottoman central administration regarded this traditional practice as definitive, and tended to support the demands of established guild masters, ruling, for example, against trainees who wanted to open their own stores or against particularly enterprising craftsmen who tried to expand their market share at the expense of their colleagues.

Trade as a Possible Source of Wealth

The older secondary literature tended to assert that there was a division of labor according to religion in the Ottoman Empire, with the Muslims concentrating on the service of the sultan and agriculture, but limiting their participation in trade to providing supplies for the city of Istanbul, an enterprise which was strictly controlled by the state. But recent research has shown that this assumption is quite mistaken: just as we have noted in the case of religious and political organization (*millet* system), conditions that may have existed in the mid-19th century have simply been superimposed on older periods without any documentary evidence. A late 15th-century register listing customs payments for Black Sea trade shows that Muslim merchants constituted the vast majority of the people paying customs dues. Many Muslims were also active in Bursa at this time, and, as we have seen, 16th-century Cairo was a center of rich Muslim merchants with broad trade networks.

The Ottoman territory did not constitute a single customs unit, and inland duties represented an important source of income for the exchequer. But the points where such dues were collected were limited in number. Furthermore, if violations occurred it was possible to lodge a complaint with the local *kadı*, and, if necessary, in Istanbul; such recourse against abusive tax collectors also must have stimulated commerce. After 1516, the Syrian trade center of Aleppo in particular experienced a new period of prosperity which resulted in an extensive construction of khans (caravanserais) and covered shopping streets.

As we have already observed in the case of Istanbul, cities expanded with the aid of large pious foundations. Examples from the later 16th century include Üsküdar, on the Asian side of the Bosporus, the Thracian town of Lüleburgaz, and the harbor of Payas along the eastern Mediterranean coast.

Moreover, "ideological" reasoning used to legitimate the supposed division of labor on a religious basis simply did not apply to the 15th- and 16th-century situation. The Islamic prohibition on charging interest has been cited in this context: but the latter did not impede money transactions any more than the corresponding prohibition to which the Catholic Church adhered throughout the Middle Ages. It was either circumvented or openly disregarded. To mask the collection of interest, people often "sold" a house, but the seller continued living in it and paid a rent amounting to a specific percentage of the sale price, while retaining the right to eventually "buy back" the property. Even in Anatolian provincial towns, money was lent by a multitude of small investors; women in particular often earned an extra income by doing so. Pious foundations in Istanbul and big cities in Anatolia extended loans with interest. This practice was roundly condemned by strict legal and religious scholars, but Sultan Suleiman's Grand Mufti Ebusuud Efendi felt that the advantages of these money-lending pious foundations for the Muslim community made it reasonable to tolerate them. All these financial sources were used not only for consumer credit, but sometimes for commercial investment as well.

Another "ideological" rationale for the alleged avoidance of foreign trade by Muslim merchants is based on several misconceptions. It is claimed that good Muslims shied away from contact with "infidels" and that this attitude severly restricted their commercial opportunities. But we need to keep in mind that religious regulations that insist on separateness are usually obeyed only by those who can afford to do so. Second, there was the vast area of domestic trade and, especially in Egypt and Syria, of trade with India that could be accomplished without ever coming into contact with "infidels." Although trade with Europe was certainly important, it would be a major mistake to assume that it was as significant in the 16th century as it was to become in the nineteenth. Moreover, Muslim Ottomans quite often did visit Venice, at least in times of peace.

Ottoman merchants of all religions operated in a political environment that limited their opportunities to accumulate capital. The Ottoman administration regarded economic life from the viewpoint of the consumer, and thus gave priority to supplying the urban market with commodities. On the other hand, merchants rarely had direct access to the ruler; the Jewish banker Joseph Nasi, financier of Sultan Selim II (1566–74) and Duke of Naxos, was a rare exception. Urban producers, most of whom were craftsmen with small businesses, had a much tougher time asserting their interests. Although it was considered the duty of the sultan to give the "poor subjects" a chance to earn money, craftsmen were under strict supervision, at least in the capital, and the opportunities to amass wealth were therefore limited.

The Ottoman administration considered the protection of native craftsmen a high priority when their products were needed for the army, the navy, the court, or the capital. For example, the export of leather or cotton was tightly controlled, and in times of war it was stopped altogether. In some businesses that yielded large tax revenues, such as a mohair-processing mill in Ankara, the raw material used by the craftsmen was protected by export bans. But there were no corresponding import bans to protect newly developing areas of production, because the sultan's administration felt that a greater abundance of goods on the market held prices down. In view of keeping the expenditure for wars and building projects within limits, this consideration was given high priority.

The consumer perspective was not even modified by the interests of certain members of the Ottoman upper class, who—sometimes quite actively—got involved in trade and land speculation. One famous example is Rüstem Paşa, the grand vizier and son-in-law of Suleiman the Magnificent. But an attitude widespread among Ottoman bureaucrats more closely resembled the ideas of the North African historian and social thinker Ibn Khaldun, who held that the subjects could not pay any taxes if the ruler and his privileged inner circle took away their opportunities to earn.

In one regard, the economic attitude of the Ottoman upper class can certainly be compared with that of European potentates of the 16th century, namely when considering the importance attached to gold and silver as the raw material for coinage. In both cases it was assumed that the import of precious metals could be regarded as positive, and the export as negative. The guiding idea was that the state's display of power, that is, its warfare, was possible only when the coffers were full. In Ottoman territory there were some deposits of silver, but very few of gold; the gold came either from Africa by way of Egypt or from European tribute payments. From the mid-16th cen-tury on, the "Spanish" silver from America reached the trade centers of Izmir, Salonika, and Aleppo, since the Ottoman trade balance with the European countries was positive and would remain so for centuries to come. The influx of silver contributed here, as elsewhere, to a rise in price. How great this increase was, however, is difficult to determine because the secular trend since Roman times had been for precious metals to be siphoned off to South Asia. The Ottoman sultans of the 16th century made every effort to stop this depletion, but the large sums that they paid each year to support the pilgrimage to Mecca and Medina must have greatly facilitated the import of Indian goods and thus an outflow of money as an unintended consequence.

CHAPTER 3
Hard-Earned Successes and Serious Setbacks (ca. 1600-1774)

Mercenaries, "Zealots," and State Dignitaries

At the end of the 16th century and the beginning of the 17th, the sultans' control over Anatolia was seriously compromised. Sizable gangs of armed men who claimed—with more or less justification—to be serving the ruler or one of his governors ravaged the country. In response the sultans allowed villagers to create militias and in emergencies to refuse outsiders access to their settlements. But this measure was of only limited effectiveness, in part because so many armed people actually did serve one office-holder or another and thus had the power to enforce their demands.

Very few of the rebelling mercenary leaders seem to have planned to form independent polities. Normally the leaders of insurgent troops were quite willing to accept an assignment at the border and thus join the Ottoman governing system. We have scant information as to what simple mercenaries hoped to gain from rebellions of this kind. But it stands to reason that they wanted to trade their uncertain status for the tax exemptions and other privileges that the janissaries enjoyed. The large-scale looting campaigns of these mercenaries, who even briefly occupied important cities in Anatolia including Bursa and Urfa, interrupted trade routes and hence forced some bazaars to shut down.

The use of portable firearms in waging war was on the rise, and the cavalry's reliance on swords and sabers was diminishing. For the *timar* holders who had always fought with swords, on horseback, this often meant a major loss of income and status. The Ottoman state did not try to develop any central organization for the new weaponry and thereby enable the "retrained" cavalrymen to assume a new role. Instead the state relied on a kind of "private initiative," putting Ottoman administrators in charge of recruiting troops.

Ottoman governors thus employed their own armed militias to collect taxes in their provinces and put a stop to robbers. However, these troops were frequently replaced, and since each new administrator brought along his own mercenaries, the number of unemployed armed men was quite high. In some cases the soldiers appear to have pressured their commander to rebel, so as not to lose their employment. While the number of mercenary leaders operating on their own initiative decreased after about 1630–40, rebellions by soldiers under the leadership of a vizier or pasha occurred throughout the 17th century.

The civil wars of the 1600s were further aggravated by the increasing political activity of the janissaries and other troops stationed in Istanbul, Cairo, and Damascus. Their activity was prompted in part by their uncertain financial circumstances. Like many European sovereigns of their time the Ottoman sultans of the 17th century lacked the means to pay a large standing army on an ongoing basis. Debasing the coinage was one of the common means of covering expenses when the treasury was nearly empty. As a result, soldiers and officers lost buying power, and tried to recoup their losses by stirring up rebellions. During the 17th century, these rebellions often had dire consequences for grand viziers, who stood to lose their heads, and sultans, who could lose their thrones. But tactics of this kind had only a temporary effect; in the long run, the soldiers had no choice but to seek out additional sources of income in the cities where they were stationed.

In some cases, janissaries and others engaged in crafts "on the side." But at least in the case of Cairo, which has been quite thoroughly examined, it was far more common for soldiers to declare themselves "protectors" of craftsmen and merchants and to demand compensation. Sometimes regular protection money was paid over, but often Muslim craftsmen were offered the opportunity to sign up as members of a military corps. In the long run, these units were downgraded to militias by the influx of craftsmen with no previous military training.

Since the privileges of a militiaman included tax exemptions, there were sound economic reasons for artisans to join up. Particularly in Cairo, the militias protected the interests of the craftsmen. However, when after 1750 these units lost power in comparison with Mamluk households, the tax pressure mounted to the point that the daily existence of the lower classes became quite shaky.

Explosive situations in the capital could quite easily result from alliances between military officers, dissatisfied men of religion, and palace dignitaries. These situations were further aggravated by the social situation of many Istanbul residents. In apparent reaction to the economic and political difficulties that "little people" so often had to suffer in the 17th century, a movement took hold in the capital that preached a return to the simplicity of the original Islam. Displays of wealth often triggered loud protests, as did the circumvention of the ban on charging interest and the use of coffee and tobacco. This movement considered the religious practices of many dervish orders, especially the whirling dances of the Mevlevis, abhorrent novelties. Murad IV formed an alliance with members of this movement and tried to make his subjects follow their teachings—without doing so himself. However, after the death of this sultan in 1640, the Ottoman upper class was more inclined to neutralize the leaders of this movement by appointing them to high positions, or by simply banning them from the capital.

The Restoration of the Köprülüs

Mehmed Köprülü, who was appointed grand vizier by Mehmed IV in 1656, preferred to take the latter route. Taking office in the middle of a war with Venice that was going badly for the sultan's navy, the ruler granted him extraordinary authority to avert this crisis. Despite his advanced age, Mehmed Köprülü proved to be a successful officer who in 1657 reconquered two Aegean islands that had recently been occupied by the Venetians and thereby eliminated the danger of a surprise attack on Istanbul. Rebellious soldiers were stricken from the muster rolls and numerous members of the subject class who had been appointed to public office were transferred back to their old positions. This action necessitated mass killings, especially of insurgent cavalrymen. When

Mehmed Köprülü died in 1661, however, the mutinies had ceased for the time being.

Köprülü's son Fazıl Ahmed, who was named his father's successor and remained in office until his death in 1676, was by training a teacher of religious law and theology. This background, unusual for a vizier, leads us to assume that he had originally aspired to become a judge. Fazıl Ahmed Köprülü was also quite successful in most of his military enterprises, notably when the Ottoman armies succeeded in restoring the sultan's hegemony in Transylvania. A campaign against the Habsburgs ended with the Treaty of Vasvar (1665), which was quite favorable to the Ottomans despite a severe defeat against the troops commanded by Montecuccoli; the Habsburg emperor had serious concerns on his western frontier, where the "Sun King" Louis XIV had embarked on a career of conquest. Moreover, with the capture of Kandia (Heraklion) in 1669, Fazıl Ahmed Paşa succeeded in completing the Ottoman conquest of Crete after decades of warfare. A series of campaigns in Poland and Lithuania brought the Ottoman Empire to its maximal expansion with the capture of Kamenets-Podolsk in 1672. While several other members of the Köprülü family who also advanced to high offices in the following years did not enjoy the great political fortune of Mehmed and Fazıl Ahmed Paşa, their influence on Sultan Mehmed IV, who was relatively inactive in political matters, assured two decades marked by continuity, political neutrality on the part of the soldiers, and successes in both foreign policy and the military realm.

Changes on the Domestic Front (from the Late 17th Century to 1774)

With the exceptions of Murad IV and Mustafa II (1695–1703), 17th-century sultans played no outstanding role; as far as the 18th century is concerned only Ahmed III (1703–30) and Selim III (1789–1807) have aroused interest among scholars today. Under the vizierate of the two Köprülüs, the office of grand vizier was enhanced, as we have seen. There were also several strong personalities who served as grand viziers in the 18th century, in particular İbrahim Paşa, often referred to as Nevşehirli İbrahim Paşa (Nevşehir being the city he founded on the site of this natal village) to distinguish him from another grand vizier with the same name.

A distinctly new development was the strong position of other members of the Ottoman bureaucracy, especially of the 'secretary of state' (*reisülküttâb* or *reis efendi*). He was a member of the grand vizier's staff, and his jurisdiction included correspondence with foreign dignitaries. With the increasing significance of diplomatic relations with European states in the 18th century, this office was greatly enhanced. Back in the 16th century, former envoys to European courts rarely attained a high rank in their later careers, but by the second half of the 18th century, such people often had special opportunities for advancement, based on their knowledge of foreign courts. This phenomenon, which would be formative in the Ottoman bureaucracy after about 1840, can thus be regarded as a continuation of older trends.

Other office-holders also achieved an impressive political career: thus Mustafa II appointed his former teacher Feyzullah Efendi as *şeyhülislam* and thereby made him the head of the Ottoman legal and religious scholars. Taking a close interest in military matters, Feyzullah Efendi was also in a position to make decisions concerning the conduct of the Ottoman-Habsburg war, a situation which resulted in protests by the soldiers. However, by taking an active political role, the *şeyhülislam* also lost the protection from corporal punishment that Ottoman *ulema* normally enjoyed: in the rebellion of 1703, Feyzullah and his eldest son were killed while the sultan lost his throne.

In the Ottoman Empire of the 17th and 18th centuries, the ruler thus receded into the background and various office-holders achieved increased power and visibility. Older research tended to consider this development a symptom of Ottoman decline. Scholars today are less inclined to subscribe to this idea: it is useful to recall Max Weber's remark that bureaucratization and routinization typify the modern exercise of power. Overall the Ottoman elite had created stable institutions. Viziers and governors recruited trainees for the state machinery, but the bureaucracy also developed its own dynamic. It can certainly be considered a sign of strength that the Ottoman polity was now able to function without an active sultan if the need arose.

In the provinces, by contrast, the governors who had earlier been appointed by the central administration lost their importance vis-à-vis local tax farmers, who were able to extend their contracts for life after 1695. In the 18th century there were governor dynasties in many places, such as the Jalilis in Mosul and the 'Azms in Damascus, who ruled "their" territories more or less autonomously. In the past, researchers considered this phenomenon a mark of the beginning of 20th-century nation-states, an interpretation that is being rejected by more recent historians. Today we emphasize the considerable Ottoman loyalty of these provincial magnates, which is not to say that they did not pursue their own agendas, for instance in their dealings with the European merchants conducting trade on their territories. The result was an incipient and rather uneven integration of the Ottoman territories into the new capitalist world economy.

War and Peace at the Iranian Border

In 1590, the Shah of Iran, Abbas I (1587–1629), who was still quite young, negotiated a peace agreement with the Ottomans that was favorable for the latter. The sultan gained Azerbaijan, hegemony in the Caucasus, which was previously regarded as an Iranian sphere of influence, and considerable prestige. However, in the following years, Shah Abbas consolidated his rule in the territories that remained under his control and created an army of Georgian slaves, comparable to the janissaries. In 1603/04, Shah Abbas attacked once again and reconquered not only Azerbaijan, but also the important fortress of Revan (today Erivan in Armenia). An additional campaign led into Iraq, which had been an Ottoman province for nearly a century, and resulted in the conquest of Baghdad. Diyarbakir, the political and commercial center of southern Anatolia, was also captured by Safavid troops in 1623/24. In 1635, however, Sultan Murad IV (1623–40) regained territory taken by Shah Abbas, who had died by this point, in a campaign he personally commanded. These reconquests included Revan and Baghdad. In honor of these two successes, Murad IV had two elegant kiosks built in the garden of the Topkapı palace; they are still standing today. The Treaty of Zuhab or Kasr-i Shirin (1639), which brought several decades of peace, confirmed the Ottoman reconquest of Baghdad.

A new Ottoman-Iranian war was not waged until 1726, this time by Sultan Ahmed III (1703-30), when the Safavid dynasty was drawing to a close and a campaign of Tsar Peter I in the Caucasus had made the weakness of the Iranian defenses manifest. But the Ottoman conquests, including Tabriz, were soon taken back by the Afghan commander Nadir Khan (later Nadir Shah). When a peace treaty was signed in 1730, and again after an additional war in 1746, the border that the two sides agreed upon was based on the old treaty of 1639.

Last Wars against Venice; the Conflict with the Habsburgs

After the loss of Cyprus (1571-73), Venice had little remaining of its colonial empire, which had been in existence since the Late Middle Ages. There were now only a few harbors on the Dalmatian coast, some islands in the Ionian Sea, and the much larger island of Crete, which governed the sea route between Istanbul and Egypt. This latter province continued to play a key role in supplying Istanbul with food, as it had done in late antiquity. The weakened situation of Venice in the 17th century must have prompted the Ottoman campaign of conquest, which dragged on from 1644 to 1669, until, as we have seen, the Köprülüs completed the takeover. When the loss of Crete began to loom on the horizon, the Venetians tried to find a substitute in what is today Greece, especially on the Peloponnesus; in the course of these battles an explosion destroyed the Parthenon in 1687. But in 1715, when these attempts had clearly failed, Venice had to confine its ambitions to its function as a northern Italian regional port, art center, and travel destination for European nobility. Clearly the shift of European long-distance trade routes to the Atlantic and to the Indian Ocean, coupled with the crisis in the German hinterland of Venice during the Thirty Years' War (1618-1648), played an important role in the decline of this commerce-based republic. But it is important to keep in mind the simple fact that the Venetian colonial empire was now essentially in Ottoman hands.

The so-called Long War for control of Hungary was waged with the Habsburgs between 1593 and 1606 (Treaty of Zsitva Torok). Despite a significant Ottoman victory at Mezőkeresztes/Haçova in 1596, the sultan's gains were modest, limited to a few Hungarian fortifications. Until 1663, there was a period of peace at the Ottoman-Habsburg border. The sultans stayed out of the Thirty Years' War and the English Civil Wars, which ended with the execution of Charles I in 1649. In the former conflict, the Calvinist king of Bohemia, Frederick V, had tried to win support from the sultans before his defeat in the battle of the White Mountain in 1620; in the latter, Charles sought Ottoman backing before his demise.

New Ottoman advances on Habsburg territory did not occur until the 1660s; a defeat of the Ottoman troops at St. Gotthard on the Raab in 1664 resulted in a nearly twenty-year hiatus from war. In 1683 a new Ottoman campaign led to the famous second siege of Vienna. Top-level Ottoman dignitaries made serious diplomatic and strategic missteps in preparing for this action. When planning its campaign, the Ottoman court had evidently not been informed that the Polish king, Jan Sobieski, who originally had been elected as the representative of the "French" party in the Polish parliament (Sejm), had changed sides after his enthronement and established good relations with the Habsburgs. Or if the relevant information reached Istanbul on time it evidently had not been taken seriously. Ottoman misjudgment of the situation led the Grand Vizier Kara Mustafa Paşa to overlook the possibility of a Polish-Habsburg relief army providing help for the besieged city.

The failure of the Vienna siege in 1683 was a far more serious setback for the Ottomans than the withdrawal had been in 1529, because this time the Habsburgs were able to pursue the retreating Ottoman troops over the border into Hungary. In 1686, the fortress of Buda fell; part of today's Budapest, Buda had been the capital of Ottoman Hungary for about 150 years. The Habsburg troops and their allies occupied a territory the size of the kingdom of Hungary in the Late Middle Ages, including, at least for a brief time, the city and fortress of Belgrade. Transylvania now lost its independence and became a Habsburg territory as well.

Poland, the Russian Empire, the Tatars, and the Cossacks

Already in the second half of the 16th century, Ottoman sultans showed a pronounced interest in the occupants of the Polish royal throne; given that the king was elected by the nobility, it was the major concern to prevent any of the Habsburgs or a prince close to this dynasty from becoming king. Between Poland-Lithuania and the Ottoman state there was a sparsely populated border zone in which the Tatar princes of Crimea waged constant battles with the Cossacks loyal to Poland-Lithuania or to the Russian tsar.

The Cossacks comprised quite diverse groups; in the early period those who recognized the sovereignty of the tsar were often Tatar princes who had lost out in succession battles in their own polity. But a good number of Cossacks were country dwellers who wanted to escape the serfdom that was spreading in Poland and Russia. They spent the summer season hunting and fishing in the estuaries of the Dnjepr and Dnjestr. The Polish aristocracy regarded the Cossacks as a political threat, because they violated the principle of rural serfdom. In the course of the 17th century, their numbers were increasingly restricted by the administration.

For many Cossacks at the beginning of the 17th century, piracy on the Black Sea became a source of income and way of life. They crossed the water on small flat boats, and repeatedly pillaged both Anatolian coastal towns and the area around Istanbul. The difficulty in fighting the pirates was undoubtedly one of the factors that caused the sultans to try to gain control of the borderland inhabited by the Cossacks, which was traversed by major rivers, namely the Prut, Djnestr, Bug, and Dnjepr. The most important Ottoman border fortification was Hotin on the Dnjestr, which was often under attack. After long battles between the three rulers with claims in these areas, which dragged on throughout the 17th century, the borderland was mostly deserted; and the Treaty of Radzin (1681) established the no man's land as an internationally recognized separation zone.

The Tatars formed a principality that was subject to the sultan, the last remnant of the Golden Horde, which had ruled all of Russia in the

13th and 14th centuries. In accordance with standard practice for dependent principalities, the khan was appointed by the Ottoman government, but had to be a member of the ruling family, which regarded itself as descendants of Genghis Khan. In the Ottoman view, this family was the noblest in the empire, just after the sultan's. In times of war, the Tatars formed part of the Ottoman force, but often acted independently of the sultan. Their quick campaigns enabled them several times to burn down Moscow or at least the city's suburbs. Only as part of the Treaty of Radzin (1681) did the sultans promise that forays of this kind would not recur in the future. But enforcing this promise was often a problem, and in the second half of the 18th century, the Ottoman statesman and historian Ahmed Resmi stated baldly that the Tatars were the major cause of wars between sultans and tsars.

The expeditions of Tsar Peter I against the Ottomans did not result in lasting Russian conquests, but when the tsar appeared on the border, Demetrius Cantemir, the scholarly prince of Moldavia and a vassal of the sultan, was easily persuaded to switch sides. To preclude a repetition of this kind of betrayal in the future, the practice of nominating local personages as princes of Moldavia and Wallachia, both located in today's Romania, was henceforth given up. From the early 1700s governors from prominent Greek families of Istanbul, the so-called Phanariots, took the place of locally-based dynasties.

The effects of the Russian-Ottoman War of 1768–74 were more serious and lasting than those of the conflict with Peter I. The sultan had become embroiled in this war to contain the influence of the tsar in Poland and to win back Podolia, which had been lost in 1699. A Russian fleet sailed from the Baltic Sea to the eastern Mediterranean in 1770 and destroyed the Ottoman warships near Çeşme. The commanders of the Tsarina Catherine II also ignited a revolt on the Peloponnesus, which was crushed by the Ottoman vizier Muhsinzade Mehmed Paşa. But the Albanian irregular troops recruited during this campaign were not paid, and in reprisal, they soon terrorized the inhabitants of the peninsula to the point that an additional Ottoman campaign was necessary to dislodge them from their positions. The long-term bitterness that these anarchic wars aroused helped set the stage for the Greek revolution of 1821. The Treaty of Küçük Kaynarca (1774), which finally ended the war after several unsuccessful attempts at peace-making, resulted in severe losses for the Ottoman Empire. Crimea was the first Muslim territory to be lost; it was finally annexed by the Russians in 1783. Equally critical was the fact that the Black Sea, which had been an Ottoman lake closed to foreign ships for about three centuries, now had to be opened to European navigation.

Succession to the Throne and Dynastic Self-Representation

Until quite recently, historians have used the expression "sultanate of women" in describing the late 16th and the first half of the 17th century, when the mothers of the sultans (Valide Sultan) played an important political role. Contemporaries tended to react quite negatively to the great power of these women. But a feminist approach in historiography has made us aware of just how widespread misogyny "on principle" was, not only among the Ottomans, but also in Europe. Consequently, historians today are less inclined to take accusations against the sultans' mothers at face value.

When the rulers were themselves underage, their mothers had reason to become active; and both Murad IV and Mehmed IV (1648–87) acceded to the throne as small children. It is by no means certain that the sultans' mothers in this period were really as inexperienced in political matters as is often claimed; after all, the harem was a complex, sophisticated, and exceedingly hierarchical institution, and those who rose within this context acquired considerable political skill.[1]

New research has shown that the importance of the sultans' mothers in the life of the dynasty shifted when the system of succession changed. Until the mid-16th century, it had been standard practice for a concubine who had borne the sultan a son to move to the provinces with her offspring as soon as the prince was old enough to assume a governorship—albeit with a tutor in the background.[2] But when Suleiman the Magnificent, Kanuni in Turkish parlance, married Hürrem (Roxelane), their relationship was so close that most of the sons of this ruler competing for the throne had the same mother. In the disputes between her sons, Hürrem Sultan's hands were tied. But when it came to Sultan

Suleiman's sons from earlier unions, Hürrem Sultan "went by the book" when she took action against her stepsons and promoted her own descendants as best she could. The only difference was that these maneuvers no longer took place in the seclusion of a provincial palace, but in full view of the court in Istanbul. This situation probably explains why Hürrem Sultan was regarded as a schemer exceeding her proper limits, especially by those who wanted to see a prince from one of Suleiman's earlier unions accede to the throne.

The princes' mothers of the following generations, toward the end of the 16th century, encountered an altogether different situation, because the regulations governing succession that had been in effect since the reign of Mehmed the Conqueror were once again in flux. Selim's successor, Murad III, was the last to have been educated in the provinces. From then on, princes remained in the palace, under the watchful eye of the ruler, and nearly devoid of contact with the outside world. By the 17th century, the rule that the sultan have his brothers killed when acceding to the throne was implemented far less often and finally lapsed. Instead, an institutionalized succession to the throne was developed in which the oldest member of the House of Osman acceded to the throne.

As a consequence, a prince's mother no longer left the sultan's palace for the provinces. By remaining in Istanbul, these women had opportunities to wield political influence right in the center of power. Besides taking part in palace intrigues, they could cultivate connections with janissaries stationed in the capital. The elaborate pious foundations that some sultans' mothers established are evidence of their power, although the buildings they constructed generally bore only the title of the donor (Valide Sultan) rather than her personal name. The status of the sultans' mothers at this time was even enhanced when the ruler relocated his royal residence to the harem in the second half of the 16th century. Because his mother was in charge of this institution, the monarch thus spent a good deal of his time in the Valide Sultan's territory.

In the mid-17th century, under the pressure of wars abroad and crises at home, a reform of government structures took place, which granted the grand vizier a great deal of power and severely restricted that of the palace women. But by the 18th century, the female members of the sultan's family were again playing a visible role. Rather than the mothers, however, it was now the daughters and sisters of reigning sultans who occupied center stage. These young women were given palaces at the Bosporus when they married high dignitaries. They had an important role in shaping the image of the sultan's family until a "neo-absolutist" sultan's regime was installed in the 19th century, which limited their influence once again.

Scholars, Travelers, and Political Writers[3]

In the 17th century, the Ottoman capital developed an active and multifaceted intellectual life despite all its domestic and foreign crises. Kâtib Çelebi ("the scribe" and "the gentleman"; real name: Mustafa bin Abdullah, 1609-57; also called Haji Khalifa in European sources) produced a major bibliography of Islamic works that is still used today, as well as a chronicle and writings on state reforms. But the most famous of his numerous works was likely his book on geography, "View of the World" (*Cihân-numâ*), which set out not only to summarize geographical knowledge about the Ottoman provinces, but also to incorporate this knowledge into the categories that he had discovered in translations of Dutch atlases, especially the *Atlas minor*. The author rewrote his work several times, integrating the findings of new publications he had come across. At his death it was still unfinished, and had to be completed by his friends. The book was published in 1732, as one of the first Ottoman works to appear in print.[4]

Kâtib Çelebi's contemporary Evliya Çelebi (ca. 1610–1685) was less scholarly, but most original. Evliya had been educated at the palace, but he kept rejecting offers of influential posts, preferring instead to travel throughout the Ottoman Empire, as well as to several areas near the border, such as the Sudan, West Iran, and Vienna.[5] Evliya knew the geographical literature of both the medieval Arabic and the Ottoman traditions, but giving an exact account of them and revising them where necessary, the way a scholar would have approached the project, was not his intention. Instead, he made his knowledge and experiences the basic framework of a travel narrative, a genre that was previously unfamiliar in Ottoman literature and which disappointed readers who wanted to use Evliya's work as a geographical source. But for readers who accept the fictional element, the travel narrative is exciting and instructive to read.

Kâtib Çelebi and Evliya Çelebi were Ottomans by birth, but several notable new arrivals from Europe who converted to Islam also bear mention. Ali Ufki (ca. 1610-1675) was originally Polish; his Latinized name had been Albertus Bobovius. For a long time he directed the choir of the pages in Topkapı Sarayı. Because of the high value that was placed on music in palace culture, this activity carried a great deal of responsibility. He used the musical knowledge he evidently had acquired in Poland to record the notes sung by the choir of pages. Many of his musical notations have been preserved. Ali Ufki's intellectual life seems to have kept oscillating between the Ottoman-Islamic and the European-Christian worlds. He spent his entire later life in Istanbul and made friends there with learned Ottomans, as well as with Antoine Galland (1646–1715), the translator of the *Thousand and One Nights* into French, who also lived in the Ottoman capital for a long time. Most of his works are now in European libraries, but during his lifetime, Ali Ufki's knowledge was beneficial primarily to the pupils in the palace school, whom he tutored in singing.[6]

In the 17th and 18th centuries, there were also notable Ottoman historiographers. Mustafa Naima (1655–1716) came from the northern Syrian city of Aleppo and thus spoke Arabic as well as Ottoman-Turkish. His major historical work covers an epoch that he did not experience as an eyewitness (1591–1660), as is often the case in this genre. An introduction contains Naima's thoughts on history and politics. His argument is based on the social theories of the Northern African scholar Ibn Khaldun (1332–82), who felt that a high degree of social solidarity makes it relatively easy for inhabitants of the steppe and desert to found states. But after settling in, this solidarity invariably dissolves and the states in question undergo stages of development analogous to those normally attributed to living beings. Ibn Khaldun's ideas had a pronounced impact on members of the sultan's inner circle who wrote analyses of the situation in the Ottoman state. In his Ottoman chronicle, Naima discussed by what ways and means it could be possible to prolong the life of the sultanate while accepting that in Ibn Khaldun's terms it had passed its prime.

Ahmed Resmi (1700–83) is notable among the historians and political writers of the 18th century because of his own long political and diplomatic experience. His travel reports as an ambassador to Berlin amusingly describe the curiosity of the residents in the Prussian capital, who had never seen a real Turk before.[7] But Ahmed Resmi had the most significant experiences of his life during the Russian-Ottoman War of 1768-1774. Resmi had warned against this venture, but was unable to prevail over the pro-war party. He concluded that Muslim and non-Muslim states were subject to the same political rules, the most important of which entailed the suitability of ends and means. A ruler who overestimated the "natural opportunities" available to his empire would only weigh down his subjects with excessive taxes.

The Ottoman View of Europe and the Enhancement of Local Traditions

It would be a gross oversimplification to assume that there was no cultural contact between the Ottoman Empire and Europe before the 18th century. There certainly was contact—however sporadic—in the realm of courtly art once Mehmed the Conqueror had invited the Venetian painter Gentile Bellini to Istanbul. When Evliya Çelebi visited Vienna in 1665, he was particularly impressed by the organ in the St. Stephen's Cathedral, and he also admired the architecture of the St. Stephen's Tower and the skill of Viennese surgeons. He pointed out the error of the assumption that Christians worshipped images; these images, he explained, were actually used as pedagogical tools (*Biblia pauperum* [Paupers' Bible]).[8] We can only speculate how he came up with this information.

In the 18th century, Ottoman courtly contacts with Europe, especially with France, increased substantially. A first attempt occurred during the reign of Sultan Ahmed III (1703–30), who dispatched an ambassador to provide a detailed report on life at the court of the young Louis XV and on the highlights of Paris. The report of this Ottoman ambassador, named Yirmisekiz Mehmed Çelebi, is full of sharp-eyed observations.[9] Selected on the basis of his ability to interact with people, he traveled with his son, who soon struck up a friendship with young French noblemen, who provided yet another source of valuable social contacts.

Ottoman interest in European art is apparent in the courtly art of miniature painting. This art was shaped by Levni, a miniaturist who was commissioned by Ahmed III to provide a series of illustrations commemorating the circumcision ceremonies for Ahmed's sons in 1720. But he also produced elegant individual sheets portraying young people in various kinds of traditional dress, including European clothing. Levni and his students experimented with themes that posed new artistic challenges. Abdullah Buhari depicted a young woman bathing, while an anonymous painter in the same circle sought to recreate festive fireworks, and produced the first Ottoman representation of a night sky.

The fashion of decorating elegant houses and mosques with pictures of landscapes was also remarkable in this context. At the beginning of the 18th century, there was a quest in courtly circles to find alternatives to the customary flowers and ornaments without violating the Islamic law forbidding representations of people and animals. Urban vedute were especially popular. Local dignitaries in the provinces were quite fond of pictures of the capital with its mosques, boats, and islands. These pictures were essentially derived from miniatures in manuscript illuminations, but there were also experiments with light and shadow and the recreation of three-dimensional space. Unfortunately we have no information as to the identity of the painters and their work methods.

Ottoman interest in European art was only one form of the quest for new inspirations in the art of the 18th century. Egyptians looked to Mamluk models; an innovative patron, such as Abd al-Rahman Katkhoda (ca. 1714–76), could even inspire a new style. The family of İshak Paşa, whose power basis was the town of Doğubeyazit at the Ottoman-Iranian border, took a highly unconventional approach when having their palace built in the second half of the 18th century. The palace was clearly based on Seljuk architecture, which had had its heyday a good five hundred years earlier.

Life in the Country

After the 16th century, central registers of Ottoman taxpayers were no longer compiled, and we have to rely on local or regional sources for this information. It is therefore difficult to make supraregional comparisons. We have already discussed the civil wars of the period around 1600, which resulted in a considerable loss of population in central Anatolia and elsewhere. In some parts of Anatolia, taxes could no longer be collected because the peasants had fled; sometimes they settled in remote areas that appeared to offer better protection. The Ottoman office-holders thus located villagers from the eastern portion of central Anatolia in the extreme western part of the peninsula, right next to the capital. In other cases, the peasants who remained built refuges in which they barricaded themselves to avoid robbers and fugitive soldiers—and the tax collector.

In a clear overestimation of his own success at establishing peace, Sultan Murad IV (1623-40) tried to make the refugees return to their former provinces. In reality, that was possible only in isolated instances, because often the peasants had sold their property before fleeing, or it had been occupied by others. Frequently these usurpers were people who had used their influence in the Ottoman state to get estates. The forests and steppes did not offer much in the way of security either, as is evident from a fascinating report by Grigor, an Armenian priest from the eastern Anatolian town of Kemah, who had to return to his home with a caravan of Muslims and Christians by order of Murad IV. It was a true odyssey.[10] Thus the unrest in the period around 1600 had a lasting impact on patterns of settlement, at least in Anatolia. While the well-situated areas around the harbor city of Izmir that began to prosper in the 17th century probably recorded an increase in population, the villages of the Central Anatolian steppe often diminished in size or even disappeared. Only in the hill country, on inaccessible islands in rivers and moors, and in the better-protected areas near major towns could many villages remain intact.

During the 16th century, numerous western and central Anatolian nomads had settled down more or less permanently, but new tribal groups from the eastern part of the country immigrated after 1600, apparently attracted by the open areas between the settlements. It is reasonably easy to trace the advance of one group of this kind. After a stop along the way west of Konya, it eventually showed up on the island of Rhodes. The peasants often complained about these newcomers, who owned horses and weapons and thus were militarily superior to the villagers unless the state intervened. Camels or sheep were often driven into the fields before they had been harvested, and into the gardens as well, which was at least as damaging. While there were also peaceful relations between villagers and nomads, these complaints were taken very seriously by the Ottoman central government.

Farmers were easier to tax than tribal groups, so the Ottoman government began systematic attempts to settle nomads toward the end of the 17th century. The border area between present-day Syria and Turkey was taken into consideration as the land for development; the Ottoman office-holders evidently hoped that the new settlers would maintain their military potential for a while and defend themselves and their neighbors against attacks by desert nomads. But in the end, the tribal groups were allotted land that was not very suitable for farming. Although the Ottoman administration had sent specialists ahead to figure out where wells could be dug, it is far from certain that their recommendations were followed. Also, the new settlers were not given any means to tide them over during the first difficult years in their new way of life, so many of them soon gave up their residences again, and because they had lost a large portion of their livestock, they had little choice but to resort to robbery.[11]

Village-style farming and cattle breeding by tribal groups were at first meant for personal use, although a portion of this production was also put on the market. In some areas, however, agricultural products were intended chiefly for sale. Olives were grown in northern Syria, in the region around Jerusalem, in the vicinity of the northwestern Anatolian district of Edremit, and above all in Tunisia and on the island of Crete, which was conquered by the Ottomans in 1645–69. Olive oil did not have the dominant place in the Ottoman diet that it holds in today's Turkish cuisine. For this reason, the oil was used either for illumination—olive oil was sent as far as Mecca and Medina for use in mosque lamps—or to make soap. Northern Syria, the area surrounding

Jerusalem, and Crete were known for their soap making. Significant amounts of olive oil were exported from Crete, Tunisia, and the Peloponnesus to Marseilles, where it was also used for soap making. In the coastal area of Tunisia, the export of olives resulted in a close tie to the southern French economy in the 18th century, that is, to a regional "incorporation."

The cultivation of cotton was also often market-oriented. This plant had a long tradition in the coastal plains of the eastern Mediterranean; because of the importance of cotton in the production of sailcloth, the Ottoman authorities often forbade the export of this product in the 16th century. But this practice changed after about 1600, and by the 18th century, cotton, both raw and spun and dyed, was one of the Empire's important exports, and drew merchants from Marseilles to Izmir or to Sayda in Southern Syria. The cultivation seems to have been left to small farmers rather than being undertaken by plantation owners. The local tax collectors had an important role only in marketing, and some were able to earn enough money to become local magnates.

Ottoman and European Economy

Between about 1720 and 1765, business and trade experienced a period of expansion in many centers of the Ottoman Empire. In the Balkans, mule drivers sometimes became shippers or businessmen who specialized in long-distance trade; in these capacities, they attended the Leipzig Fair. The first step in this direction was for the mule drivers to take along products made during the winter at home to sell them in the spring at markets far from home. This is how the weaving of coarse and sturdy wool fabrics developed in present-day southern Bulgaria, in the area of Plovdiv. The local merchants were able to increase their sales quite substantially by using strategies we would today describe as aggressive marketing.

There were signs of economic expansion in other parts of the Ottoman Empire as well. In the Ottoman port cities, European merchants were feeling stiff competition from local Christian merchants. Cotton print fabrics and copper goods were also produced in the inland Anatolian city of Tokat, while cotton and light silk fabrics were woven in Bursa. The manufacture of silk also flourished on the island of

Chios. In present-day southeastern Anatolia and northern Syria, the manufacturers of cotton prints sought to attract customers who had been buying imports from India since the 17th century. Skillful copies of Indian fabrics from these eastern Mediterranean centers were at times even exported to France.

We can only speculate as to the reasons for this expansion and why it came to an end between 1760 and 1770. It appears significant that only brief periods of war punctuated the decades after the Treaty of Pasarofça in 1718, at least at the western and northern fronts, and the Ottoman state undertook serious efforts to make the trade routes safe again for merchants. Fortified stopping points for caravans were built, and they sometimes developed into small urban centers. These measures were attempts to reverse the damage caused by the wars in 1683-99, when the concentration of all resources in the Balkans had led to the uncontrolled spread of robbers on the roads of Anatolia and Syria.

It is also of some interest that in France, the economy expanded during the mid-eighteenth century; in other words during approximately the same years as the flourishing of Ottoman trade and manufactures. This convergence might indicate an integration of the Ottoman Empire as a whole into the "world economy" dominated by Europe. If so, this integration must have occurred earlier than is assumed by most experts today, namely in the 17th century or possibly even in the late 16th. However, this parallel growth may be more or less coincidental; and many historians today consider the closing decades of the 18th century as well as the first quarter of the 19th the crucial period of change. Exporting craft products was of moderate importance to Ottoman and foreign traders during the 1700s; and the work of local craftsmen typically went to the Ottoman domestic market. Quite possibly developments outside the empire's borders were still of limited importance for the fate of its industries.

But after about 1750, the world economic integration of coastal regions, such as the area around the Aegean, seems to have progressed rapidly. This process did not always go hand in hand with a decline in local industrial production, even though that was often the case. Thus in the late 1700s merchants and spinners in the small Thessalonian town of Ambelakia supplied Austrian and Bohemian workshops with high-quality cotton thread; and some local merchants profited substantially.

But when hand-spun yarn was no longer in demand the industry rapidly declined; as this example shows, Ottoman producers and merchants were now at the mercy of fluctuations in demand in very remote economic centers, where they did not have the least bit of control.

There has been some reflection as to why the wars in the late 18th century did not lead to an economic boom in the armaments sector, but rather to a crisis in which weapons manufacturers and food purveyors were no longer able to provide adequate supplies to the Ottoman armies. It has been suggested that the financing methods of the Ottoman central administration were the root cause of this problem, because it was common to pay the producers of these war supplies far less than their production costs, or even to demand these supplies for free. The result was a lack of capital and long-term economic weakness. But why had similar methods had better outcomes in the 16th and 17th centuries? Part of the reason appears to be that waging war in the early modern age was becoming more and more costly. Without a corresponding economic expansion no capital could be accumulated; and as a result it became impossible to satisfactorily supply the sultans' armies. The limits placed on the accumulation of capital had been a perennial weak point in the Ottoman economy; given rising costs, by the later 1700s the empire no longer could mobilize the resources needed for modern war.

Ottoman Women

There are more locally oriented sources available on the subject of urban women outside the realm of palace circles after about 1600 than for older periods. Many of these sources revolved around questions pertaining to the assets held by women. Islamic religious law granted the right to inherit—albeit only half the share that would have been accorded to a man of the same degree of relationship. Still more significant was the fact that a married woman was able to control her assets on her own, had legal capacity, and was entitled to file suit in court, even against her husband. Many women complained that their male relatives were trying to force them out of their share of the inheritance. The archives of the *kadı* offices often list unpaid debts as well, because many urban women earned a modest income by lending money. Albeit to a lesser extent women also owned houses and gardens.

Our sources thus reflect the problems facing women who had some money to their names. The very poorest women—and men—were rarely documented. Still, we learn that in Ankara in the period around 1600, families without resources were known to press their small daughters into service as maids (*besleme*). Other texts record women who were freed from slavery and received a dowry. There are also reports of spinners who worked for merchants. Textile centers such as Bursa and Ankara seem to have offered women greater opportunities to earn money working at home.

The activities of well-to-do women were most likely to be recorded when they established a pious foundation. Existing family foundations could be expanded, and freed slavewomen could be supported when a foundation belonging to a woman who had owned them gave them a roof over their head. Foundations to benefit mosques were common, but at least in 18th-century Bursa, women were also known to take care of street and bridge repair.

An area of additional research interest is the religious, artistic, and literary activity of women. In theory, prepubescent girls could attend a Koran school, but most women who learned how to read and write were instructed at home. Particularly in families of religious and legal scholars, and of dervishes, women could typically read and write. As far as "official" religious doctrine, they were granted the authority to transmit sayings of the prophet (*hadis*), in accordance with early Islamic traditions. The letters a female dervish from the Macedonian city of Üsküb (today: Skopje) wrote to her sheikhs in the 17th century have been preserved. The fact that her family kept the drafts of her letters is evidence of the esteem they felt for her.

There were also occasional female voices in Ottoman poetry. In 18th-century Istanbul, Fitnet Hatun made a name for herself in this field; her assertiveness seems to have intimidated her male colleagues. Nothing is known about works by the fairly numerous female musicians in pre-19th-century upper-class houses. In the fine arts, there were embroiderers and carpet weavers, but before the 19th century, works of this kind were rarely signed. Still, recent findings suggest that new discoveries may be forthcoming.[12]

CHAPTER 4

"The Longest Century of the Empire"[1]
(From Küçük Kaynarca to the End of World War I)

Political and Military Crises at the Turn of the Nineteenth Century

The crushing defeats in the wars of 1768-74 led the Ottoman political establishment to focus squarely on the introduction of European military technology, especially after Sultan Selim III's accession to the throne (1789-1807). These efforts were continued throughout the 19th century, but even so, few wars ended successfully for the Ottomans. The reasons are more likely economic and political than military in the narrower sense. Until the end of the 18th century, the majority of Ottoman subjects, including the Christians in the Balkans, had not been inclined to obey conspirators' calls to action against Ottoman rule, although there were plenty of these calls, particularly in the 16th century. That changed in the 19th century, when the idea of nationalism, with or without religious overtones, mobilized the provincial elites, and soon thereafter the "ordinary" subjects as well.

Moreover, by 1800, the opponents of the Ottoman Empire had gained novel resources that allowed them to engage in power politics on a scale unimaginable two centuries earlier. England had made great strides on the path to industrialization and acquired a great number of colonial possessions in India, the defense of which required active involvement in the Mediterranean region. Napoleon did not succeed in acquiring Egypt as a colony for France, but Algeria was conquered in 1830, and in 1881 Tunisia became a French possession. Moreover, during the late 17th and early 18th centuries the Habsburg monarchy had made major advances into the Balkans. But the most dangerous enemy for the Ottoman state was without a doubt tsarist Russia. For one thing, the tsars laid claim to a kind of protectorate over the Orthodox Christians of the Balkans; for another, the Russian rulers had built up important military power since the early 18th century.

If one adds to these political factors the "incorporation" into the world economy, dominated by Europe, that had been taking place rapidly since the end of the 18th century, it is clear that especially after about 1815 the Ottoman Empire was in an extremely precarious position.

Despite the sultans' interest in initiating structural changes in the military in the early 19th century, opportunities for innovation in this area were severely restricted, at least until 1826. The new technologies required specially trained soldiers, but these soldiers would have competed with the janissaries, who had close ties to the craftsmen in the big cities, as we saw earlier. But the craftsmen's ability to eke out a living depended on the tax privileges they enjoyed because of their membership in the military corps, which had evolved into militias. This limited economic leeway also explains why the janissaries adamantly opposed all innovations that would have compromised their privileges.

Craftsmen doubling as militiamen found support for their position among the less prosperous legal and religious scholars (*ulema*). Those who did not belong to established families and had completed their education in the provinces found that they were forced into less lucrative offices. Under conditions of financial stringency it made sense for these people to link the legitimacy of the state with the fulfillment of religious precepts. The *ulema*, even those in modest positions, thus justified their status as guardians of the Muslim community. If the Muslims lived according to the precepts of Islam, so the argument went, victorious campaigns could not fail to materialize with God's help, and there was no need to copy the habits of the "infidels."

By contrast, members of the Ottoman upper class, such as the aforementioned Ahmed Resmi, had a very pragmatic attitude. In order to emerge victorious once again, they reasoned, they would first have to compensate for previous political and military errors. The result was a demand for strategic and tactical reform. But diplomacy also gained in importance, so as to anticipate the shifting alliances that were so typical of European politics.

An argument advanced by certain Ottoman chroniclers of the late 16th century now reappeared in this context, namely that it would be a serious mistake to assume that God would automatically bring about the victory of the Muslims against the infidels. Ahmed Resmi for instance emphasized that the rules of politics and war apply to all states, and anyone who did not go by these rules was only setting himself up for defeat. This issue gave rise to a conflict of the sort we continue to encounter in diverse forms until 1918 and beyond. A split occurred between many members of the governing classes, which by and large were prepared to experiment with modern technical and institutional imports from Europe in order to preserve the empire, and the lower class, many of whose members considered this route fundamentally wrong. An extreme divergence between the culture of the upper and lower classes emerged at this time, a divergence that would characterize the 19th century as a whole. It goes without saying there had been socio-cultural differences between upper and lower classes in earlier epochs as well, but those differences had never had a bearing on such fundamental issues as the relationship between religion and politics. The fact that the Ottoman upper class did not succeed in holding the empire together in the long run fueled the arguments of those who opposed "Ottoman pragmatism."

Sultan Selim III tried to introduce military reforms by forming a special military corps called the "New Order." European instructors conducted the training, and the soldiers were equipped with better weaponry. But the sultan was deposed and eventually murdered. In view of this threat, when Selim's nephew, Mahmud II (1808-39), acceded to the throne, he spent more than a decade merely consolidating his power. He built a base for himself in the provinces by driving back the notables and magnates who had come to power during the 18th century; those who survived his centralizing drive settled for non-political landownership or else went into the service of the central administration.

This policy was largely successful in the central provinces. Then the sultan again created a modernized military. The janissaries rebelled and suffered a devastating defeat, and the military corps was dismantled. Now the lower *ulema* had lost their strongest social support, and urban revolts of the kind that had been frequent in the 18th century were virtually out of the question. Sultan Mahmud II thus established a neo-absolutist regime of a sort that had been absolutely unknown to his predecessors in the 17th and 18th centuries.

Egypt and the European Great Powers

Mahmud II was adhering to patterns of behavior that had previously been practiced by Mehmed Ali (Muhammad Ali), his governor in Egypt. From the Ottoman conquest of 1517 to the early 19th century, this province had been governed by freed military slaves (Mamluks). While Mamluks had controlled Egpyt since the 13th century, the conditions under which they operated came to differ radically once an Ottoman garrison was established in Cairo and they owed an annual tribute to the central government in Istanbul. Since the late 17th century, however, the politically relevant households in which the Mamluks (and many other officers in Cairo) came to be organized had become increasingly autonomous. From Istanbul's perspective, the rule of the Mamluk households had proved counter-productive when their army was defeated by Napoleon in a single battle in 1798. Napoleon's attempt to control Egypt ultimately failed, but the Ottoman reconquest was a long, drawn-out process, despite the support of England, and in 1805, Selim III recognized Mehmed Ali, the second-in-command of this campaign, as governor. Mehmed Ali consolidated his rule by having the heads of the leading Mamluk households and many of their supporters killed in 1807 and putting a stop to the recruitment of new military slaves.

Even in this early phase, however, Mehmed Ali set his sights on more than a typical governorship. Initially his support was crucially important to the new sultan, Mahmud II, since the Egyptian army was the only strong military force available to the Ottoman central government at this time. Egyptian troops quelled the Greek revolution; the fact that a Greek state was founded anyway was a consequence of the interests of the great powers of Europe.

Mehmed Ali's successes resulted from a standing army that was recruited from the Egyptian peasant class. Their provisions were supplied by a system of state-owned factories, which in turn received raw materials from the ruler's trade monopoly. The factories that produced weapons, ammunition, and textiles were able to stay afloat financially as long as the army was a steady purchaser. Between 1830 and 1840, it seemed as though the foundations of industrialization were being created with state capitalist methods in Egypt. A war between Mehmed Ali, who was aiming for autonomous rule in Egypt and Syria, and his Ottoman overlord from 1831 to 1833 did little to impede Egyptian progress. In several battles, the armies of the Egyptian magnate, commanded by his son Ibrahim Paşa, did extremely well.

The sultan ultimately survived by mobilizing the support of the European great powers, especially England. The industrialization of Egypt posed a threat to European, especially British, markets and sources of raw materials. Moreover, many Europeans were dismayed at the notion of an "Oriental" ruler competing for equal power and status, who ought to be "put in his place." In 1840, Mehmed Ali was confronted with the alternative of facing the ordeal of a war against England or returning to the sovereignty of the sultan and giving up the conquered territories, including Syria. The end of Egyptian expansion signified the acknowledgement of the Ottoman customs regime, making it impossible to continue state-sponsored industrialization, which was already in trouble because of the inadequacy of many goods produced by inexperienced factory managers to the requirements of the Egyptian domestic market. Even so, Mehmed Ali's attempt to industrialize a province of the empire largely failed because incorporation into the European economic system had already taken place.

National Movements in the Balkans (1803–1912)

The activities of the Greek merchant fleets laid the economic foundations for the Greek revolution of 1821. In the wars of the revolutionary epoch, such as the Napoleonic era (1792–1815), Greek merchants did not face any competition from the French, who had traditionally been active in this sector, and they exploited this opportunity for powerful expansion and capital accumulation. Control of ships and maritime routes enabled the Greeks to foster key international connections, in particular with the tsars of Russia, who had just acquired new territories in the Black Sea region and were seeking capital and know-how. The Greeks seemed especially suitable partners because they shared an Orthodox creed with the Russians.[2] This "Russian connection" explains why the Greek revolution of 1821 was initiated by an exile organization based in Odessa.

From the perspective of the tsars, the Greek desire to found a state represented a golden opportunity to expand Russian influence to the Balkans. Given the powerful English naval presence in the Mediterranean, it was important for the emerging state to maintain a good relationship with England and to promote English trade. Moreover, the Greek merchants were regarded as creditworthy in Europe, thus enabling the insurgents to finance their war against the Ottoman Empire with loans. In 1830, the European great powers enforced the establishment of a Greek state on the Peloponnesus and in Attica that was independent on paper but was actually under their protectorate. Prince Otto of Bavaria (1833–62) became king for a time.

The beginning of the Serbian revolt dated back to the years around 1800, when the many aggressions of the Belgrade janissary garrison set the population against them. Sultan Selim III, who, as we have seen, was pursuing military reform, initially supported the efforts of his Serbian subjects to contain the janissaries. But the defeat of this sultan on the domestic front turned the Serbian revolt into an uprising against Ottoman rule as a whole. The principality of Serbia had been recognized internationally as a small autonomous entity since 1830, although it was still part of the Ottoman Empire. In Greece, there were two distinct social groups engaged in a degree of political competition: a small, quite wealthy class of merchants at the Mediterranean coast, and poor peasants and herdsmen who plowed barren mountainous fields or tended flocks. The principality of Serbia, by contrast, was an entirely rural society, with the export of livestock as the only "currency earner."

As for present-day Romania, Transylvania was part of the Habsburg Empire in the 19th century. Moldavia and Walachia were Ottoman territories, but these areas were ruled by Christian governors in the name of the sultan. In the course of the 19th century, this local autonomy increased. The social structure also differed fundamentally from the centrally ruled Ottoman provinces. The local nobility ("boyars") established the institution of serfdom, which was otherwise unknown in Ottoman territory.

Because of its geographical position, the territory comprising present-day Bulgaria developed autonomy and independence movements far more slowly than the rest of the Balkans. Dependence on the policies of the Russian Empire was even greater here than in the other Balkan states. As in Greece, a period of economic development preceded the blossoming of the national movement. After 1826, the manufacturers of woolen cloth in the Plovdiv area became suppliers for the Ottoman army. But early industrial production expanded even apart from this new market. Notable cultural endeavors also preceded the political movement. Bulgarian merchants objected to the preeminence of the Greek language in ecclesiastical practice, and the so-called exarchate was established as a church organization independent of the ecumenical patriarch residing in Istanbul. Ottoman policy tolerated this church that competed with the "Greek" one, and for the Bulgarians, affiliation with the exarchate constituted a form of pre-national organization.

All the territories discussed here were rural societies without the kinds of factories and industry that typified the 19th century in western and central Europe and the United States. While in Bulgaria a few factories had been established in the mid-19th century to service the Ottoman military, their economic impact was limited and for the most part they faded away after the Bulgarian provinces gained a degree of independence through the Russo-Ottoman War of 1877-78. This meant that military supplies often had to be imported. In Greece, Serbia, and Bulgaria, the political landscape was dominated by groups of politicians who aimed to annex additional areas into the "motherlands." In many cases irredentism was supported by the local rulers, who were often members of foreign dynasties and tried to legitimize their new positions by promoting territorial expansion. No Balkan state regarded itself as what the diplomatic language of the 19th century might have described as "saturated." Relatively large armies were maintained, which contributed to a high national debt and in some cases even to national bankruptcy.

Yet until the 1870s, such campaigns for expansion quite often failed because they conflicted with British interests; for until this time British government circles preferred to maintain the Ottoman state as a bulwark against the expanding tsarist empire.

Until the last quarter of the 19th century, since the territories they sought to acquire were always Ottoman, the Balkan principalities had common interests; and only one single Balkan power laid claim to a given territory. But this changed after about 1870, when rival nation-states demanded the integration of ethnically mixed or not easily classifiable areas. Adherents of the so-called Megali Idea ("Great Idea") in Greece hoped to acquire the entire territory of the former Byzantine Empire, and the Greek government under Venizelos attempted to achieve this plan after the end of World War I by means of a campaign in western Anatolia. Only the utter failure of this enterprise in 1922 discredited the project.

A point of contention between Bulgaria, Greece, and Serbia was Macedonia, which was still in Ottoman hands. Since it was assumed that the future affiliation of the area would essentially be determined by the self-identification of the inhabitants, each of the three neighboring states had its own school system, with a curriculum tailored to the propagandistic needs of the particular state. Worse still for the residents of Macedonia, Bulgarian guerrillas attempted to draw Macedonians to their side by means of terrorist actions. The frustration of the Ottoman officers at the prospect of a long guerrilla war—entailing a loss of salary and home leaves—would play a significant role in the revolt against Sultan Abdülhamid in 1908.

Another source of tension was the situation of the Albanians, who by the 19th century had largely become Muslims. Opposition to the Ottomans was here triggered by the military reforms of the period, which involved the disarming of local populations, as well as universal taxation and conscription. Many Albanians had hitherto served in the Ottoman military, often as irregulars, either in the armies of the central government or in those of local magnates. However, those clansmen who had provided soldiers were categorically opposed to conscription and new-style military discipline. In addition, once the Ottoman Empire began to lose territory in the Balkans on a massive scale, educated Albanians started to demand autonomy so as to avoid becoming part of Orthodox national states that often expelled their Muslim subjects.

Enshrined in a document that became known as the Fourteen Points, concrete demands included the concentration of all lands inhabited by Albanians in a single province that was to be administered by officials of local background. Except in wartime, Albanian recruits were to serve only in their home territory; this was an attempted compromise between the central state's demand for conscripts and the insistence of local clans on a volunteer army. In addition, schools in the province were to teach in Albanian. In the early 20th century an Albanian uprising whose leaders put forth these demands was to trigger a series of wars that would end with the collapse of the Ottoman Empire.

There is no need to go into detail here about the wars in which the Ottoman Empire was embroiled between 1803 and 1912. In all cases, the success or failure of the Ottoman troops was only one of the—less important—variables that determined the outcome. What mattered was the attempt on the part of the great powers involved in the Balkans and in the Mediterranean region not to let any rival become too powerful in this strategically important area, which is why the peace treaties focused on provisions on which the great powers in question were able to agree. The government of the sultan had no more than a secondary role in all of this.

Even a list of the military entanglements clearly reveals the burden facing the subjects of the empire. Apart from the Egyptian advances between 1831 and 1833, and again between 1839 and 1841, the Greek revolution lasted throughout the 1820s. In 1828–29 there was a war with tsarist Russia. For a short time, it appeared as though the Ottoman Empire would become a Russian protectorate. In the Crimean War (1853-56), the sultan was on the side of the victors, but that had no long-term consequences. In 1878, the armies of the tsar actually advanced into the periphery of the Ottoman capital. The Treaty of San Stefano/ Yeşilköy (now the site of the main Istanbul airport) aimed to establish a Greater Bulgarian principality that would have been a satellite state of the tsar in the immediate vicinity of the Ottoman capital. This was unacceptable to the other great powers, and a revision providing for a greatly reduced Bulgaria was introduced at the Congress of Berlin in the same year.

By the end of the century, when war was being waged between Greece and the Ottoman Empire, the English government had given up its opposition to the division of the empire. Since the Ottomans won this war, however, drastic measures were put off for the time being. In 1908, a new series of complications ensued when Austria-Hungary annexed the provinces of Bosnia and Herzegovina, which had been occupied since 1878. This act gave rise to lasting hostilities in Istanbul, as these territories, with their largely Muslim population, had been Ottoman possessions since the 1400s, but also in Belgrade, where the government hoped to annex a large group of people speaking a language closely related to Serbian. Moreover, the Kingdom of Serbia could count on the support of Russia in this matter. These conflicting interests had a significant role in the formation of European alliances when World War I was fought just a few years later.

In many cases, Ottoman territorial losses were coupled with expulsions and emigration. Some Muslims emigrated in a reasonably orderly fashion, but many more had to flee due to acts of war and massacres of the Muslim population, which were part and parcel of the wars of independence in the Balkans. Entire populations, such as the Circassians, were forced to emigrate after the annexation of their territory by the Russians in 1863. The refugees often lost everything they owned; they lived in Istanbul, generally in deplorable conditions and racked by disease, until the Ottoman government was able to provide them new places to live.

This situation was the backdrop for the so-called Bulgarian Horrors. During a Bulgarian revolt in 1876, numerous Muslims living in the affected area had been massacred. To suppress the revolt, the Ottoman government mobilized irregular troops. These regiments, which consisted in large part of Circassians recently driven over the Russo-Ottoman frontier and traumatized by hunger, epidemics, and expulsion, slipped out of the control of their commanders and killed large numbers of Bulgarians. There are widely divergent estimates as to the number of victims. English and American sources conjectured that about 12,000 to 15,000 people must have fallen victim to this repression. The ensuing press coverage was largely responsible for the conservative English Prime Minister Disraeli's decision to bow to the pressure of the opposition and distance himself from his former ally, the sultan.

Reorganization of the State and the Military (1839–1878)

In 1839 a new proclamation guaranteed all subjects the right to life, property, and honor, and thus redefined the relationship of the ruler to the classes representing the state. This imperial decree marked the beginning of a period of extensive reform from 1839 to 1876 known as the Tanzimat ("reorganization"). The slave-like status of all Ottoman dignitaries apart from the legal and religious scholars (*ulema*) that had prevailed since the 15th century vis-à-vis the sultan was now abolished. In 1856, this decree was supplemented by an additional one that retained Islam as the state religion but declared the equality of all male subjects under the law, and thereby went a step further in adopting the model provided by the European great powers.

A revision of property law was introduced in 1858. The state's *dominium directum* (formal ownership right) over meadows and fields remained in place; owners who did not use their land might find that it was subject to confiscation. In all other instances, however, possession rights over state land (*miri*) were made to resemble private ownership (*mülk*). The aim of this revision was to reduce the multitude of legal claims to the same piece of land and thus to give new impetus to the property market. The idea was also that the free negotiability of land would lead to better use. In this connection it was also decreed that only single individuals would be recognized as owners. In areas where communal ownership of land was common, such as parts of Syria and for the nomads of southern Anatolia, this regulation had unintended consequences: powerful members of a tribe registered the land in their names, and the remaining members of the community forfeited their rights.

Reforms of this kind were also intended to strengthen non-Muslim subjects' ties to the government of the sultan by opening up opportunities for political participation to their local dignitaries. This policy evoked considerable interest in the Jewish population, which was largely concentrated in Salonika at that time. The Christians in the Balkans were less enthusiastic; when given the choice, most of them opted for the new nation states.

Rulers and Bureaucracy until 1908

After the death of Sultan Mahmud II in 1839, domestic power devolved to the grand vizier and his ever-increasing numbers of subordinates. This change was facilitated by the gradual establishment of special ministries and by codifying the rules for the training and careers of civil servants. The old rules of promotion by patronage and the unconditional loyalty of the beneficiary to his patron did not disappear, but their purview was increasingly restricted. The grand vizier thus had a modernizing bureaucracy at his disposal, even though the new professional requirements, which included proficiency in French, furthered careers in some ministries more than others.

A group called the Young Ottomans protested vehemently against this power on the part of high bureaucrats who were accountable only to a relatively passive ruler. The writer Namik Kemal, who preached a blend of Islamic values and political and cultural renewal, was regarded as the group's leading exponent. Namik Kemal and his associates are mentioned here not so much because of their achievements in practical political matters as because of the impetus their ideas gave to the Turkish nationalism that arose several decades later.

The crisis that followed the defeats of 1878 culminated in the acceptance of a constitution and the election of a parliament. The constitution reiterated the guarantee of equality to all subjects, thereby checking the attempts of the great powers of Europe to attain more and more privileges for their Christian charges. This process was headed by Midhat Paşa, who had already made a name for himself as a successful and innovation-minded governor.

The new constitution, which the new sultan, Murad V, supported, was short-lived. Murad, who ruled for a mere three months in 1876, suffered a nervous breakdown when confronted with the foreign and domestic demands of the office. After his deposition, Abdülhamid II acceded to the throne (1876-1909). Abdülhamid was an exceptionally controversial sultan. In the area of foreign policy, he succeeded in delaying the dissolution of the Ottoman Empire for several more decades. On the domestic front, his rule was absolute, and the palace was once again the center of power. An ingenious system of reciprocal espionage by current and potential dignitaries was designed to keep the sultan informed about the loyalty of his subordinates, especially of the intellectuals among them. Particularly in his later years, the sultan feared being assassinated to the point that he rarely left his palace in the hills over Beşiktaş.

The fact that Abdülhamid increasingly used Islamic motifs to legitimate his state earned him great loyalty among the Muslim population and several dividends in foreign policy. The Indian Muslims, for example, regarded the caliph, as Abdülhamid liked to be called, as a source of moral support vis-à-vis the English colonial power and the Hindu majority population.

Abdülhamid also adapted to the new situation by attempting to integrate his Arab subjects more fully into the Ottoman body politic. These subjects now made up a far greater proportion of the population than before the losses in the Balkans. Sons of Arab dignitaries were encouraged to complete the sultan's school of public administration and take up new bureaucratic careers. Cadet training was open to them as well. In eastern Anatolia, the sultan focused on the "divide and conquer" principle by exploiting the differences between Armenians and Kurds. The Hamidiye regiments, which consisted of Kurdish irregular soldiers and were ordered to quell Armenian nationalist unrest, contributed in large part to intensifying tensions in eastern Anatolia.

The Tripoli and Balkan Wars (1911–1913)

The period that followed the reintroduction of the constitution in 1908 brought a quick succession of foreign crises, and any hopes for liberalization and domestic peace that many Muslims and non-Muslims had cherished were soon dashed. Apart from Austria-Hungary's annexation of Bosnia, Italy attacked Tripoli, the last Ottoman possession in North Africa, and rapidly occupied the area. As we have seen, major revolts in Kosovo and other territories largely inhabited by Albanians between 1910 and 1912 were followed by an attack on the Balkan provinces in 1912 by a coalition of Greece, Serbia, and Bulgaria. The allied armies conquered Kosovo, and many of the previously rebellious Albanians joined the Ottoman army in a last-ditch effort. The Ottoman forces, however, were disorganized and outnumbered, and they soon were forced to retreat. The coalition armies took Edirne and once again stood just a few miles away from the capital. Moreover, in 1912 Greece annexed the island of Crete, and Greek armies entered Salonika, one of the Empire's most modern cities and the starting point of the Committee for Union and Progress. At that time, Salonika still held an ethnically mixed population of Jews, Muslims, and Greeks. However, many of the non-Greek inhabitants soon emigrated; many Muslims moved to Istanbul, and others went to the United States and elsewhere.

Since the three Balkan states could not agree on the division of the Macedonian spoils of war, however, another war broke out between them in 1913 which enabled the Ottoman army to reconquer Edirne. The Albanians achieved the sovereignty they had sought. As a result, the Ottoman Empire was essentially pushed back to the European borders of present-day Turkey even before the beginning of the First World War.

Politics and Survival in the Countryside

The retreat of the Ottomans from the former Balkan provinces in the course of the 19th century meant big changes for the farmers and nomads of Anatolia. For one thing, a new existential basis had to be created for exiles and emigrants. For another, it became increasingly necessary to change the regions from which Istanbul received its grain supplies. Most of the grain had come from the coastal areas of present-day Bulgaria and Romania, but now it was brought from Anatolia instead. There were certainly sparsely populated expanses in central Anatolia, used almost exclusively by semi-nomads, that could be put to agricultural use. But the local inhabitants were quite hostile to the reduction of their traditional pastures, and in the face of problems both natural and man-made, quite a few settlers, who in any case were often townspeople, soon left the areas allotted to them. Others went on the offensive, especially the Circassians, who traditionally bore arms, and whose social structure deviated from the traditional norms of Anatolia; this situation may have prompted the Ottoman government to allocate land to some Circassians in the sparsely populated steppe of present-day Jordan. In southern Anatolia, large-scale projects for new settlements also served to provide more agricultural products for both the domestic and the international market; these pushes for settlement now affected larger numbers of nomads and half-nomads, and the state authority was heavily involved. Later in the 1960s and 1970s the traumatic events connected with forced sedentarization found expression in the stories of Yaşar Kemal.

In spite of it all, the second half of the 19th century was a time of redevelopment in Anatolia. Villages that had been abandoned since about 1600 were repopulated, and former summer pastures were redesigned as permanent settlements. Local administrative centers that were required for these endeavors were established at this time; while the larger urban centers of Anatolia quite often go back to Roman or even pre-Roman antiquity, the network of small towns is mostly a product of the 19th-century settlement process.

Since very few bodies of water in Anatolia are navigable, agriculture was profitable only when there were reasonably priced train connections. Track systems were usually built by foreign companies interested in branch lines to coastal harbors, but these companies were less inclined to build a comprehensive railway system. The financial outlay to construct a railway system placed a great strain on the national budget. For the Ottoman government, military considerations often outweighed economic factors; as a result of these conflicting pressures, no railway network, as opposed to individual lines, was built in Turkey until the early years of the republic. Nevertheless, the completion of the railway link to Ankara in 1892 had a profound impact on the agriculture of northwestern Anatolia. Feeder services were provided by peasant carts and camels. As a result, the economic significance of these animals did not decline during the first stage of railway transport, but actually increased.

Through it all, Anatolia remained a land of small farmers. There were large estates (*çiftlik*), cultivated by paid laborers, in the Aegean area and in the region of Adana, where cotton was grown for the world market, as well as in the southeast, which had a less commercial orientation. Besides the merchants who acquired land as a second source of investment, there were also families that had been powerful since the

17th or 18th century as tax lessees and local magnates in a particular region. Some of these well-established families had acquired land back in the 17th or 18th century (the legality of their acquisitions was not always clear), and had it cultivated by sub-lessees. In the Balkans, especially at the Bulgarian coast of the Black Sea and in Macedonia, large estates were also common; in 1849-50, for example, Bulgarian peasants rebelled against the large estate owners in the area of present-day Vidin.[3] It is important to keep in mind, though, that historians of the new Balkan states after 1945 tended to overestimate the number and economic significance of these possessions when using national and social arguments against Ottoman rule. In Syria and southeastern Anatolia, the development of large estates was often a result of the reorganization of ownership regulations in the Ottoman Land Law of 1858. But rural economists who studied the region of today's Keban dam in the Anatolian southeast around 1970 found out to their surprise that large landholdings were less prevalent than they had anticipated.

Anatolian agriculture remained vulnerable, especially in times of drought, notably in central Anatolia in 1873–74, when an estimated 250,000 people and a large number of cattle and sheep succumbed to famine. In some places, the number of casualties was far higher than the number of those presumed to have fled. There had already been signs of a catastrophic drought several years earlier, with below-average rainfall over an extended period of time. A lack of transport links played a decisive role in the catastrophe, but quite possibly the government's indifference to this remote region was also detrimental: the tax breaks that would have allowed local peasants to form some reserves even in times of mediocre harvests had not been forthcoming.

Ottoman Manufacturers and the Capitalist World Economy

There has been a recent resurgence of a longstanding debate about the economic implications of the independence movement in the Balkans. Until a few years ago, scholars concurred that whatever the weaknesses of the new Balkan principalities, each carried out important modernization projects. But a new study by Michael Palairet disputes that this was the case in the economic sector.[4] Palairet's study shows that the conditions for the growth of proto-industry in the Ottoman Empire were relatively favorable after the establishment of peace under Mahmud II, because the provinces paid their taxes to the central government and thus had to replenish their monetary holding with the sale of goods. As a result, money was transferred from the center to the provinces that made it possible to pay the next round of taxes. Independence transformed the situation. The market contracted sharply, land was now easier to acquire, and many farmers returned to subsistence farming. One could of course argue that the new nation-states demanded higher taxes from their farmers than the sultan had, and that it became more difficult to avoid paying them. However, the decline of the cities in many autonomous or independent Balkan principalities shows that economic and social development was by no means an automatic consequence of independence.

European observers who reported on Ottoman artisan production in the mid-19th century painted a uniformly bleak picture. The import of European (particularly British) goods took business away from domestic manufacturers of textiles, especially because the customs regime was quite favorable to imported goods. European importers paid only a modest import duty, as stipulated in treaties with their respective governments known as "capitulations." These capitulations that by the mid-19th century had been granted to all the Empire's trading partners constrained the sultan's government in other economic matters as well.

More recent studies prove that Ottoman commerce and artisan production were more varied than they might appear at first glance. Many manufacturers adapted to changing circumstances. Imported thread, for instance, was woven into cloth suited to the needs of the local market. But the new industries often paid low wages. There were instances of machine-breaking, mechanized looms being destroyed, particularly in the carpet industry in western Anatolia. Quite possibly the total Ottoman industrial output in the late 19th century was no less than a century earlier, but this production was now integrated into the world market dominated by Europe, and large amounts of foreign capital were invested in many branches of industry.

All these developments meant that tax revenues remained limited;

and the Ottoman government resorted to borrowing to finance infrastructure and also—it must be admitted—the building of luxurious residences for the sultans and their court on the shores of the Bosporus, including the still extant palaces of Dolmabahçe and Çırağan. By and large, however, Ottoman debts resulted from the bonds the government had issued to pay for the modernization of the army and navy after the Crimean War. The guarantees for a specific return on investment that investors in railway lines demanded also put a strain on the budget. These bonds yielded high interest rates, and the accumulation of debt led to state bankruptcy in 1875. Beginning in 1881, a consortium of European financial backers called *Dette ottomane* administered important Ottoman public revenues. Although the Ottoman Empire was never added to a European colonial empire, toward the end of the century its dependency was considerable.

Nationalism among Turks and Non-Turks

In the 19th century, the Ottoman elites initially promoted a loyalty to state and dynasty that transcended ethnic and religious differences. By 1878, however, it had become apparent that at least in the Balkans, this ideology was not working. In the following decades, Sultan Abdülhamid tried to hold together the empire by emphasizing Islamic solidarity. Opposition to his neo-absolutist regime brought the theme of Turkish nationalism to the fore. The economic aspect was of particular importance in this development. The trade bourgeoisie in the Ottoman central provinces consisted in large part of Greeks and Armenians, whose nationalist efforts were directed against the territorial integrity of the Ottoman Empire. One idea under discussion was to have the state help create a Turkish-Muslim bourgeoisie to counterbalance the "foreign" one; in this period the attitude took hold that any given state would promote the interests of the dominant ethnic group/groups living in its territory and more or less wash its hands of those people classified as minorities. Creating a Turkish-Muslim bourgeoisie also was a policy directed against integration into the European world economy; for Christian merchants were regarded as the accomplices in that integration. The first step was to eliminate special rights for foreigners, which inhibited the Ottoman state's freedom of action. This goal was attained during World War I. However, the establishment of a Muslim bourgeoisie with the help of the state did not really take effect until after 1923, in the republican period.

Opposition to Abdülhamid gathered steam in the so-called Committee for Union and Progress, a loose consortium of several groups, but the supporters of this opposition, known as Young Turks, largely shared a fundamentally secular view of the world even though a few religious scholars adhered to the movement as well. Many intellectually-minded supporters were deeply influenced by the materialism of Ludwig Büchner. Léon Cahun's writings about the Turks were also read, while in later years, many supporters of the movement were drawn to the racism then popular in Europe. Besides their secular view of the world, the opposition found common ground in their call for the restoration of the constitution of 1876. Despite the great authority this latter document granted the sultan, the 1908 coup, which forced the ruler to reintroduce the constitution, signified a transition to a constitutional monarchy. The new sultan, Mehmed V Reşat, who followed the deposed Abdülhamid in 1909, had little power beyond signing the bills of his Council of Ministers.

The open nationalism of the Young Turks became a model for other incipient nationalist movements, including groups that had shown little previous interest in this issue, such as many Syrian Arabs. Official insistence on the use of Turkish and perhaps preferential treatment given to Turkish candidates for civil service positions and other jobs apparently led to lingering resentments. But in this region it was the repressive government measures of 1914–18 that de-legitimized Ottoman rule in the long run.

The Press, Theater, and Photography

In the capital, and to a lesser extent in large provincial towns such as Izmir and Salonika, the second half of the 19th century was a period of innovation in the areas of literature and the fine arts. Before and after 1900, a media landscape was rapidly taking shape that featured increasing specialization of individual journals in particular fields. One journal that was originally designed for a general readership, for instance, narrowed its focus to music criticism. This was of course possible only because public concerts and opera performances were an integral part of the cultural life of Istanbul by this time.

The circulation of newspapers and magazines was hampered not only by censorship, but also by low literacy rates and poor distribution. By the time a publication made it to the provinces, the news it contained was often out of date. Many readers relied on the newspapers in coffee houses, which made them accessible to men of modest means, but limited the number of potential buyers. Even so, the newspaper business enabled some entrepreneurs in Istanbul to establish themselves as publishers. In this industry, the market for printed books, apart from textbooks, was quite limited. Many 19th-century booklovers continued to prefer the aesthetic charm of handwritten manuscripts.

Armenians, who generally spoke fluent Ottoman as their second language (it was sometimes even their native language), had a very prominent position in the Istanbul book trade. In 1854, Vartan Paşa, a high-level civil servant, as his title indicates, published the first Ottoman novel that is still known today, a variation on the theme of Romeo and Juliet. The plot revolves around Istanbul Armenians whose different religious denominations set them apart as enemies. Armenian theater professionals had a key role in the development of Ottoman drama, which increased in popularity during the second half of the century. Güllü Agop, the impresario who directed the theater that introduced the public to the plays of Namik Kemal and other outstanding writers of contemporary Ottoman literature in 1870-80, also instituted a training program for correct Ottoman pronunciation and established a commission that was to select suitable plays and adapt them to the exigencies of his stage.

In early photography, there were also a good many foreigners and members of Christian minorities. Prominent photographers included Pascal Sébah, originally from Lebanon, who won several prizes at international exhibitions in Vienna and Paris, and Abdullah Frères, a firm of three related Armenians. They were soon joined by Ottoman officers and former officers who had learned the use of photography in artillery training. The work of Ali Sami, who taught photography at the military school, shows not only scenes of Istanbul street life but also his emphatically "modern" family: both male and female members, all fashionably dressed, were shown with their books and newspapers. Sultan Abdülhamid became an enthusiastic supporter of the new art form, and commissioned lavish albums to highlight the "modern" sides of Ottoman life: schools, hospitals, factories, and of course the omnipresent military. Members of the Ottoman upper class were quite fond of calling cards with portraits, which were in vogue at the end of the 19th century and are today a favored collector's item and a valuable resource for social historians.

"New-Style" Education and Instruction

There was no continuously functioning Ottoman university until 1900. Earlier attempts failed not only because of a lack of qualified teachers and books, but also because many members of the administration mistrusted students, who might prove hostile to the government, as had happened in quite few European countries. By contrast, service academies for future military officers (and, increasingly, for civil officers as well) dated back to the late 18th century. The army engineering school was renowned for its well-rounded curriculum and its publications. The school of administration (Mülkiye) was a leading civil institution that imbued its graduates with a strong esprit de corps. Moreover, students had been sent to France and Belgium for their education since the Tanzimat period, even though the Ottoman authorities were always concerned that these young people might encounter politically radical ideas. French as a language of literary education thus gained importance, in addition to the traditional triad of Arabic, Persian, and Ottoman Turkish.

Well into the second half of the 19th century, however, Ottoman students were inadequately prepared for these institutions of higher education. State-sponsored secondary instruction was slow in emerging. In 1867, an elite secondary school was founded in a former Istanbul palace, which still exists today. The curriculum was adapted from the French *lycée*; the language of instruction was also French, and the faculty included renowned literati. The school was open to members of all religions. But the great majority of those who sought an elementary education still relied on private instruction, local schools teaching the Koran on an elementary level in addition to the "three Rs," and parochial schools, to which Christians had relatively easy access. For in addition to the schools for Greek Orthodox and Gregorian Armenian children, there were others run by Catholic and Evangelical missions. For Jewish students, there was the Alliance Israélite Universelle, a set of schools based in France, which offered a modern practical curriculum.

In the epoch of Abdülhamid, public Muslim elementary and middle schools also received official support, although they were few in number, especially in the provinces. Even in schools supported by the state and not by Muslim pious foundations, religious instruction was strongly emphasized in the early grades. The goal was to educate students to be pious and devoted to the sultan; the Ottomans described this aim as loyalty to "religion and state" in a manner reminiscent of Metternich's "alliance of throne and altar." In largely Shiite provinces such as Iraq, government support of education was used as a means of spreading Sunni Islam; Christian missions provided the model, even though Abdülhamid was otherwise very critical of them. Teacher training seminars rounded out the educational offerings.

The World of Women

For a long time, historians of modern Turkey considered it axiomatic that the political rights and the enhanced educational opportunities for Turkish women after the 1930s were not attained by the actions of the women concerned, and were in fact not even demanded by them. However, feminist-inspired historiography over the past thirty years has shown that this is a crass oversimplification. In Istanbul and several large cities, including some located in today's Syria and Lebanon, groups of women in the late 19th and early 20th centuries advocated better education for girls. Among Arab-language journals, publications addressed to women began to appear in the 1890s. Their editors were typically Christian women; the journalist Labība Hāshim was noted for her distinguished style and gave guest lectures at Cairo University.

These female journalists were supported in their efforts by men, who, at least where the Turkish-language press was concerned, wrote a good many essays in women's magazines, usually in a nationalist framework.[5] Nationalist discourses rejected the notion that ignorant women could be suitable "mothers of the nation." Moreover, more and more educated men expected their wives to possess at least a certain degree of schooling. After all, hygiene and nutrition in the everyday life of a family were contingent on female education, to say nothing of the fact that literate men might be familiar with the belles-lettres of the time in which love and the joys of educated conversation were important topics. Widespread interaction with male "allies" explains why women who demanded better educational opportunities emphasized the good of the coming generation and not merely—or even primarily—their own.

One sphere of activity open to educated women was journalism. Fatma Aliye (1862–1936), the daughter of Grand Vizier Ahmed Cevdet Paşa, combined a rather traditional marriage with successful work as a journalist and as an author of popular novels. Halide Edib (later surname: Adıvar, 1884–1964) also wrote newspaper reports and stories that are still widely read today. She was active in Istanbul as a political orator after the collapse of the Ottoman army in 1918, when the city was occupied by the Allies, becoming (as it says on the monument to her memory) the symbolic female figure of the Turkish War of Independence. Sahiba (later surname: Sertel, 1895–1968) began writing for newspapers when she was still in school, and met her husband when they both worked as journalists. The couple became well-known figures in the early republican media landscape after their move from Salonika to Istanbul.

A number of Ottoman Armenian women made names for themselves as actresses. After all, Muslim women were only allowed on the stage after 1923; but in Istanbul, the theater flourished from the 1850s onwards. Ottoman literary theater, as promoted by Namık Kemal and others, thus relied on Armenian female performers, some of whom took special courses in elocution so as to become the models of educated speech that theatrical authors of the time envisaged.

Some women of the Ottoman upper class, both Muslim and Greek, got their first taste of participation in the public sphere by working for charitable organizations. In Salonika during the late 19th and early 20th centuries a charitable association of Greek women gave aid to old people and especially to students. The necessary funds were provided by people like Elissavet Kastritsiou, a rich woman who died in Bucharest in 1862 and left half of her estate to the Greek community schools of Salonika and Jannina.[6] Muslim women worked for the Red Crescent Society (Hilal-i Ahmer, the counterpart to the Red Cross), especially during World War I. As girls' schools were run by females, some women were able to work as teachers; unfortunately, this area is much less well researched than journalistic activity. Clearly these types of work in the public sphere were restricted to a very small group of mostly upper-class women in the late Ottoman era. But the example they set is of great significance for women today.

CHAPTER 5
The Ottoman Military, World War I, and the End of Empire

Military Rule

Significant politicization of the Ottoman officers' corps had already been observed during the reign of Abdülhamid. At this time, quite a few competent commanders esteemed by their subordinates had been appointed to non-command posts or even sent abroad on diplomatic missions, because the sultan feared that they might lend their prestige to a future military rebellion. In fact, the coup d'état or revolution of 1908—the events have been interpreted differently by historians—was partly initiated by the dissatisfaction of officers combating guerillas in Macedonia who felt that they were not given the necessary support (see Ch. 4); certainly soldiers' pay was notoriously in arrears.[1]

During the following years, top-level commanders were closely involved in politics: thus a rebellion in 1909 that aimed at the restoration of Abdülhamid as an absolute ruler was put down by the intervention of a military corps from outside Istanbul. When Italy occupied Tripoli in 1911, many officers accused their government of all too rapidly abandoning the last North African province to the enemy. Several young men who were to play an important role during the World War served with distinction in the small military force that the Ottoman central government was able to send to Tripoli. Here, a circle of politically active officers emerged, of which Enver (later: Enver Paşa, 1881–1922) was the emblematic figure. In 1912 the Committee for Union and Progress suffered a brief setback when Nazım Paşa, the commander of the First Army corps stationed in Istanbul, opposed any activity on its part within the military and the same year, the veteran General Gazi Ahmed Muhtar Paşa formed a cabinet in which the Committee was not represented.

In January 1913, however, after only a few months in office, this government was overthrown when the seat of the Prime Minister was attacked by a detachment of soldiers (*Bab-ı ali baskını*) in which Enver participated. The Minister of War was killed and the so-called "military wing" of the Committee seized power. This coup d'état was a direct consequence of the threat to Edirne (lost in March 1913; see Ch. 4), whose loss many Ottoman officers were not willing to countenance under any circumstances. Mahmud Şevket Paşa, who became the pivotal figure in the new government until his assassination later that year (June 1913), was also a soldier. Moreover military rule did not end once Edirne had been recovered in July 1913 and in fact continued until the very end of World War I. It was after the assassination of Mahmud Şevket Paşa that repression of real and suspected enemies of the Committee began in earnest.

As this account shows, during the Balkan wars and particularly the crucial summer of 1914 the Ottoman government was in the hands of the military. Enver Paşa, who commanded the army, supposedly as a stand-in for the elderly sultan, had also become the key figure in the Ottoman government, along with his colleagues Cemal and Talat Paşa. Yet serious divisions within the officer corps continued; politically active soldiers could be found among the Unionists but also among their opponents. In addition, Enver Paşa had enemies within his own movement. Acrimonious discussions concerning the responsibilities of individual commanders for the recent defeats, and particularly the fall of Edirne, further accentuated divisions.

Another type of tension was structural and long-term, namely the confrontations between officers trained in military schools (*mektepli*) and those who had been commissioned after extended service as non-commissioned officers (*alaylı*). While the former had been trained in the conduct of modern warfare, they were often socially remote from the men they commanded and thus found it difficult to instill confidence. As for the *alaylıs*, while often able to share the concerns of their men and thus to provide effective leadership, their lack of experience with modern weapons was a major drawback, to say nothing of the fact that they often lacked the general education needed for the comprehension of tactics and strategy. Added to the insufficiencies of the communications system—in many cases there were no railroads to bring armies rapidly to the field of battle, and roads were often of poor quality—these divisions within the officer corps explain at least in part the difficulties of late Ottoman armies in the field.

A host of further problems was connected with conscription, which remained highly unpopular, especially when service in remote provinces such as Yemen was involved. The Committee of Union and Progress as a matter of principle had instituted the draft of non-Muslims, which had been on the books since the mid-1800s but rarely applied in practice. Even in 1908, the inclusion of non-Muslims in the army was viewed as a long-term project. At the first stage, men of military age but over twenty-four years old still were excused from active service: they were liable for the exemption fee that previous generations of Jews and Christians also had paid. While Jewish soldiers in particular often served with devotion and distinction during the Balkan wars, refusing the draft and fleeing to foreign countries was frequent, especially among soldiers of Christian and southeastern European backgrounds.[2] Particularly during World War I, the authorities therefore mobilized many non-Muslims not as soldiers but as conscript laborers. As living conditions in the labor corps were often poor and political conflicts in the relevant regions tended to "spill over" into the military, the number of casualties in the labor battalions was quite high.

The German Connection

It was probably the Prussian victory over the armies of Napoleon III in the war of 1870-71 that first attracted the attention of Ottoman military men. A further factor was presumably the lack of any common borders and the absence of the fledgling German navy from the Mediterranean: thus it seemed probable that the newly formed German state (1871) did not aim for territorial acquisitions at Ottoman expense. In spite of limited financial resources, however, the German ruling group did aim for economic predominance. In the reign of Abdülhamid II (1876-1909), known as the Hamidian period, Ottoman officers were sent to Germany for training in sizeable numbers; and German military missions were sent to the Ottoman Empire.[3]

In 1913 the government of the Kaiser supported the demands of the military for a "revanche" and reconquest of the territories lost in the Balkan war. Arms and ammunition of German make, purchased on credit, helped re-equip the Ottoman army, while a further loan from the same source enabled the government to pay the long overdue salaries of its officials. The debacle of 1912–1913 was not attributed to the German military advisors who had been in place up to that time, but rather to the Ottoman commanders who had disregarded their advice.

In 1913, just when peacetime recruitment patterns were being revised so that Ottoman draftees would do their military service within their regions of origin—as we have seen, this had been a major demand of the Albanian insurgents—a new German military mission was instituted under the command of Otto Liman von Sanders. The latter became inspector of military schools and reorganized the college of Istanbul/Pangaltı according to the German model. He also fortified the defenses of the Bosporus and Dardanelles (often called the Straits in the relevant literature), an act that was violently opposed by Tsarist Russia. Promoted to marshal in the Ottoman army, this officer played a major role throughout World War I.

It has been concluded that in the Great War, the deliveries of German-made arms and military equipment to the Ottomans were modest in quantity when compared to total production in Central Europe. But these supplies certainly enabled the Ottoman armies to hold out longer than would have been possible otherwise. As for the military value of the German officers on active command in the Ottoman army, it is now regarded as less significant than in the past. Liman von Sanders did make a contribution, but his problems in communicating with his fellow Ottoman officers, including Mustafa Kemal Paşa (later: Atatürk, 1881–1938), significantly limited his effectiveness; he even aroused the opposition of the minister of war Enver Paşa, otherwise known for his pro-German attitude. Colmar von der Goltz, the former teacher and mentor of quite a few Ottoman officers, died before he could put his capabilities to full use. By contrast, the work of staff officers in the planning of campaigns was very valuable, as were the technical services that made locomotives and other equipment function under often very difficult conditions.[4]

The Ottoman Entry into the War

Conscious of the need for a period of recovery after the wars of 1911–1913, the Ottoman government approached the Great Powers of the time for an alliance, even including—rather to his surprise—the Russian foreign minister Sergei Sazonov, who after all represented the Ottomans' principal long-term opponent. Thus the alliance with Germany was not the more or less automatic result of German influence in the military; a first approach by the Ottoman side to the Kaiser's ambassador Hans von Wangenheim in the summer of 1914 was unsuccessful, as the German government did not believe the Ottoman armies capable of serious action against the Russians. But when war actually was declared on August 1, the ambassador, under pressure from Kaiser Wilhelm, did conclude an alliance with the Ottoman government.

At the same time, relations with Great Britain were thoroughly compromised by a fortuitous event: in the summer of 1914 two warships close to completion in British shipyards, which had been paid for by a public subscription of Ottoman citizens, were confiscated by Winston Churchill, First Lord of the Admiralty, at the outbreak of war: historians are divided over the question whether Churchill's action had any legal basis.[5] On the other hand, two German warships in the Mediterranean at that time escaped their British pursuers and arrived in Istanbul on August 10, 1914; they were taken over into the Ottoman navy for action against the Russian Black Sea fleet, which was not yet ready for battle. A couple of weeks later, Enver Paşa, with the support of Admiral Souchon, who commanded the two newly acquired warships, seems to have placed the remaining members of the Ottoman government before a fait accompli: an attack on the Russian Black Sea coast brought the Ottoman Empire into the war on the side of the Central Powers.

Entry into the war provided the Ottoman government with a long-awaited opportunity to abolish the so-called capitulations, the rights of foreigners to be judged by their consuls and the far-reaching immunities from Ottoman law that these people also enjoyed (see Ch. 4). In addition, the repayment of foreign debts was largely interrupted; as a result, the Ottoman government regained control of the revenue sources that had been at the disposal of its creditors through the Dette Ottomane ever since the bankruptcy of 1875. These measures caused a certain amount of dissatisfaction among the Empire's German and Austro-Hungarian allies; however, on this issue, the latter were not in a position to influence the course of events. Long after the end of the war, the Republic of Turkey was to take over and pay off a certain share of this debt; payments were finally terminated in 1944. Other rather smaller shares fell to the "successor states" that had also once been part of the Ottoman Empire.[6]

The Ottoman armies entered the First World War already in a parlous state due to the losses of 1912–13. Even worse, this war was based on the performance of industrial economies, and some of the Ottoman territories that were most advanced in terms of industry and infrastructure, such as Salonika, had been lost during recent decades.

Remarkably enough, given the amount of work that has been done on World War I, there are still quite a few areas where information is vague. One of the most obvious examples concerns casualty estimates. When discussing the Gallipoli (Çanakkale in Turkish parlance) campaign of 1915, one observer has claimed that there were about 300,000 Ottoman casualties versus 265,000 on the side of the Allies. But other sources give considerably lower figures: in one case 210,000 Allied losses correspond to 120,000 Ottoman casualties; by yet another author we are informed that the Allies lost about 70,000 men and the Ottoman side about 90,000.[7] Some of the discrepancies may be due to the manner of counting: those men who were ill or wounded but soon returned to their units may or may not have been included. An American military historian working with Turkish and Ottoman sources has concluded that where Ottoman and Allied combatants were concerned, the numbers of dead and wounded were about equal, in the range of 200,000 each.[8]

Other discrepancies involve the evaluation of certain battles: thus most authors consider the confrontation of Sarıkamış between the Russians and Ottomans in the winter of 1914-15 as an unmitigated catastrophe for the Ottomans. But at least one military historian has claimed that from the perspective of the sultan's commanders, the enterprise should be regarded as a qualified success.[9] For a non-specialist in military history it is only possible to record these discrepancies; they show that our data often is much weaker than we would like it to be.

Major Theaters of Conflict

To understand the catastrophes of the war years, events on the northeastern front need to be narrated in some detail. As we have seen, in the late fall of 1914 Enver Paşa ordered a winter campaign against the Russians in the Caucasus, the battle plan being to attack on a broad front in eastern Anatolia, draw the Russians deep into Ottoman territory, and then cut them off from their supply bases by an attack from the rear. However, in this region there were almost no railways, and the few existing roads were impassible during the long and severe winters. Moreover, the troops had not been issued any kind of protective uniforms or equipment. According to western sources, the Ottoman army thus lost over 80,000 men—more than half of the army engaged on this front—within a few months of warfare; 30,000 soldiers died of the cold alone. Ottoman sources record 50,000 casualties.[10] Russian armies entered Erzurum in November 1914 and Trabzon somewhat later.[11]

The Russian invasion encouraged attacks on the part of local Armenians against the Muslim population. Especially grave was a rebellion of Armenian nationalists in the town of Van, which was occupied by the Russian army with great loss of Muslim life. This was the background for the Ottoman government's order to move the Armenians out of most parts of Anatolia and relocate them in northern Iraq. Settlement was to be at least 40 km from the Baghdad railway, a ruling which limited settlement to arid and infertile areas where it was almost impossible to make a living.[12] Originally conceived as a wartime measure, the government soon reversed its position and ordered the sale of the deportees' property to refugee Muslims. On the road, the deportees were given almost no supplies or protection; sometimes those detailed to guard them made common cause with robbers and other attackers. Mass killings were the result. The number of people that perished through hunger, cold, disease, revenge attacks, and banditry is not exactly known. A figure of 200,000 has been suggested by an American scholar sympathetic to the Turkish position, while a demographic historian has suggested a loss of almost 600,000, and others assume even higher casualties, up to a million and more.[13]

At present this is the most contentious topic of Ottoman history. One point of dispute is whether the government—or perhaps mainly its secret service—had a hand in planning the massacres in order to promote a more homogenous population in Anatolia.[14] On this and related issues, opinions have become so much polarized that no consensus is in sight; and for a non-specialist on the period, informed judgment at present seems impossible. Only at some future date, when the question hopefully will have become less politically loaded, will we gain a clearer picture and view the issue more dispassionately. In any case, it is important to keep in mind that in 1915 parts of eastern Anatolia were in a state of civil war that to some extent had preceded the 1914-15 conflict but was exacerbated by the Russian advance—Russian policy of the time included using Ottoman Armenians for purposes of destabilization and territorial acquisitions—and that the losses of the Muslim population through massacres committed by Armenian bands also were horrific.[15] The observations of two American observers who visited Bitlis, Van, and Doğubeyazit in the summer of 1919 reflect the devastation that both sides had suffered.[16]

Another significant rebellion involved the Hashemite ruling family in the Hijaz, where the Muslims' Holy Cities of Mecca and Medina are located. Here, outside support for the revolt came from the British, who were concerned about the influence that the caliph, who for centuries had been the Ottoman sultan, might exercise over their own Muslim subjects in India and elsewhere. In fact, Abdülhamid II had made considerable and often successful efforts to promote the prestige of the caliphate among the colonial Muslim subjects of Britain and the Netherlands. In the early days of the war, the Ottoman sultan had issued a call to holy war (jihad), which however had little practical effect in India and elsewhere. At this time British policy planners anticipated that Istanbul and thereby the sultan-caliph would soon fall under Russian control. This consideration was behind their offer to the Sharif Husayn, ruler of Mecca under Ottoman suzerainty, that the caliphate might be transferred to the Holy City if an Arab rebellion against the Ottomans could be brought about. In this case, Sharif Husayn was to become the new caliph. It is impossible to summarize in a few sentences the tortuous negotiations between the various British agents and the ruler of Mecca. Suffice to say that the British never intended to allow this Arabian prince to exercise real power; he was to be a figurehead through which the authorities in London and the colonial bureaucracy under the viceroy of India hoped to rule the area. The military forces at Sharif Husayn's disposal were limited. Even so, the Arab revolt in the desert caused the Ottoman army considerable problems, if only by the interruption of railway lines and the harassment of troops moving through the area.[17]

Until the collapse of Russia in 1917, the Ottoman armies did not score very many successes over the armies of the Tsar. However, against the British and their Dominions, the Ottomans did gain a major strategic victory during the summer of 1915, when the British navy, with considerable army support, attempted a landing. The original idea was to create a diversion from what was viewed as the principal theater of war, namely the western front. While this view prevailed, supplying the armies of the Tsar through the Black Sea was the true purpose of the campaign. However, in the minds of certain military planners, this enterprise was to serve more ambitious purposes as well: they envisaged occupying Istanbul and perhaps even winning the war against Germany by a piecemeal defeat of the Ottoman and Austro-Hungarian Empires. Because the British command did not wish to draw away many troops from the west, the landing was attempted with a limited number of soldiers, many of them Australians and New Zealanders (ANZACS).[18] A distinguished British war historian has concluded that even if the landing had succeeded, the enterprise as a whole would probably have failed.[19] After extremely hard fighting, the Ottoman troops were able to dislodge the invaders and force them to withdraw; Mustafa Kemal, then a colonel and corps commander, emerged as the outstanding figure of this campaign. The battle of Çanakkale/Gallipoli is today a major subject of historical memory, not only in Turkey but also in Australia, where the narrative of events connected to the battle has served as a kind of "foundation myth" of the state, at that time still a very recent political formation.

In addition, the Ottoman armies succeeded in containing a British invasion of southern Iraq, at least for a time. The invaders reached the vicinity of Baghdad but were decimated by fighting on the way. As for the survivors, they took refuge in the fort of Kut al-Amara but were cut off by the floods of the Tigris and after a lengthy siege were obliged to surrender to their Ottoman opponents in April 1916. However, the British took Baghdad in 1917, and late in 1918, after the armistice had already been concluded, occupied Mosul, a coveted prize because the region was known to contain oil supplies. Farther to the west, Cemal Paşa's attempt to seize the Suez Canal in February 1915 was not supported by the local uprising that he had apparently anticipated. Most of the troops were unable to approach the Canal and the campaign failed with a considerable loss of Ottoman soldiers.

The collapse of Russia's war effort in 1917 also entailed the breakaway of the empire's Caucasian possessions. For a brief moment, a Transcaucasian state was formed, but it soon dissolved into the three small republics of Georgia, Armenia, and Azerbaijan. While Azerbaijan was a Muslim state with a largely Shiite population, the other two were Christian. The Germans patronized Georgia in an attempt to gain access to the oilfields of Baku. In Ottoman government circles, there was an inclination to make up for the loss of long-standing possessions in the Balkans and the Arab world with conquests in this region, especially important because of the large local oil resources. It was also hoped that in this way a contact might be established with the Turcophone Muslims of Central Asia. For this purpose, an army was formed which scored some successes. But due to the ultimate victory of the Bolsheviks in Central Asia, these Ottoman attempts to establish a presence in the region failed just as badly as those undertaken by their opponents, the British, who had similar ideas in mind. Moreover, due to rivalry over the Baku oilfields, the Ottoman-German alliance in 1918 was strained to the breaking point.

The Arab revolt was secondary to the advance of regular British troops in Palestine. General Allenby took Jerusalem at the end of 1917 and in the course of the following year advanced steadily northward. But the Ottoman retreat took place in an orderly fashion and the British themselves did not anticipate an end to the war before 1919 or even 1920. That the Ottomans were forced to surrender in late 1918 was not because of any collapse on the Syrian front but because of events farther to the west. First, Bulgaria sued for an armistice, thus compromising the supply of German military material. Shortly afterwards, the Germans were beaten in France, and in November 1918 a revolution swept away the Kaiser and his government. Under these conditions, the Ottomans had little choice, and the armistice of Mudros was concluded on October 31, 1918. The principal Unionists left the country; Enver Paşa continued to chase his dream of establishing a Turkic state in Central Asia. After moving to the fledgling Soviet Union, he seemed at first to go along with the Bolsheviks, but he soon changed over to the anti-Bolshevik side and in 1922 was killed in battle in what is today Tajikistan.

War Financing and the Lives of "Ordinary People"

The sequence of wars that began with the confrontation over Tripoli in 1911 and continued until 1923 completely disrupted Ottoman finances and the livelihoods of ordinary people as well.[20] As the government was concerned about the possible failure of a drive to secure loans for the conduct of war from the citizenry, such an attempt was only made in 1918 under pressure from the German government. The drive was well publicized and even netted the Ottoman exchequer a significant sum during the last year of the war. Financing by means of taxes, by contrast, only covered a small part of expenses. German loans amounted to about 235 million Turkish liras; however, Ottoman war expenditures were largely financed by printing money.[21] As a result, the cost of living rose faster in the Ottoman Empire than among its allies or opponents. An economic historian specializing in the period even has claimed that inflation was introduced into the world's [economic] literature by the Committee of Union and Progress.[22]

Paper money and the concomitant inflation resulted in social upheaval. Receivers of fixed incomes and pensions suffered heavily; and as the public expected the devaluation of the currency to continue, there was a general flight away from money and a concomitant rise in demand for goods in the civilian market, quite apart from enormous war-related government purchases. Even worse, customers not only experienced bottlenecks in essential goods but expected worse hardship in the future: this anticipation encouraged not merely traders but also ordinary consumers to accumulate stocks of whatever commodities became available. As a result, price increases even went far beyond the levels that could have been expected in the face of rising military demand and currency inflation.

Traders were best placed to profit from stockpiling, and those that were in a strong position locally, perhaps because they also operated as money-lenders, obliged their dependents to sell them their small properties against paper currency. These processes resulted in a class of nouveau-riches and a concomitant loss of property among people of modest means. While in pre-war Istanbul people typically had owned their homes, these property sales and the influx of large numbers of refugees resulted in the emergence of a rental market, accompanied by numerous confrontations between landlords and tenants.

Another cause of distress was the difficulty of distributing food and other necessities to the civilian population. While the government entered the war with significant stocks, the interruption of trade with the numerous countries that aligned themselves with the Entente soon resulted in shortages. Wartime speculation included rapid resales of goods that were never consumed but gained in value each time they changed hands. Government attempts to foil speculators by ordering them to sell their wares back to the original owners at the prices they originally had paid for them were at best of limited effectiveness. Rationing was instituted and "official" prices were strictly controlled. But loopholes were numerous and no effective measures were taken against the "black market," partly because the Committee of Union and Progress wanted to establish a Muslim bourgeoisie and regarded war profits as a convenient way of providing candidates with the necessary capital. In addition, some Istanbul guilds were still powerful and generally supported the Committee, so that the government did not wish to alienate them. Those traders that were punished for profiteering thus were often either non-Muslims or people who for one reason or another had fallen afoul of the Committee of Union and Progress.[23]

Market connections between Istanbul and the provinces, problematic even in pre-war times because of the lack of transportation, were interrupted more often than not. Consequently, prices in Anatolian towns were frequently several times higher than those demanded in the capital. On the other hand, farmers were encouraged to increase production by the government's policy of paying primary producers relatively high prices. Many villagers thus were involved in the interregional market economy for the first time; but these economic advances were soon dwarfed by the enormous losses of manpower due to battles, expulsions, and epidemics.

Plans for Dismembering the Ottoman Empire

Plans to divide up Ottoman territories after the eventual fall of the ruling dynasty were certainly not a novelty of the early 1900s, having been made by various opponents of the sultan from the late sixteenth century onwards, and with special frequency during the 1800s. In the course of the First World War such projects once again emerged, this time the brainchild of Allied war planners. On the Russian side, the demand to control Istanbul and the Straits had been voiced many times over; but during the 1800s other European powers, especially Britain, had always rejected proposals of this kind. However, while Russia was an ally in the Great War, in other words until 1917, British politicians now were willing to concede this demand, perhaps in exchange for Russian concessions elsewhere. On the other hand, French colonialist circles demanded a controlling influence in the Ottoman provinces making up Greater Syria. Italy, neutral until 1915, was induced to enter the war on the side of the Entente not only by promises of Austro-Hungarian territory, but also by gains in the eastern Mediterranean. In 1916 a formal agreement was signed between Mark Sykes, who spoke for the British Minister of War Lord Kitchener, and François Georges Picot on behalf of the French Foreign Minister; later on, the French also came to an understanding with Sergei Sazonov of Russia. Differences in details notwithstanding, the three powers through these arrangements demarcated the Ottoman lands that after the war they intended to annex or at least control indirectly.[24]

Moreover, in 1917 the former British Prime Minister Balfour issued a declaration since known by his name that promised British aid in the establishment of a "Jewish homeland" in Palestine. This declaration was made in order to gain support from Zionist organizations; apparently British policy-makers of the time tended towards a somewhat exaggerated notion of Jewish power in the sultans' realm that they hoped to use in order to undermine Ottoman rule—in the early stages of the war they likewise had vastly overestimated the influence of a small number of Jews that were members of the Committee of Union and Progress.[25] In view of the alliance with Sharif Husayn, the wording of the declaration was intentionally kept vague. In the aftermath of the war, when Britain controlled Palestine, the contradictory promises made to Zionists and Arabs made for a host of political problems.

By the time the war ended, the Sykes-Picot-Sazonov agreement was considered irrelevant both by the British and by the Russians; for the October revolution of 1917 had brought the Bolsheviks to power in the territory that was to become the Soviet Union. The Bolsheviks denounced the imperial ambitions of their predecessors and published the secret treaties and understandings that their predecessors had concluded. As a result, the British government, now hoping for a larger share of the Ottoman booty, no longer felt bound by the agreement.

From Empire to Republic: Anatolia and Istanbul against the Treaty of Sèvres

The set of treaties that ended World War I but singularly failed to bring peace were negotiated between Britain, France, Italy, and the United States. However, the latter government ultimately withdrew from the peace agreement. Many organizations and states—including the sultan's government—sent delegates to plead their respective causes, but these demands were only taken into consideration insofar as it suited the small group of victorious Great Powers. For the most part, the defeated Central Powers were in no condition to continue fighting and could only accept the conditions imposed upon them.

The dismemberment of the Ottoman Empire decreed by the Treaty of Sèvres included the loss of the Arab provinces. This arrangement conformed to the Sykes-Picot-Sazonov agreement but was somewhat modified because of the American President Woodrow Wilson's disapproval of the institution of new colonies. Instead, France received the Syrian provinces apart from Palestine as so-called mandates from the newly formed League of Nations; as we have seen, Palestine was taken over by the British. The difference between colonies and mandates was on the whole minor, but mandates were—in principle at least—intended to be temporary. However, after having driven Sharif Husayn out of the Syrian cities that he previously had been promised, the French government made it fairly clear that it regarded the takeover as permanent.

From the viewpoint of the Ottoman elite, a much more serious loss was the division of the Turkish-speaking area, which had not been occupied by the Allies when the armistice of Mudros was concluded. By the Treaty of Sèvres, territories in eastern Anatolia were awarded to the Republic of Armenia and promises of autonomy were made to the Kurds. In addition, it was foreseen that after a transition period, Izmir would go to the Greeks. France appropriated territories adjacent to its Syrian mandate, particularly Maraş (today: Kahramanmaraş) and Ayntab (today: Gaziantep). Italy was assigned certain Aegean islands, including Rhodes, and the mainland town of Antalya. But the British government seems to have had second thoughts: when in 1919 the Italians did land in Anatolia, the British Prime Minister David Lloyd George encouraged Britain's client state of Greece to occupy Izmir right away in order to forestall any further territorial gains on the part of Italy. The Allies completely occupied Istanbul in March 1920 and remained until 1923. Many non-Muslims welcomed this occupation; the local Greek community even declared that it no longer owed allegiance to the Ottoman government. These events, singularly humiliating for the Muslims, left a legacy of lasting bitterness.[26]

The recently enthroned Sultan Mehmed VI Vahdeddin seems to have accepted his position as an Allied figurehead because he viewed this as the only way to retain his throne. In Anatolia, however, sections of the former Ottoman army were still intact. In the spring of 1919 Mustafa Kemal Paşa, the victor of Gallipoli who was largely responsible for the orderly Ottoman retreat through Syria in 1918, was given a mandate to use these troops in order to suppress the banditry, both political and non-political, that was rife in many parts of Anatolia during that period. The date of his landing in Samsun (May 19, 1919) is today celebrated as the beginning of the struggle for a Turkish national state.

A degree of political organization was also present in postwar Anatolia; while the government of Enver, Cemal, and Talat had disappeared, the "Unionist factor" was still a force to be reckoned with in many Anatolian towns.[27] Local societies "for the defense of rights" that organized resistance against the Treaty of Sèvres were typically created and run by former Unionists. However, because in the country as a whole the Committee was widely regarded as responsible for the recent lost war, and also to facilitate future relations with the major Allies, the delegates assembled at a founding congress in Sivas in 1919 swore that they would not revive the Committee of Union and Progress.

In this assembly and others of similar purpose held at this time, in which Mustafa Kemal Paşa took on the key role, the delegates agreed on the demand for an independent state within the borders of what had been Ottoman territory not occupied by the Allies at the time of the Mudros armistice.[28] Later in 1919 Mustafa Kemal Paşa and his closest collaborators, now often known as the Nationalists, established themselves in Ankara, which in 1923 became the capital of the newly founded Republic of Turkey.

In January 1920 the last Ottoman parliament began its work in Istanbul: the largely Muslim voters returned a body that was overwhelmingly in favor of the Nationalists and out of sympathy with Sultan Vahdeddin. This split between the monarch and the politically minded elite made it possible for officials technically in the service of the sultan to give assistance to what had become the de facto government in Ankara. Even after the delegates assembled in this town had declared themselves the National Assembly in April 1920 and thereby embarked on a collision course with the sultan, unofficial cooperation between certain administrators of both sides continued. As for Sultan Vahdeddin, he was adamant in his opposition to the Nationalists, and quite a few rebellions in Anatolia against the rule of the National Assembly were undertaken in the name of the sultan-caliph. However, to placate conservative adherents of the sultanate in Anatolia, the National Assembly steadfastly claimed to be acting in the name of the monarch, no longer a free agent because of the Allied occupation. Therefore speakers of the National Assembly were able to argue that the ruler's condemnation of their actions was not to be taken seriously. This contradiction was only resolved when Sultan Vahdettin went into exile in November 1922. A year later, in October 1923, the sultanate was abolished and the republic instituted; at the same time, the British finally evacuated Istanbul.

The Wars in Anatolia and the Greco-Turkish Population Exchange

The Allies thus were unable to enforce the Treaty of Sèvres without major armed intervention. In addition, the Italian government was not convinced that its best interests were served by such a policy.[29] Both Britain and France were exhausted by the war and unable to pay large bodies of troops, and the latter demanded demobilization at the earliest opportunity. Given this situation, the Italian government soon sought to come to an understanding with the Nationalists, with whom economic relations might be instituted in the future. Italian troops accordingly pulled out of Antalya, and in the fall of 1921 the French followed suit, evacuating Maraş and Ayntab.

On the eastern border, the Nationalist government, at war with Armenia over the territory that the latter state had been promised by the Allies, reached an agreement with the Soviet Union; for the Bolshevik government was intent on regaining Armenia, Georgia, and Azerbaijan, which, as we have seen, had previously declared independence. A pact concluded between the Ankara government and the Soviet Union in March 1921 netted the Nationalists money and supplies that could be used on the eastern front against Armenia. But just as importantly, through this treaty the government of the National Assembly gained international recognition by a major power for the first time. At the end of the Caucasian war, the borders with Armenia were determined by agreements concluded in the towns of Kars and Gümrü in October and December 1921, respectively; they are valid to the present day.[30]

Fighting in the west was much more prolonged and serious. In June 1920 Greek troops left Izmir, aiming at further conquests in Anatolia. In this military adventure the Prime Minister Venizelos had the support of his British colleague David Lloyd George. But Venizelos was voted out of office, and it fell to his successor to take responsibility for the ensuing defeat. While Greek troops were within a few miles of Ankara in 1921, they were driven off by the Turkish army in a series of battles and suffered the decisive defeat in August 1922. A few days later, in September 1922, the Greek troops were back at their starting point in Izmir. The war was fought with much brutality: the destruction of villages and massacres of civilians were commonplace occurrences; and after the Nationalist takeover, a fire devastated mainly the non-Muslim parts of Izmir, leaving one of the formerly most active and thriving cities of the now defunct Empire a mere smoking ruin.[31]

It was against this background of mutual hatred that the Treaty of Lausanne (July 14, 1923), which finally concluded the series of wars that had plagued the inhabitants of Thrace, Istanbul, and Anatolia since 1911, stipulated a compulsory exchange of populations between Turkey and Greece. Muslim refugees had left Greece and quite a few Greeks had fled Anatolia "on their own" especially in the days before Mustafa Kemal Paşa's army entered Izmir. Now the remainder were also obliged to leave. Greece was saddled with approximately 1.1 million immigrants, while about 380,000 refugees arrived in Turkey. In what might be viewed as a throwback to Ottoman times, religion, rather than language or cultural identity, was deemed the criterion by which the authorities determined who had to leave. Thus at a late stage of the negotiations, the Orthodox Karamanlıs were included in the exchange even though they spoke Turkish as their native language; and the same procedure was applied to Greek-speaking Cretan Muslims.[32]

Many of the new arrivals in both cases were completely destitute, and for several decades the loss of the non-Muslim populations hampered the development of trade and crafts in Anatolia. In Greece, refugees from the same region were encouraged to form new communities whose names were often reminiscent of the places the refugees had left; and state aid to the newcomers was financed by foreign loans. In Turkey, by contrast, such loans were on the whole avoided; in addition, building a homogenous nation was a priority, and the newcomers were thus directed to whatever town quarters and villages had been vacated by the Greeks. For several decades, immigrants from Balkan countries typically had a higher degree of schooling than many locals, and thus some of them were able to build careers in the professions. Memories of the "old country," however, were relegated to the private sphere; and there they have remained.[33]

In Lieu of a Conclusion: Continuities and New Beginnings

Consonant with the radical modernizing project of Mustafa Kemal Paşa, soon to be known as Atatürk, the proclamation of the republic in 1923 was, for a considerable time, viewed as a clean break with the past, not only by politicians but also by historians. The transition to the Latin alphabet in 1928, the expansion of schooling, the restructuring of Istanbul University and the founding of its Ankara counterpart, the vote given to women, who now were able to enter professional life—all these factors were regarded as indications of a new society in the making.

Continuities over Long Periods

On the other hand, some historians born in the 1950s and thus viewing the early republic from a certain distance have concluded that the continuities between the late Ottoman Empire and the early republic are more significant than the differences. A social and economic historian of Marxian inspiration has even proposed that a strong thread of continuity connects Byzantine, Ottoman, and early republican history.[1] The two empires both experienced periods of centralization and decentralization; but the fundamental socio-political setup—relations of production in the author's terminology—did not change. In both cases, a central administration consisting of military men, bureaucrats, and officers of the palace taxed the peasants and attempted to keep local aristocrats or notables under control. Traders and artisans, while not unimportant as purveyors and producers of goods, were never able to challenge either the central government or local power-brokers. A transition to capitalism was thus out of the question in either case.

From this perspective, the early republic did not bring any dramatic change: on the contrary, due to the disappearance of the non-Muslim bourgeoisie of the late Ottoman Empire, officials and military men dominated the life of the country without significant challenges until the period following World War II. After all, the world economic crisis of the 1930s and the Second World War greatly impeded trade. A low degree of integration into the market, in turn, meant widespread poverty made worse by the fact that the country had not yet been able to compensate for the exodus of entrepreneurial talent before, during, and after the First World War. Only in the 1950s, after the single party system had been dismantled and the newly formed bourgeoisie, both urban and rural, was able to make its voice heard politically, was there a "real" transition into the modern world. Doubtless, this perspective was inspired by the much fuller integration into the world market that Turkey experienced after 1980, when the author conceived his study.

On a more short-term political level, the continuity problem has been tackled by a researcher studying the Committee of Union and Progress.[2] Here, the continuities in terms of personnel form the crucial issue: as we have seen, the provincial cadres whose mobilization made military victory in Anatolia and revision of the Sèvres treaty possible quite often had been involved to some extent with the Committee of Union and Progress. Given the narrow basis for political participation in the late Ottoman Empire, it could scarcely have been otherwise. These men had quite often benefited materially from the war and could only hope to hold on to their gains if the Nationalists were able to take power.

On the other hand, it is important to avoid over-simplification: we have seen that in the Sivas congress the delegates swore that they would not revive the Committee. Moreover, shortly after the republic had been established, the Kemalist group, now securely in power, divested itself from a number of former Committee members through a series of show trials.[3] These latter events were in fact instrumental in making historians wonder about the specific relationship between Unionists and Kemalists. If viewed in this light, continuity and contradiction thus are closely intertwined.

Modernity, No Brainchild of the Early Republic: The Re-valuation of Sultan Abdülhamid

Mostly undertaken in the 1980s, other studies emphasized that significant steps towards modernity had already been carried out in the late nineteenth century. In this period a few regions of the Empire experienced significant population growth—a fact often forgotten because the wars and expulsions of 1911-1923 largely nullified its effects. Trade expanded and artisan producers, far from disappearing, often adapted to the changing conditions of the world market, albeit at the price of long hours and minimal wages.[4] Although the Ottoman Empire was not well supplied with railways, enough of them had been built by century's end to encourage agriculture in western Anatolia by allowing producers access to the Istanbul market. Educational opportunities also expanded, as modern schools were founded to train officers, administrators, and professional men, although non-Muslims tended to benefit more from these advantages than Muslims did.

In addition, the state apparatus was overhauled: even if bureaucratic inefficiency remained a common problem, many aspects of the legal system had been changed in order to facilitate trade, with the institution of private property in land a crucial factor. In the second half of the nineteenth century modern-style urban administrations were founded not only in big cities like Istanbul, Izmir, and Salonika, but also in some small Anatolian towns.[5] While often limited in their endeavors by lack of funds, the councilmen who administered these places raised money for urban improvements like street widening and paving, for public construction in general, and for fire-fighting. Now that many sections of the nineteenth-century Ottoman archives have become accessible, their efforts are more widely appreciated than they were thirty years ago. Recent studies of Ottoman towns in the late 1800s and early 1900s have also discussed the crucial question of agency: to what extent were reforms imposed by governors and edicts from the center, and to what extent were local elites and sometimes even artisans able to contribute toward determining the shape that their home towns were to take?

Even feminist historians have submitted some positive findings concerning the situation of women in the years before and after 1900.

Certainly it would be difficult to claim that the Hamidian regime, or the Committee of Union and Progress for that matter, did much to enhance the status of women. Even under the Unionists, rhetoric trumped action; schools for girls always lagged far behind those for boys. Yet historians of the press have pointed out that contrary to the widespread assumption that Turkish women did not struggle for their rights but were simply granted them during the early republic as part of the modernizing "package," around 1900 a small but active minority of women did campaign for education and a role in the public domain. However, because the modernizing package was put together by men, they were obliged to be circumspect in their demands. Very often it seemed more effective to advocate education so as to further the health and safety of future generations.

As a result of these studies, the reign of Sultan Abdülhamid II, previously abhorred by most authors of even moderately liberal persuasions, has received some belated recognition.[6] While the stultifying effects of censorship upon literature and intellectual life in general are acknowledged, the use of religion as a means of building solidarity is no longer regarded as incompatible with a modernizing project. Thus recent historians have come to regard Abdülhamid's attempts to strengthen the Empire by establishing contact with Muslims under colonial domination as a viable effort, especially where India is concerned. The sultans interest in modernizing projects also has emerged, in rather a backhanded way, from his attempts to promote conversion to Sunnite "right belief" among his subjects in Iraq in order to make attempts at subversion more difficult: for the tactics applied in this campaign owed something to those of Christian missionaries, otherwise Abdülhamid's *bête noire*.[7]

Art and Culture in the "Modernity" Project of the Late Ottoman Empire

Historians of art have made a particular contribution to the reassessment of late Ottoman modernity. In part, this move is connected to the fact that the architecture of the Belle Époque is now esteemed by many post-modernists; as a result, buildings in the eclectic/historicist style of the Hamidian period in Istanbul have also been regarded as worthy of protection. In addition, the sultan was a patron of photography and photographers; these works are now viewed not merely as historical documents but also as important cultural contributions. Thus this ruler has enjoyed some reflected prestige because he sponsored the works of artists, including the Armenian family of photographers known as Abdullah Frères.

Furthermore, the publication of memoirs by numerous figures born into elite families during the early 1900s has demonstrated that during that period many upper-class Ottoman Muslims were widely traveled, had visited European countries at length, and possessed a good grasp of the realities of the societies they had visited. But the wars of 1911–1923, the world economic crisis, and World War II and its aftermath produced a generation many of whose members regarded travel and the concomitant knowledge of foreign languages and the world at large as strange and somewhat objectionable luxuries. The renewed emergence of a cosmopolitan outlook has probably made us more sensitive to such issues. Children of Turkish workers educated in European countries, but also scholars, artists, and others who have spent a considerable portion of their lives abroad, all have connections to relatives, friends, and colleagues outside of Turkey. The strident nationalism which can be observed in other sections of present-day society may well be at least in part a reaction to such (re)emerging cosmopolitanism: the historian will soon discover that a comparable conflict existed at the time of the Committee of Union and Progress.

But even if we admit strong elements of continuity between late Ottomans and their great-grandchildren of Republican times, there are sharp breaks that must also be taken into account. Language and literature are prominent examples. A journal recently published two translations of Hamlet's famous monologue: while the translation from the 1940s or early 1950s is perfectly comprehensible to the modern public, that of 1912 appears to have been written in another language. Moreover, it is not only a question of vocabulary: during the forty years that encompass the end of the Ottoman Empire and the early republic, sentence structure also has changed significantly.[8] Literary taste is a related example: while the modern reader of Ottoman poetry needs to reconstruct a whole different world before he/she can appreciate a work of the eighteenth or even nineteenth century, authors who flourished in the 1940s or 1950s still find their reading public without too much difficulty.

Summing Up the Debate: Nostalgia versus Realism

Thus it does not seem reasonable to simply deny discontinuities. But even so, if the re-valuations we have briefly introduced here are at all realistic, the early republic deserves less credit for setting the Ottoman provinces that now form Turkey on the road to modernity than had previously been assumed. However, we must not forget that many achievements of the late nineteenth century disappeared without a trace during the wars that followed. In quite a few cases, people who lived in the 1920s and 1930s thus had to begin all over again; and only half a century later, in the 1970s and 1980s, did historians rediscover the modernizing impulses of the years before and after 1900.

It is interesting to see, however, that the renewed esteem for the Ottoman past does not include sympathy for monarchy. Certainly the artistic contribution of the last caliph Abdülmecid, who developed a second identity as an academic painter, is highly valued today, but that is not a political matter. While members of the Ottoman dynasty are now allowed to live in Turkey, they are not known to the public at large and play no political role.

Certainly the mere passage of time has encouraged the growth of nostalgia: people who have personal memories of the Hamidian period are no longer alive, but the same cannot be said of the early republic. As a result, the difficulties of life in the late 1800s are less present in the public mind than those of the 1930s or 1940s. People choose to remember horse-drawn coaches and ladies with parasols, the celebrated "life in the villa," preferably located on the shores of the Bosporus (*köşk hayatı*). As for the troubles of immigrants, servants, and widows, who made up a large part of Istanbul's population, they have long since been forgotten.

Given this state of affairs, it is only prudent to make allowances for the effects of the nostalgia culture that exists all over the world but is especially pronounced in Istanbul. The renewed prosperity of the city after several decades in limbo has entered the public consciousness largely through its negative effects. Destruction of monuments to allow street widening or new construction, the use of concrete instead of wood as a building material, the often remarkable lack of aesthetic values, and sensitivity to the natural environment in public building projects have all encouraged the glorification of the late 1800s, when supposedly life was simpler and more beautiful. Interestingly, the public discourse about the disadvantages of change in the urban fabric was already well developed before there was much construction in real life, in the 1950s if not earlier. But with prosperity and the gentrification of previously poor town quarters, Istanbul nostalgia for the Belle Époque Ottoman style seems to grow apace.[9]

However, as a female scholar—and the gender component must be taken very seriously—I have doubts that this laudatory discourse really captures reality "on the ground" in the late Ottoman period; and I remain convinced that historians should try to the best of their abilities to keep a distance from nostalgia and fantasy.[10]

Chronology

1326	Ottoman conquest of Bursa
1331	Conquest of Iznik (Nicaea)
1352	Beginning of the Ottoman conquests in Thrace
c. 1361	Conquest of Edirne (Adrianople)
1376	Andronicos V crowned as Byzantine emperor with Ottoman aid, hands over Gelibolu (Gallipoli) to the Ottomans
1389	Battle of Kosovo. Death of Sultan Murad I; Sultan Bayezid I accedes to the throne
1389–92	Ottoman conquest of numerous small Anatolian principalities
1396	Bayezid I defeats European Crusader army near Nicopolis
1398	Ottoman conquest of the Bulgarian principality of Vidin
1402	Bayezid I defeated by Timur and taken prisoner. Restoration of the Anatolian principalities
1402–13	Interregnum; the sons of Bayezid I fight each other for the Ottoman throne
1430	Ottoman conquest of Salonika (Thessaloniki), formerly Byzantine and recently handed over to the Venetians
1444	Defeat of European coalition army near Varna
1451–81	(Second) sultanate of Mehmed II, "The Conqueror"
1453	Conquest of Constantinople (Istanbul) by Mehmed II
1460–64	Ottoman conquest of the Peloponnesus
1468–74	Definitive conquest of the central Anatolian principality of Karaman
1470	Completion by Mehmed the Conqueror of a major complex of mosque, theological colleges, and other charities in Istanbul, in the urban quarter today known as Fatih (meaning "Conqueror")
1473	Mehmed II's defeat of Uzun Hasan, ruler of the Ak Koyunlu
1483	A struggle for the throne between Bayezid II (r. 1481–1512) and Prince Cem ends with Cem's flight to Rhodes
1484–91	War between Ottomans and Mamluks
1500–04	Shah Ismail consolidates his power in Iran and Iraq
1514	Selim I defeats Shah Ismail at Çaldıran (Iran); short-lived Ottoman occupation of Tabriz

1516–17	Ottoman conquest of Syria and Egypt; end of the Mamluk sultanate. Mecca and Medina become Ottoman cities
1521	Conquest of Belgrade, until then the southern border fortress of the kingdom of Hungary
1522	Conquest of Rhodes, previously occupied by the Order of St. John
1526–41	Battle of Mohács. Hungary becomes an Ottoman province
1529	First siege of Vienna
1543	Capture of Nice by French-Ottoman fleet
1551	Conquest of Tripoli (Lybia)
1556	Completion of the Süleyman Mosque along with the adjacent schools and other charities (Istanbul)
1570–73	Ottoman conquest of Cyprus
1571	Defeat of the Ottoman fleet at Lepanto
1574	Third (and final) conquest of Tunis
1574	Completion of the Selimiye Mosque (Edirne)
1578–90	War with Iran
1593–1606	Ottoman-Habsburg War ("Long War") in Hungary
1596	Ottoman victory near Mezőkeresztes
1617	Completion of the Sultan Ahmed Mosque (Istanbul)
1623	Conquest of Ottoman Baghdad by Shah Abbas of Iran
1638	Campaign of Murad IV against the Shah; reconquest of Baghdad
1645–69	Ottoman conquest of Crete
1656–61	Grand Vizierate of Mehmed Köprülü
1660–64	Ottoman-Habsburg War
1661–76	Grand Vizierate of Fazil Ahmed Köprülü
1663	Defeat of Ottoman troops near St. Gotthard/Raab
1672	Ottoman conquest of Kamieniecz-Podolsk (greatest territorial extent of the empire)
1681	Friede of Radzin; a no-man's-land divides Russian from Ottoman territory
1683	Second siege of Vienna
1686	Habsburg conquest of Buda (present-day Budapest)
1687	Venetian attacks on Ottoman territory in Greece; destruction of the Parthenon. Deposition of Mehmed IV

1697	Defeat of the Ottomans near Zenta
1703	Deposition of Sultan Mustafa II
1703–30	Reign of Sultan Ahmed III; height of courtly elegance in the so-called Tulip Age
1705	Beginning of autonomy of Tunis under a local dynasty
1716–18	Habsburg-Ottoman War
1720	Recovery of the Peloponnesus, previously occupied by the Venetians
1725–83	The 'Azm rule Damascus as local potentates
1755	Completion of the Nuruosmaniye Mosque (Istanbul)
1763–73	The Mamluk lord (bey) Ali al-Kabir controls Egypt
1768–74	Russo-Ottoman War, which ends with the Treaty of Küçük Kaynarca, results in heavy losses for the Ottomans
1783	Tsarina Catharina II annexes the Crimea
1788–1822	Tepedelenli Ali Paşa controls a large portion of the western Balkans
1791	Selim III creates a new army corps, known as the "New Order"
1798	Napoleon's invasion of Egypt
1807	Deposition of Selim III following a janissary revolt
1808–39	Government of Mahmud II; he breaks the power of numerous local rulers in the Balkans and in Anatolia
1821–30	Greek revolt crushed by the troops of Mehmed Ali/Muhammad Ali Pasha, governor of Egypt. The European great powers, however, install a Greek state on the Peloponnese and Attica
1826	Mahmud II destroys the janissaries. Formation of a new army corps, the "Victorious Soldiers of Muhammad"
1828–29	Russo-Ottoman War
1830	Recognition of Serbia as an autonomous principality
1831	The troops of Mehmed Ali Pasha, now in rebellion against the sultan, reach the town of Kütahya in western Anatolia
1833	Russians offer military assistance to the Ottomans. Treaty of Hünkâr İskelesi
1839	Ottoman troops defeated by Mehmed Ali's troops at Nizip
1839	Edict of Gülhane: Tanzimat era begins

1840	Mehmed Ali is forced by the intervention of the European great powers to once again recognize the Ottoman sultan as his sovereign
1853–56	Crimean War
1856	Second Tanzimat Edict ends the legal privileges of the Muslims
1876–77	First Ottoman constitution; soon suspended by Abdülhamid II
1878	Russian troops reach the suburbs of Istanbul; Treaty of San Stefano; Congress of Berlin: creation of an autonomous principality of Bulgaria
1897	Greek-Ottoman War ends with Ottoman victory
1908	"Young Turk" revolt forces Abdülhamid II to restore the constitution
1909	After a failed anti-constitutional revolt, deposition of Abdülhamid
1911	Occupation of Tripoli by Italy
1912–13	First Balkan War: Serbia, Montenegro, Greece, and Bulgaria capture Macedonia and Edirne
1913	Second Balkan War; Ottoman re-conquest of Edirne
1914	Participation in World War I on the side of the Central Powers; heavy losses at Sarıkamış
1915	Successful defense of Gallipoli (Çanakkale in Turkish parlance) against British Commonwealth and French troops
1915	Sykes-Picot Agreement to divide the Empire into English and French colonies or spheres of influence
1918	Advance of Ottoman troops in the Caucasus territory; retreat of Ottoman troops in Syria and Palestine; Armistice of Mudros
1920	Division of the Ottoman Empire through the Treaty of Sèvres
1919–22	Greek attack on Western Anatolia; then defeated by Ottoman army corps, reinforced by locally recruited troops under the command of Mustafa Kemal Pasha
1922	Flight of Sultan Mehmed VI Vahdeddin; abolition of the sultanate
1923	Treaty of Lausanne; recognition under international law of the Republic of Turkey; Greco-Turkish population exchange

Ottoman Sultans

(According to Halil Inalcik, *The Ottoman Empire.
The Classical Age 1300–1600*. Some sultans have sobriquets;
in some cases, these are as widely used as the names.)

Osman I (died 1326)

Orhan (1326–1362)

Murad I Hüdavendigâr (1362–1389)

Bayezid I Yıldırım (1389–1402)

Civil war among Bayezid's sons until 1413

Mehmed I Kirişçi (1413–1421)

Murad II (1421–1444, 1446–1451)

Mehmed II Fatih (1444–1446, 1451–1481)

Bayezid II Veli (1481–1512)

Selim I Yavuz (1512–1520)

Süleyman Kanuni/Suleiman the Magnificent (1520–1566)

Selim II (1566–1574)

Murad III (1574–1595)

Mehmed III (1595–1603)

Ahmed I (1603–1617)

Mustafa I (1617–1618, 1622–1623)

Osman II Genç (1618–1622)

Murad IV (1623–1640)

İbrahim, Deli (1640–1648)

Mehmed IV Avcı (1648–1687)

Süleyman II (1687–1691)

Ahmed II (1691–1695)

Mustafa II (1695–1703)

Ahmed III (1703–1730)

Mahmud I (1730–1754)

Osman III (1754–1757)

Mustafa IV (1757–1774)

Abdülhamid I (1774–1789)

Selim III (1789–1807)

Mustafa IV (1807–1808)

Mahmud II Adli (1808–1839)

Abdülmecid I (1839–1861)

Abdülaziz (1861–1876)

Murad V (1876)

Abdülhamid II (1876–1909)

Mehmed V Reşad (1909–1918)

Mehmed VI Vahdeddin (1918–1922)

Abdülmecid II (only caliph, 1922–1923)

Notes

Acknowledgments

1. Caroline Finkel, *Osman's Dream. The Story of the Ottoman Empire 1300-1923* (London: John Murray, 2006).

Introduction

1. The work of Charles Wilkins on 17th century Aleppo, currently in press, has shown that slaves in that city were in their overwhelming majority Russian-Ukrainian as well as Georgian.
2. Martin Hinds, Victor Menage (eds.), *Qasr Ibrīm in the Ottoman Period: Turkish and Further Arabic Documents* (London, Egypt Exploration Society, 1991), pp. 103-106.
3. Cengiz Orhonlu, *Osmanlı İmparatorluğunun Güney Siyaseti, Habeş Eyaleti* (Istanbul: İ.Ü. Edebiyat Fakültesi, 1974); Salih Özbaran, *Yemen'den Basra'ya Sınırdaki Osmanlı* (Istanbul: Kitap Yayınevi, 2003).
4. Halil Inalcik, "Ottoman Methods of Conquest," *Studia Islamica*, III (1954), pp. 103-129.
5. Abdul-Rahim Abu-Husayn, *Provincial Leaderships in Syria 1575-1650* (Beirut: AUB, 1985).
6. Ariel Salzmann, "An Ancien Régime Revisited: 'Privatization' and Political Economy in the Eighteenth-century Ottoman Empire," *Politics and Society*, XXI (1993) 4: 393-423.
7. Kate Fleet and Maurits H. van den Boogert (eds.), *The Ottoman Capitulations. Text and Context* (Naples/Cambridge: Istituto A. Nallino and Silliter Centre, 2003).
8. Oliver Jens Schmitt, *Levantiner. Lebenswelten und Identitäten einer ethnokonfessionellen Gruppe im osmanischen Reich im „langen 19. Jahrhundert"* (Munich: Südost Europa Institut, 2004); Marie-Carmen Smyrnelis, *Une société hors de soi. Identités et relations sociales à Smyrne aux XVIIIème et XIXème siècles* (Paris, Leuven: Peeters, 2005).
9. Virginia Aksan, *Ottoman Wars 1700-1870. An Empire Besieged* (London, New York: Pearson Longman, 2007), pp. 59-69.
10. The prospective authors are Ali Yaycıoğlu and Esra Danacı for the period of Selim III, and Meinolf Arens, Denise Klein, and Natalia Krolikowska for the khanate of the Crimea, in addition to Alp Yücel Kaya on private

property and economic data collection during the Tanzimat. See Huri Islamoğlu (ed.), *Constituting Modernity: Private Property in the East and West* (London and New York: I. B. Tauris, 2004).

11. For a polemical but stimulating discussion of Turkish nationalism in the late Ottoman Empire see Halil Berktay, "Küme Düşme Korkusuna Osmanlı-Türk Reaksyonu," in *Dünyada Türk İmgesi*, ed. Özlem Kumrular (Istanbul: Kitap Yayınevi, 2005), pp. 179-204.
12. Maurus Reinkowski, *Die Dinge der Ordnung. Eine vergleichende. Untersuchung über die osmanische Reformpolitik im 19. Jahrhundert* (Munich: Oldenbourg, 2005).
13. Carter Findley, *Bureaucratic Reform in the Ottoman Empire, The Sublime Porte 1789-1922* (Princeton: Princeton University Press, 1980), p. 85.
14. Ferdan Ergut, *Modern Devlet ve Polis, Osmanlı'dan Cumhuriyet'e Toplumsal Denetimin Diyalektiği* (Istanbul: İletişim, 2004).
15. A Turco-French conference on this issue was held at the University of the Bosporus/Istanbul in January 2008.
16. Compare the recent doctoral theses of Betül Başaran and Cengiz Kırlı.
17. Paper given orally by Cengiz Kırlı, who is preparing an edition.
18. Nora Lafi, *Une ville du Maghreb: Tripoli entre Ancien régime et réformes ottomanes (1795-1911)* (Paris, L'Harmattan, 2002).
19. I owe this information to Erdem Kabadayı, who is about to defend a dissertation on the subject.
20. Donald Quataert, *Miners and the State in the Ottoman Empire, The Zonguldak Coalfield 1822-1920* (New York, Oxford: Berghahn Books, 2006).
21. John Chalcraft, *The Striking Cabbies of Cairo and Other Stories, Crafts and Guilds in Egypt 1863-1914* (Albany NY: SUNY Press, 2004).
22. Fatmagül Demirel, *II. Abdülhamid Döneminde Sansür* (Istanbul: Bağlam Yayınevi, 2007).
23. Yavuz Selim Karakışla, *Women, War and Work in the Ottoman Empire. The Society for the Employment of Ottoman Muslim Women 1916-1923* (Istanbul: Ottoman Bank Archives and Research Centre, 2005).
24. Zafer Toprak, *İttihad-Terakki ve Cihan Harbı, Savaş Ekonomisi ve Türkiye'de Devletçilik 1914-1918* (İstanbul: Homer Kitabevi, 2003), p. 175.
25. Selçuk Esenbel, "Japanese Perspectives of the Ottoman World," in *The Rising Sun and the Turkish Crescent, New Perspectives on the History of Japanese-Turkish Relations*, ed. by Selçuk Esenbel and Inaba Chiharū (Istanbul: Boğaziçi University Press, 2003), pp. 7-41. I am most grateful to the author for her advice on this section.
26. İsmail Hakkı Uzunçarşılı, *Osmanlı Tarihi*, 4 vols. (Ankara: Türk Tarih

Kurumu, reprint 1977, 1982, 1983); Halil Inalcik, *The Ottoman Empire, The Classical Age, 1300-1600* (Weidenfeld & Nicholson, 1973); Stanford J. Shaw, *History of the Ottoman Empire and Modern Turkey*, 2 vols., vol. II coauthored with Ezel Kural Shaw (Cambridge: Cambridge University Press, 1977).

27. Robert Mantran (ed.), *Histoire de l'Empire Ottoman* (Paris: Fayard, 1989); Ekmeleddin İhsanoğlu (ed.), *Osmanlı Devleti ve Medeniyeti Tarihi* (Istanbul: IRSICA, 1994); Halil Inalcik with Donald Quataert (eds.) *An Economic and Social History of the Ottoman Empire, 1300-1914* (Cambridge: Cambridge University Press, 1994); Halil İnalcık and Günsel Renda eds., *Ottoman Civilization*, 2 vols. (Ankara: Ministry of Culture, 2002).
28. Justin McCarthy, *The Ottoman Turks, an Introductory History to 1923* (London: Addison Wesley Longman Ltd., 1997).
29. *The Cambridge History of Turkey* (Cambridge/Engl.: Cambridge University Press, 2006-). Volumes 4 (ed. by Reşat Kasaba) and 1 (ed. by Kate Fleet) are to be published in 2008, while volume 2 is scheduled for 2009. As for volume 3 (ed. by this author) it was published in 2006. Virginia Aksan, *Ottoman Wars 1700-1870* and Caroline Finkel, *Osman's Dream. The Story of the Ottoman Empire 1300-1923* (London: John Murray, 2005).
30. Evliya Çelebi, *Evliya Çelebi Seyahatnamesi, İstanbul Üniversitesi Kütüphanesi Türkçe Yazmalar 5973, Süleymaniye Kütüphanesi Pertev Paşa 462, Süleymaniye Kütüphanesi Hacı Beşir Ağa 452 Numaralı Yazmaların Mukayeseli Transkripsyonu-Dizini*, ed. by Seyit Ali Kahraman, Yücel Dağlı, Robert Dankoff (Istanbul: YKY, 2007).

Chapter 1

1. Sources differ on Ibn Battuta's year of death.

Chapter 2

1. The official explanation was that coffee had an intoxicating effect similar to wine, which Islamic religious law forbids. But it appears more likely that the objection was rooted in the sociability of the coffee house, where it was difficult to monitor what the male residents of the city were discussing.
2. This expression was used to designate a heterodox group that is still found today in Anatolia; it is now considered disrespectful and has been replaced by "Alevi."

3. Seyyidî Alî Reîs, *Le Miroir des pays. Une anabase ottomane à travers l'Inde et l'Asie centrale*, trans. Jean-Louis Bacqué-Grammont (Paris: Sindbad, Actes Sud, 1999).
4. See Cornell Fleischer, *Bureaucrat and Intellectual in the Ottoman Empire, The Historian Mustafa Âli (1541-1600)* (Princeton: Princeton Univ. Press, 1986), p. 298. As modern as this argumentation sounds, it is in line with the thinking of many Islamic legal and religious scholars. It was considered excusable for a man in dire economic straits to limit the number of his children, as long as his wife consented. It is revealing to compare this attitude to a Western practice, still widespread in the Victorian Age, that a woman with a known susceptibility to tuberculosis would be expected to endure numerous pregnancies if her "loving" husband so desired.

Chapter 3

1. Leslie Peirce, *The Imperial Harem, Women and Sovereignty in the Ottoman Empire* (New York, Oxford: Oxford University Press, 1993).
2. In the mid-15th century, the Ottoman sultans abandoned the custom of marrying daughters of neighboring rulers. The end of the Anatolian small principalities contributed to this development, as did the fact that after 1500, Shiite princesses from Iran were not regarded as suitable candidates for marriage because of their religious convictions. Also the organization of the male section of the sultan's palace seems to have provided a model for the harem. Yet even more than the pages who were dependent servitors (*kul*), the women of the harem were subordinate to the ruler, as they had entered the palace as his slaves. Daughters of Indian or central Asian rulers would have had a great deal of difficulty adapting to an organization of this kind.
3. The people discussed here have been chosen because there have been recent monographs about them; Gottfried Hagen, *Ein osmanischer Geograph bei der Arbeit. Entstehung und Gedankenwelt von Katib Celebis Ğihannüma* (Berlin: Klaus Schwarz Verlag, 2003); Robert Dankoff, *The World of Evliya Çelebi* (Leiden: E. J. Brill, 2006).
4. On Kâtib Çelebi's autobiography, see his *The Balance of Truth*, translated by G.L. Lewis (London, 1957).
5. Evliyâ Çelebi, *Evliya Çelebi in Diyarbekir,* ed. and trans. by Martin M. van Bruinessen et al. (Leiden, 1988); this volume contains an exhaustive commentary by a team of Dutch specialists.
6. Albertus Bobovius, *Topkapi, Relation du sérail du Grand Seigneur*, ed. and annotated by Annie Berthier and Stéphane Yérasimos (Paris: Sindbad,

Actes Sud, 1999); Cem Behar, *Saklı Mecmua. Ali Ufkî'nin Bibliothèque Nationale de France'taki [Turc 292] Yazması* (Istanbul: Yapı ve Kredi Yayınları, 2008).

7. [Ahmed Resmi] *Des türkischen Gesandten Resmi Ahmed Efendi gesandtschaftliche Berichte von Berlin im Jahre 1763* (Berlin, rpt. 1983); Virginia Aksan, *An Ottoman Statesman in War and Peace, Ahmed Resmi Efendi, 1700-1783* (Leiden: E. J. Brill, 1995).
8. This expression is used to describe a series of illustrations of biblical stories found primarily in churches and intended for people who have no access to books.
9. For a French translation, see Mehmed Efendi, *Le paradis des infidèles, un ambassadeur ottoman en France sous la Régence*. Trans. Julien Claude Galland, annotated by Gilles Veinstein (Paris: François Maspéro-La Découverte, 1981).
10. Andreasyan, Hrand, "Bir Ermeni Kaynağina göre Celali İsyanları" In *Tarih Dergisi*, XIII, 17-18, pp. 27-42.
11. Cengiz Orhonlu, *Osmanlı İmparatorluğunda Aşiretleri İskân Teşebbüsü (1691-1696)* (Istanbul: İstanbul Üniversitesi Edebiyat Fakültesi, 1963).
12. We have very little information at this point about Christian women in the Balkans, but we know somewhat more about the Jewish women of Istanbul, particularly in more recent periods.

Chapter 4

1. This title has been borrowed from İlber Ortaylı, *İmparatorluğun en Uzun Yüzyılı* (Istanbul: Hil Yayınevi, 1983).
2. Since the events that culminated in the founding of Serbia, Greece, and Bulgaria are discussed in detail in any history of the Balkans, the reader is referred to the literature on this subject, such as Barbara Jelavich, *History of the Balkans, Eighteenth and Nineteenth Centuries* (Cambridge: Cambridge Univ. Press, 1983). For a novel perspective see Noel Malcolm, *Kosovo. A Short History* (New York: Harper Collins, 1999); this book is much wider than the title suggests.
3. Halil İnalcik, *Tanzimat ve Bulgar Meselesi* (Ankara: TTK, 1943).
4. Michael Palairet, *The Balkan Economics, c. 1800-1914, Evolution without Development* (Cambridge: Cambridge University Press, 1997).
5. Only the magazine *Kadınlar* was produced by an all-female group.
6. Meropi Anastassiadou, *Salonique, 1830-1912. Une ville ottomane à l'âge des Réformes* (Leiden: E. J. Brill, 1997), pp. 376-378.

Chapter 5

1. Odile Moreau, *L'Empire ottoman á l'âge des réformes. Les hommes et les idées du "Nouvel Ordre" militaire 1826-1914* (Paris: Maisonneuve & Larose, 2007).
2. Uğur Gülsoy, *Osmanlı Gayrimüslimlerinin Askerlik Serüveni* (İstanbul: Simurg, 2000).
3. İlber Ortaylı, *Osmanlı İmparatorluğunda Alman Nüfuzu* (reprint Istanbul: Alkim, 2006), pp. 89-108.
4. Edward J. Erickson, *Ordered to Die. A History of the Ottoman Army in the First World War* (Westport, London: Greenwood Press, 2001), pp. 231-235.
5. David Fromkin, *A Peace to End All Peace, The Fall of the Ottoman Empire and the Creation of the Modern Middle East* (New York: Henry Holt & Company, 1989), pp. 56-57 states that there was no legal basis; Hew Strachan, *The First World War* (Simon & Schuster UK Ltd., 2003), p. 105 contends the opposite.

   Throughout, this chapter owes a great deal to Fromkin's narrative; to keep the number of footnotes within bounds, not all statements derived from his study have been documented individually.
6. Stanford Shaw and Ezel Kural Shaw, *History of the Ottoman Empire and Modern Turkey* (Cambridge: Cambridge University Press, 1977), vol. 2 *Reform, Revolution and Republic. The Rise of Modern Turkey 1808-1975*, p. 367.
7. John Keegan, *The First World War* (London: Hutchinson, 1998), p. 268; Justin McCarthy, *The Ottoman Peoples and the End of Empire* (London: Hodder, Arnold, 2001), p. 102; the lowest figures are from Strachan, *The First World War*, p. 120; the author is vague about British losses.
8. Erickson, *Ordered to Die*, p. 94.
9. Erickson, *Ordered to Die*, p. 61.
10. Keegan, *The First World War*; p. 242; Erickson, *Ordered to Die*, p. 60.
11. Keegan, *The First World War*, p. 242.
12. Keegan, *The First World War*, p. 243; McCarthy, *The Ottoman Peoples*, p. 111 records slightly over 800,000 refugee survivors in 1920. See also Erickson, *Ordered to Die*, pp. 95-104.
13. Shaw; History, vol. 2, p. 316; Sina Akşin, *Turkey: from Empire to Revolutionary Republic. The Emergence of the Turkish Nation from 1789 to the Present*, tr. by Dexter H. Mursaloğlu (London: Hurst, 2007), p. 110; Justin McCarthy, *Muslims and Minorities.. The Population of Anatolia and the End of the Empire* (London, New York: New York University Press, 1983),

p. 130. Erickson, *Ordered to Die*, p. 104 says "hundreds of thousands." Donald Bloxham, *The Great Game of Genocide. Imperialism, nationalism and the destruction of the Ottoman Armenians* (Oxford: Oxford University Press, 2005), p. 89, "over a million."

14. Caroline Finkel, *Osman's Dream. The Story of the Ottoman Empire 1300-1923* (London: John Murray, 2007), pp. 534-536 focuses on current debates.
15. Bloxham, *The Great Game*, p. 91; McCarthy, *The Ottoman Peoples*, pp. 106-12.
16. McCarthy, *The Ottoman Peoples*, p. 202.
17. Fromkin, *A Peace*, pp. 218-228.
18. On the violent disagreements among politicians and military men concerning the conduct of this campaign, see Fromkin, *A Peace*, pp. 152-165.
19. Keegan, *The First World War*, p. 261.
20. Zafer Toprak, *İttihad-Terakki ve Cihan Harbı, Savaş Ekonomisi ve Türkiye'de Devletçilik 1914-1918* (İstanbul: Homer, 2003), pp. 99-126.
21. Toprak, *İttihad-Terakki*, p. 113.
22. Toprak, *İttihad-Terakki*, p. 197.
23. Toprak, *İttihad-Terakki*, pp. 172-175.
24. Fromkin, *A Peace*, pp. 188-196.
25. Fromkin, *A Peace*, pp. 41-43.
26. Andrew Mango, *Atatürk* (London: John Murray, 1999), p. 210.
27. Eric Jan Zürcher, *The Unionist Factor. The Role of the Committee of Union and Progress in the Turkish National Movement 1905-1926* (Leiden: Brill, 1984).
28. Mango, *Atatürk*, p. 245.
29. Nur Bilge Criss, *Istanbul under Allied Occupation* (Leiden: Brill, 1999), p. 15.
30. Mango, *Atatürk*, p. 294.
31. Michael Llewellyn Smith, *Ionian Vision: Greece in Asia Minor 1919-1922* (London: Allen Lane, 1973).
32. Mango, Atatürk, p. 390; Onur Yıldırım, *Diplomacy and Displacement: Reconsidering the Turco-Greek Exchange of Populations, 1922–1934* (New York: Routledge, 2006).
33. Bruce Clark, *Twice a Stranger: The Mass Expulsions that Forged Modern Greece and Turkey* (London: Granta Boks, 2006).

Conclusion

1. Çağlar Keyder, *State and Class in Turkey. A Study in Capitalist Development* (London, New York: Verso, 1987).
2. Eric Jan Zürcher; *The Unionist Factor. The Role of the Committee of Union and Progress in the Turkish National Movement 1905-1926* (Leiden: Brill, 1984); Şükrü Hanioğlu, *A Short History of the Late Ottoman Empire* (Princeton: Princeton University Press, 2008) appeared after the present volume had gone to press.
3. Andrew Mango, *Atatürk* (London: John Murray, 1999), pp. 443-453.
4. Donald Quataert, *Ottoman Manufacturing in the Age of the Industrial Revolution* (Cambridge: Cambridge University Press, 1993).
5. Zeynep Çelik, *The Remaking of Istanbul, Portrait of an Ottoman City in the Nineteenth Century* (Seattle, London: University of Washington Press, 1986); Nora Lafi, *Une ville du Maghreb entre ancien régime et réformes ottomanes. Genèse des institutions municipales à Tripoli de Barbarie (1795-1911)* (Paris: L'Harmattan, 2002); Huri Islamoğlu (ed.), *Constituting Modernity Private Property in the East and West* (London: I. B. Tauris, 2004).
6. François Georgeon, *Abdülhamid II. Le sultan calife (1876–1909)* (Paris: Fayard, 2003).
7. Selim Deringil, *The Well-Protected Domains. Ideology and the Legitimation of Power in the Ottoman Empire 1876-1909* (London: I. B. Tauris, 1998), *passim*.
8. Zeki Arıkan, "İstanbul 1912, Hamlet'in temsili," *Toplumsal Tarih*, 170 (February 2008), 56-63.
9. I owe this observation to my colleague Christoph Neumann.
10. Richard J. Evans, *In Defence of History* (London: Granta Books, 1997).

Suggestions for Further Reading

The Cambridge History of Turkey, vol. 3 *The Later Ottoman Empire*, ed. by Suraiya Faroqhi (Cambridge: Cambridge University Press, 2006); vol. 4 *Turkey in the Modern World*, ed. by Reşat Kasaba (Cambridge: Cambridge University Press, 2008); vol. 1 *Byzantium-Turkey, 1071-1453* (Cambridge: Cambridge University Press, 2008). (A collective work; unfortunately, vol. 2, encompassing the period of Suleiman, will not come out until 2009-10.)

Davison, Roderic. *Turkey: A Short History*, ed. by Clement Dodd. 3rd ed. (Huntingdon: The Eothen Press, 1998). (Discussion of the earlier Ottoman history is now somewhat outdated, but the book is very informative on the 19th and 20th centuries.)

Faroqhi, Suraiya. *Approaching Ottoman History: An Introduction to the Sources* (Cambridge: Cambridge University Press, 1999). (Discussion of Ottoman and non-Ottoman archives and literature.)

———. *Subjects of the Sultans*, translated by Martin Bott (London: I.B. Tauris, 2000). (Extensive bibliography on the everyday lives of Ottoman townspeople.)

Finkel, Caroline. *Osman's Dream. The Story of the Ottoman Empire 1300-1923* (London: John Murray, 2006). (Both scholarly and readable: the best single-volume history currently in print.)

Hanioğlu, Şükrü. *A Brief History of the Late Ottoman Empire* (Princeton, NJ: Princeton University Press, 2008). (By a connoisseur of the documents left by the Committee of Union and Progress, with an emphasis on intellectual history.)

Hathaway, Jane, with contributions by Karl Barbir. *The Arab Lands under Ottoman Rule, 1516-1800* (Harlow, London: Pearson Longman, 2008). (Wide-ranging survey that includes social and cultural history while emphasizing the Ottoman framework in which provincial history took place.)

Howard, Douglas. *The History of Turkey* (Westwood, CT: The Greenwood Press, 2001). (Ottoman "background information" to the history of modern Turkey, which is the major subject of this book; by an author who has done significant work on the early modern period as well.)

Inalcik, Halil. *The Ottoman Empire: The Classical Age 1300-1600*, translated by Norman Itzkowitz and Colin Imber (New York: Praeger Publishers, 1973). (This book, now a classic, has been reissued several times and remains a great introduction; of course, by this time the bibliography is outdated.)

Inalcik, Halil. *The Ottoman Empire, Conquest, Organization and Economy*

(London: Variorum Reprints, 1978). (A collection of classic essays by the master of Ottoman history.)

——, with Donald Quataert, eds. *An Economic and Social History of the Ottoman Empire, 1300-1914*. 2 vols. (Cambridge: Cambridge University Press, 1997, for paperback version). (Informative essays by various authors, especially by the two editors, and comprehensive bibliographies.)

Issawi, Charles. *The Economic History of Turkey, 1800-1914* (Chicago: The University of Chicago Press, 1980). (In contrast to the expectations raised by the title, it is not an economic history like that of Owen or Pamuk, but an anthology of primary and secondary sources, the originals of which are often difficult to find.)

Jelavich, Barbara. *History of the Balkans,* vol. I *Eighteenth and Nineteenth Centuries* (Cambridge: Cambridge University Press, 1983). (Comparative account of Habsburg and Ottoman history.)

Kafadar, Cemal. *Between Two Worlds: The Construction of the Ottoman State* (Berkeley: University of California Press, 1995). (Highly recommended; especially effective discussion of the state of research and about the Ottomans and the intellectual history of the 20th century as well.)

Malcolm, Noel. *Kosovo: A Short History* (New York: New York University Press, 1998). (This book is both learned and well written but certainly not short; presents the story from the Albanian viewpoint but invites us to rethink late Ottoman history as a whole.)

Mango, Andrew. *Atatürk* (London: John Murray, 1999). (A "life and times" in the positive sense of the phrase; says a great deal about the history, both cultural and military, of the late Ottoman Empire and the early Republic of Turkey.)

Mantran, Robert, ed. *Histoire de l'Empire ottoman* (Paris: Fayard, 1989). (Essays by several authors. The bibliography focuses especially on the extensive French production; political history emphasized more than in Inalcik and Quataert. Especially strong in the history of the Arab provinces.)

McCarthy, Justin. *The Ottoman Turks: An Introductory History to 1923* (London: Longman, 1997). (A historian of demographics takes into account the otherwise often neglected sufferings of the Muslim population during the dissolution of the Ottoman Empire; unfortunately lacks a bibliography.)

Ortaylı, İlber. *İmparatorluğun en Uzun Yüzyılı* (Istanbul: Hil Yayınevi, 1983). ("The Longest Century of the Empire" refers to the nineteenth; excellent portrayal of the Ottoman upper class.)

Owen, Roger. *The Middle East in the World Economy 1800-1914* (London: Methuen & Co., 1981). (A classic; deals primarily with the Arab provinces. No Ottoman archival sources, but outstanding knowledge of research.)

Pamuk, Şevket. *A Monetary History of the Ottoman Empire* (Cambridge: Cambridge University Press, 2000). (Much wider than the title suggests; a great introduction to Ottoman economic history.)

Quataert, Donald. *The Ottoman Empire, 1700-1922* (Cambridge: Cambridge University Press, 2000). (Late Ottoman history, by a specialist on the social and economic history of the 1800s.)

Sugar, Peter. *Southeastern Europe under Ottoman Rule, 1354-1804* (Seattle: University of Washington Press, 1977). (Pioneering effort: attempts to incorporate cultural history into the study on an equal footing.)

Turan, Şerafettin. *Türk Kültür Tarihi: Türk Kültüründen Türkiye Kültürüne ve Evrenselliğe* (Ankara: Bilgi Yayınevi, 1990). ("Turkish Cultural History: From the culture of the Turkic peoples to the culture of Turkey and to universalism"; as the title indicates, this book tackles the difficult issue of considering the national cultural history as a part of larger contexts.)

Zürcher, Erik Jan. *Turkey: A Modern History* (London: I. B. Tauris, 1993). (Good depiction of the last decades of the Ottoman Empire and the lines of connection between this state and the Republic of Turkey.)

IRAN

A SHORT HISTORY

Monika Gronke

Translated by Steven Rendall

Introduction

In 628, the sources would have us believe, a letter from the Prophet Muhammad arrived in Ctesiphon, the ancient Sasanian capital on the Tigris. This letter urged the Great King of Persia to convert to Islam, and it inaugurated a new era, although contemporaries were surely not aware that this was so. Only a few years later the Arabs, inspired by their new religion, overthrew the Sasanian Empire, which then became part of the Islamic world. The Arab conquest was the most profound rupture in the history of Iran, and may even be a unique historical phenomenon. It led to a whole people abandoning its own manifold religious tradition and adopting a new faith. Iran became an Islamic country, and it made this momentous change in a relatively short time, in comparison with its long past. However, during the intervening period of more than a thousand years, the Islamic history of Iran has shown that the country was not absorbed by the massive Islamic expansion of the seventh century, nor did it completely forget its pre-Islamic history. Instead, it blended Islam, which was originally alien to it, with its own ancient heritage to create a unique Iranian-Islamic culture. Over the centuries, the latter set its stamp on large parts of the Islamic world, and also inspired a number of works by European writers, among which Goethe's *West-Östlicher Divan* is one of the best known and finest.

The territory of present-day Iran (officially the Islamic Republic) includes an area about one-sixth that of the United States, and its latitude is roughly that of the southern United States. It is a land of high mountains and dry, desert-like basins between the Caspian Sea—which is actually an enormous inland lake with no outlet to the ocean—in the north and the Persian Gulf in the south. The Iranian high plateau is surrounded in the north by the lofty Alburz Mountains, in the west by the Zagros Mountains, which broaden into parallel ranges stretching toward the southeast, and in the east by a mountain range running along the border with Afghanistan and Pakistan and merging in the north with the Hindu Kush. Smaller mountain ranges divide this central highland into several large basins of differing sizes. These basins most commonly consist of gravel and salt deserts like the Kavir Desert and the Lut Desert to the south, with completely sterile salt plains. The few rivers mostly peter out in the gravelly debris of these low places. Iran is primarily a dry land of low rainfall where since antiquity agriculture has been dependent on artificial irrigation. Farming without irrigation was and is possible only in a few areas such as the lowlands near the Caspian.

During long periods of its history in Islamic times, the sphere of Iranian culture nonetheless extended far beyond the geographical borders of the present-day Iran. Mesopotamia—which had been part of the Sasanian Empire, while the emperor's residence was in Ctesiphon, not far from the later site of Baghdad, the capital of the ʿAbbasid caliphate (749–1258)—also belonged to the Iranian cultural sphere, as did the region corresponding to present-day Afghanistan and Transoxania, that is, the land between the Amu Darya and Syr Darya rivers (in ancient times, these were known as the Oxus and the Jaxartes). The name "Iran" is derived from Middle Persian, *Iran*, whose complete form was *Iranshahr* or *Iranzamin* ("Land of the Aryans"; *Iran* is the genitive plural of *ir*, "Aryan"). Although the concept "Aryan" was already found in the ancient Persian Empire of the Achaemenids (558–330 BC), *Iran* first became an established, meaningful term referring to a political, religious, and ethnic unit under the Sasanian dynasty (224–651), the last pre-Islamic dynasty on Persian soil. After the Arab conquest, the country of Iran—which was now part of the extensive Islamic empire—no longer represented a clearly defined territory, but instead disintegrated into individual provinces with their own names (such as Khurasan, Fars, and Azerbaijan), whereas the old term *rân* survived as a historical name for the Sasanian Empire. Persia appears in Firdawsi's so-called Iranian "national epic," the *Shahnameh* ("Book of Kings," c. AD 1000) under the old name *Iranzamin*, which was directly derived from the Middle Persian original. However, "Iran" first reappears as the name of an empire under the rule of the Mongols in the thirteenth century. Since then, the concept "Iran" has been connected with the idea of the greatness and unity of Persia, an idea into which later dynasties, and finally that of the Pahlavis (1925–1979), tried to breathe life. The term "Persia," on the other hand, referred originally to an area in the southwest part of the country, the Old Persian Parsa, which the Greeks called "Persis" and the Arabs "Fars"; it was therefore a purely geographical concept.

Iran's lengthy pre-Islamic past, during which there were three great Persian empires—the Achaemenid, the Parthian, and the Sasanian—may be responsible for the fact that today historians often tend to see Iran as a unity in Islamic times as well, and to seek everywhere for signs of an Iranian national feeling distinguishing Iranians from other peoples. On this view, Arabs and Iranians are fundamentally inimical groups; after their initial conquest by the Arabs, the Iranians are supposed to have later achieved a new national assertiveness under native Persian dynasties. This kind of thoroughgoing nationalist interpretation of Iranian history inevitably leads to a distorted picture, since it applies a narrowly defined concept in modern European history to ancient periods that were shaped by entirely different factors. Similarly, it overlooks the fact that even in antiquity Iran was a multi-ethnic state and remains one today, and thus cannot be seen as a nation connected with a single people. However, in the course of Persia's pre-Islamic history, political and cultural traditions as well as a peculiarly Iranian idea of the state and ruling power emerged, and these unified the Iranian cultural sphere and lent it its special characteristics. At least as ideas, these traditions survived the Islamization of Persia, and they contributed to the development of a peculiarly Iranian variant of Islamic culture. The consciousness of a great past expressed itself in Iranians' marked sense of superiority both with regard to other peoples, even if the latter subjected Iran to their rule—as did Arabs, Turks, and Mongols—and in Iranian-Islamic literature. The Iranians' adherence to their own traditions is shown with particular clarity by the fact that although like other peoples they ultimately abandoned their ancient religion, they did not give up their language. Persian is the only language in the areas of the Middle East conquered by the Arabs that not only survived this upheaval but early on established its position alongside Arabic as a major language in the Islamic cultural sphere.

This book will describe the chief processes of development and change that have shaped Iran's history since its Islamization, and that have given the country its present character. The material is divided into four main chapters, each defined temporally and dealing with an extensive historical period during which important changes and shifts in direction can be observed.

The first of these periods stretches from the Arab conquest of Iran, which culminated in the Muslim victory at the Battle of Nihavand (642), to the Saljuqs' conquest of Baghdad, the capital of the caliphate (1055). During this period, the ʿAbbasid caliphate came to power and did much to establish the contours of "classical" medieval Islamic culture. This culture was greatly indebted to pre-Islamic Iranian culture. The period was, however, characterized by frequent conflicts over the question of legitimate rule.

With the Saljuqs began the centuries-long influx from Inner Asia into Iran of Turkish and later Mongol nomads; in 1258 the latter overthrew the ʿAbbasid caliphate. This period was characterized by increasing nomadism and economic decline in many parts of the country, but also by brilliant achievements in art and literature.

In 1501, the Safavids put an end to Iran's political fragmentation by reunifying it and making Shiʿism the state religion. The conversion to Shiʿism divided Iran from its Sunni neighbors, but in the long run it also lent the country's various peoples a new spiritual unity. For Iran, the modern age began with the Safavids: diplomatic contacts with Europe were established, economic and commercial relationships broadened.

After further political division in the eighteenth century, military and economic confrontation with the European powers began around the turn of the nineteenth century under the Qajar dynasty. This fourth period is marked by debate regarding the idea of a national state, the secularization of public life, and increasing interest in pre-Islamic Iran. Since the Islamic Revolution ended the country's long monarchical tradition in 1979, Iran has been seeking a new way for itself, for the time being under the rule of Shiʿite religious scholars.

Because of the length of Iranian-Islamic history and the multiplicity of historical materials, a Western historian who wishes to provide a wide readership with a brief history of Iran from Islamization to the present inevitably encounters the difficult question of what can be omitted without doing excessive damage to the overall picture. I have nevertheless decided to attempt such an overview because I hope to contribute to a better understanding of the historical development of one of the most important countries in the Islamic East. If this book makes the long history of Iran and the fascinating culture it has produced since its Islamization more familiar to its readers, leading them to further investigation, it will have achieved its purpose.

CHAPTER 1
The Early Islamic Period (642–1055)

The Arab Conquest

Islam is the youngest of the three monotheistic world religions. It was founded by the Prophet Muhammad (c. 570–632) on the Arabian peninsula. Islam proclaims belief in a single God, whom Muhammad named "Allah" (in Arabic, "the God," that is, the one and only God), and maintains that it is the original revelation of God. According to Muhammad, over time God has made his unvarying revelation known to the peoples of the earth through a series of prophets, to the Jews through Moses and to the Christians through Jesus; in Islam's strictly monotheistic conception, Jesus was a prophet, and not the son of God. However, Muhammad, who had come in contact with Jews and Christians living in Arabia, was convinced that in the course of history Judaism and Christianity had deviated from the original divine revelation and that both had retained only an incomplete and distorted version of it. It is Muhammad, seen as the last of the series of prophets, who restores the original divine revelation and thereby concludes it. Islam's sense of superiority to all other religions, including the other monotheistic ones, is based on this claim to have brought men back to the original divine message.

Just two years after the Prophet's death, Muslim Arabs set out on campaigns of conquest and quickly subjugated Byzantine Syria and Egypt as well as the whole Persian Empire of the Sasanians. The defeat of the Sasanian army in 637 at the battle of al-Qadisiyya on the Euphrates, where Rustam, the imperial commander-in-chief, was killed, left the Arabs in control of Iraq and the Sasanian capital, Ctesiphon.

In 642, the Arabs won a decisive victory at Nihavand, in western Iran; in 644 they took Isfahan and in 649 Istakhr, which had been built on the site of the ancient Persepolis; starting in 650, they subdued the northern province of Khurasan. The last Sasanian king, Yazdgard III, fled and was murdered in 651. Thus the whole territory of the Sasanian Empire was henceforth under Arab control and became part of the Islamic realm.

Many reasons have been given for the astonishing speed of Arab expansion: the Sasanian Empire's internal instability during the crucial period of conquest (the empire had been exhausted by a long war with Byzantium that had only recently ended); the unifying and motivating effect of Islam that inspired the Arabs in their campaigns, especially since those who fell in battle were promised immediate entrance into Paradise; the Arabs' mobility and gift for military improvisation, which gave them an advantage over the slow-moving Sasanian mercenaries; the nearly unlimited supply of fighters from the Arabian heartland; and the fact that the Sasanians seem to have initially underestimated the Arab advance and considered it just another of the regular but not really dangerous attacks on the empire. However, a truly decisive and for the most part overlooked basis for Arab expansion was the support—despite all the warfare—for Muslims among both Arabs living on the borders of the Sasanian Empire and the native Persian population. This was connected first of all with the status of the so-called *ahl al-kitab* ("People of the Book"). In the Muslim view, human beings were divided into three groups: (1) Muslims, (2) pagans, and (3) Jews and Christians. Jews and Christians could not be put on the same level as the pagans, because they were both in possession of a divine revelation and sacred books, even if these had become incomplete and obsolete. Pagans who fell under Islamic rule had to choose between conversion to Islam and death, whereas Jews and Christians still had the option of putting themselves under the protection of the state and paying the so-called poll tax (Arabic *jizyah*). In return, the state guaranteed their lives, their property, and their right to practice their own religion, though it imposed a number of restrictions and prohibitions intended to symbolize the subjection and degradation of non-Muslim minorities with respect to Muslims (for example, rules regarding clothing and prohibitions on riding horses and carrying weapons). The source for these regulations, which eventually developed into a complex system of prescriptions, were the past relationships between Muhammad and Jewish and Christian groups in other parts of Arabia and certain guiding principles announced in the form of revelations and later recorded in the Qurʾan. Originally, only Jews and Christians, since they were expressly mentioned in Muhammad's revelations, were granted the status of "people of the book." After the conquest of Iran, Muslims also granted this status to adherents of Zoroastrianism, which was the state religion of Sasanian Iran, relying on a tradition according to which Muhammad was supposed to have accepted poll tax payments from Zoroastrians in Bahrain.

Therefore, in accord with the Prophet's practice, the Arabs generally did not force the peoples they conquered to convert to Islam; instead, they entered into agreements with them in return for payment of the poll tax. The Arabs ensured the progress of their conquests and their ongoing presence in the areas they conquered by building new garrison cities in the course of their military campaigns—cities such as Basra and Kufah in the southern part of present-day Iraq. Finally, in a second wave of campaigns at the beginning of the eighth century, Transoxania was conquered. By this point large numbers of Arabs had settled in almost every part of Iran and intermarried with the native population. Even today the Arab heritage of many Iranian tribes and families can still be traced.

In the territories the Muslims conquered real property was usually not taken away from its owners, but they had to pay a property tax (Arabic *kharaj*) if they did not convert to Islam. Only at the beginning of the eighth century, when the number of Muslims significantly increased, did the latter have to start paying this property tax as well in order to fill the state's coffers. Land that was left practically ownerless because the owners had died or fled was appropriated by the authorities and awarded to Arabs. Naturally, this was not always done in an orderly way; illegal appropriations of land and even unauthorized divvying-up of provinces—as in Kirman in southeast Iran—by Arabs also occurred. In rural areas the *dihqan* (landlord) played an important role after the conquest. Since the late Sasanian era these landlords had constituted a lower level of landed aristocrats who owned lands of a certain size and who were responsible for local administration. They maintained their land holdings by means of payments in cash or kind to individual Arab military leaders and often, to be sure, by converting to Islam. As was already the case under the Sasanian Empire, in the early Islamic period the dihqans were also responsible for collecting taxes as well as for cultivating the land and maintaining roads and bridges. Some dihqans were almost independent local rulers, particularly in Eastern Iran. Only at the end of the tenth century did this modest form of landed property gradually disappear, and along with it the importance of the dihqans.

The Arabs incorporated the whole Sasanian territory into their empire (which they had not done in the case of the Byzantine areas they had conquered), but they were not prepared to govern so enormous a territory. For that reason they adopted the Persian model of a self-contained imperial government and left the existing administrative apparatus untouched. Persian remained in use as the language of the chancellery, and began to be replaced by Arabic only toward the end of the seventh century as a result of a general Islamization of the administration. Similarly, the Arabs kept in place trained officials in various branches of the administration. This Persian bureaucracy, referred to in Arabic as *kuttab* (sing. *katib*, "scribe, secretary"), had extensive knowledge and experience that could only be of use to the Muslims. From the ranks of the *kuttâb* emerged numerous dignitaries, statesmen, and literary figures who enjoyed complete mastery not only of their native tongues but also of Arabic. It was the secretaries who, by keeping alive old Iranian traditions and combining their own spiritual world with the new faith, made an important Iranian contribution to the development of Islam and universal Islamic culture. During the first Islamic century—from the reign of the first four caliphs to the end of the Umayyad dynasty (600–749)—a distinction was still drawn between Muslims who were of Arab descent and those who were not, even though this was incompatible with Islam's later egalitarian claim that all Muslims, regardless of their ancestry, are equal. Muslims who were not of Arab descent—and this included almost all new converts—had to become the "clients" or "mawali" (Arabic *mawali*) of an Arab tribe or prominent Arab individual. Even if they were wealthy and educated, they did not enjoy all the rights of Arab Muslims, and their social standing was lower. Although *mawâlî* were of differing ethnic heritage, the majority of them were Iranians, and hence as a whole the problem was an Iranian one. Therefore the mawali felt a certain sympathy for other groups that were opposed to Umayyad rule. The fourth caliph, ʿAli (656–661), with whom the origin of the Shiʿite faith is connected, is said to have made the mawali the equals of the Arabs, much to the annoyance of the latter. In particular, the mawali living in Kufah were among ʿAli's adherents. This explains the strong early response that Shiʿism among Iranians, as well as the fact that many Iranians participated in the Shiʿite rebellions against the Umayyads, including for instance the one that ultimately led to the Umayyads' fall in 749.

The Islamization of Iran

Although there were some local skirmishes, the Islamization of Iran was achieved largely without fighting. It took place over several centuries, continuing to advance slowly and gradually until the middle of the eighth century. It has occasionally been said that whole sections of the population converted to Islam, but this seems seldom to have been the case. However, it is difficult to determine exactly what was meant by a true conversion to Islam—whether, for instance, it was necessary to demonstrate that one was familiar with Islamic forms of worship and that one was able to read the Qurʾan. Presumably many people converted formally to Islam without really knowing what duties were connected with being a Muslim; often enough, they have have given it no more than lip service. Moreover, depending on the region, Islamization proceeded in entirely different ways. In some provinces, such as Fars, Jibal, Gilan, and Daylam, most of the people initially kept their old religious beliefs. Some documents suggest that significant Zoroastrian minorities continued to exist in these areas well into the tenth century, and in southeast Iran the Zoroastrians' holy fire seems to have burned even into the thirteenth century. We can assume that much the same can be said for other areas of Iran; since Zoroastrians were recognized as "people of the book," they were able to go on practicing their religion without serious restrictions.

Conversion to Islam often depended on membership in a specific social group. For instance, tradesmen and workers in cities belonged to a group more open to conversion to Islam than were farmers or the Zoroastrian priesthood. Craftsmen and workers were considered impure by the priests because their occupations inevitably led them to violate numerous Zoroastrian regulations, such as the taboo on polluting fire, water, and earth. Islam, which does not have these rigid regulations, therefore constituted an acceptable alternative. As in these cases, social or economic grounds may often have been crucial factors in the decision to convert to Islam. Many members of the Iranian upper class apparently converted quite rapidly in order to preserve their property, their social standing, or their fiscal privileges, to escape paying the poll tax, or to make it easier to join the new Muslim elite.

Although social and economic reasons played a far larger role than force employed by the conqueror, there was evidently no lack of missionary zeal and even coercion on the part of the Muslims, and this makes it only too clear that the conversion of many Iranians to Islam was at first merely superficial. It appears that the number of conversions to Islam sharply increased after the ʿAbbasids rose to power because they put Arabs and non-Arabs on the same level, thus eliminating the problem of the mawali. This must have significantly increased Iranians' willingness to adopt Islam. It may also be that there was already—as later historical sources indicate—a tendency to resist allowing non-Muslims to participate fully in community life or hold high political and social positions. The longer Muslim rule continued, the more the Islamization of Iran became an irreversible process that ultimately benefited the new religion. Nonetheless, the long survival of Zoroastrianism was manifested in the second half of the eighth and the first half of the ninth centuries in Iran, and especially in eastern Iran, by a series of syncretistic religious movements that combined elements of Zoroastrianism, Manichaeanism, and Mazdakism with Islamic ideas or expressed overt hostility to Islam; they were suppressed by the ʿAbbasid caliphs in Baghdad only with difficulty.

Shiʿism

Since the early modern period—and up to the present day—Iran has been a Shiʿite country. Shiʿism originated in the uncertainties that followed the death of the Prophet Muhammad. When the latter died in Medina in the summer of 632, he left behind no surviving male heir of his own, and had apparently established no rules regarding his succession. Thus the young Muslim community was forced to decide for itself who was to be the leader—that is, the caliph (from Arabic *khalifah*, "successor," "deputy," i.e., of the prophet Muhammad)—of the post-Prophet community. In determining the group of legitimate candidates for the leadership of the Muslim community, the genealogical principle played an important role, as did also early credit for spreading and supporting the new religion. In the end, family ties to the Prophet proved to be the decisive factor. It was this—only superficially political—question of the legitimacy of the caliph that resulted in the split between Sunnis and Shiʿites in the Muslim community that has persisted to the present day.

The term *Shiʿah* means "party" in the sense of faction. It refers to those contemporaries of the Prophet who sought, during the conflicts regarding succession that broke out after his death, to reserve the leadership of the community for ʿAli, Muhammad's cousin and son-in-law (he was married to the Prophet's daughter Fatima). Contrary to many popular Western and Sunni notions that often tend to equate Shiʿism with Iran and thus to suggest a historically doubtful opposition between an ethnically defined Arab Sunnism and an Iranian Shiʿism, Shiʿism is anything but a special Iranian variant of Islam. The origin of Shiʿism lay in intra-Islamic conflicts in the Arab milieu of Medina; shortly afterward it was further developed in the equally Arab city of Kufah in what is now southern Iraq.

However, after Muhammad's death the leading members of the community in Medina first chose, from their own ranks, his father-in-law, Abu Bakr, as caliph (reigned from 632 to 634). The second caliph, ʿUmar (reigned 634–644), who was also one of the Prophet's fathers-in-law, was designated by Abu Bakr. The reign of the third caliph, Uthman (reigned 644–656), the Prophet's son-in-law, was chosen by an electoral committee. After Uthman was murdered by rebellious soldiers, ʿAli finally became the caliph (reigned 656–661). However, ʿAli's caliphate was disputed from the outset. Above all, Uthman's relatives from the Umayya clan did not recognize ʿAli as caliph, and they left Medina and moved to Syria. ʿAli, for his part, went to the garrison city of Kufah, where he had faithful supporters who helped him in his battle for the caliphate. The five years of ʿAli's reign, during which his supporters fought the Umayya clan's followers for power, and therefore Muslims battled members of their own religion, ended in a final schism of the Muslim community. In the summer of 657, at Siffin on the banks of the Euphrates, ʿAli's army and that of his rival Muʿawiyah, a cousin of the murdered caliph Uthman, met in battle. After weeks of fighting, it was decided to resolve the whole question of the rightful ruler by referring it to a panel of arbitrators whose deliberations were to be guided by the Qurʾan. Reports regarding this panel are contradictory, so that the question about who had a legitimate right to the caliphate remains unanswered. In any case, ʿAli's agreement to abide by the arbitrators' decision proved fateful, since some of his supporters were angered by these events and deserted him. In their view, ʿAli had abdicated the caliphate that was rightfully his by making his claim to it subject to the decision of human judges. In 661, ʿAli was murdered by one of these dissidents (Arabic *khawarij*, "seceders"). The preceding year his rival Muʿawiyah had already proclaimed himself caliph in Jerusalem, thereby founding the Umayyad dynasty (661–749). The problem of the caliph's legitimacy had thus become a pure battle for power, even if it was conducted by means of religious arguments.

For the Shiʿites, the "party of ʿAli," ʿAli is the sole legitimate successor of the Prophet Muhammad as the leader of the Muslim community. ʿAli's close genealogical relationship to the Prophet spoke in his favor, and he was also among the first to convert to Islam. However, the Shiʿite's base ʿAli's claim to be the Prophet's immediate successor primarily on a series of traditions of which the most important is an utterance Muhammad is supposed to have made on his return from his last pilgrimage from Mecca to Medina in 632, the year of his death. On March 16—according to the Muslim calendar, the eighteenth day of the pilgrimage month Dhu al-Hijjah—the pilgrims were resting by the pool of Khumm, halfway between the two cities. There Muhammad is supposed to have said, "Whoever accepts me as master (*mawla*), ʿAli is his master too." Shiʿites interpret this statement as the Prophet's designation of ʿAli as his successor. For them, that day at the pool of Khumm has extraordinary meaning, and from the tenth century on, it became the second most important Shiʿite holiday and is still celebrated today. Sunnis also recognize this tradition, but they consider it less important, and in any case they do not regard it as an express command regarding the succession; instead, they interpret it as merely expressing the Prophet's desire to strengthen ʿAli's status within the community, in which he had for various reasons made himself unpopular.

The first three caliphs, Abu Bakr, ʿUmar, and Uthman, are not recognized by Shiʿism as legitimate rulers; they are seen as having usurped a position that should by rights have gone to ʿAli from the outset. For the Sunnis, in contrast, the first four caliphs were all equally legitimate leaders of the community and deserve the same respect, since according to Sunnis the only requirement is that the caliph belong to the Prophet's tribe, the Quraysh. Thus Sunnis and Shiʿites have completely opposed views of the course of early Islamic history. The ferocity of the conflicts between the two groups, which continues today, becomes comprehensible when we consider that according to Islamic belief, a divine plan of salvation underlies history, and that this plan culminates in a final judgment day. Since in Islam the religious and secular communities are completely fused, the task set for the community consists in making this divinely willed form of the state manifest in the temporal world, thereby fulfilling the divine plan so far as possible. This view gives political events their religious meaning, and it is the reason for the enormous importance of the question regarding the legitimate caliph: only a legitimate leader of the Muslim community can guide it through worldly life in accord with God's will. According to Shiʿism, the Sunnis, who did not support ʿAli's claim to the caliphate, disregarded God's will and thereby committed a grave sin. In the Shiʿite view, the history of the early Muslim community did not unfold in accord with God's will, and since it cannot be undone, the Sunnis can in principle never atone for the sin they committed against ʿAli.

At the present time, about 10 to 15 percent of all Muslims world-wide adhere to Shi'ism in one form or another. The most important and numerically largest group among these is "Twelver Shi'ism" (*Ithna 'Ashariyyah*), the current state religion of Iran.

The Doctrine of Twelver Shi'ism

Regarding the question which of 'Ali's descendants had the right to lead the Muslim community after his death in 661, the views of the various Shi'ite factions differ. For Twelver Shi'ism, only 'Ali's descendants from his first marriage with the Prophet's daughter Fatima count as legitimate. The term "Twelver" is derived from the number of the leaders of the Muslim community considered legitimate, beginning with 'Ali himself. Twelver Shi'ites are also called "imamites," after the title "imam" ("leader or head of the community") accorded to 'Ali and his successors. A third name for the Twelver Shi'ites is "Ja'fariyyah," after the sixth Imam, Ja'far (d. 765), who played an especially important role in shaping the Twelver Shi'ites' doctrine.

The Twelvers' eleventh imam was not yet thirty when he died (sometime between 873 and 874) without—according to the general tradition—having left a male heir. At this point the unresolved question of who was his legitimate successor as the community's new imam divided the imamites into various sects and factions. However, one of these groups had from the outset disputed the notion that the eleventh imam had left no heir, maintaining that he had a young son born in 869, and that it was no accident that his name was Muhammad, like the Prophet's. Through a miracle, they claimed, this Muhammad had gone into occultation. Since then, he is supposed to have resided somewhere in the world, invisible, hidden. One day, no one knows when, the hidden twelfth imam is expected to return. His is called al-Mahdi ("divinely guided one") and he will return as a redeemer after a series of heavenly signs; it is for him to complete the Prophet's task, to overthrow the rule of usurpers and tyrants, and to establish the realm of justice, a paradise on Earth. This belief in the existence of a hidden twelfth imam and his future return became the most important characteristic of Twelver Shi'ism.

Twelver Shi'ism was given its special religious imprint by the fate of ʿAli's younger son Husayn, the third imam. When the Umayyad caliph Muʿawiyah died in Damascus in 680 and the son he had named as his heir, Yazid, succeeded him, Husayn attempted to take over the caliphate by force of arms. Relying on his supporters in Kufah, he invaded Iraq along with a small group of faithful followers from Medina. However, the help he expected to receive from the Shiʿites in Kufah was not forthcoming, and his troops were almost wiped out in a battle fought on October 10, 680 (according to the Muslim calendar, on the tenth day of Muharram in the year 61) near the little town of Karbala, some 70 kilometers north of Kufah. The day of this battle, known as "ʿAshura" ("the tenth," i.e., the tenth day of Muharram) signifies both Shiʿism's political failure and the true beginning of Shiʿite religious feeling. With the defeat at Karbala, Shiʿism was politically played out, and for centuries it was merely a movement opposing Sunni rule. However, it was only after Karbala that Twelver Shiʿism developed its typical religious rituals of penitence and mourning. For Twelvers, the day of Karbala is the day of Husayn's martyrdom, which he suffered blamelessly. On this day—ʿAshura—and the nine days preceding it in the month of Muharram, Twelvers commemorate his death. The rituals carried out on this occasion, which outsiders often see as mere expressions of mourning, are far more than that: they are rituals of penitence, through which the believer seeks to atone for his own guilt with regard to the fate of the third imam. The origin of this is apparently the feeling of the Shiʿite supporters in Kufah that at Karbala they had left Husayn in the lurch. In the fall of 684, a group of "penitents" left Kufah for Karbala in order to sacrifice themselves. The participants in this effort were in fact almost all killed by Umayyad troops at the beginning of January, 685. The acceptance of self-sacrifice, together with lamentation over the fate of the imam, is still today the most prominent mark of Twelver religious feeling.

According to Twelver tradition, not only Husayn but all the other imams—except for the twelfth—died a violent death: they were murdered by their enemies or perished in the latter's dungeons. Like Husayn, they had all innocently suffered and are therefore regarded as martyrs, just as he is, and Shiʿites celebrate the days of their martyrdom as holidays, with the sole exception of the twelfth imam, whose birthday is celebrated. The graves of the first eleven imams are greatly venerated by believers and are the goals of many Shiʿite pilgrimages. The Muharram celebrations, which are attested as early as the tenth century, at first included publicly performed songs of lamentation and processions. Starting in the seventeenth century, European travelers reported bloody processions of flagellants that sometimes degenerated into street fighting in the course of which people were killed. Finally, among the characteristic customs of Muharram celebrations are dramatic representations of the events in Karbala—so-called "passion plays" (taʿziyeh, "expressions of mourning") performed in public.

Processions of flagellants during the month of Muharram, which are often regarded with mistrust by Shiʿite theologians and sometimes prohibited by the authorities, are now common everywhere in Iran. The excited atmosphere during these occasions, on which thousands of believers come together, has proven to be politically explosive right down to the present day. The story of Husayn and his opponent Yazid can easily be given a contemporary context whenever it is a question of protesting what is seen as a tyrannical or unjust government. How effectively the events of early Islamic history can be instrumentalized politically has been impressively shown by the 1979 Islamic Revolution in Iran.

According to their own conception, Twelver Shiʿites have lived under what they consider legitimate rule only once: during the five years of ʿAli's caliphate. None of the imams following him ever succeeded in taking power again, the Shiʿite community has ever since lived under authorities it considers illegitimate. Moreover, after the concealment of the twelfth imam the Twelvers have remained entirely without leadership, for only the returned twelfth imam can be their legitimate leader. Even in seclusion he is the sole legitimate authority for Twelver Shiʿites, so that until he returns no earthly power can enjoy more than a temporary and strictly limited legitimacy. The problem that confronted the Shiʿites was who could rightfully lead them while they awaited the return of the hidden imam. After many disputes, this task was finally assigned to the Shiʿite scholars. The most current formulation of the principle that only this group, as representatives of the hidden imam, are allowed to lead the Shiʿite community, is found in the Ayatollah

Khomeini's doctrine of the "representative governance by the jurist" (in Persian, *vilayat-i faqih*). The representative ruling power of the Shiʿite scholars during the absence of the twelfth imam is also established in the Islamic Republic's constitution.

The ʿAbbasid Caliphate

The ʿAbbasid dynasty (750–1258) traced its lineage back to al-ʿAbbas, an uncle of the Prophet's. As members of Muhammad's family, they were in the Sunnis' opinion legitimate rulers, from a religious point of view. The ʿAbbasids had promoted the fall of the Umayyads by means of clandestine propaganda they entrusted to Abu Muslim, one of their freedmen of Iranian descent. Officially, Abu Muslim supported a pretender from the Quraysh clan of Hashim, which was Muhammad's and ʿAli's clan, thereby gaining the support of Shiʿites. However, Abu Muslim was for an imam whom he named only indirectly as "the one from Muhammad's house who wins approval." The center of his propaganda efforts was in Marv, in Khurasan, where Arabs had settled in great numbers with their *mawali*, in order to continue Muslim expansion toward Inner Asia. Starting in 747, at the head of his rebel army Abu Muslim conquered eastern Iran and then drove westward, where he took Kufah in 749. There Abu al-ʿAbbas, a member of the ʿAbbasid family, suddenly emerged and had himself honored as caliph; the overthrow of the Umayyads by ʿAbbasid troops came soon afterward. The Shiʿites, who had wanted to fight to win the caliphate for one of ʿAli's descendants, were now forced to recognize that they had helped a new usurper take power. It is clear that the Shiʿites, deprived of their hopes, saw the ʿAbbasids' action as a betrayal.

The ʿAbbasids followed the Prophet's original idea and abolished the clientele relationship. By making Arab and non-Arab Muslims legally equal, the Islamic state acquired a cosmopolitan character. The "Arabian Empire" of the Umayyads, as it is often called because of the privilege it accorded Arabs, was transformed into an "Islamic Empire" in which the concept of the *mawali* eventually became obsolete and in the ninth century disappeared entirely. Only then did the old culture of the Near East, whose traditions were transmitted by non-Arabs who had gone over to Islam, fuse with the new Islamic religion. Pre-Islamic Iranian ideas must have played a major role in this process.

In order to escape the Shiʿite milieu of Kufah, the caliph al-Mansur (reigned 754–775) founded in 762 the city of Baghdad in present-day Iraq, which remained—with a short interuption in the ninth century—the residence of the ʿAbbasid caliphs until it was taken by the Mongols in 1258. The choice of a site near the ancient Sasanian capital of Ctesiphon (Arabic *al-Madaʾin*, lit. "cities") and the city's layout make the shaping influence of pre-Islamic Iranian concepts of power clear. Baghdad is a remarkable example of purposeful city-planning. It was laid out as a round city, resembling a fortress with its three concentric walls; the caliph's palace, the main mosque, and the state administration were all inside the innermost wall. The city had four gates and was divided into four districts of equal size that could be closed off and guarded during the night. This round city, praised by Arab chroniclers as unique, and of which nothing has survived, was probably modeled on the round city layouts of the ancient Near East; we know of several round or oval layouts for cities dating from the age of the Sasanians, including Ctesiphon itself. The separation of the caliph from the people, which al-Mansur's Baghdad makes visible, along with the ruler's ability to exercise surveillance over his subjects at all times, correspond entirely to the position of an ancient Sasanian Great King. The administration was also obviously modeled on Sasanian institutions: religious, civil, and military responsibilities, which under the Umayyads had been vested in one person, were now separated and a supreme administrative official, the vizier, was introduced; he was the caliph's direct subordinate. Often it was officials of Iranian descent who rose to high administrative positions and even to the post of vizier. Ancient Persian notions of royal splendor may also have influenced the sumptuous character of life at the ʿAbbasid court, with its magnificent buildings, opulent banquets, and varied courtly ceremonies. The caliphs celebrated Iranian holidays, especially the spring festival of Noruz, and they enjoyed playing polo, one of the ancient Persians' favorite sports. All this, together with a high regard for Iranian craftsmanship, gave the culture of the ʿAbbasidian court a distinctly Persian appearance.

Militarily the ʿAbbasids no longer relied, as had the Umayyads, on

Arab tribal fighters, but instead, to an increasing extent, on soldiers recruited from Khurasan. The caliph al-Muʿtasim (reigned 833–842) created a bodyguard that was under his direct command and was composed of military slaves, chiefly of Turkish descent, who were bought on the steppes of Inner Asia when they were still children and raised as soldiers. They constituted the heart of the ʿAbbasidian army. However, this quickly proved to be a fateful step: instead of being a militarily effective instrument in the hands of the caliph, these guards increasingly gained political power. Frequent encroachments by the Turks, which al-Muʿtasim was unable to keep under control, on the people of Baghdad led to fighting in the streets and revealed the caliph's military weakness with regard to his army. The removal in 836 of the imperial residence to the newly founded garrison city of Samarra in northern Iraq was not to be a long-term solution; in 892 the ʿAbbasid court returned to Baghdad because a similar intolerable situation had developed in Samarra. The Turkish guards installed and overthrew the caliphs at will, so that by the ninth century the caliphate lost all real political power. The authority of the caliphs was no more than a fiction maintained for the benefit of outsiders, whereas the caliphate itself now represented only ideally the vanished unity of the Muslim universal community. Under these circumstances, independent territorial rulers began to appear as early as the beginning of the ninth century, at first on the periphery of the empire, and then also in its core lands, so that the actual territory controlled by the caliphate finally shrank to the immediate environs of Baghdad. However, many of the new dynasties had their rule confirmed by the caliph and thereby religiously justified, so that at least in theory the unity of the caliphate was preserved.

In 945, finally, the imperial residence of Baghdad was itself conquered by the Buyids, a mountain people from northern Iran. The Buyids "liberated" the ʿAbbasids from their Turkish guards, but they also seized political power for themselves, leaving the caliph only his moral authority. In 1055, the Saljuqs succeeded the Buyids, and ruled just as independently. After a short revival of the caliphate in the twelfth century, it was overthrown by the Mongols, the successors of Genghis Khan, in 1258, when they sacked Baghdad and killed the last ʿAbbasid caliph.

The Samanids

Starting in the first half of the ninth century, following the disintegration of the vast ʿAbbasid Empire, dynasties came to power in Iran that ruled de facto autonomously, even if—like many others—they nominally supported the caliph and made no claim to his title. Here, on the eastern edge of the caliphate, pre-Islamic Iranian traditions had remained alive that –now associated with the religion of Islam—shaped Iran's new cultural independence within the Islamic community and also gave Islam itself a new direction.

After the Tahirids (821–873), the earliest autonomous dynasty in Iran, which ruled the province of Khurasan practically independently, and after the Saffarids (867–903), who created a short-lived but enormous empire extending from Kabul in present-day Afghanistan to Isfahan, the Samanids (892–999) established in Transoxania, the caliphate's frontier province, a stable rule that they then extended to Khurasan. Their ancestor Saman—who lived in the eighth century—is supposed to have been a dihqan. According to the unanimous testimony of Muslim chroniclers he had fled, for unknown reasons, to Khurasan, where he converted to Sunni Islam. As a reward for their faithful service, the Caliph named Saman's grandsons to various gubernatorial positions in Transoxania. Under Ismaʿil (reigned 892–907), the true founder of Samanid rule, an empire emerged that was de facto independent of the caliphate and was at that time the greatest power in the Islamic East. In their capital, Bukhara, the Samanids created a centralized administration modeled on the caliph's court that became in turn a model for the Saljuqs and other dynasties: the ruler appointed provincial governors who were responsible for collecting taxes and were required to provide troops when needed. Militarily, the Samanids succeeded in making their territory safe for Sunni Islam by protecting it against attacks by the pagan Turks of the steppes of Inner Asia. Like the Tahirids before them, the Samanids imported Turkish military slaves into the caliphate's lands, but no longer for the caliph's court alone. Since its beginning under al-Muʿtasim, military slavery had developed into the basis of the army, so that the need—together with the price—had significantly increased. This profitable business, coupled with a prudent encouragement of trade to which the spread of Samanid coins as far as Scandinavia and the Rhine testifies, led to greater economic prosperity.

The Samanids turned their residence in Bukhara into a cosmopolitan center of artistic and intellectual creation that was also the center of what is often called the "Iranian Renaissance." Their own affinity with the Iranian past is shown in the old Persian title *shahanshah* ("king of kings") that they bore, and in their claim to be descended from the Sasanian military commander and later Great King Bahram Chubin (ruled 590-591). At their court, the Samanid rulers generously promoted New Persian language and poetry. The language of the court was Persian, which may at this early date have already been used alongside Arabic in the administration. In Samanid Bukhara a revival of pre-Islamic Iranian traditions took place that should not, however, be misunderstood as a mere return to the past, as is suggested by the term "Renaissance," and certainly not as a reaction of an Iranian national consciousness to Arab Islam. Instead, the return to old Iranian traditions occurred in combination with Islam, so that we might more properly speak of an Islamic-Iranian Renaissance. It was the Samanids' achievement to have shown that Islam as a religion, and above all as a culture, need not remain bound to the Arabic language. By separating it from its purely Arab background, they freed it from the narrow, Bedouin conditions in which it had originated. They showed the way to make the new religion more flexible and adaptable than it had earlier been, and to ensure that it would have a future beyond the Arabs. Just as the Samanids had combined their own—Old Persian—tradition with Islam, other peoples could do the same in the future. Thus Islam became a truly universal religion and culture, open to all people.

The Samanids were the last dynasty of Iranian descent in Transoxania. Their decline and fall had many causes. Internal rebellions weakened the empire; the Turkish military slaves who made up the Samanid army seized power, as they had already done in Baghdad. Finally, Khurasan fell to the Turkish Ghaznavid dynasty (977–1186), which invaded the province from eastern Afghanistan, while Transoxania fell to the Turkish QaraKhanid dynasty (992–1212), which advanced from the north. Only one architectural testimony to the artistically brilliant

Samanid age is still extant in Bukhara: the mausoleum of the founder of the dynasty, Isma'il. This is a four-arched edifice built on the model of Sasanian fire-temples and completely covered with tiles in which patterns were inscribed with great craftsmanship; it is one of the great masterpieces of Islamic architecture.

The Buyids

The family of the Buyids (Arabized as "Buwayhids"), who took their name from their ancestor Buyeh, came from the Daylam region on the southern coast of the Caspian Sea. In this mountainous area Islam established itself only relatively late. The inhabitants of Daylam were known as courageous foot soldiers; they had fought in the Caucasus as the Sasanians' allies and more than once repelled Muslim attacks on their homeland before in the ninth century they gradually began to open up to Islam, which was spread in Daylam chiefly by Shi'ite groups. The Buyids, like most of the people of Daylam, belonged to the Zaydiyyah, a moderate Shi'ite branch that considers the succession of imams after Husayn to be still open and does not believe in a hidden imam. However, they especially encouraged the Twelvers, probably under the influence of their viziers. Like the Turks, the people of Daylam had already served as mercenaries before the reign of the Buyids, and Buyeh's three sons—Ali, Hasan, and Ahmad—also began their careers in the army of Mardaviz (reigned 931–935), who came from the Daylamite clan of the Ziyarids and had brought the greater part of northern Iran under his rule. After Mardaviz was murdered by his Turkish mercenaries in 935, his short-lived kingdom rapidly fell apart. In only a few years the three brothers of the Buyid family had established their control over central and western Iran and Mesopotamia, which they were to rule for over a century (945–1055). In 945, Ahmad took Baghdad and made himself the caliph's "protector."

The third Buyid ruler, 'Adud al-Dawlah (reigned 978–983) united all the Buyid territories in Iraq, Iran, and Oman. As a result, the center of power—at least after the fall of the Samanids—was shifted to western Iran, the area of the former Sasanian Empire. Like the Samanids before them, the Buyids assumed the old Persian title of *shahanshah* ("king of kings"); Adud ad-Daula had himself formally crowned as king by the caliph, and it is no surprise that he now also claimed to be descended from the Sasanian emperor Bahram Gur (reigned 421–439). Although in the meantime many Iranians had gone over to Islam, and Adud ad-Daula considered himself a devout Muslim, the pre-Islamic idea of kingship was—in parallel with the "Iranian Renaissance" in eastern Iran—still important in the west.

From a religious point of view, the Buyids were in no way legitimate rulers, so that they urgently needed the Sunni caliphate, especially since the large majority of their subjects were Sunnis. In addition to their old Persian title the Buyids therefore assumed the already existing title of commander-in-chief (*amir al-ʿUmara*). In the Buyids the Shiʿah nonetheless found powerful protectors and promoters. Under the first Buyid ruler, Ahmad, the main Shiʿite holidays—ʿAshura and the commemoration of ʿAli's designation at the pool of Khumm—were for the first time publicly celebrated. The Buyids frequently made pilgrimages to the graves of the Shiʿite imams, whose shrines they enlarged and surrounded with walls to protect them from Bedouin attacks. ʿAli's and Fatimah's many descendants received privileges such as annual pensions or payments made from revenue derived from pious donations if they could prove the authenticity of their descent. A special office of the *naqib al-ashraf* ("marshal of the nobility") was set up, presumably in the ninth century, to record and verify genealogical connections with ʿAli's family. Insofar as the descendants of ʿAli and Fatima—who were allowed to use the titles *sharif* ("noble," for the descendants of ʿAli's son Hasan) and *sayyid* ("lord," for the descendants of ʿAli's son Husayn)—developed into a kind of religious aristocracy, the office of *naqib al-ashraf* also acquired social prestige. During the Buyid dynasty the standard canonical books distinguishing the Twelvers' religious doctrine and law from those of other Shiʿite denominations appeared, about a century after the corresponding Sunni books were written. It is moreover interesting to note that the authors of the canonical works of the Buyid period already made Shiʿite scholars, as representatives of the twelfth imam, responsible for leading the Shiʿite community. Although the scholars' representative leadership of the Shiʿite community long remained in dispute, the direction it would take is already foreshadowed here.

From the outset the Buyids had no established regulation regarding succession to the throne; usually, various branches of the family ruled in the cities and provinces of Iran and Iraq unless an energetic personality like Adud ad-Daula was able to gain their general support. However, this political fragmentation benefited the various seats of government—such as the cities of Rayy, Isfahan, and Shiraz—whose rulers erected splendid edifices and were active as patrons and promoters of the arts. The frequent internal conflicts between the later Buyids made it easier for their opponents to take one province after another away from them. In 1055 the Saljuqs conquered Baghdad, and thereafter the Buyids continued to rule only in Fars, until this province also fell to the Saljuqs.

The Continuing Existence of Iranian Traditions

The Islamic civilization of the Middle Ages, as it developed under the ʿAbbasids, may initially appear to outsiders to be an Arabian culture, because of the dominance of Arabic as the language of the Qurʾan, science, and literature, but its content has in fact been essentially shaped by Iranian culture. Scholars and men of letters of Iranian descent, many of whom came from bureaucratic families, concerned themselves with the pre-Islamic past of Iran, which they sought to harmonize with their own time and with the religion of Islam. In the eighth century, Iranian Muslims started producing numerous translations of Sasanian court literature from Middle Persian into Arabic, and thereby introduced Iranian historical traditions into the Muslim view of history. The dominant model of this Persian tradition of rulership and the statecraft was the empire of the Sasanians, who had amalgamated the Persian past with their own dynasty to produce a more or less official view of history. The latter was expressed in the Middle Persian "Book of Kings" (*Khoday-Namak*), composed under the rule of Khusraw Parviz (reigned 590–628). This work compiled mythical, legendary, and historical material and provided a chronological history of Iran beginning with the first king, Gayomart. The translation of this work into Arabic by the Iranian state secretary Ibn al-Muqaffa (d. 757) made this self-image of the Sasanian kings known to the educated Muslim world. The

Sasanian Empire thus became the standard model of the traditional conception of state rulership and thinking in connection with pre-Islamic Persia.

During the period of governmental and social reorientation under the first ʿAbbasid caliphs, a new literary genre emerged that was concerned with statecraft and became a favorite vehicle for the expression of Islamic-Iranian traditions of rulership: the "mirror for princes," which was addressed with admonitory intention to kings and rulers and that sought to instruct them regarding the ethical and moral principles of government. Since the subjects these works dealt with did not exist in the original Islamic tradition, their authors were from the outset Iranian Muslims, even if they wrote at first in Arabic, and only later, at the beginning of the tenth century, in New Persian. However, these authors provided the traditional concept of the king with new traits in order to adapt it to the Islamic religion. The mirrors for princes thus clearly testify to the consciousness of political and cultural continuity that motivated their Iranian authors, and are at the same time our most important source of information regarding the development of the image of Iran in the Islamic age.

A basic feature of the Persian conception of the ruler was the doctrine of charisma, *khvarnah*, the possession of which distinguished the king from other men and legitimated him. Charisma was seen as a light that radiated from the ruler; hence its Arabic translation as *nur*, "light." God gave the Persian king the gift of wisdom, and this enabled him to exercise justice and do good. The king acted on behalf of God, and just as God ruled over the heavenly sphere, so did the king rule over the earthly sphere. The equivalent juxtaposition of prophet and king, of the Islamic and non-Islamic, in the mirrors for princes—a juxtaposition that is of course entirely impermissible from a theological point of view—necessarily led to many reinterpretations of the Iranian idea of rulership that made it compatible with the Islamic conception of rulershi, which demanded that the caliph be in immediate contact with his subjects. The absolute ruler thus became—according to the traditional model of the first four caliphs, to whom this attribute was ascribed—a king who was close to his people and always available to them. The Iranian ruler's throne, which was originally a symbol of his distance from the people, was interpreted in the mirrors for princes as a means of giving the king a better overview during audiences.

The Persian monarchical tradition remained alive in the history of Iran down to the modern period. Under the Qajar rulers of the nineteenth century, for instance, the "chest of justice" that was sent to the provinces so that even subjects living in the most remote parts of the country might send their petitions to the capital symbolized the accessibility of the rulers. In the twentieth century, the Pahlavis repeatedly invoked old Iranian ideas that could in case of need be visually represented: thus during the coronation ceremonies in 1967, the crown and the Qur'an were presented to the Shah by two soldiers walking side by side—the Iranian idea of the state and Islam symbolically appearing as completely equal in importance.

The Beginnings of New Persian Literature

Persian belongs to the Indo-Iranian (Aryan) group of the Indo-European family of languages. In the first centuries after the fall of the Sasanian Empire, the official language of which had been Middle Persian, or so-called Pahlavi, New Persian developed and was henceforth written in Arabic script. Thereby it constituted the basis for a peculiarly Iranian cultural development that in the course of its later history put its stamp on large geographical areas reaching as far as the Near East, Central Asia, and India.

The first examples of New Persian literature appeared in the east, far from the center of the caliphate, and until the tenth century they were limited to Transoxania and Khurasan. There, without strong competition from other languages, New Persian could more freely develop as a literary medium. As sparse early reports suggest, New Persian was at first used in courtly poetry addressed to local potentates, princes, and dignitaries. Many of these understood little Arabic or none at all, so that poets had to compose their panegyrics in New Persian, which was widely understood. Except for a few examples, early poetry in New Persian has been lost; the oldest poetic fragments extant go back only as far as the ninth century, complete poems to the tenth century. The most impressive figure among the early New Persian poets is the blind singer Rudaki (d. 940 or 950), who was active at the court of the Samanids and whose works are also extant only in fragments. According to the unanimous judgment of his contemporaries, his verse was regarded as the inimitable model of poetic language, so that he is often considered the father of Persian poetry. In addition to poetry, prose works were also written before the eleventh century in New Persian, among them books on geography, the exegesis of the Qurʾan, and medicine, but few of these have survived. At the court of the Samanids, the vizier Abu Ali Bal'ami wrote a history of Iran (completed in 963), which he took from the annals—composed in Arabic—of al-Tabari (d. 923), who was also an author of Iranian descent, and reworked or expanded here and there. It is still the oldest known prose work in New Persian and until the time of the Mongols it remained the standard book on the history of Iran.

The Persian epic is a uniquet Iranian creation that grew out of the pre-Islamic royal tradition. Among the numerous epics in New Persian literature, there is basically only one outstanding heroic epic, which is often called the Iranian "national epic," though it also contains many romance-like elements: Ferdowsi's *Shahnameh*. Ferdowsi (d. after 1020) came from a wealthy dihqan family in Tus (modern Mashhad) in Khurasan. His *Shahnameh* (completed in 1010), which is more than 50,000 verses long, is a monumental epic on the early, pre-Islamic history of Iran that goes back into distant, mythical ages, and concludes in the age of the Sasanians. It weaves historical events and legends together. In this way it became a compendium of the Iranian heritage that provides an all-encompassing history of pre-Islamic Iran and presents all the numerous kings and heroes constantly encountered in later Iranian literature. In the early twentieth century, Iranian nationalists rediscovered Ferdowsi as the "re-awakener" of a particular Iranian identity (after the Arab conquest of Iran in the seventh century) and the *Shahnameh* as the literary monument of this identity.

CHAPTER 2
Iran under the Turks and Mongols (1055–1501)

The Eleventh Century

In many respects, the eleventh century represents a significant turning-point in the history of Iran and of large parts of the Islamic world. From then on, and for many centuries, dynasties of Iranian descent were displaced by Turkish dynasties. Thus ended the "Iranian interlude," as scholars came to refer to the ninth and tenth centuries—the era of the Tahirids, the Safarids, the Samanids, and the Buyids. Although for a long time Turks had already played an important role in the armies of the caliphate and its provinces, up to that point they had been individuals separated from their former tribe or clan. Now, however, wave after wave of Turkish tribes from Central Asia began to migrate toward the west, streaming into the Islamic world and founding their own states and dynasties. Where Turks settled permanently, they changed the character of the country. The ethnic and linguistic layering of various peoples is visible in the spread of Turkish and Turkish-derived place names in the areas particularly favored by Turkish settlers. Turkish peoples appeared as advocates and defenders of Sunni Islam; after the end of the Buyid dynasty, Twelver Shi'ites were eliminated as a political force almost everywhere for the next five centuries. Despite the Turks' military ability, most of the states they founded proved to be relatively unstable; because of the lack of a fixed order of succession and the idea that subjected territory "belonged" not to the ruler alone but to his whole clan, sooner or later they disintegrated into various small regional states—an almost inevitable consequence of the battles over succession that regularly occurred when a sovereign died. This process took place repeatedly in Iran from the eleventh century on, until at the beginning of the sixteenth century the Safavid dynasty once again welded the various regional states into a single empire.

Originally, the Turks of Central Asia were nomads, but—unlike the Arab conquerors of Iran—they had very robust animals for riding and carrying loads. The Bactrian camel can endure cold and climb high mountains. Thus the advance of the Turks also spread their own way of life: nomadism. Unlike in Europe, where the role it played was small or non-existent, nomadism was an important factor shaping the Middle East. From that point on, relationships between nomads and sedentary peoples were marked by constant conflicts that led to devastation and a long-term decline of agriculture. To a large extent, climatic conditions determined the direction taken by the spread of the Turks, since for their animals they needed cool mountain meadows in the summer and mild lowland plains in the winter, moving back and forth semi-annually between the two. Thus, for instance, Azerbaijan in northwest Iran became one of the natural Turkish settlement areas.

The processes of change described above began on a large scale under the Saljuqs (1040–1194), but the Turkish dynasty of the Ghaznavids (977–1186) was in many ways already typical of the new situation. Its founder was a military slave in the Samanid army who had risen to a high position and had brought a small territory in Ghazna (in modern Afghanistan) under his rule. The greatest ruler of the dynasty, Mahmud (reigned. 998–1030), was a devout Sunni who regarded himself as the defender of the caliph in Baghdad against inimical Shiʿite activities. He conquered a large empire that included Afghanistan, Khurasan, Khwarazm, and parts of northern India. Since it was essentially tailored to him as an individual, under his successor his empire was quickly lost to the Saljuqs, but the Ghaznavids held on in eastern Afghanistan and northern India for about a hundred and thirty years. The short-lived Ghaznavid Empire is the first example showing how the Turks from the steppes of Central Asia who came into contact with the high civilization of Iran claimed it as their own. On the military basis provided by the Turks, the court and the administration were organized on the Iranian model of the Samanids, while the official language of government remained Arabic. Despite their Turkish descent, the Ghaznavids bestowed upon themselves a genealogy that went back to a daughter of the last Sasanian king, Yazdgard III (reigned 633–651). The Ghaznavids, and especially Mahmud, enthusiastically supported and promoted Iranian culture and literature, as had the Samanids. Mahmud sought to emulate the already waning splendor of the Samanid court in Bukhara. He made his court in Ghazna into a widely known cultural center that attracted many scholars and poets.

From the Saljuqs to the Khwarazm-Shahs

The Saljuqs, who traced their name back to their ancestor Saljuq, were originally the leading family of a clan belonging to the Turkish tribal confederation of the Oghuz (Arabic *Ghuzz*) that lived during the tenth century on the steppes north of the Aral Sea and the Caspian Sea. Toward the end of the century, they converted to Islam, which had been spread in these regions on the frontiers of civilization chiefly by merchants and wandering preachers. After a crushing victory over Ghaznavid troops in 1040, near Dandanqan (between Marv and Sarakhs) in present-day Turkmenistan, the Saljuqs moved farther west and conquered the lands ruled by the Buyid family. In 1055, their leader Toghril Beg took Baghdad and thus ended the 110-year-long Shiʿite domination over the Sunni caliphate. As devout Sunnis, the Saljuqs revived the religious war, seeing themselves as holy warriors (Arabic *ghazi*) for orthodox Islam, which they sought not only to defend against heterodox denominations within the Islamic world, but also to spread to heretofore non-Islamic areas. The Saljuq Empire achieved its greatest extent under Malik-Shah (reigned 1073–1092). In 1071, he defeated the Byzantine emperor Romanos Diogenes (reigned 1068–1071) at Manzikert (now Malazgird, north of Lake Van in present-day Turkey), with the result that the enormous area between Anatolia and Transoxania now fell—at least nominally—under Saljuq rule.

Shortly after Malik-Shah's death, the Saljuq Empire collapsed into various regional powers. The situation remained relatively ordered and stable only in Transoxania, during the long rule of Malik-Shah's son Sanjar (reigned 1097–1157). The Saljuq Empire's tendency to disintegrate into smaller and smaller powers was promoted by the custom of appointing an Atabeg (Turkish "Prince Father") as tutor to the Saljuq princes who were given a province to govern. The Atabegs were Turkish military leaders who had their own following, who ruled with increasing independence, and who deprived their pupils of power and secured rulership for their own descendants. From the twelfth century, Atabeg dynasties ruled autonomously in various parts of Iran: in Shiraz, the Salghurids (1148–1282), in Tabriz, the Eldiguzids (1145–1225), and in Maragheh the Ahmadilis (1122–after 1220). Other Atabeg dynasties and local rulers from various branches of the Saljuq family composed a patchwork of new small states that ultimately reached across the whole of the Near East as far as Central Anatolia. At the beginning of the thirteenth century, the many Saljuq regional rulers were eliminated by the Khwarazm-Shahs (1077–1231), who conquered a large but very short-lived empire that extended from the boundaries of Anatolia to those of India. They started out from the remote Khwarezm oasis south of the Aral Sea. A governor installed there by Malik-Shah had bequeathed his office to his own descendants, who in turn took the title "Khwarazm-Shah" ("Ruler of Khwarezm"). Their empire, which was established at the beginning of the thirteenth century, soon fell victim to the Mongols led by Genghis Khan.

The Saljuq State

Like the Buyids before them, the Saljuqs, who had no religious legitimation, had their rule confirmed by the caliph. The latter granted their founder, Toghril Beg, various titles, including that of Sultan (Arabic *sultân*, lit. "power," "rule"). In earlier times some princes had used this title informally; now, however, it became an official title designating the independent—and usually Sunni—ruler of a territory. Characteristic of the Saljuq period was the dichotomy of caliph and sultan, which referred to two de facto separate spheres of authority. Whereas the caliph was now only the supreme religious and moral authority of the Muslim community, the sultan combined in his person the real political and military power. This new dichotomy, which was alien to the original Muslim conception of the state, actually only made the caliph's longstanding weakness more obvious.

For the government of their empire the Saljuqs adopted the traditional Iranian-Islamic institutions. Whereas the court offices responsible for organizing ceremonies and receptions were chiefly occupied by Turkish military leaders, the civil administration, with its numerous departments, remained in the hands of Iranian officials, who usually came from the bureaucratic class. Under the Saljuqs the vizier, as the highest civil official, was a very influential and powerful figure; he controlled the financial and fiscal department, the ruler's correspondence, and the military department, which was responsible for recruiting and paying soldiers and for maintaining the army. One of these viziers, Nizam al-Mulk, who held this office for thirty years under the sultans Alp Arslan (reigned 1063–1072) and Malik-Shah (reigned 1073–1092), composed the *Siyasat-nameh* ("Book of Government"), which is one of the most important Persian prose works both because of its historical and cultural content and because of its outstanding language and style. Although during their campaigns of conquest the Saljuqs had relied on the support of their warlike nomadic hordes, once they took power they quickly replaced these troops with an army composed of military slaves and mercenaries. Nonetheless, familial bonds between the sultan and the tribes continued to exist. On the other hand, the Saljuqs were never able to find a satisfactory solution for the problem of integrating the nomadic tribes and their herds into the economy and society of Iran's sedentary population. Because additional Turkish groups were constantly emigrating from the steppes into Iran, and especially into Khurasan, the number of nomads steadily increased. However, the damage done to Iranian agriculture by these nomads was at first kept within limits—unlike what happened later on under the Mongols. Although many Turks remained in Iran, others moved westward in great numbers, where they found—in the Caucasus, Anatolia, and Syria—ample opportunities to fight for Islam. As a result of these migrations the number of nomads markedly increased in various areas of Iran where the climate suited them.

In order to meet the material demands of an excessively powerful army, the Buyids had already begun rewarding leading military figures by assigning them the tax income from a certain area instead of paying them in cash. In medieval Iran, this practice was designated by the

Arabic word *iqtâ* ("separation") and became a typical economic institution that was, depending on the period and geographical region, implemented in different ways and sometimes known by other names. However, the Saljuqs' army—which as a standing army was typically composed of military slaves of Turkish and, later on, Kurdish descent, among others—was considerably larger than that of the Buyids, if only because the geographical extent of their empire was far greater. For that reason the system of grants made to military leaders had to be systematically expanded and extended to areas in which it had earlier been practiced little or not at all. Increasingly, grants were accompanied by additional authority for the holder. Frequently the latter was given full administrative powers and could appoint his own officials in his grant. This broadened form of *iktâ*, which scholars usually call "administrative grants," became common everywhere under the Saljuqs, and was ultimately awarded even to meritorious officials and court dignitaries. In times when there was a strong central power, the system certainly had advantages, and often had a stabilizing effect on internal conditions. On the other hand, in this way more and more local and regional centers of powers with their own troops came into being. As a consequence of the increasing decline of the Saljuq central government in the twelfth century and the emergence of Atabeg dynasties, the grants, which had originally been granted for a limited period of time, became de facto and then also de jure hereditary, remaining in the permanent possession of the military leaders and provincial governors. In the later Saljuq period the granting of *iktâ* by the state often amounted to no more than the legalization of an already existing situation. After a few decades' interruption caused by the Mongol invasion in the thirteenth century, this tendency resumed in the fourteenth century.

Like other areas controlled by the Saljuqs, until the end of Malik-Shah's rule Iran's cities enjoyed widespread internal peace. Many of them profited from their position on the great trade routes, as did, for example, Kirman and Nishapur on the important route from the Persian Gulf to Khurasan. During the whole of the Saljuq period this latter route was a very important link between the Indian Ocean and the Arabian peninsula and Central Asia. Mediated by the Crusader states on the Syrian-Palestinian coast, the widespread trade network reached as far as Europe.

The Saljuq rulers admired Iranian culture, which they generously promoted. In their era, architecture and craftwork, for which the rulers presumably employed almost exclusively native Iranians, flourished. The Saljuqs, whose court language was Persian, also were active as patrons of Persian literature. Panegyric court poetry achieved perfection in the work of Anvari (d. c. 1170), who lived at Sanjar's court, and that of Khaqani (d. c. 1199), who wrote at various courts between Khwarezm and Shirvan; the great ruins of ancient Ctesiphon (al-Mada'in), whose vanished splendor seemed to him an admonition regarding the transience of all human striving, inspired Khaqanii to write one of the most famous poems in Persian literature. Nizami (1141-1209), who lived in Ganja, in Azerbaijan, under the rule of the Atabeg dynasty of the Eldeguzids, is considered the greatest representative of the romantic verse epic. His famous *Five Epics* (Arabic *khamseh*, "five," and Persian *panj ganj*, "five treasures"), which emphasize the ethical principle of humanity and are committed to the ideal image of the just ruler, became the classical model for later generations of Persian poets and for Turkish and Indian authors as well. Attar (d. between 1220 and 1234), who was from Nishapur and was one of Iran's greatest mystical storytellers, wrote in the eastern part of the Saljuq Empire; Jalal al-din al-Rumi (1207–1273, generally known in Iran as Mawlana) wrote in Anatolia (Rum) under the rule of the Anatolian branch of the Rum Saljuqs (1081–1307); his mystical epic was praisede as the "Qur'an in Persian language." Here we must not forget to mention Omar Khayyam ("the tent-maker," died c. 1122), among the greatest figures of the Saljuq age. In Iran he famouse chiefly as a brilliant mathematician and natural scientist, but in the West he is best known for his skeptical, ironic-satirical verse quatrains.

Sunnism and Shi'ism under the Saljuqs

The age of the Saljuqs was a time of intense religious unrest. At this point Shi'ism had split into two different factions: alongside "Twelver Shi'sm") and the moderate Zaydiyyah emerged the extremist Isma'iliyyah, which was itself divided into various smaller sects. The Isma'iliyah takes its name from Isma'il, the son of the sixth Shi'ite imam Ja'far.

Although Ismaʿil predeceased his father, all the Ismaʿilite groups recognize him as a true imam, whereas the Twelvers continue the succession of imams after Jaʿfar through the latter's younger son Musa (d. 799). The Ismaʿilites developed an esoteric doctrine that included Gnostic and later also neo-Platonic elements. They assumed that there was a cyclic revelation that took place through six prophetic eras. Isma'il's hidden son Muhammad—who bore the same name as the Prophet—is expected to return as the *mahdi*. According to Ismaʿilite doctrine, the mahdi will then do away with all religious systems, including Islam, and re-establish the paradisiacal, original religion of Adam; the latter has no fixed forms of worship and consists solely in God's creatures' praise of their Lord and in their recognition that he is the one and only God. Certain Ismaʿili sects developed different conceptions of the mahdi, and some even proclaimed their leaders to be divine. In so doing, they clearly went beyond the limits set by orthodox Islam, which as a strict monotheistic religion does not allow any divine persons or beings other than God. Therefore many of the Ismailis' contemporaries no longer considered them Muslims at all.

By 900, the Ismaʿilis had already created, by means of trained propagandists, a far-flung network that covered the whole Islamic world. Soon thereafter they gained political power and established an Ismaʿilite counter-caliphate, that of the Fatimids (909–1171) in North Africa, and from the middle of the tenth century, in Egypt and Syria as well. The Ismaʿilites' political goal was to overthrow the ʿAbbasid caliphate and, from 1055 on, the battle against the Sunni Saljuq sultans and their followers.

In Iran, the Ismaʿilite propaganda campaign was led by Hasan-i Sabbah (d. 1124) from Qum, who had originally been a Twelver Shiʿite but converted to the Ismaʿiliyah while he was young, and who had since 1072 been active as a propagandist in various parts of the country. In 1090 he conquered the fortress of Alamut in the eastern Alburz Mountains, where he henceforth resided. From there, he sent out envoys who were to incite open insurrection against the caliphs and the Saljuq rulers. The numerous political assassinations carried out by Hasan-i Sabbah's followers to weaken the Saljuq Empire became notorious. In Syria, they were given the Arabic name *hashishiyya*, "hashish-eaters," from which the Western term "Assassins" is derived, although their use of hashish and other drugs has not been proven. The "Assassins" referred to themselves as "devotees" (Persian *fidaʾin*, "those who sacrifice themselves"), since their activities usually cost them their lives. During Hasan-i Sabbah's lifetime, they thoroughly infiltrated the Saljuq army and court. One of the Assassins' most prominent victims was the vizier Nizam al-Mulk, who was stabbed by a disguised attacker in 1092. After Hasan-i Sabbah's death a dynasty of propagandists ruled in Alamut. They assassinated two caliphs, a Saljuq sultan, several governors and viziers, and numerous jurists who had preached or written against the Assassins. In 1256 the Mongols put an end to the rule of this sect, wrecked Alamut and other fortresses held by the Assassins, and destroyed the Ismaʿilite library at Alamut. As late as the sixteenth century there were still Ismaʿilite groups in the region, and today small Ismaʿilite communities persist in Khurasan, Kirman, Yazd, and elsewhere.

The Saljuqs did all they could to establish orthodox Sunnism in their empire. To this end they promoted Sunni schools and teachers of the recognized Sunni schools of law. Theological seminaries or madrasahs (Arabic *madrasah*, lit., "place of teaching and learning") were set up throughout the empire, and thus education, which had previously been dispensed for the most part privately in mosques, was institutionalized. While the sultans had already distinguished themselves as founders of madrasahs, the latter are associated above all with the vizier Nizam al-Mulk. He established numerous madrasahs, named "Nizamiyyah" in honor of him, and staffed them with the most learned men of his time. The most famous Nizamiyah was in Baghdad; others were in Basra, Mosul, Isfahan, Nishapur, Herat, Marv, and Balkh.

Although the relationship between Sunnis and Shiʿites was seldom without tension, in general the non-Ismaʿilite Shiʿites, a religious minority, seem to have lived quite peacefully alongside the Sunnis. Their common opponent, the Ismaʿilites, seems to have ensured a relatively calm relations between the two sects. After an initial decline at the beginning of the Saljuq period, the importance of Twelver Shiʿism gradually increased again. Many Twelvers rose to high administrative posts and even became viziers. These officials were inclined to provide money for the tombs of the imams and to build mausoleums for the imams' descendants (Persian *imamzadeh*). Twelver dignitaries created their own Shi'ite educational institutions on the model of the Sunni madrasahs, and financed them—as did the Sunnis—by means of revenues provided by religious donations.

The Mongol Invasion and Its Consequences

The Mongol invasions under Genghis Khan (d. 1227) and his successors constituted a deep rupture in Iranian history. While it is true that there had already been a decline of cultivated land and an increase of nomadism in Iran since the Saljuq invasion in the eleventh century, the Mongol invasion greatly accelerated this process, and this fact clearly distinguishes Mongol rule over Iran from the conquests and dynastic shifts of the preceding centuries. The Mongol homeland lay in the steppes of Central Asia, near the headwaters of the great Siberian rivers west and northwest of China, where they were nomadic shepherds and horsemen divided, like the Turkish peoples, into tribes living in the same region. Through a series of battles the Mongol prince Timujin succeeded in uniting all the warring Mongol tribes under his leadership. In 1206 he was formally recognized as the master of all Mongols, and assumed the title Genghis Khan. The meaning of this title is not clear; a connection with the Turkish *tengiz*, "ocean," has often been suggested, so that the title might be rendered as "universal ruler." After conquering Transoxania and Khwarezm in the fall of 1219, the Mongols invaded Iran, penetrating as far as the Caucasus. However, when in 1224 Genghis Khan moved back toward the east, with the exception of Khurasan the country was once again left to itself until Genghis Khan's grandson Hülegü renewed the campaign of conquest in the West and founded the Mongol Il-Khanid Empire.

The Mongol invasion was for Iran a catastrophe of unprecedented magnitude. The regions conquered by the Mongols were left completely in ruins. Many areas recovered only slowly, others not at all. The merciless cruelty with which the Mongols carried out their campaigns, the countless massacres of the male population of the cities they conquered and their enslavement of women and children severely damaged the country. Political and intellectual centers of the Iranian cultural sphere such as Nishapur, Balkh, and Marv never regained their earlier significance as foci of Islamic civilization. Numerous other cities dwindled into villages. During their campaigns of conquest in Iran the Mongols spared only those craftsmen, artists, scholars, and families of notables in the cities who could be of use to them because of their experience in administration and jurisprudence. In this way the Iranian upper class remained, at least in the cities, relatively stable.

The conflicts between Iranians and Turks that arose during the Saljuq period were intensified by Mongol rule because many Turkish warriors followed Genghis Khan's army from Central Asia. It is generally thought that far more Turks than Mongols reached Iran. In the course of time the Mongols as a race were completely absorbed by the Turks. Hence in the long run Iran was not so much Mongolized as Turkified. After the Mongol invasion, the twofold ethnic nature of the population and thus of the society became a permanent feature of Iran. Even in today's Iran, Turks constitute independent population groups in northwest Iran, on the southern coast of the Caspian Sea, and in Khurasan.

The Mongols left neither longstanding ethnic nor linguistic traces on Iran. In particular, the Turkish language gained importance at the expense of Mongolian, but far more at that of Persian. Many areas of Iran became primarily Turkish-speaking and have remained so down to the present day. In the thirteenth century northwest Iran in particular became an area settled almost exclusively by Turks. Azari, the language of Azerbaijan, was originally the name for the Persian dialect spoken in that area; it was later transferred to Turkish, which is still called Azeri there.

The Il-Khans

Genghis Khan decreed that after his death the vast empire he had conquered should be divided among his four sons by his first wife. At the beginning, the empire was still headed by a Great Khan elected by a general assembly of Mongol notables. His seat was Karakorum on the upper reaches of the Orchon River in modern-day Mongolia. But in the course of the following decades the ties holding together the Great

Khan's far-flung empire had grown so loose that by the end of the thirteenth century independent Mongol states had sprung up. From Iran, Mesopotamia, the Caucasus, and Anatolia emerged the Il-Khanid Empire (1256–1335). Its true founder was Hülegü (reigned 1256–1265), a grandson of Genghis Khan who had continued the Mongol campaign of conquest in West Asia. He began his campaigns in the spring of 1253; in 1258 he took Baghdad and overthrew the ʿAbbasid caliphate, which was thus extinguished after a rule of more than five hundred years and found only an insignificant epilogue in the Egypt of the Mamluks (1250–1517). It was also the Mamluks who in 1260 defeated Hülegü's troops in Palestine and put a definitive end to his conquests in the West. As nomadic shepherds and horsemen, the Mongols settled—like the Turkish tribes that had immigrated from Central Asia—particularly in areas that offered suitable climatic conditions for their flocks: in northwest Iran, in the area around Baghdad, and in eastern Anatolia. It was here that the centers of Il-Khanid rule developed. The title "Il-Khan" which means something like "subordinate Khan," was assumed by Hülegü and his successors in deference to the Great Khan in Karakorum. Only toward the end of the thirteenth century did the Il-Khanid Empire finally detach itself from its subordination to the Great Khan. The Il-Khan Ghazan (ruled 1295–1304) formally cut his ties to the Great Khan and abandoned the title "Il-Khan" in favor of "Khan" on his coins and in his documents.

The Il-Khans succeeded in defending their empire against pressure exerted by neighboring states: in the east, against the Mongol autonomous region Chagatai, where the Amu Darya river (the ancient Oxus) became a permanent barrier; in the Caucasus, against the Golden Horde—also an autonomous Mongol state; in Egypt and in Syria, where the Euphrates formed the border, against the Mamluk state. Thus the Il-Khans ruled approximately the area that corresponded to Persia in both earlier and later times. The Il-Khanid Empire was essentially an Iranian state, whereas the center of Arab-Islamic culture shifted definitively to the west, away from conquered Mesopotamia and toward Cairo and Damascus. The increased division between the Arab and Iranian parts of the Islamic world ensuing from this situation becaem even deeper in later times, because the Mongol and Turkish rulers of

Iran, Asia Minor, Central Asia, and India increasingly integrated themselves into the Iranian world with respect to language, government, and cultural orientation.

At the head of the state stood the Il-Khan, along with the imperial assembly of Mongol nobles and high dignitaries, and especially the vizier, who was usually of Iranian descent. Il-Khan rulers did not, however, govern the state in accord with any firmly established forms. For example, over long periods of time there was not a single vizier, but rather two viziers holding office at the same time, and their rivalries made consistent exercise of the office impossible. Throughout the rule of the Il-Khans, the highest levels of government remained erratic, and this contributed to the relatively short duration of their empire. To this also contributed the numerous economic ills that became habitual under the Il-Khans. The henceforth constantly high level of nomads among the population was accompanied by systematic transformations of large areas of farmland into the pastures needed by the nomads for their herds. Together with the devastation that resulted from the Mongol invasions, this practice eventually led to a dramatic decrease in agricultural production. Because of these changes, the situation of the sedentary population grew more difficult, especially because the Mongol rulers and their followers were not competent in financial management. External wars and internal power struggles, extravagant expenditures at the imperial court, excessive distributions of money on the occasion of important events, and not infrequent successions to the throne—all this led inevitably to the financial draining and impoverishment of the sedentary population and in the long run undermined the country's fiscal resources.

In Iran, Mongol rule left a permanent mark on the system of government. The taxes arbitrarily introduced by the Il-Khans (e.g., on cattle and various commercial articles) were never rescinded; despite the fact that they were unsanctioned by Islamic law, they were preserved very officially. In later times no serious effort was made to bring these un-Islamic administrative factors into compliance with Islamic religious law. From the time of the Mongols, there was a de facto separation between government and Islamic law, and this situation was ultimately—after initial but increasingly muffled criticism from learned circles—tolerated by Muslim theologians as well.

The end of the Il-Khanid Empire came in 1335 with the assassination of the Il-Khan Abu Sa'id; he was the last Mongol ruler whose power still extended over the whole empire. After his death the country was fought over by warring emirs, tribes, and clans that sought to raise to power princes descended from Genghis Khan who were likely to benefit them; but in this they failed. Around the middle of the fourteenth century Mongol rule over Iran came to a definitive end, and the country disintegrated once again into various small regional states.

In this time of turmoil there lived in Fars—where the Atabeg dynasty of the Salghurids held power until 1282—one of the greatest poets of Iran, Sa'di (1213/1219–1292), who had settled in his home town of Shiraz after years of journeying. His *Gulistan* ("Rose Garden") is a masterpiece of Persian prose with intercalated verses that conveys general wisdom about life in the form of ethical and didactic stories and anecdotes. Sa'di's poetry is also highly regarded, especially his ghazals. In the twelfth century the *ghazal*, a short lyric form with erotic-mystical content, became a favorite poetic genre. The main figure in the ghazal, the poet's handsome young male friend and lover, was often transformed by the poets into an abstract symbol in which they celebrated the appearance of divine beauty in this world. Hafiz (c. 1325/1326–1389)—who also came from Shiraz, which was then ruled by the Musafirids (1334–1393), a successor dynasty of the Il-Khans—is considered Iran's greatest ghazal poet; Goethe described him as his twin brother. With incomparable mastery Hafez makes the earthly and sensible converge with the divine and supersensible, keeping them both in play, and repeatedly completely transcends any univocal meaning.

Concepts of Rulership and Empire

By conquering Baghdad, Hülegü destroyed not only the center of the Islamic world, but also posed a serious challenge to the Muslim community's self-conception, because through this event Islam at first ceased to be a principle of political authority. Alongside legitimation based on Islam, after the Mongol invasion other views emerged that were based on nomadic traditions. For the next century and a half,

Genghis Khan, the founder of an empire, became the quintessential model of the nomadic ruler. He was characterized by his mobility. His true residence was not a city, but rather the *ordu*, a mobile royal court-camp with no fixed location that accompanied him on his travels around his territory. The *ordu* was located outside fortified sites or cities and consisted of an extensive tent that could be expanded at any time. In the *ordu*, important political and military decisions were made, celebrations and entertainments held, ambassadors received, and, when necessary, documents prepared. The *ordu* usually included the ruler's family and entourage, military and civilian dignitaries, along with numerous servants, administrative employees, and poets and chroniclers who entertained the ruler with their art and recorded his deeds in writing. The notion that a ruler descended from nomads should have no fixed capital city was traced in later tradition back to Genghis Khan, although no categorical assertion to that effect has come down from him. While Mongols and Turks made certain centers into their capital cities and equipped them with splendid edifices, these could hardly be considered residences in the true sense, and they did not play a major role in the political and military domains. Instead, the capital city represented primarily a forum for scholarly and artistic activities that could not be pursued in the *ordu*, such as astronomy, architecture, and plastic arts. The *ordu* thus became a characteristic institution in the eastern Islamic lands between the thirteenth and the sixteenth centuries, even if in later times individual rulers sometimes also lived in the city and no longer exclusively in the *ordu*.

The Il-Khans called their empire "Iran." The idea of "Iran" as not only a purely geographical concept but also as a political concept, as it was defined in the age of the Sasanians (224–651), had by this time no longer existed for six centuries, as a result of the changed power relationships under the caliphate. Muslim geographers and chroniclers, even those who had been born in Iran, knew "Iran" only as a historical term designating the long-past Sasanian Empire. It is one of the notable facts of history that after all these centuries the name "Iran" came into use again as a political concept and an idea of empire under the Mongol Il-Khans, i.e., under non-Iranian sovereigns, and already occurs in the early chronicles of the age. This is also connected above all with the fact that with the end of the Baghdad caliphate, the Islamic universal empire also collapsed, so that other notions of rule could come into effect. In the extensive historical writing in Persian that was produced during the Il-Khanid age—during the Saljuq period, for the most part only works originally written in Arabic were translated into Persian—chroniclers saw in retrospect the centuries of the caliphate as a kind of interregnum, the rule of "regional princes," so to speak, between the Sasanian Empire and that of the Il-Khans, who had brought the individual provinces of Persia together into a unified empire again. That this occurred under non-Iranian rulers seems to have posed no problem for the chroniclers; perhaps the factual power of the Il-Khanid Empire reminded them of the old Iranian concept of empire known from Ferdowsi's *Shahnameh*. The city of Tabriz, the Mongols' most important city of residence, was apparently indivisibly associated with "Iran" as a political conception. The idea developed that Tabriz was—also after the Il-Khans—the "natural" capital of Iran. This idea lived on after 1600, when other cities—such as Isfahan and later Tehran—had assumed the role of capital. Tabriz continued to bear, as henceforth the second most important city in Iran, its official title of "Ruling City" (*dar al-saltaneh*, lit. "house of power"), which went back to the age of the Il-Khans, and in addition it was the usual residence of Persian crown princes and heirs to the throne.

Islam under Mongol Rule

The Il-Khans, their wives, and their entourage belonged to different religions, Buddhism in its Tibetan-Lamaist form and various kinds of Christianity being at first by far the most dominant. Until the end of the thirteenth century, the Il-Khans encouraged one or another of these religions, but never attempted to force their subjects to adopt a specific faith, because Genghis Khan was said to have ordered that all religions be tolerated in his empire. The Il-Khan Ghazan was the first to convert, in the initial year of his reign, 1295, to Sunni Islam. Ghazan's conversion, which made Islam the dominant religion once again, resulted in a far-reaching elimination of religious differences between the Mongols and their Iranian subjects, on the one hand, and on the other between the Mongols and the Turks living in the country, most of whom were also Muslims.

From the thirteenth century on, a popular form of religiousness emerged that was characterized by certain phenomena that may have existed earlier as well, but whose frequency under the disastrous conditions of life in the Mongol period was nonetheless unprecedented. These included religious views and practices that deviated from orthodox Islam or that were compatible with it only with restrictions, such as belief in miracles, the veneration of saints, tomb worship, pilgrimages to non-canonical religious sites—in short, a mystically-colored religiousness that was chiefly a matter of invididual feeling and had little to do with orthodox theo-logy; in Western scholarship, it is often termed "popular Islam." However, it was not connected solely with the common people; quite a few members of the wealthy and educated classes, military and civilian dignitaries, and even the rulers themselves often turned to this kind of religiousness.

Islamic mysticism sees its goal above all in the personal, individual experience of God. The mystics spoke of a "mystical path" on which the believer was driven forward by his love of God and at whose end stood a vision of the Divine or even a fusion of the soul with God in a state of supreme ecstasy. By means of a gradual overcoming of the ego and the rationality that they considered an impediment to the experience of the Divine, the mystics sought to eliminate this-worldly impressions from their consciousness and to achieve a state of inner purification in which it would be possible for human beings to become one with God. The practices developed with this goal in mind include especially the repetition of a certain religious formula that can be recited individually and silently or aloud in the community, and also ecstatic dancing. The mystics were called "Sufis" because of the woolen robe (from Arabic *suf*, "wool") they wore, or "dervishes" (from Persian *darvish*, "poor"). Whereas originally these seekers after God generally gathered around a mystical master who provided spiritual guidance for them, in the time of the Mongols this personal master-pupil relationship was already largely institutionalized, and the previously small, mystical groups became communities living in their own convents under definite, if still not very rigid, rules. In the thirteenth and fourteenth centuries the dervish communities increasingly lost their earlier esoteric character. The dervishes and their leader, the sheikh (Arabic *shaykh*, "venerable elder, master") were more and more seen as the true representatives of Islamic religious belief. Their convents and tombs were places of popular worship. People ascribed miraculous powers to many dervishes and sought their help against repression and financial exploitation by officials.

Under the repressive living conditions connected with Mongol rule, some dervish communities developed into genuine mass movements. The common people came to them in droves because they hoped that a miracle-working sheikh could provide them with protection and help in everyday life. In fact, quite a few sheikhs saw themselves as advocates for the Iranian people in opposition to the rulers, and when conflicts arose they acted—sometimes successfully—as mediators between the two parties. On the basis of their growing economic prosperity resulting from the donations, endowments, and privileges they received from their followers, in the fourteenth century many dervish groups became well-organized, militant associations whose explosive political power repeatedly manifested itself, initially in a local and later in a wider, super-regional framework. Exemplary in this regard is the dervish community of the Safaviyyah, from which the Safavid dynasty (1501–1722) emerged.

Certain features of popular Islamic religiousness, such as a particularly intense reverence for ʿAli, show Shiʿite influences. However, it would be an error to deduce from this a formal conversion to Shiʿism, since popular Islam is characterized precisely by an oscillation between Sunnism and Shiʿism. On the other hand, it is understandable that the vast geographical spread of the mystical communities, from Anatolia to Central Asia, promoted veneration of ʿAli and his descendants and thus prepared the way for later Shiʿite propaganda. Thus, for example, Shiʿism could spread in Anatolia—a center for the Safavids—even though in that area there was as yet no Shiʿite literature.

Timur and His Successors

Timur (1336–1405), called "the lame" because of an injury he had received in his youth—hence the European corruption of his name from the Turkic Timur Lenk, "Timur the lame," to Tamerlane—came from the nomadic tribe of Barlas, which was probably Turkish, in Transoxania. After Genghis Khan, he was the greatest nomad ruler and founder of a major empire, and he caused further significant changes in the Iranian cultural sphere. The old Iranian area of Transoxania had been particularly severely affected by Mongol rule. Around 1370, Timur exploited the anarchical conditions there to make himself, as the young leader of a group of warlike adventurers who came chiefly from nomadic backgrounds, the supreme ruler of Transoxania. Ten years later he undertook the first campaign from Transoxania toward the west.

The model Timur sought throughout his life to emulate was Genghis Khan, whose empire he wanted to restore. Toward the end of his life he had almost achieved his goal: his empire reached from Transoxania to the Euphrates and the Caucasus. By conquering this enormous territory Timur, who was particularly drawn to Iranian culture, reunited for the last time the extensive ancient Iranian cultural sphere into a single empire. He died in 1405 during a campaign on the way to China. All in all, Timur's campaigns, which were as famous as they were feared among his contemporaries, were conducted with unbridled cruelty and even beastliness. As a symbol of this we can take the pyramids of skulls he caused to be piled up outside the gates of rebellious cities; these were the skulls not only of fallen opponents but also of the male and female inhabitants of the cities. Timur's reverence for his Mongol model Genghis Khan completely determined his image of himself. He never assumed the title of Khan; instead, throughout his life he ruled in the name of the puppet khans descended from Genghis Khan who were supposed to lend his rule a formal legitimation. He married a princess from Genghis Khan's family, so that he could claim affliation with his role-model. He called himself "amir" (Arabic, "commander"), and used the honorific *gurgen* (royal son-in-law), which identified him as related by marriage to Genghis Khan's descendants. In accord with nomadic tradition, he also clung to the *ordu* or mobile court-camp.

Despite his firm connections with Mongol tradition, Timur often emphasized his Islamic belief; he was strongly influenced by the Sufi dervishes whom he kept in his entourage as spiritual advisors.

At the time of his death, Timur had established neither an arrangement for the appointment of the successor to his enormous territory nor even a stable institutional organization for it. Throughout his life he had sought to govern his empire through his personal authority and to ensure that he retained control over the conduct of state affairs. Therefore after his death the Timurid princes who had issued from his family were free to govern their various provinces with almost complete independence. This quickly led to the fragmentation of the territory he had conquered. The Timurid princes' neighbors took advantage of this situation: from the west Turkmen tribal confederations advanced from eastern Anatolia, first the Kara Koyunlu ("Black Sheep"), later the Ak Koyunlu ("White Sheep")—so called, perhaps, because of their totemic animals—while the Turkish Uzbeks invaded Transoxania from the north and northeast. In 1507 the rule of the Timurid rulers came to an end when the Uzbeks conquered Khwarazm after taking Transoxania.

Thus the significance of the Timurid rulers hardly lies in the area of military efficiency and statecraft. Above all, it was their cultural and artistic achievements that made Timur and his successors famous. In addition to Timur's capital of Samarkand, which he ornamented—chiefly by employing craftsmen and artists he had brought in from the areas he had conquered—with splendid edifices built on Persian models, in the second half of the fifteenth century Herat emerged as another important Timurid cultural center. The rulers and their dignitaries were major patrons of literature and poetry, miniature painting, the art of bookbinding, and calligraphy. Islamic Iran's greatest miniature painter, Bihzad (d. 1535/1536) worked in Herat, as did the dervish and poet Jami (1414–1492). The most important achievement of the latter, who is considered the last classical Iranian poet, were his epics, collected under the title *Haft Owrang* ("The Seven Thrones" or "Ursa Major"). However, in accordance with the still vital traditions of the steppes, under Timur and his successors the *ordu* remained the political and military center of the empire. In order to combine nomadic life in tents with the advantages and comforts of sedentary existence, the Timurids created exceptionally splendid gardens on the traditional Persian model, in which the *ordu* frequently resided. Around old cities such as Samarkand and Herat extensive garden areas were developed that differed from the suburbs of earlier times not only by their size, but also by the magnificent pavilions that were erected in them.

One of Timur's last descendants—and on his mother's side, a descendant of Genghis Khan himself—Zahir al-Din Babur, sought in vain to bring Transoxania back under Timurid control. After his final defeat, he moved into northern India, where he founded his own empire, that of the Mughals. There the flourishing culture of the Timurids, enriched by new elements, enjoyed a no less brilliant continuation.

The material basis for the Timurid state was also provided by the usual granting of fiscal grants in return for personal military assistance in the event of war. In the fourteenth century, the word *iqtaʿ* was increasingly replaced by the Mongol term *soyurghal* ("reward"); until the seventeenth century the term *tiyul* (also *toyul*, possibly an Iranized misspelling of the Turkish *yatul*, "landed property") was also used as a synonym of *soyurghal*. Typical phenomena of the fifteenth century were the grant-holder's independence in fiscal, administrative, and now even juridical matters, along with the inheritability of the grants and the considerable extent of the territories granted, which sometimes included whole provinces. Around this time the rural population had almost completely lost the right to own cultivated land; very few of the formerly free village communities still existed, and their further decline could not be prevented. The imperial administration under Timur's successors was the result of the now long-established ethnic dichotomy between Iranians and Turks. The supreme state authority (*divan*) was responsible, among other things, for maintaining the army, which consisted largely of Turks and Turkified Mongols. The civil and financial administration lay traditionally in the hands of native Iranians. This state of affairs was altered by neither the Mongols nor the Timurids, and thus a financial bureaucracy composed of Iranian officials working independently of the supreme *divan* continued to exist. The Mongol tradition also remained alive in fiscal institutions, and this meant above all that the Timurids also levied un-Islamic taxes, since the state was neither able nor willing to forego these lucrative sources of income.

Like the preceding centuries, that of the Timurids was essentially shaped by Islamic folk belief and its representatives, the popular mystical dervish communities. Because of the constant attraction the dervishes' religiousness had for the people and many rulers, the theological oppositions between Sunnis and Shiʿites became less manifest, so that it is often difficult to ascertain to which denomination a given individual or group belongs. Of course, orthodox Sunni theology continued to live on, but in the fifteenth century it had already largely fossilized into scholastic forms and limited itself—with a few exceptions—to composing countless glosses, commentaries, and commentaries on commentaries. Thus the representatives of Sunnism ultimately proved incapable of competing with the multiplicity of Shiʿite or heterodox movements. When one of these movements, the Safaviyyah, succeeded by force of arms in establishing itself and in making Twelver Shiʿism the state religion of Iran (1501), the fate of Sunnism in large areas of Timurid territory was sealed, though not in Transoxania, where the Uzbeks who invaded in the early sixteenth century were Sunnis.

CHAPTER 3
Iran in the Early Modern Period (1501–1779)

Turkish Immigration from the West

Toward the end of the fifteenth century the Islamic East was in a state of upheaval, after which new power blocs appeared: the Safavid Empire in Iran, with the Ottoman Empire on the west, and on the east the Uzbek Khanate in Transoxania and, about two decades later, the Indian Mughal Empire. Whereas since the eleventh century waves of Turkish immigration from Central Asia had essentially shaped Iran's history, at the beginning of the fifteenth century a reverse movement began to emerge that brought three great waves of Turkish nomads into Iran, this time coming from the west. The first two of these waves occurred under the Turkmen tribal confederations of the Kara Koyunlu and Ak Koyunlu, which came out of eastern Anatolia and overran large parts of the Timurid empire. Beginning in the age of the Saljuqs, Muslim chroniclers and geographers generally used the term "Turkmen"—which today generally designates the Turkish tribes that have spread since the Middle Ages over the Near and Middle East and Central Asia—to refer to the tribes of Oghuz origin that had converted to Islam. Since the Mongol periods, the term "Turkmen" had largely replaced the term "Oghuz." For nearly a century (1380–1469) the Kara Koyunlu ruled in Iran and Azerbaijan, but they were then displaced by the Ak Koyunlu (1396–1508), who for a short time controlled the whole area from Anatolia to Khurasan and as far as the Persian Gulf, so that it seemed to many contemporaries that they were to be the future dominant power in the East.

The third wave of Turkish immigration from Anatolia to the Iranian plateau, which took on significant proportions, involved the Turkmen tribe of the Kizilbash (Turkish, "red heads"), fanatical adherents of the Safavids who at the beginning of the sixteenth century had broken the power of the Ak Koyunlu and seized power in Iran for themselves. The beginnings of the Safavid dynasty first become visible in northwest Iran in the time of the Il-Khans. The ancestor from whom they took their name, Safi al-Din (d. 1334), had around 1300 established an originally Sunni-oriented dervish convent, called Safaviyyah after him, in the city of Ardabil. We know very little about Safi al-Din's ancestors, except that he came from a well-to-do family of farmers and cattle-breeders that resided near Ardabil and presumably had Kurdish roots.

At the outset, the order of the Safaviyyah may not have differed from many other dervish communities, yet the political development to which it led was unique. Its founder Safi al-Din was a typical figure of folk Islam, venerated as a saint by his followers, who attributed various miracles to him.

As the leader of an order, Safi al-Din achieved considerable success and laid he foundation for his community's future prosperity. His no less gifted successors at the head of the order amassed immense wealth and systematically sought to organize their numerous followers into military units. For a long time the order attracted enormous numbers of recruits from Turkmen nomadic tribes in eastern Anatolia, Azerbaijan, and northern Syria—areas that belonged at least in part to the Ottoman Empire, but in which Safavid agents nevertheless openly carried on deliberate and successful propaganda efforts. Although they were nominally Muslims, the Turkmen tended to adopt extreme religious views, so that their Islamic creed is with some justification interpreted as only a superficially Islamized paganism in which the shamanistic traditions of their homeland on the steppes of Inner Asia can still be clearly discerned beneath a thin overlay of Islam. The long-standing, close connection between these nomads and Sufism, combined with their enthusiasm for religious war, led Turkmen to join the Safaviyyah in large numbers. A further factor was the policy pursued by the Ottomans, who had by this time expanded their territory far to the east and were now seeking to subject the Turkmen tribes of Anatolia to the rigid administrative structures of their empire. The Turkmen, whom the government had up to that point left largely undisturbed, rejected the Sultan's demand that they pay taxes and provide soldiers for the Ottoman army, and increasingly they shifted their political and religious allegiance to the leaders of the Safavid orders. Haydar (d. 1488), the head of one such order, wore, allegedly because of a dream in which ʿAli had appeared to him, a red cap with twelve pleats that has often been interpreted as a symbol of the twelve imams of Shiʿism. Because of the cap's color, its wearers were called Kizilbash ("red heads") by their opponents, but they themselves quickly adopted this name as an honorary title. Sometime around the middle of the fifteenth century the Safaviyyah order was transformed from a mystical popular movement into a tightly organized and well-armed community of Turkmen religious warriors.

For Iran, and especially for the Iranian plateau, the three waves of immigration by Turkish nomadic tribes meant a further increase in the number of nomads; the latter could not move on beyond Iran because since the sixteenth century the Uzbeks had constituted an unrelenting military barrier in the east. In this way Iran became for centuries afterward a permanent homeland for countless hordes of Turkish nomads, whom the emergence of the new power blocs prevented from spreading to new territories. The disputes over pastureland that inevitably resulted from this led many conflicts between tribes and tribal confederations. In the long run, did not induce the tribes to abandon their nomadic way of life but it did induce them to change the way they were organized: they transformed themselves from originally economically-determined communities into more or less military structures. Only the nomads' politico-military authority over the sedentary population that fed them permitted them to survive in their traditional way of life. It is no wonder that under these conditions the repression and exploitation of the Iranian people working the land once again greatly increased. The military supremacy of the nomadic tribes continued to be a factor in Iranian history over the following centuries as well. Only at the beginning of the twentieth century was the central government able gradually to supplant the tribes as the dominant military power.

The Safavids

The Safavid period (1501–1722) is another crucial turning point in Iran's history. Whereas since the Arab conquest in the seventh century Iran had been part of the great Islamic community that was disintegrating into regional powers after eight and a half centuries of foreign domination and political fragmentation, the Safavids reestablished a strong and enduring state on Iranian soil. This was the dynasty that introduced Twelver Shi'ism as the state religion of Iran and thereby brought the Shi'ah to power on its territory. Thus began the religious shaping of Iran—which was at that point still primarily Sunni—as a Shi'ite country, which it has remained down to the present day, even though this process went on at least until the end of the Safavid period. The conversion to Shi'ism is the element that most obviously distinguishes modern Iran from its neighbors. The process of transforming Iran into a homogeneous Twelver Shi'ite land, along with Iran's geopolitical situation between the Sunni blocs of the Ottoman Empire, the Uzbek Khanate, and the Indian Mughal Empire, over time contributed to the development among most of Iran's heterogeneous population of a new-found feeling of religious unity on the basis of Twelver Shi'ism. However, the unification of extensive Persian-speaking areas of the Islamic East under Safavid rule should not be interpreted, as it sometimes has been, as the beginning of a future Iranian nation-state or as a breakthrough of Iranian national consciousness. Until the twentieth century the self-conception of both Iranians and Turks living on Iranian soil was based on their common adherence to Shi'ism, which for them represented true Islam.

In 1501 Isma'il, the young head of the Safavid order, conquered the city of Tabriz with the help of the Kizilbash tribes and resumed an ancient Iranian royal tradition by taking the title *shahanshah* ("king of kings"). During the following nine years he extended his control over all of Iran, Mesopotamia, and western Afghanistan. This first Safavid shah already entered into military conflicts with the Ottomans in the west and the Uzbeks in the east that continued under the following Safavid rulers. In general, this enmity is blamed on the religious opposition between Shi'ite Iran and the Sunni Ottomans and Uzbeks, but at least as great a role was played—regardless of religious propaganda on both sides—by substantial political and territorial interests. The Safavids competed with the Uzbeks for possession of the province of Khurasan, which they were eventually able to secure for themselves. However, border cities such as Herat and Mashhad repeatedly fell under the temporary control of the Uzbeks. Well into the nineteenth century the Turkmen carried out attacks over the border in search of booty and slaves.

Conflict with the Ottoman Empire, which in the sixteenth century was at the height of its power, was inevitable. The Ottoman sultans sought to control the unrest among the Kizilbash in eastern Anatolia, who were devoted to the Safavids, in order to provoke a military decision. In the fall of 1514 Sultan Selim I (reigned 1512–1520) soundly defeated the Safavid army at the battle of Chaldiran in eastern Azerbaijan. The Ottoman victory was due above all to their being equipped with modern artillery and firearms, which the Iranian army still lacked. The new weapons had been known in Iran for a long time, but in contrast to the Ottomans, the Iranians at first accepted them only with a certain hesitation. The Kizilbash voluntarily forewent firearms because this way of fighting seemed to them unmanly and cowardly; their persistence in fighting a moving battle on horseback led to their doom, because the Ottoman artillery did devastating damage to their cavalry. With the defeat at Chaldiran ended the previously successful expansion of the Safavid Empire; still more, it caused Shah Isma'il's aura of invincibility among his Kizilbash followers to evaporate. During the last decade of his reign he no longer engaged in any military campaigns. However, contrary to the earlier notion that at this point the shah entirely ceased any politico-military activity, Ottoman and Venetian sources show him to have been a clever organizer and farsighted politician who undertook many and diverse diplomatic efforts to modernize his army's weaponry and—successfully—to protect the young Safavid state against further Ottoman attack and thus to ensure its survival.

Under Isma'il's successor Tahmasp (reigned 1524–1576), invasions by the Uzbeks and conflicts with the Ottomans continued; Mesopotamia was lost to the Ottoman Empire. Despite the continuing clashes between Safavids and Ottomans during the whole sixteenth century, attempts at diplomatic contact were repeatedly undertaken. The Safavids had a great interest in ensuring that Shiʿite pilgrims could safely visit the shrines of their imams in Iraq and the holy cities of Mecca and Medina; since the Hijaz had fallen to the Ottomans (1517), these places were also under Ottoman control.

The reign of Shah ʿAbbas I (1588–1629), commonly called "the Great," marks the highpoint of Safavid rule. Under his rule the empire reached its greatest extent; he centralized governmental administration, encouraged economic development, and promoted architecture and art. He was able to recover most the territory that had been lost under his predecessors as a result of internal conflicts: he took Khurasan back from the Uzbeks (1598/99), Azerbaijan (1603/04) and large parts of Iraq, including Baghdad and southeast Anatolia from the Ottomans (1623/24), and the area of Kandahar in western Afghanistan from the Mughal emperors (1622). After the shah's death, however, many of the territories he had subdued were once again lost to the Ottoman Empire. In 1639 the treaty of Zuhab (or Qasr-i Shirin) settled the boundaries between Safavid and Ottoman territory, and except for the northern section these boundaries have lasted down to the present day. For Iran, however, this treaty brought about the final loss of Iraq and the Shiʿite holy sites.

The successors of ʿAbbas I were for the most part incompetent rulers, with the sole exception of his namesake ʿAbbas II (ruled 1642–1666). Toward the end of the century, when the Safavid shahs' loss of power could no longer be ignored, internal economic problems and religiously motivated rebellions brought the empire into a crisis. In 1722, the Afghan Ghalzai tribe invaded Iran and conquered large areas of the country. The last Safavid shah, Sultan Husayn (ruled 1694–1722) was forced to abdicate in the fall of the same year.

During the Safavid period diplomatic and commercial contacts with Europe of an unprecedented extent were established. Europe's interest in Safavid Iran was directly connected with the threatening power of the Ottoman Empire, to which both parties were exposed. Religious considerations apparently played no role for either side. Despite numerous embassies, however, no tangible military result was achieved since the distance separating Europe from Iran, with its strains and dangers, proved too great an impediment. Toward the end of the sixteenth century the focus of European-Iranian contacts shifted increasingly from foreign policy toward trade and economic relations. In the wake with European diplomatic missions and trading came numerous researchers eager to learn about the country, and they left us an abundance of informative travel reports about Safavid Persia.

Again, it was chiefly Shah ʿAbbas I who took a great interest in promoting foreign trade and who sought to attract European merchants to the country. On the European side, since the sixteenth century foreign trade had increasingly been conducted by large state companies that had the advantage of a broad capital base. During the seventeenth century the British East India Company, founded in 1600, and the Dutch East India Company (*Oost Indische Compagnie*, founded in 1602) competed with each other for trade with Asia, and both were inerested in establishing commercial relationships with Iran. Commercial goods from Iran—chiefly silk, cloth, and spices—were transported over the traditional caravan routes by way of Baghdad and Aleppo to the Mediterranean or by way of Tabriz and Trebizond to the Black Sea. However, since both routes passed through Ottoman territory, they were burdened with transit tolls and were not usable in times of war. The sea route to Europe that the Portuguese under Vasco da Gama (1469–1524) had opened as early as 1497/98 by sailing around the Cape of Good Hope remained for the time being unavailable to Iran. The Portuguese had immediately recognized the strategic and commercially favorable situation of the island of Hormuz at the entrance to the Persian Gulf and took permanent control of it in 1515. During the sixteenth century the Portuguese held a virtual monopoly over sea trade on the Indian Ocean, which Shah ʿAbbas was first able to break in 1623 with the aid of a fleet provided by the British East India Company. After he had reconquered Hormuz and destroyed the island city, the settlement on the south coast of the mainland, where British, Dutch, and French agents had established themselves some time earlier in competition with Hormuz, was developed under the name of Bandar ʿAbbas (Persian *bandar*, "harbor") into a major trading post.

The destruction of the Portuguese commercial base in Hormuz

opened the way for trade activities in the Persian Gulf on the part of the new sea powers Great Britain and Holland. On the Iranian side, Armenian merchants played an important role by establishing trade depots in Europe. In order to take advantage of the Armenians' commercial experience and craft abilities, Shah 'Abbas had several thousand Armenian families from Azerbaijan transferred to his new residence of Isfahan (1604), where he assigned them their own quarter that bore the name of their old home city of Julfa and has remained the city's Armenian neighborhood down to the present day.

By the end of the seventeenth century the rivalry between the British and Dutch East India Companies for dominance in the Persian Gulf had been settled in favor of the former. However, the decline of the Safavid Empire was accompanied by a decline of security in the Gulf, which was increasingly plagued by pirates (mostly Arab, but also British). Nonetheless, the East India Company continued its trade activities in Bandar 'Abbas and later in Basra, in southern Iraq, even though they were reduced in scope. During the eighteenth century trade relationships with Czarist Russia were intensified. After the eighteenth century, European interests in Iran, which had previously been oriented exclusively toward trade, turned into a power struggle among the great European nations for political influence in the Middle East.

The Safavid State

The Safavids claimed to be descended from the seventh imam, Musa al-Kazim ("the self-controlled," d. 799), in direct lineage from the Prophet Muhammad. This claim cannot be proven beyond doubt, but in any case the oldest extant sources for the early history of the Safavids explicitly state that they were members of 'Ali's family. This ancestry of the Safavids was nonetheless considered to be authentic, and it lent them great religious prestige that allowed them to present themselves as the sole representatives and deputies of the hidden twelfth imam. Thus the highest religious and worldly authorities were united in the person of the Safavid shah and formed the basis for a claim to universal power such as had not been made since the fall of the 'Abbasid caliphate. At the same time, in this personal union the Safavids were the leaders of the Safaviyyah order. However, they were not able to integrate the Sufi organization of the order into the state administration, so that as time went on Sufism became increasingly insignificant. It can be said that through Sufism the Kizilbash were affiliated in a special way with the shah, but when Shah ʿAbbas succeeded in weakening the power of the tribes, Sufism lost all political influence. The Safavids' legacy of the long Iranian royal tradition was taken over by later dynasties, but they could not lay claim to the religious aura that surrounded the Safavid shahs. Thus, after the fall of the Safavid Empire in 1722, numerous princes who were genuinely or allegedly descended from the Safavid family arose throughout the land as pretenders to the throne and were used by the new holders of power to legitimate their own rule.

During the sixteenth century the Kizilbash tribes, with whose help the Safavids had come to power, were able to assert their predominant position in the government. Turkmen were appointed to military offices and provincial governorships, and the Kizilbash leaders to whom a province was given to administer generally took their tribesmen with them, thus preserving the tribe's unity. Consequently, the Safavid Empire was at first in no way a centralized state, but instead was based on the rule of nomadic tribes; to this corresponded the Safavid shahs' continuing use of the *ordu*. Militarily, the Safavids long remained completely dependent on the Kizilbash. In addition, the shahs followed the usual practice of rewarding Kizilbash leaders for their military service by fiscal grants. As under earlier dynasties, under the Safavids these grants were de facto inheritable and the property of the military leader. From the outset, the Safavids tried to control the latent instability of the empire, which was in constant danger of disintegrating into independent areas under the rule of Kizilbash tribes, by filling posts in the civil administration with Iranian officials, whereas military posts went largely to the Kizilbash. Because of their experience and sedentary way of life these Iranian officials represented a more reliable foundation for the State than did the Kizilbash.

Shah ʿAbbas I was the first to succeed in centralizing the state administrative apparatus and eliminating the predominant position of the Kizilbash. Under his government began the steady decline of the Turkmen tribes and the decay of their military influence. Soon after he mounted the throne, ʿAbbas created—largely following the model of the janissaries in the Ottoman Empire—a standing army with cavalry, infantry, and artillery units. He admitted two British adventurers, the brothers Robert and Anthony Sherley, to his court in order to take advantage of their knowledge of the techniques of artillery. However, the notion that the Sherleys actually introduced artillery in Iran is erroneous, because it was already known there in Ismaʿil's time. The shah's new army was composed of the so-called "king's servants" (Persian *ghulaman*, Turkish *kullar*, "military slaves"), for the most part Caucasian Christians (Georgians, Armenians, etc.) who had been taken prisoner during the Safavids' campaigns, converted to Islam, and trained for service at the court. These military slaves were no longer loyal to a particular tribe but exclusively to the shah, who found in them valuable support against the Kizilbash. Caucasians were appointed to newly created military posts such as the supreme commander of the king's servants and the riflemen, and ultimately also to the new posts of supreme commander of all the Safavid military forces (Persian *sardar-i lashkar*). Thereby the inevitable disputes between Turkmen and Iranians regarding these high posts were effectively forestalled, because depriving the Kizilbash of power had inevitably increased the influence of the Iranian civil officials, and especially that of the vizier. Filling the new posts with king's servants, who by the beginning of the seventeenth century held about a fifth of all the high state offices, ensured the cohesion of the army. In addition, Shah ʿAbbas systematically resettled Kizilbash groups and scattered them over Iranian territory in order to weaken their tribal ties.

Although Shah ʿAbbas managed to establish a balance between the three groups that provided the basis for the state—the Turkmen, the Iranians, and the Caucasians—the measures he took proved to be only temporarily successful and in the long run contributed to the decline of the Safavids. The new royal troops were paid—unlike the Kizilbash—from the revenues of the estates under the crown's direct control. At the expense of the Kizilbash, large tracts of land in the provinces were now added to the royal domains, and members of the king's servants were appointed to manage them and to collect taxes for the state coffers.

However, in the long run the decrease in the number of Kizilbash governors was accompanied by increased financial exploitation of the royal domains, since the king's servants did not live from the land itself as did the Kizilbash but rather, during their tenure of office, tried to squeeze as much as possible out of the lands under their control. Excessive taxation (which impoverished the rural population and consequently increased the already considerable burden of taxes) imposed to meet the demands of the court and the military was one of the main causes for the decline of the state.

A further factor was the incompetence of Shah ʿAbbas's successors. This can also be traced back to a fateful step taken earlier, because for fear of conspiracies ʿAbbas had abandoned the previous custom of sending young princes to the provinces, where they were supposed to gain practical experience in administration under the guidance of Kizilbash leaders. Instead, ʿAbbas shut up his own sons in the harem, where they were exposed to the influence of the women and eunuchs at the court and could acquire no experience of government. When later on they themselves came to power, they often showed little inclination to devote themselves to affairs of state. The shahs who succeeded ʿAbbas continued to raise the princes in the harem; intrigues woven by military officials, court officers, eunuchs, prin-cesses, and concubines were the result. Increasing economic problems as well as religious unrest and rebellions, provoked especially by the last Safavid Sultan Husayn's ill-fated persecution of the Sunnis living in Iran, contributed to the further destabilization of the empire, whose end—despite an epilogue played out during the short reign of various Safavid puppet rulers—was finally sealed with the abdication of Sultan Hoseyn in 1722.

The cultural legacy of the age of the Safavids is inseparable from the city of Isfahan, which Shah ʿAbbas I chose as his capital around 1600 and developed into a splendid residence that can still rightly claim to have some of the most beautiful architectural monuments in the world. To the south and southwest of the old city center with its winding streets, which dates primarily from the age of the Saljuqs, the shah built his splendid new residence area with ingeniously planned avenues and extensive gardens. At its center is the enormous royal square, which at that time, according to reports by European travelers, surpassed anything in the Western world. In Isfahan, Iran's artistic creation reached another highpoint: Shah ʿAbbas called upon craftsmen, architects, and artists from all over the country to produce the city's many incomparable edifices covered with bands of decorative script and complicated patterns of glazed faience. Under Shah ʿAbbas Isfahan became a cosmopolitan city that is said to have rapidly grown from an original population of about 60,000 inhabitants to ten times that number. Many European contemporaries provided a colorful picture of the city: they described a lively mixture of Iranians, Turks, Europeans, Chinese, and Indians; Muslims, Zoroastrians, Christians, Jews, and Hindus.

Shiʿism under the Safavids

Immediately after taking Tabriz, the young Shah Ismaʿil declared Twelver Shiʿism to be the state religion. What led him to do so has still not been fully explained. It is certain that along with its growing militancy the Safaviyyah order had also undergone a fundamental religious transformation. Although this process of transformation is not clear in every detail, it is noteworthy that none of the main chroniclers of the time, not even those who opposed the Safavids, described any of Ismaʿil's ancestors as a Shiʿite. The Turkmen's idolization of their Safavid leaders, which was noted by contemporaries and which spurred them to an almost unbridled willingness to sacrifice themselves on the battlefield, profoundly influenced Ismaʿil himself. The *Divan* (collection of poems) in Turkish, the language of the Kizilbash, that Ismaʿil composed in his youth and which is programmatic in nature, reveals a very personal, extremely religious sense of mission that has nothing to do with orthodox Twelver Shiʿism and everything to do with the views of the Kizilbash tribes: in his poems Ismaʿil describes himself as an incarnation of divine substance and even as the returned twelfth imam, the mahdi. Although this extreme conception did not prevail in the long run, it nonetheless remains a remarkable fact that the introduction of Twelver Shiʿism as the state religion was initiated by a man whose understanding of the elaborate Twelver theology was hazy at best. In any case, with Ismaʿil begins a new polarization between Sunni and Shiʿite Islam. His strong, indeed aggressive anti-Sunni animosity culminated in his demand that all his subjects publicly curse the first three caliphs as an outward sign of their Shiʿite attitude. Here began an ideologization of Shiʿite religion that created a deep gulf between Sunnis and Shiʿites and reawakened acute oppositions that had become less sharp by the fifteenth century.

The Twelver Shiʿite state religion imposed from above was at first accepted by the still mainly Sunni population of Iran with the greatest reluctance and could be spread only by means of coercive measures. Many scholars who refused to adopt the new religious direction lost their lives or fled to the neighboring Sunni states. At the beginning of the sixteenth century, there was as yet no Twelver Shiʿite tradition in Iran. Thus it is questionable whether Ismaʿil and his followers could have succeeded in forcing a whole people to adopt a new faith without the support of Arab Shiʿite scholars from Bahrain, southern Lebanon, and southern Iraq—traditional Shiʿite centers—who were brought into the country to explain the doctrine of Twelver Shiʿism and make it accessible to the population. It was because of their work that Shiʿism finally abandoned its extreme elements and its popular form. These scholars developed the learned structure of Twelver orthodoxy into the form it has kept down to the present day, so that the religious orientation of the Safavid Empire became increasingly distant from its popular origin as represented by the Kizilbash, and thereby from Sufism as well. In the course of the seventeenth century, the term "Sufi," which was once an honorable name for the Safavids' followers, came to mean "heretic."

Under the rule of the Safavids, for the first time in the history of Twelver Shiʿism scholars were able to form independent social groups without being repressed by the state. The Shiʿite clergy first achieved its final form in the eighteenth century, but in the age of the Safavids the foundations were already laid for the development of a status that can properly be called "clerical"; however, unlike in Christianity, "clerics" are not ordained priests, but rather simply scholars (Arabic *ulama*) who have completed studies of the religious and legal traditions of Shiʿism. The Persian title of these scholars, which is also used in a very similar way by Sunni Islam, is "mullah" (from Arabic *mawla*, "master") or "akhund" (Persian, "teacher").

The hierarchical organization of the Shi'ite clergy began under Shah Isma'il. He reintroduced the "sadr" (Arabic *sadr*, leader), an office that had already existed in a similar form in the time of the Timurids and that was responsible for supervising religious institutions and endowments. With a view to transforming Iran into a Shi'ite state, the sadr was also assigned the task of disseminating Twelver doctrine and defending its dogma against unorthodox deviations. The office of the sadr thus served as a counterweight to the unorthodox fanaticism of the Kizilbash, who still venerated Isma'il's successor Tahmasp. When orthodox Twelver doctrine was finally established in the country, the office of sadr lost its political importance, whereas the influence of Twelver legal scholars, the mujtahids, grew.

The Arabic word *ijtihad* (lit. "exerting oneself") refers to the individual deduction of legal rules on the basis of intellectual reasoning. The principles underlying Twelver *ijtihad* were outlined during the Mongol periods by the scholar Al-'Allama (Arabic "the greatly learned") al-Hilli (1250-1325), who was active in Hilla, in southern Iraq, which was at that time the center of Twelver Shi'ite learning. In his view, only scholars possess the ability to arrive at valid knowledge by means of rational reflection, and they must have completed the appropriate course of training for this purpose. However, the mujtahid—that is, a scholar who practices *ijtihad*—is fallible, because only the twelfth imam can claim to be infallible. So long as the latter remains hidden, all results at which scholars arrive by means of reasoning are only provisional, so that the juxtaposition of contradictory decisions can be tolerated. Moreover, the mujtahid may not appeal to or cite an already deceased colleague, because each generation is supposed to come through discussion to its own consensus regarding the questions it faces. This conception of rational *ijtihad*, which was definitively developed in Twelver Shi'ism during the eighteenth century, establishes the authority of the mujtahid in matters of religion and law and thus provides the basis for the increasing influence—which was also political—of Twelver scholars.

The Safavids, especially Shah 'Abbas I and his court dignitaries, arranged extensive endowments for the benefit of Shi'ite holy places and institutions; Shi'ite scholars managed these endowments and drew revenue directly from them. Since according to Islamic law such endowments are inalienable and valid until Judgment Day, large amounts of money that accumulated from income on these endowments—as well as from the exercise of well-paid religious offices—passed into the hands of the mujtahids. The Shiʿite shrines in Mashhad and Qum, as well as the tombs of the imams in Iraq—Najaf, Karbala, Kazimayn, and Samarra—flourished anew. The endowed wealth of all these sites has continued to grow immeasurably through donations and endowments made either by the rulers of Iran or by believers throughout the world.

The increasing power of the mujtahids inevitably proved to be a threat to the position of the Safavid shahs. Like the shahs, the mujtahids claimed to be the sole legitimate representatives of the hidden imam. Although until the end of the Safavid dynasty the monarchy was strong enough to assert its role as the leader of the Shiʿah, the scholars' influence grew significantly under Shah ʿAbbas's successors, most of whom were incompetent. It is true that there were periods when tensions declined, and when there was even a certain collaboration between rulers and scholars, but principally the mujtahids called the shah's authority into question. When the Safavid Empire came to an end, so did the only dynasty that could claim the aura connected with descent from the Prophet by way of the seventh imam and the authority to lead the Shiʿite community. The disappearance of this rival made the scholars an important power factor opposing the autocratic rule of later dynasties and providing a rallying point for all opponents of the monarchy. Furthermore, the final military loss of Iraq in 1639, which helped Shiʿite shrines located in Iran itself, such as Mashhad and Qum, gain new prestige, also favored the clergy's growing independence from the monarchy. When conflicts arose, the scholars could now evade the shah's immediate power by establishing themselves in one of the Shiʿite holy places in Iraq. In 1979, the mujtahids finally abandoned the role of opposition to the monarchy that they had occupied since the seventeenth century by overthrowing the shah and seizing power themselves. In this respect Iran is unique, since no Sunni country has ever undergone a similar development.

Iran in the Eighteenth Century

The Afghan invasion of Iran in 1722, which put an end to the Safavid dynasty, was beaten back by Nadir Khan of the Turkmen tribe of Afshar. The Afshars, who had been members of the Kizilbash, lived a nomadic life in northern Khurasan. Nadir (b. 1688) was a military adventurer who spent his life in an almost unbroken series of wars and campaigns of conquest. Having begun his career as a military commander in the service of Safavid pretenders to the throne, in 1736 Nadir finally had himself crowned in the Mughan steppe in northwest Iran and henceforth took the name of Nadir Shah (reigned 1736–1747). He moved his capital city from Isfahan to Mashhad in Khurasan, which lay within the pastureland area of the Afshar tribe. His many military campaigns—through which he conquered large parts of Afghanistan, brought back from India the Peacock Throne and the famous Kohinoor diamond (from Persian *kuh-i nur*, "mountain of light") in 1739, and in 1746 re-established the border between Iran and the Ottoman Empire that had been set by the 1639 treaty of Zuhab—required enormous expenditures to maintain his huge army and in the long run depleted the country's resources. The inevitable consequence—oppressively higher taxes—soon made Nadir hated by the majority of those who felt the squeeze.

In particular, Nadir Shah's religious policies alienated the Twelver clergy when he tried to declare that the Twelver Shi‘ism was a fifth school of law on an equal footing with the four already established orthodox Sunni law schools; he named it Ja‘fariyya, after the Twelvers' sixth imam, Ja‘far. This adaptation of a Sunni institution could not but arouse the opposition of the Shi‘ite clergy. What they saw as Nadir Shah's attempt to reintroduce Sunnism in Iran (in which the shah himself may have seen an opportunity to ease tensions with the Ottoman Empire and destroy the influential position of the Shi‘ite clergy) succeeded only in driving many members of the clergy out of the country. They considered the shah's action to be a form of religious persecution and established themselves near the holy Shi‘ite tombs in Ottoman Iraq. In the summer of 1747 Nadir Shah was murdered by a group of leading members of the Afshar and Qajar tribes.

Nadir Shah's death threw northern and northeastern Iran into chaos, with numerous military leaders fighting for power and territory. Only southern Iran, ruled by the Zand dynasty, experienced a period of peace and prosperity. The Zands came from the Iranian nomadic tribe of the same name, which lived in the central Zagros Mountains. One of their leaders, Muhammad Karim Beg, who was later known as Karim Khan and was one of the dynasty's most important rulers, reigned as a *wakil* (Arabic "deputy," "authorized representative"), initially as the deputy of the Safavid prince Isma'il III (reigned 1750–1753), whom he held in honorable imprisonment until his death in 1773. After Isma'il III's demise, Karim Khan did not install another puppet king, so that the idea of a possible restoration of the Safavid dynasty was finally abandoned. When he moved to Shiraz, which he made his capital at the beginning of the 1760s, Karim Khan changed his title to wakil al-ra'aya ("regent for the people").

After seven hundred years of Turkish and Mongol domination, the Zands were the first dynasty of Iranian descent. Their state, which lasted only a short time (1751–1794), brought peace and economic growth to southern Iran, especially under the rule of Karim Khan (reigned 1751–1779). Karim did not engage in unnecessary, ruinous wars of conquest and sought successfully to bring order and a certain level of prosperity to his devastated and impoverished country by imposing moderate taxes and reviving trade. The Zands claimed no religious authority, but in contrast to Nadir Shah they again encouraged Twelver Shi'ism. Each of the twelve districts of Shiraz was dedicated to one of the twelve imams, and the religious courts that had been abolished by Nadir Shah were reintroduced. Shiraz flourished anew as a trade and cultural center in which Karim Khan undertook an active building program that gave the city much of its present-day character. Among other things, he restored the memorials to the famed poets Sa'di and Hafiz.

After Karim Khan died in 1779 his four sons immediately became instruments serving the ambitions of his relatives. By 1789 almost all male successors and relatives had either died in battle against each other or been executed, so that within a few years the country fell under the rule of the Turkish Qajar dynasty.

CHAPTER 4

From the Qajars to the Islamic Republic (1779 to the Present)

The Qajars

The history of the nineteenth century is shaped essentially by the massive expansion of the great European nations that pursued their competing colonial interests in the extra-European world by political and economic means. Inevitably, Iran was drawn into these conflicts: the Qajar dynasty (1779–1925), which had reunited Iran after the fall of the Safavid Empire and made it an important power in the Middle East, carried on a constant battle to maintain the country's political sovereignty and to preserve its territory. In the long run, however, the Qajars were unable to prevent either continuing territorial losses or the Europeans' increasing economic penetration of Iran. The military and technical superiority of Europe had become only too clear; this led to reflection on internal reforms whose urgency and necessity had become obvious, but also to stormy debates about the adoption of European secular ideas of the state and nation. The violent dispute that then began over Iran's adaptation to Western civilization, the danger of excessive Westernization, and a return to Iran's own traditional values continued unabated into the twentieth century.

Shah ʿAbbas I had resettled the Turkmen tribe of the Qajars, which belonged to the Kizilbash, along the northern border of Iran, which it was supposed to guard against attacks from the outside. After Karim Khan's death in 1779, Agha Muhammad, the son of a Qajar leader, was able to flee to northern Iran, win the support of the Qajar tribal groups there, bring most of the northern provinces under his control, and put an end to the Zands' rule in southern Iran. After he had conquered Azerbaijan, Armenia, and Georgia, in the spring of 1796 he had himself crowned as shah in the Mughan steppe; by assuming the old Persian title of *shahanshah* he also connected himself and the dynasty he founded—as many rulers before him had done—with the long Iranian tradition of kingship. Since the Qajars could claim no religious legitimation, Agha Muhammad strove to make his coronation an act of legitimation by using the ceremony that had been customary under the Safavids, thereby seeking to associate himself with the religious aura that surrounded them. A few years earlier, Agha Muhammad had already chosen as his capital Tehran, a provincial city near ancient Rayy, because it was close to the Qajar tribe's pasturelands southeast of the Caspian Sea. However, Tehran first began to grow significantly under Nasir od-Din (reigned 1848–1896), who, inspired by his travels in Europe, made the city into a genuine metropolis.

The foreign policy goal of the Qajar dynasty was to restore the borders of Iran as they had been under the Safavids, but they were unable to achieve this. Agha Muhammad was still able to conquer without great difficulty the province of Khurasan. However, after he was murdered in the summer of 1797 by two of his servants, his unworldly nephew Fath ʿAli Shah (reigned 1797–1834), who succeeded him on the throne, suffered considerable territorial losses. During his reign the European powers began to intervene directly in the internal affairs of Iran. Toward the end of the eighteenth century, Great Britain and Russia were the European nations with the greatest influence in the Middle East. During the whole of the nineteenth century they battled for military and economic predominance in Iran, which directly involved the interests of both countries: whereas Russia wanted to enlarge its national territory in the Caucasus, Great Britain wanted to acquire a land route to its Indian colonial possessions and keep Russia out of the Indian Ocean. The course of the war between Iran and Russia, which had annexed Georgia in 1801 and in 1804 advanced into Iranian territory in the Transcaucasus, was in large measure determined by the changing alliances among France, Great Britain, and Russia during the Napoleonic wars. As a consequence of these changing alliances, which the Iranians found unfathomable, the country lost large areas in the Caucasus that ultimately fell to Russia by the 1813 treaty of Golestan. Urged by the Shiʿite clergy to defend Muslims living in the Caucasus, the shah got involved in another war with Russia (1826) that ended in 1828 with the treaty of Turkmanchay (in Iranian, Azerbaijan) and resulted, through the loss of further Caucasian provinces, in the establishment of the present-day border. In 1813 Iran had already been forced to accept the humiliating provision that future heirs to the Iranian throne would have to be endorsed by Russia. Now it was made to pay enormous damages and grant Russia full consular jurisdiction over Russian citizens in Iran, who were thereby completely exempted from Iranian legal authority. The notorious system of "capitulations," as they were called, which originated in this situation, was later expanded to include other European and Ottoman citizens in Iran as well.

In Nadir Shah's time, Iran's borders with the Ottoman Empire remained relatively stable, despite frequent tensions, but a definitive determination of its eastern border was not achieved until the middle of the nineteenth century. After unsuccessful attempts (1833, 1837) to reconquer Herat and western Afghanistan—formerly Iranian territory—Nasir al-Din undertook a new advance and seized Herat in the spring of 1856. The conflict that then broke out with Great Britain, which regarded Afghanistan as an indispensable buffer for its Indian colonies, ended in the 1857 treaty of Paris, by which Iran was forced to give up Herat and recognize the independence of Afghanistan. In 1872, through British mediation, the province of Sistan was divided between Iran and Afghanistan. Thereafter, the country's borders were, with few exceptions, those of present-day Iran.

The impression of Iran's unquestionable military inferiority led to the insight that if the country was to resist the European powers' threat effectively, reforms would have to be made. As in the Ottoman Empire, in Iran it was primarily the army that was to be transformed in accord with Western standards. At the beginning of the nineteenth century, Crown Prince ʿAbbas Mirza (1789–1833), the governor of Azerbaijan and one of the most enthusiastic advocates of reform, made great efforts to bring French and British military instructors to Iran, and at the same time to send Iranians to study in Europe. However, because they were not supported by the shah and the leading government dignitaries, his plans did not produce any decisive effect.

The reformers who vigorously pursued ʿAbbas Mirza's efforts were for the most part men who had come into contact with Western ideas while traveling in Europe. Among them was Nasir al-Din's prime minister, Emir Kabir (Mirza Taqi Khan, 1807-1851), who during his short term in office engaged in an energetic activity of reform, though once again primarily in the military sector. His efforts soon aroused the hostility of the bureaucracy and the court, resulting in his dismissal and eventual execution. In order to educate personnel capable of modernizing the army, he had founded in Tehran the polytechnic school *Dâr al-Fonûn* (Persian "school of the new sciences"), the first and for a long time the only institution of higher learning in Iran. In addition to military studies, it offered, under the guidance of foreign teachers, curricula in the natural sciences, medicine, and other areas, and thus abandoned the traditional theological studies in favor of European subjects (known as *fann*, plural *fonûn*, lit. "art, branch of knowledge"). The education provided by the new schools, in which European books were translated into Persian and Persian textbooks were written, thus disseminated European ideas and over time led to the development of a new class of intellectuals who had been influenced by Western ideas. Except for the *Dâr al-Fonûn*, none of the attempts at reform made during Nasir al-Din's long reign were able to move beyond their initial stages for lack of the financial means to carry them out. Only a Cossack brigade composed of Iranian, Turk, and other troops commanded by Russian officers was set up (1879); as long as it existed, it was the most powerful force in the Iranian army.

Iranian students and travelers who had resided for a considerable length of time in Europe—even if for the time being there were not many of them—made European political and legal structures and technical advancements known to a broader public in Iran. Their reports led to a new literary genre, travel memoirs. In addition to the translation of an increasing number of European books on various subjects, the new media of the telegraph and the printing press (the first one was set up in Tabriz in 1812, the second in Tehran in 1824) helped spread Western ideas. In the context of the expanded diplomatic contacts with the

West that had been established since the beginning of the nineteenth century, Nasir al-Din was the first Iranian monarch to visit Europe; altogether, he made three such trips, leaving behind interesting travel journals.

The hesitation to undertake truly fundamental and certainly costly, but nonetheless necessary, reforms characterized the unsystematic modernization policies of the Qajar rulers throughout the nineteenth century. In comparison with the Ottoman Empire, efforts to implement reform in Iran were far less frequent and more hesitant. The reason for this—apart from the attitude of the shahs themselves, who feared losing their power and having to make large expenditures—may be found above all in Iran's social structure, in which the tribal leaders, the great landowners, and the clergy enjoyed greater independence than in other Islamic countries and, like the corrupt bureaucracy, vehemently defended their own interests.

The growing discontent with Iran's political dependence on foreign powers and the increasing economic selling-out of the country provoked, in the final years of Nasir al-Din's reign, a protest movement in which conservatives and modernists joined in resisting the government and that finally led to the Constitutional Revolution (1905–1911). The shah had already been assassinated by a dissident in 1896.

The Qajar State

The Qajars saw themselves, as their title *shahanshah* clearly indicated, as associated with the ancient Iranian tradition of kingship. At the same time, the Qajars considered themselves the successors of the Safavids, whose administrative structure they adopted. As absolute ruler, the shah stood above all state officials, but he nonetheless ceded them the power to make the real political decisions. However, the dependency of government officials on the shah and the ensuing insecurity of their positions induced them to strive to enrich themselves during their terms of office, constantly plotting against each other and attempting to retain their positions with the help of foreign powers, again particularly Great Britain and Russia.

From the outset, the Qajars were confronted by financial problems resulting from wars, weapons purchases, and the growing consumption of Western luxury goods, and these problems made repeated tax increases necessary, so that the situation of the rural population steadily deteriorated. Instead of establishing a regularly paid bureaucracy, the Qajars auctioned off public offices—such as those of customs officials and provincial governors—to the highest bidders. In turn, the officials who received high posts in this way leased out subordinate posts. The set sums of money that the governors were required to send annually to the capital, as well as those needed to finance the provincial administration and the governors' own often extravagant lifestyle, were collected on the spot. Provincial officials' nearly complete military and financial independence encouraged them to exploit their subjects, inciting ambitious types to rebellion and, given the lack of state control, leading local tribal leaders and major landowners to levy excessive taxes on the inhabitants of their own estates.

The West's political influence was accompanied by the European powers' attempts to make Iran economically dependent on them as well, and by demanding concessions, to gain control over at least part of the Iranian economy at low cost. The Iranian state's persistent liquidity problems made it easier to carry out this "peaceful" economic penetration of Iran, which by the end of the nineteenth century was headed for bankruptcy. After concessions for the construction of a telegraph network were granted to Great Britain in the 1860s, in 1872 the British citizen Julius de Reuter received a very far-reaching concession that put large parts of the Iranian economy under his control; however, in the following year pressure exerted by conservative groups, and especially by Russia, forced the shah to rescind this concession. For some time afterward, continuing rivalry between the two European powers providing "development aid," Great Britain and Russia, prevented the granting of further concessions that had been planned for the construction of a railway network. Only in 1879 did Russia acquire fishing rights in the Caspian Sea; additional concessions were awarded in the early 1880s. Toward the end of that decade, requests for concessions were piling up: the previously mentioned Baron Reuter received, through the mediation of the British envoy Sir Henry Drummond Wolff, permission to set up the Imperial Bank of Persia in Tehran—which, despite its name, was under British control. As a countermove, in 1890 the Russians were allowed to open their own credit bank, which later became a branch of the State Bank of Russia.

These unscrupulous concessions reached their apex in March 1890, when the Imperial Tobacco Corporation of Persia, which was controlled by a British consortium, was granted a fifty-year monopoly on the production, purchase, and export of all Iran's tobacco. This concession was initially kept secret, but when toward the end of the year it became generally known, it provoked a mass protest. A religious edict (*fatwa*) issued in December 1891 and attributed to one of the leading Shiʿite scholars, Mirza Muhammad Hasan Shirazi, which declared any use of tobacco to be an offense against the hidden twelfth imam, led to a complete tobacco boycott throughout the country. As a result, the tobacco concession was rescinded in early 1892, and shortly thereafter another religious edict—of which this Shirazi was clearly the author—declared that the use of tobacco was now allowed again. However, the real importance of the conflict over the tobacco monopoly lies in the fact that here, for the first time in modern Iranian history, a successful mass movement came into being in which the clergy, the urban middle class, and intellectuals oriented toward modernity joined together in opposing the government and thereby made it clear how much influence such an alliance could have on the leadership of the state.

Shiʿism in the Nineteenth Century

During the nineteenth century, the Shiʿite clergy were able to increase their independence from the state. Since the Qajars lacked the religious legitimacy that the Safavids had enjoyed, the mujtahids considered them purely worldly rulers who did not have the religious authority that they themselves claimed. In addition, since the eighteenth century many clerics lived outside Iran in the Shiʿite holy places in Iraq and received revenues from endowments, donations, and so on. In modern times, the Shiʿite shrines in Iraq had become important centers of Shiʿite scholarship—and also centers of Shiʿite agitation. From these bases the mujtahids rigorously advocated their view that only the limited circle of specially trained scholars was qualified to make—by means of individual logical deduction—valid, authoritative decisions in religious matters, decisions that ordinary believers were required to accept without question (Arabic *taqlid*, lit. "imitate," i.e., submission to or acceptance of authority). Moreover, according to their own doctrine, which was definitively formulated in the Qajar period, only the mujtahids, as the deputies of the hidden imam, were qualified to perform the latter's functions until he returned. The mujtahids and their theory were ultimately able to prevail over all competing intra- and extra-Shi'ite religious movements, whether those of traditionalists who held that every believer was able to fulfill his own religious duties adequately without guidance by scholars, or those based on Sufi or Gnostic speculations, which did not recognize the authority of the mujtahids in religious matters. After the middle of the nineteenth century, with the emergence of a supreme theological authority, the clerical hierarchy assumed its present form. A particularly outstanding, exemplary scholar who was generally recognized within the clergy could be seen by his colleagues as the highest religious authority, as *marja'-e taqlid* (Arabic *marji' al-taqlid*, "source of emulation" or "model for reference"), but who is nonetheless fallible, like every mujtahid. This rank can be assigned to a single mujtahid or to several simultaneously—or to no one, since there are not always enough respected scholars who can be considered a mardsha. The title of mardsha is an honorary title that may be offered to a scholar, but not—for lack of an authorized institution—formally conferred upon him.

In view of the European powers' increasing intervention in internal Iranian affairs, especially in the economic sphere, the clergy acquired a somewhat "national" role: that of the protectors of the Iranian people's interests against foreign influences, on the one hand, and against the Qajar shahs' granting of concessions and their attempts to modernize the country on the other. The clergy thus represented a strongly conservative element in the society that saw itself as opposing, for the sake of Iran and of Islam, the influence of the West as well as the worldly power of the monarchy; and this was precisely the role that the mujtahids also played in the twentieth century under the Pahlavi dynasty. Since the age of the Safavids, in which state promotion of trade and industry led to a significant increase in the number of craftsmen in urban bazaars (*bazar*), a particularly close connection between these craftsmen and the clergy could be observed. Often the clergy came from the social stratum of these bazaar craftsmen, with whom they shared a common interest in resisting foreign control over whole sectors of the economy—an alliance that still exists and in the modern history of Iran has more than once been an important determinant of the course of events.

Around the middle of the nineteenth century Shi'ism underwent a period of religious unrest during which new religious directions were established. The "Shaykhis," named after their founder, Shaykh Ahmad al-Ahsa'i (1754–1826), were a group that had its roots in Twelver Shi'ism and who maintained that there must always be a man in the world who is capable of communicating with the hidden imam, and who can know and interpret the latter's will at all times. Under the influence of this movement, the theology student Sayyid Ali Muhammad (1819–1850) declared himself to be this intermediary. He proclaimed himself as the *bab* (Arabic "door," "gate," i.e., to the hidden imam) and representative of the twelfth imam; later he even claimed to be the mahdi himself. The Babi movement rapidly won many followers, especially since the *bab* proclaimed a new social order that was divinely willed and would produce greater social equality. Babi revolts against the government were cruelly suppressed, and in 1850 the *bab* was executed. However, his successor, Mirza Yahya Nuri (c. 1830–1912), who took the title Subh-i azal (Persian, "dawn of eternity"), retained on a minority of the Babis (the Azali-Babis, today a small, dwindling group with about 2000 members). Most of the Babis followed Mirza's half-brother Baha'i Ullah (Arabic "divine splendor"), who in 1863 declared himself to be the spiritual reincarnation of the *bab* and further developed the latter's messianic teaching. The Baha'i community quickly grew and spread over all the continents. In Iran, the Baha'i were subjected, under the autocratic rule of the Pahlavi dynasty, to a series of repressive measures. In the Islamic Republic, which does not count the Baha'is among the officially recognized religious communities, its situation has once again drastically worsened.

From the Constitutional Revolution to the Pahlavis

In the events that culminated in the so-called Constitutional Revolution and the constitutional movement (Persian *mashrutiyat*) of 1905, Shiʿite scholars played, because of their social position, a leading role in the opposition to the new shah Muzaffar al-Din (reigned 1896–1907). The general protest against the absolutism of the monarchy and the continually growing foreign influence on Iran—which was still a bone of contention between Great Britain and Russia—united the clergy with secular elements and progressive intellectuals. In the 1880s, the Iranian intellectual Jamal al-Din al-Afghani had already called for religious and non-religious opponents of Western colonial expansion to join forces. Al-Afghani greatly contributed to the spread of reformist ideas in Iran, including in religious milieus. More a political activist than a systematic thinker, throughout his life he propagated the idea of a spiritual—and not necessarily political—Islamic unity, the political cooperation of Muslims against overwhelming European superpowers, and an active, dynamic Islam. During two sojourns in Iran (1887, 1889–1891), al-Afghani gained influence over the younger generation of reform-minded Iranian intellectuals, whom he also introduced to the methods of organized resistance.

When the Iranian court's constant shortage of money—caused by the extravagant expenses incurred during the shah's stays at expensive European health spas—made it necessary to contract two large loans from Russia and forced new economic concessions, complete Russian control over Iran seemed dangerously near. Opposition to this development, which led to the founding of many secret societies comprising clerics and progressive secular thinkers, was stirred up by critical writings produced by expatriate Iranians. As a result of these writings, many who had up to that point never had an opportunity to visit other countries gained a new perspective on the conditions in Iran. Revolutionary feeling was strengthened by the victory of Japan, a country that had until recently been technically backward, over the great power Russia in early 1905, as well as by the Russian revolutionary uprising that had begun shortly thereafter. Starting in December 1905, this climate led to months of unrest in the course of which the original demand for representative institutions administering justice (using the vague Persian expression ʿ*adalatkhaneh*, "house of justice") escalated into a call for a new constitution. Muzaffar al-Din was eventually compelled to consent to the election of a parliament (Persian *majlis*), and in October 1906 the latter actually convened. On December 30, shortly before he died, the shah signed the constitution (Persian *qanun-i asasi*), modeled largely on the Belgian constitution. The following year several amendments (Persian *motammemât*) to the constitution were drafted and signed by Muzaffar al-Din's successor, Muhammad Ali Shah (reigned 1907–1909). The absolute monarchy that had ruled Iran since time immemorial was thereby transformed into a constitutional monarchy in which the ministers were no longer accountable to the shah but to the parliament. This weakening of the monarchy benefited the Shiʿite clergy more than it did the progressive forces familiar with Western ideas that had fought for the democratization of Iran. An amendment to the constitution passed in 1907 provided that all parliamentary decisions should be submitted to a committee of five Shiʿite clerics which was to evaluate their compatibility with Islamic law (Shariʿah). This amendment meant that the mujtahids could now revise all proposed laws in accord with their own views or even block them altogether.

The new form of government in Iran was short-lived, because it brought the country neither stability nor progress; above all, financial problems persisted. In 1907, in order to settle their mutual differences in Asia, Great Britain and Russia signed a treaty dividing Iran into three areas corresponding to their spheres of interest: the northern zone was assigned to Russia and the southern to Great Britain, with a neutral buffer zone separating them. Muhammad Ali used a failed attempt to assassinate him as a pretext for suppressing the parliament with the help of the Persian Cossack Brigade and for suspending freedom of the press. Rebellions flared up in the provinces, especially in northwest Iran, that forced the shah to abdicate before the year was out. His son Ahmad (reigned 1909–1925) was still a minor, but he was nonetheless designated as the new ruler by the rebels and was recognized by Great Britain and Russia. In 1911, in order to resolve Iran's persistent budgetary problems, the government—whose previous experiences with Great Britain and Russia had led it to mistrust both these nations—

hired the American expert William Morgan Shuster to reorganize the government's finances. Shuster's plan to have taxes collected by special police units headed by an officer of the British Indian Army aroused Russia's protest. When the parliament refused to dismiss Shuster and Russian troops advanced toward Teheran, the regent, Nasir al-Mulk, who administered the government's affairs on behalf of the still-underage shah, dissolved the parliament and fired Shuster. Nonetheless, Russia continued to occupy areas of northern Iran and, in conjunction with Great Britain, saw to it that press censorship remained in force and that a parliament acceptable to the two countries was installed. This put a de facto end to the Constitutional Revolution as well; the constitution was suspended.

In the First World War, Iran officially declared its neutrality, but the latter was not respected by the great powers. Russia, the Ottoman Empire, and Britain all fought battles on Iranian soil, with the result that the central government almost completely collapsed and the country was thrown into chaos. The Russian revolution in October 1917 found many sympathizers in Iran, especially since the new Bolshevik government promised henceforth to respect Iran's territorial sovereignty. Thus after the Russian troops' withdrawal from Iran, Great Britain remained the only militarily and economically significant power in the Middle East. In 1919, after the failure of its attempt to make Iran a kind of British protectorate, Great Britain changed its policy and began to support the installation of a strong Iranian central government that could establish internal order and at the same time ward off the threat of expansion on the part of the new Soviet Union. Therefore Britain welcomed it when in February 1921 Reza Khan, an officer in the Persian Cossack Brigade, staged a coup d'etat and installed a new premier. As minister of war in the new government, Reza Khan reorganized the army and put down rebel movements in the provinces of Azerbaijan, Gilan, and Khuzistan. By means of a second coup d'etat carried out in 1923, he made himself prime minister and was able to get through a series of laws that strengthened the central government: compulsory military conscription, the standardization of weights and measures throughout the country, the introduction of family names and birth certificates, and the use of revenues from the state tea and sugar monopoly for the construction of a Trans-Iranian railroad.

In spring 1925 the parliament decided to depose the last Qajar ruler, Ahmad (who had left Iran in 1923 to travel in Europe), and to transform itself into a constitutional assembly that in December 1925 finally agreed to raise Reza Khan to the throne as the new shah. Thus began the short-lived Pahlavi dynasty (1925–1979)—named after the language of pre-Islamic Iran, Pahlavi. Ahmad Shah never returned to his country.

The Pahlavis

Backed by the army he had modernized, Reza Shah reigned as a despot, so that the parliament, which formally approved the decisions he made, was no more than a kind of democratic veneer. In contrast to the time of the Qajars, during which only a few effective reforms were introduced, Reza Shah's primary goal was to make Iran into a progressive, secular nation-state on the European model by means of a large-scale program of modernization such as Atatürk, whom he greatly admired, had set underway in Turkey. From his coronation to his abdication in 1941, the shah implemented the first truly significant series of effective reforms and undertook to create a functioning infrastructure: the Trans-Iranian railroad from the Persian Gulf to Tehran and the northern provinces was built (1926–1938) and rapidly advancing road construction made motor vehicles the main means of transportation between small towns and villages. The development of agriculture and industry was intensified and the legal system secularized on European models through new legal codes (Commercial Code, 1925; Criminal Code, 1926; Civil Code, 1928), as was the educational system. A network of public elementary schools was established, and in Tehran the first modern university in Iran opened in 1935; Iranians were also encouraged to study abroad. Western-style clothing for men was made obligatory in 1929; in 1936 it was also made obligatory for women, and the wearing of the veil was prohibited. However, the prohibition of the veil could not be enforced even by coercion, so that after 1941 women, especially lower-class women, began to wear it again. Muharram celebrations were forbidden, and the professional activities of the clergy restricted to the religious realm alone; only the clergy was allowed to retain its traditional clothing (caftan and turban), so that it was now also defined outwardly as a separate social group. All these measures had the effect of banishing Islam from public life and undermining the position of the clergy.

The beneficiaries of the modernization of Iran undertaken by Reza Shah were the steadily growing governmental bureaucracy, which was used to keep watch over the state, the new entrepreneurs who profited from increasing industrialization, and the great landowners, since land reform did not take place and the provisions of the new Civil Code were undermined by bribery and personal connections. On the other hand, industry and the countless construction sites throughout the country required a more mobile labor force, so that workers were often forced to abandon their traditional ways of life. Social transformation manifested itself with particular clarity in the immense growth of the cities, in which large numbers of peasants—drawn to the cities by the promise of better living conditions—constituted a steadily expanding proletariat.

In order to create a strong central government, Reza Shah considered it urgently necessary to sedentarize the often more or less independent and well-armed nomadic tribes, which constituted about one fourth of the total population, the better to control them. After his power was sufficiently established, the shah began in 1927 a rigorous policy of sedentarizing the nomads, who were forcibly disarmed and compelled to settle the areas that had been designated for them—which were often unsuitable for keeping livestock. Thus the nomads' herds were prevented from making the necessary migrations between summer and winter pastures, so that many animals died. In addition to this economic disaster, health problems emerged due to the malarial diseases that often broke out during the summer and which the tribes' earlier migrations had spared them. Tribal resistance was ruthlessly put down by the army, and most tribal leaders were executed or expelled.

Reza Shah's foreign policy sought to present his country to the international public as an independent nation-state. To this end the Pahlavis attempted to return, as the name of their dynasty indicates, to Iran's pre-Islamic past; from the outset, at his coronation, the shah made this new nationalism evident by having his crown and banner made in the Sasanian style and by wearing a cloak imitating the ancient Iranian model. In 1934, the official name of the country was no longer to be the European "Persia," but rather "Iran." In 1927–28, the shah canceled nearly all Iran's agreements with foreign states insofar as they infringed on the equality of the parties, and abolished the humiliating concessions. Seeking to make Iran as independent of Great Britain and Russia as possible, Reza Shah had, after attempts to establish closer relations with the United States had failed, turned increasingly to Germany. Nonetheless, in the Second World War Iran tried to remain neutral, but once again it was unable to assert its own interests against those of the great powers. In August 1941 British and Soviet troops marched into Iran, forced the shah to abdicate, and deported him to South Africa, where he died in 1944. His son Muhammad Reza Shah (1941–1979) succeeded him on the throne with the approval of the occupying powers.

The new shah (b. 1919) cooperated with the Allies and in 1943 was recognized by treaty as an ally, but until the occupation ended in 1946 his freedom of action remained restricted. At first, Muhammad Reza endorsed the constitutional monarchy, but during these years the parliament essentially paralyzed itself by engaging in partisan factional struggles. Taking advantage of weakness of the young shah, various social-revolutionary movements that had been repressed by Reza Shah fused in the communist Tudeh party (Persian *tudeh*, "masses"); many nomadic tribes reorganized themselves and went back to their traditional way of life, and the clergy also sought to regain influence. The Muharram celebrations were gradually resumed, and in 1948 a religious edict (*fatwa*) issued by one of the leading mujtahids declared that women once again had a duty to wear the veil.

Shortly thereafter the shah found himself involved in serious conflicts with Premier Muhammad Mosaddeq, who was the head of the National Front, a coalition of liberal and religious nationalist parties. His attempt to nationalize the Anglo-Iranian Oil Company, in which Great Britain held a majority stock position and which was considered by many Iranians to be a channel for British influence in the country, ended—as a result of pressure exerted by both Britain and the United

States—in a boycott of Iran by almost all the major oil companies, and the ensuing decrease in oil revenues had a damaging effect on the state's finances. During this crisis, in which Mosaddeq had to rely on the support of the Tudeh party, the shah fled abroad, returning later in the same year after Mosaddeq had been overthrown in a coup staged by the army. The American CIA played a role in this coup, in an attempt to prevent Iran from establishing closer ties with the Soviet Union. After Mosaddeq's fall, the oil problem was settled by an agreement to apportion oil revenues to a consortium of several international oil companies and the National Iranian Oil Company. The latter's share of these revenues was henceforth considerably larger and further increased when new oil deposits were discovered near Ghom (1956).

Like Great Britain before them, during the Cold War the United States was greatly interested in binding Iran to the Western allies in order to have a reliable bulwark against communism in the Middle East. As a result, the country received extensive American military aid that enabled the shah was able to modernize and enlarge his army. Again with foreign support, the shah set up an inernal intelligence service (S.A.V.A.K.) that became active in 1957 and developed into an instrument of surveillance that was feared throughout the land. The army and the secret police were Muhammad Reza's main agents for enforcing his authority. After Mosaddeq's fall, the shah became more and more of a despot like his father, but without the latter's energy. Responding to American pressure, in 1960 Muhammad Reza began a short phase of liberalization during which the National Front was allowed to resume its activities, but in 1963 he once again shut down oppositional movements by force. As a result, not only were democratic structures eliminated, but also the idea of democracy suffered serious damage in Iran, because the West supported the shah's autocratic regime on grounds that were obviously connected with power politics. The shah himself willingly played the role of a "policeman of the Gulf," protecting Western and above all American interests. In 1975 the two authorized political parties, which in any case had only a shadowy existence, were dissolved and merged in single party, *Rastakhiz* ("resurrection"), to which most adult citizens had to belong.

Iran's economic growth, which had been greatly accelerated by oil revenues and the influx of foreign capital, especially toward the end of the 1960s, not only resulted in significant governmental and private investment, but also contributed to the increasing prosperity of a previously small middle class that was now becoming larger, and which, under pressure from the S.A.V.A.K.—and perhaps sometimes not unwillingly—turned away from politics and devoted itself entirely to Western-style consumerism. However, since as a result of this economic development basic foodstuffs became more expensive and corruption increased, over time social tensions inevitably intensified. With the development program known as the "White Revolution" (Persian *inqilab-i safid*), Muhammad Reza thus undertook the first serious efforts at reform intended to improve the situation in rural areas. Although peasants received plots of land, they nonetheless remained for the most part dependent on the great landowners because they lacked the means to farm their land by themselves. This situation led to increased migration to the cities and to further growth of the urban proletariat. In addition to land reform, the shah set as his goal the establishment of the legal equality of men and women: in 1962, women were given active and passive voting rights, and a family protection law enacted in 1967 facilitated divorce initiated by women. Both these initiatives encountered resistance from the clergy because they feared the loss of their endowments, and also because they fundamentally rejected any tendencies toward Westernization.

In the 1960s and 1970s, the shah became increasingly alienated from his own people, although he did not seem to realize it. The preparations for the celebration in Persepolis of the twenty-five-hundredth anniversary of the Iranian monarchy (1971) were extremely extravagant in view of the living conditions of the majority of the people, the introduction of a new calendar (1976) that took the year of the coronation of the Achaemenid king Cyrus the Great (550 BC) as its starting point, and a planned international symposium intended to resolve the world's problems (1977), are all indications of Muhammad Reza's fragile grip on reality. He overlooked the fact that only a minority of the population had profited from economic growth, and that his policy of Westernization deeply offended many devout Iranians for whom their religion was a basic element of their identity. On the other hand, his extremely repressive internal policy forfeited the sympathies of Western-oriented Iranians, who could not imagine progress without democratic freedoms. Because there was no channel for political co-determination and criticism of the government, the religious opposition offered the only way to articulate resistance to the shah's autocratic rule. The Shiʿite clergy thus once again assumed its traditional role of defending the Iranian people against un-Islamic influences and a despotic government.

The true cause of the Islamic Revolution was thus the political, social, and economic crisis into which the shah had led his country, yet inevitably the religious element got the most attention. In the West, where the growing gulf between the clergy and the shah had in any case not been perceived, the religious justification for the revolution created the impression that it was nothing more than a deliberate "return to the Middle Ages." When in 1978 the swelling discontent broke out in a mass protest movement, the revolution could no longer be halted. In January 1979 the shah left Iran; he died of cancer in Cairo in 1980.

Political Shiʿism and the Islamic Revolution

In the West, the Islamic Revolution and the foundation of an Islamic Republic left the erroneous impression that Twelver Shiʿism had always been a politically revolutionary ideology. It is nothing of the sort. While Shi'sm's original goal was in fact to establish at the head of the Muslim community a legitimate successor of the Prophet, but when this aspiration was not fulfilled after ʿAli's caliphate, it could henceforth only be realized through the return of the hidden imam. Traditionally, therefore, Twelver Shiʿism had been unpolitical, even quietist; and with few exceptions its clergy has kept its distance from day-to-day politics. The idea of a politically active Shiʿism is a new phenomenon and sprang not from the learned clergy's ideas but rather from Iranian intellectuals who felt that Iran was infiltrated by foreign cultural domination and economically exploited. The men who paved the way for revolutionary ideology and shaped a whole generation of young Iranians were Jalal Al-i Ahmad (1923–1969) and his student ʿAli Shariʿahti (1933–1977).

Whereas up to that point Western models had remained authoritative for most Iranian intellectuals regardless of their political direction, even though their benefit for Iran was becoming increasingly doubtful, Al-e Ahmad induced them to return to their own cultural values. His best known work, *Gharbzadigi* (1952) provided the key to a worldview in which leftists and Islamists joined together in opposition to the shah's despotism and his obedience to the West. The title of Al-e Ahmad's—which has been translated as "attacked by the West," "poisoned by the West," and "Occidententosis"—refers to the blind imitation of the West that was alienating the Iranian people from their own roots. Although personally inclined to nationalism, Al-e Ahmad saw religion as the only cultural value in Iran that had not yet been poisoned by the West and that still remained of paramount importance for the majority of Iranians.

Shariʿahti, who had been educated in France and who shared Al-e Ahmad's convictions, also attacked the cultural "colonization" of Iran by the West. He developed the notion of a combative, dynamic Islam that he thought had been realized in the original Muslim community of Muhammad and ʿAli's era. Thus Shariʿahti imparted an entirely new quality to Twelver Shiʿism by drawing a sharp distinction between "Alid or red Shiʿism" and "Safavid or black Shiʿism." "Red Shiʿism" represents the original, uncorrupted, true Shiʿism of the Golden Age at the beginning, which constitutes an active Islam, a progressive, revolutionary movement that stood up for justice and fought all kinds of foreign domination, oppression, arbitrary despotism, and exploitation. By making it the state religion, the Safavids had reduced this Shiʿism—which had always opposed tyranny—to a mere institution, a means of political enslavement. "Black Shiʿism" is thus a depraved form of religious belief that seeks to get along with worldly despots and exploiters and has replaced holy martyrdom with the pathetic—because wholly passive—mourning of the Muharram celebrations. The notion of a combative Alid Shiʿism thus freed Shiʿism from the current petrified religious tradition and obligated all believers to engage in political action. The new, subversive content of this utopian Shiʿism expressed itself in two incisive and in fact revolutionary reinterpretations of traditional Shiʿite principles. Shariʿahti urged the whole population to act as representatives of the hidden imam and to establish here and now the realm of justice as precisely this imam had been expected to do in an eschatological future. According to this conception, the mujtahids would lose their superior position and their task would be limited to organizing revolutionary movements. Second, according to Shariʿahti, every place is Karbala, every month is Muharram, every day is ʿAshura—and this became one of the slogans of the Islamic Revolution. It means neither more nor less than that the ritual of symbolic self-sacrifice that the Shiʿites perform once a year on the day of ʿAshura should be replaced by revolutionary war, and if necessary, by actual martyrdom. Notwithstanding Shariʿahti's completely ahistorical perspective on the many past centuries of Islamic history, through belief in these ideas, traditionally unpolitical Shiʿism was transformed into a revolutionary ideology that was able to unite diverse oppositional groups that had been drawn together by their collective struggle against Western imperialism, and their hatred of the shah was its tool. In 1973, Shariʿahti was forbidden to speak in public and moved in 1977 to London, where he died the same year. The Islamic Revolution, of which both he and Al-e Ahmad may be considered the ideological forerunners, nonetheless ignored many of their originally anti-clerical and to some extent even Western-influenced ideas.

Ayatollah Ruhollah Khomeini (1902–1989) became the leader of the Islamic Revolution. "Ayatollah" (Arabic *ayat Allah*, "sign of God") is a high honorary title that can be attributed to a mujtahid. Khomeini came from a family of small landowners in the town of Khumayn (between Hamadan and Isfahan) that traced its ancestry back to the seventh imam, Musa al-Kazim. After completing his education, Khomeini became a close associate of Ayatollah Husayn Burujirdi in Qum, who was averse to engaging in any political activity. It was probably his influence that at first prevented Khomeini from taking public political positions. Only in June 1963, a year after Burujirdi's death, did Khomeini begin his direct attack on the shah; in a stirring speech he denounced the shah and the Iranian nouveaux riches as parasites on the body of the people, and openly called for resistance. In 1964, after twice being imprisoned, he was sent into exile in Turkey and finally settled in 1965 at the shrine of Najaf in Iraq, where he continued to teach and give sermons; tape recordings of his speeches, in which he called for the overthrow of the shah, circulated in great numbers and, disseminated by a well-functioning network of religious groups, elicited wide interest among the Iranian people. In October 1978, having been expelled from Iraq, Khomeini continued his propaganda activity against the shah from Neauphle-le-Château, near Paris. The fact, found astonishing by Westerners, that he was able to lead a successful revolution from such a distance can be explained if we reflect that the Shiʿite clergy had long since played oppositional roles from outside Iran; whether they did so from Najaf or Neauphle-le-Château is irrelevant.

Khomeini succeeded in calling forth in Iran a mass protest movement against the shah's dictatorship that—like the Constitutional Revolution—united a spectrum of diverse opposition groups: leftists and rightists, liberals and conservatives, intellectuals, bazaar merchants, radicals and moderate groups of clergy, as well as the great mass of impoverished former landowners now living in the slums of the great cities. These groups inevitably had different ideas about the future of Iran after the shah was overthrown. Khomeini succeeded in conveying the impression that he himself was only a rallying point and that after the revolution succeeded, he and his colleagues would return to their mosques and madrasahs without trying to establish a government. In order to maintain the external unity of the revolutionary movement, he at first avoided talking about his ideas regarding a theocratic state. Instead, he promised that the social system would be retained, with democratic freedoms and equal rights for men and women. This won him wide support, especially among Iranian women. Often these women were members of liberal or leftist groups who hoped for future democratic development in Iran, and saw the full body veil (*chadur*) as only a symbol of protest against the shah. The condition that Khomeini regularly added to his promises, namely that all this must be in accord with Islam, apparently was not sufficiently noticed. Only in the fall of 1978, at an advanced stage of the revolutionary movement, did Khomeini openly demand the establishment of an Islamic Republic.

The real trigger for the revolutionary events was a newspaper article that appeared in the government-controlled press on January 7, 1978 and that violently slandered Khomeini. This resulted in demonstrations staged by theology students that were brutally suppressed by the police. The clergy sharply condemned the government and its actions as un-

Islamic, and ordered a period of mourning for the victims, during which there were further protests. A cycle of mass demonstrations, clashes with police and military forces, followed by new demonstrations, was repeated over and over. After the shah finally left Iran in January 1979, Khomeini flew on February 1 from Paris to Tehran, where he dissolved the civilian interim adminstrtion set up by the shah and called upon the devoutly religious engineer Mehdi Bazargan to form a provisional revolutionary government, thus putting an end to the revolution.

The Islamic Republic

A referendum in March 1979 proposing the establishment of an Islamic Republic was approved—as was foreseeable—by about 97 percent of the voters. The republic was officially proclaimed on April 1 and at the beginning of the following December its new constitution was endorsed by popular vote.

According to this constitution, the Islamic Republic is a theocracy in which God is the sole ruler. Until the hidden imam returns—and this is also part of the constitution—the basic principle of the "representative governance of the jurist" (Persian *vilayat-i faqih*), which Khomeini had developed in his book *Islamic Government* (Persian *Hukumat-i Islami*, 1971) is to be applied. In this work Khomeini stipulates that direct governmental power should be in the hands of the best qualified legal jurist (*fakih*) or, in case there is no generally recognized mujtahid, of a committee of jurists who are to rule as representatives of the hidden imam until the latter's return. This goes far beyond the function of supervising the government assigned to the clergy by the 1907 amendment to the constitution, and explicitly asserts the claim that only Shiʿite legal scholars are entitled to be legitimate representatives of the hidden imam. That the clergy's representative role would lead to the exercise of actual political power is no more foreseen in traditional Shiʿism than is the office of a supreme spiritual and political leader of the Khomeini type. Both are qualitatively new and so revolutionized traditional Shiʿism that they long aroused conservative clerics to stubbornly resist such innovations.

By a plebiscite held in December 1979, Khomeini was confirmed in the office, established in the constitution, of supreme religious and political leader (Persian *rahbar*) of Iran. In addition to a Supreme Leader or Leadership Council of Shiʿite jurists, the constitution provides for a Council of Guardians composed of an equal number of religious and secular jurists, and—resuming the tenor of the 1907 amendment to the constitution—entrusts it with the task of ensuring that laws passed by the parliament are in accord with Islam. Khomeini combined in his person the office of political leader with the religious authority of a *marjaʿ*. However, since his successor would not necessarily have the same rank, a 1989 amendment to the constitution separated the office of the political leader from that of the religious leader. The religious political leader, who is at the same time the head of state, need no longer be a *mardsha*, and the current occupant of this office, Ali Khameneʾi (b. 1940), is not one. On the same occasion, the office of the prime minister was abolished and the state president given the task of leading the government; the latter's position was thus significantly strengthened.

Shortly after the revolution, the differing political interests of the various groups that had lent their common support to the movement re-emerged. Nonetheless, Khomeini succeeded in eliminating the moderate, liberal, and leftist oppositional groups that rejected the clergy's seizure of power, sidelining critical liberal clerics, and realizing his conception of a theocratic state. In particular, the leftist People's Mujahidin (Persian *Mojaihdin-i khalq*), which had been founded in 1965 as a group opposing the shah's government and which had largely contributed to the revolution's victory, carried on in the early 1980s guerrilla activities against the Islamic Revolutionary Guards Corps (IRGC) established by Khomeini, and made many assassination attempts. Two bomb attacks in June 1981 killed numerous figures who had been involved in the revolution. Now the clergy finally had their own revolutionary martyrs. The government responded to the Mujahidin's terrorist attacks with an even more comprehensive campaign of persecution that resulted in thousands of victims throughout the country, not only among the Mujahidin, but also among opposition and heterodox groups of all kinds, so that democratic protests such as strikes and demonstrations became virtually impossible until Khomeini's death. Thus after 1981 a theocratic state could be implemented. The clergy also took over the office of state president, which at first had been held by religious "laymen." After Mehdi Bazargan (d. 1995) retired from the office of prime minister in late 1979 as a result of disputes with the clergy about governmental responsibility, it came as a surprise when at the beginning of the following year Abu al-Hasan Bani-Sadr, one of Khomeini's advisors in Neauphle-le-Château, was elected the first state president of the republic. After his overthrow he fled to Paris. His successor in this office was Muhammad Ali Raja'i, a member of the Islamic Republican Party (IRP), which was loyal to Khomeini. Afterward this office was held by Ali Khamene'i (1981–1989), who in 1989 became Khomeini's successor, by Ali Akbar Rafsanjani (1989–1997), and Muhammad Khatami (1997–2005)—all three of them clerics. In 2005, in another presidential election surprise, the engineer Mahmud Ahmadinejad, a former mayor of Tehran, defeated Rafsanjani, who had been especially favored by the Western powers. He is the second Iranian state president, after Bani-Sadr, not to be a member of the clergy.

After the defeat of the opposition, the clergy tried—in the name of Islam, which it praised as the solution to any problem the country might have—to Islamize Iran's culture: penal law was implemented in conformity with Islamic religious law, women were again required to wear a veil, alcohol was prohibited; school textbooks were rewritten in accord with Islamic ideas and cookbooks were revised to comply with Qur'anic food regulations. Iraq's attack on Iran in September 1980, by which the Iraqi dictator Saddam Hussein hoped to gain control over the whole Shatt al-Arab area and the oil fields in Khuzistan, plunged Iran into an eight-year-long war that claimed countless victims on the Iranian side. However, the war made it easier for the government to impose tighter internal restrictions by appealing to the necessity of defeating the external enemy, against whom all the country's resources had to be mobilized. The significant restriction of freedom of speech, along with propaganda against a Westernized, "corrupt" elite, drove many members of the intelligentsia—about a million Iranians—to leave the country. This, combined with the closing of the universities that was connected with the war and lasted for years, seriously damaged Iranian art, culture, and science. Resentment against the West led

Khomeini to issue in February 1989, shortly before his death, a fatwa in which he condemned the British writer Salman Rushdie to death because in his book *The Satanic Verses* Rushdie had satirized the life the Prophet. This fatwa, which Khameneʾi repeated after Khomeini's death to give it continuing validity, led to a rupture of Iran's relations with Great Britain and did severe damage to its international reputation. Khomeini also contributed to the isolation of Iran, which began when Iranian students occupied the United States embassy in Tehran in 1979, by his propaganda against Israel, for whose destruction clerical leaders regularly called in speeches on domestic policy given on Jerusalem Day (the last Friday of the fasting-month of Ramadan). The repetition of this already formulaic demand by the current state president, Mahmud Ahmadinejad, on the foreign policy level is a new development that is regarded with increasing concern—not least, of course, by Israel.

Above all, Khomeini failed to prove that Iran's severe economic problems could be solved by Islamic leadership. It quickly became evident that a rapidly growing population and an increasing rural exodus could not be dealt with by religious slogans. In Tehran, the number of inhabitants rose from five to nine million during the decade 1979-1989, and by 1993 it had reached thirteen million. The war with Iraq ended in 1988 with a cease-fire that did not demand that the aggressor, Iraq, pay reparations. A few years earlier, when Iranian fighters had driven the Iraqi army back over the border, it would have been possible to negotiate such payments. But since at that time Khomeini himself had ordered that the war be continued, it was inevitable that people would eventually come to the bitter realization that many thousands of soldiers had died in vain on the battlefield.

After Khomeini's death in June 1989, Rafsanjani, who became state president when Khameneʾi took over as supreme religious leader, tried to open Iran to foreign investment. This resulted in a large influx of products—for the most part financed by foreign loans—onto the Iranian market, but because the Islamic Republic was not trusted in matters of politics and the management of the economy, the desired long-term investments were not forthcoming. Instead, imports had to be drastically reduced, causing disturbances in many Iranian cities. Iran's economic problems still await solution.

In the area of domestic policy, the new state president counted on a careful liberalization of public and cultural life, for example by alleviating censorship of the press. However, Rafsanjani's policy suffered repeated setbacks because he had constantly to struggle against the predominance of the conservative clerics. In the mid-1990s, this conservative faction intensified their attacks on the easing of restrictions achieved by reform politicians. Consequently, censorship of the press was increased, writers and newspaper editors were arrested or fled, and the possession of satellite dishes was forbidden in order to cut off "un-Islamic" foreign influences.

Even under the liberal state president Khatami, who was elected in 1997 by a large majority, the conflicts between reformers and conservatives continued. Although Khatami was the first Iranian president to visit the West, and although parliamentary elections in the year 2000 gave supporters of reform a clear majority, true power remained for the most part in the hands of the religious leader, Khamene'i, who controls the police, the secret service, and the armed forces and who has the support of the council of Guardians. These power relationships were reflected in the 2004 parliamentary elections, in advance of which the council of Guardians excluded numerous candidates (about 2,500 out of 8,200), primarily on the ground that their convictions were not—or not sufficiently—Islamic. Moreover, since many reform-minded Iranians, chiefly members of the younger generation, did not vote as a protest against the exclusion of these candidates, the victory of the conservatives and their absolute majority in the parliament were assured. President Khatami's rather timid efforts on behalf reforms that the Iranian intelligentsia had long vehemently demanded thus remained for the time being unsuccessful.

Under the new president who has been in office since 2005, the radical-conservative Ahmadinejad, the trend toward a policy in strict accord with Islam has continued in accord with Ahmadinejad's campaign promise to realize the ideals of the 1979 revolution. This promise, along with promises to resolve Iran's social problems and provide food and work for everyone, won him the votes of the poorer classes as well as those of Iranians who rejected a Western orientation of their country.

However, less than two years later Ahmadinejad got the bill for his unfulfilled promises, especially in the social area: in local elections held in December 2006, his conservative opponents were very successful, and the forces of reform also made progress. Ahmadinejad's sponsor, Ayatollah Mesbah-e Yazdi, defeated his opponent, the supposedly moderate conservative Rafsanjani.

As for Ahmadinejad's foreign policy, the conflict regarding Iran's use of nuclear power has grown more intense during his term in office. The Iranian government insists that this conflict concerns only the peaceful use of nuclear energy, but it could also concern the production of nuclear weapons, and may become more acute in the future. In the 1980s Iran had already begun a nuclear program coordinated by Rafsanjani and further developed during his presidency. Understandably, the West is concerned about the uncontrolled proliferation of nuclear weapons, especially when they are in the hands of a regime that the West considers unpredictable. In the Iranian view, the international configuration of power requires Iran to be capable of effectively protecting itself against potential aggressors. Iran, which has not engaged in an aggressive war for more than a cen-tury and half but in the recent past has suffered under massive outside influence to the point of losing territory, currently sees itself—directly or indirectly—surrounded by nuclear powers (Israel, Pakistan, India, Russia, China) and American military bases (in Turkey, Afghanistan, and parts of the former Central Asian Soviet republics). In addition, the war conducted in Iraq by the United States and Great Britain since 2003 has led many Iranians to conclude that their country is surrounded on all sides by enemies and that it must be prepared to defend itself. Even President Khatami, who was seen in the West as a reformer, pursued a hard-line national foreign policy on this issue with respect to what seemed in Iran to be an arrogant intervention on the part of the West. Many Iranians, who reject the current regime, are inclined to back it on the nuclear issue because of their national patriotic feeling.

Women in Modern Iran

In Iran, the first movements toward equal rights for women, based on the unquestioned equality of men and women before God in Islam, go back to the turn of the twentieth century. They were triggered by the confrontation with Western ideas in the late nineteenth century, and at that time involved chiefly educated and influential women from the upper classes or the royal house. Thus, for example, many women from Nasir al-Din Shah's harem joined the tobacco boycott of 1890–1892. During the Constitutional Revolution of 1905–1911, champions of the women's movement, once again from the upper classes, organized themselves into groups and, supported by many male intellectuals, wrote newspaper and magazine articles advocating women's rights. However, under pressure from the clergy, most of the periodicals devoted to the women's movement had to suspend publication until about 1920. Nevertheless, between 1906 and 1910, again despite resistance from conservative clerics, about fifty schools for girls were opened in Tehran. Although up to that point all efforts to improve the lot of women had been based on private initiative, this situation radically changed under the Pahlavis. In 1935, under the rule of Reza Shah, a state-sponsored Women's Center (Persian *Qanun-i Banuvan*) was founded most of whose members had participated in the women's movement. The government was able to suppress by force the resulting outburst of clerical resistance, but it subsequently flared up again and again. As a counter-reaction, women's associations were established privately, as they had been before Reza Shah, and these associations pursued their goals by publishing periodicals advocating women' rights. Above all, female suffrage, which had been an issue ever since the Constitutional Revolution, was repeatedly demanded, but because of clerical resistance it was not granted until 1963, in the framework of the White Revolution. In 1966, fifty-five women's associations were merged in the Women's Organization of Iran (Persian *Sazman-i Zanan-i Iran*) founded under the patronage of Princess Ashraf, Muhammad Reza Pahlavi's twin sister. This organization achieved considerable progress for women, for example, an increase in the minimum age for marriage, measures making it easier for women to get divorces, the legalization of abortion, and a special provision prohibiting a husband from taking a second wife without his first wife's consent. With the exception of female suffrage, nearly all these rights prescribed by the government were revoked after the 1979 revolution, and the wearing of the veil was again made obligatory. At first, the most that could be achieved in the new Islamic Republic was to obtain a certain freedom of action for women. The eight-year war with Iraq (1980–1988) made it necessary to admit women to the world of work and professional activity. Thus at the beginning of the 1990s the debate over equal rights for women was resumed, and many restrictions have in the meantime been toned down, though not the obligation to wear the veil in public. Various women's periodicals reflect new trends seeking to reinterpret Islam in such a way as to bring it into harmony with the modern democratic world or to approach "scientifically" the problem of the inequality of women and by means of Qurʾanic exegesis show that in the holy book of Islam no gender-specific discrimination is implied. These publications promote political engagement on the part of Iranian women, whose votes made a decisive contribution to the election of the reformer Khatami to the presidency. It has to be said that moderate clerics do support greater freedoms for women. In the long run, the 1979 revolution has thus produced a new women's movement that is specifically Iranian and largely free of foreign influences. One of its outstanding figures is the attorney Shirin ʿEbadi (b. 1947), who was awarded the Nobel Peace Prize in December 2003 for her activities on behalf of human rights and the improvement of the position of women in Iran. ʿEbadi also regards her work as firmly rooted in Islam, since—as she emphasized in her Nobel Prize acceptance speech—Iran's serious shortcomings with regard to human rights and the situation of women should not be blamed on Islam, but rather on a mistaken interpretation of the Qurʾan. In 2006, another movement considerably more distant from Islam launched the "One Million Signatures Campaign Demanding an End to Discriminatory Laws against Women." According to its organizers, this campaign is neither Islamic nor secularist, and is concerned solely with ensuring equal treatment for men and women. The future of the Iranian women's movement remains for the time being uncertain.

Future Prospects

With the success of the Islamic Revolution, Iran's long tradition of monarchy, which seems to have become obsolete under the Pahlavis, has apparently come to a final end. The attempt, unique in the Islamic world, to set up an Islamic Republic under the aegis of Shi'sm has not yet come to an end. Much will depend on whether it succeeds in solving Iran's urgent economic problems and in creating some kind of partnership with the West. There are several ways to carry out these multi-leveled tasks, ranging from closer cooperation with the West, especially on the economic level, to completely sealing off the country and seeking to create an autarkic economy based on Islam.

How and whether it will prove possible to reconcile these divergent tendencies in an Iranian state cannot at this point be determined. But whatever Iran's future development, one thing seems certain: although parts of Iranian society may be alienated from the current regime, for the majority of Iranians Islam is still inseparable from Iranian identity. Therefore a democracy based entirely on the Western model, in which Islam would have a merely subordinate role, will probably not be established in Iran in the foreseeable future.

Chronology

632	Death of the Prophet Muhammad in Medina.
632–661	Age of the four "righteous caliphs": Abu Bakr (reigned 632-634), ʿUmar (reigned 634-644), Uthman (reigned 644-656), ʿAli (reigned 656-661).
642	Muslim victory in the Battle of Nihavand leads to the conquest of Iran.
651	Assassination of the last Sasanian king, Yazdgard III.
661–749	Umayyad caliphate with its center in Damascus.
680	Battle of Karbala; death (martyrdom) of the third imam, Husayn.
749–1258	ʿAbbasid caliphate with its center in Baghdad, founded 762.
821–873	Tahirids in Khurasan, the first autonomous Islamic dynasty on Iranian soil. 867–903 Safarids in Sistan; 867-901, rule over almost all Iran.
892–999	Samanids in Transoxania and Khurasan; center in Bukhara.
945–1055	Buyids in Iraq and Iran; 945, conquest of Baghdad; greatest extent of the empire under Adud al-Dawla (reigned 978-983).
977–1186	Ghaznavids in Khurasan, Afghanistan, and North India; greatest extent of the empire under Mahmud of Ghazna (ruled 998-1030).
1040–1195	Saljuqs; 1055, conquest of Baghdad; greatest extent of the empire under Malik-Shah (reigned 1073-1092) in Iraq and Iran.
1071	Saljuq victory over Byzantium at the Battle of Manzikert opens up Anatolia for Islam.
1090–1256	Ismaʿili sect of the Assassins takes control of Alamut Fortress in the Alburz Mountains; Hasan-i Sabbah (d. 1124) leader of the Ismaʿilis.
1092	Assassination of the Saljuq vizier Nizam al-Mulk.
1200–20	Khwarazm shahs; 1200-1220, rule over all Iran and Transoxania.
1219–24	Mongols under Genghis Khan (d. 1227) devastate Transoxania and Iran.
1256–1335	Rule of the Mongol Il-Khans in Iran.
1258	Overthrow of the Baghdad caliphate by the Il-Khan Hülegü.

1295	The Il-Khan Ghazan (reigned 1295-1304) converts to Islam; Islam becomes once again the principle of rulership.
1370–1405	Timur's campaign of conquest in Transoxania and Iran.
1380–1469	Kara Koyunlu (Turkmen tribal confederation) in northern and central Iran; greatest extent of the empire under Jihan Shah (reigned 1438-1467).
1396–1508	Ak Koyunlu (Turkmen tribal confederation) in eastern Anatolia and Iran; greatest extent of the empire under Uzun Hasan (reigned 1501-1534).
1405–1506	Rule of the Timurids in Transoxania and Iran.
1501	Isma'il I (reigned 1501–1524) conquers Tabriz and proclaims Twelver Shi'ism as the state religion of Iran.
1501–1722	Safavids in Iran; centers in Tabriz, Qazvin, and Isfahan.
1514	Safavids defeated by Ottoman artillery at the Battle of Chaldiran.
1639	By the Treaty of Zuhab (Qasr-i Shirin), Iran loses Iraq and the Shi'ite shrines to the Ottoman Empire.
1722	The Afghan Ghalzais attack Iran; abdication of the last Safavid shah, Sultan Husayn (reigned 1694-1722).
1722–36	Nadir Khan drives back the Afghans; nominal rule of two Safavid princes.
1736–96	Nadir Shah (reigned 1736-1747) and his descendants (Afsharids) in Iran; after 1750, only in northern and central Iran.
1750–94	Southern Iran under the Iranian Zand dynasty; center in Shiraz.
1779–1925	Qajars in Iran; center in Tehran.
1801–13	First war between Russia and Iran; 1813, Treaty of Golestan, by which Iran loses large areas of the Caucasus to Russia.
1826–28	Second war between Russia and Iran; the Treaty of Turkmanchay (1828) and further territorial losses in the Caucasus establish the present border with Russia.
1857	By the Treaty of Paris Nasir al-Din Shah Qajar agrees to recognize the independence of Afghanistan.
1872	Partition of the province of Sistan between Iran and Afghanistan.
1879	Establishment of the Persian Cossack Brigade.
1891–92	Tobacco boycott.

1906	Victory of the Constitutional Revolution; first parliamentary elections and signing of the constitution for a constitutional monarchy.
1907	Signing of amendments to the constitution.
1911	End of the Constitutional Revolution; the constitution is suspended.
1925–79	Pahlavi dynasty: Reza Shah (reigned 1925-1941), Muhammad Reza Shah (reigned 1941-1979).
1951–53	Muhammad Mosaddeq attempts to nationalize the Iranian oil industry.
1963	In June, Ayatollah Ruhollah Khomeini (1902-1989) calls for resistance to the shah; shah has subsequent popular protests put down.
1971	Celebration in Persepolis of 2,500 years of Iranian Monarchy.
1979	Islamic Revolution and overthrow of the shah. April 1, official proclamation of the Islamic Republic of Iran; December 2-3, adoption of the constitution by plebiscite.
1980–88	Iran-Iraq war.
1989	Death of Ayatollah Khomeini. Revision of the constitution.
1997	Election of Muhammad Khatami as the fifth president of the Islamic Republic.
2005	Election of Mahmud Ahmadinejad as the sixth president of the Islamic Republic.

Selected Bibliography

General Reference Works

Bosworth, Clifford E. *The New Islamic Dynasties. A Chronological and Genealogical Manual.* Edinburgh 1996.
The Cambridge History of Iran, vols. IV–VII. Ed. J. A. Boyle. Cambridge 1968-1993.
Encyclopaedia Iranica. Ed. Ehsan Yarshaher. New York 1982– 2001 (thus far, thirteen volumes reaching as far as the letter "I" have appeared).
Encyclopaedia of Islam (new edition). Selected articles. 12 vols. (complete). Leiden 1960 –2004.

Works on Iranian History

Abrahamian, Ervand. *Iran Between Two Revolutions.* Princeton 1982.
Alfons, Gabriel. *Die Erforschung Persiens. Die Entwicklung der abendländischen Kenntnis der Geographie Persiens.* Vienna 1952.
Algar, Hamid. *Religion and State in Iran 1785–1906. The Role of the Ulama in the Qajar Period.* Berkeley/Los Angeles 1969.
Amanat, ʿAbbas. *Pivot of the Universe. Nasir al-Din Shah Qajar and the Iranian Monarchy, 1831–1896.* London/New York 1997.
Amir Arjomand, Said. *The Turban and the Crown. The Islamic Revolution in Iran.* New York/Oxford 1988.
Avery, Peter. *Modern Iran.* London 1965.
Bakhash, Shaul. *Iran: Monarchy, Bureaucracy & Reform under the Qajars.* Oxford/London 1978.
Bosworth, Clifford E. *The Ghaznavids. Their Empire in Afghanistan and Eastern Iran 994 –1040.* 2nd ed. Beirut 1973.
Bosworth, Clifford E. *The Later Ghaznavids. Splendour and Decay. The Dynasty in Afghanistan and Northern India 1040– 1186.* Edinburgh 1977.
Buchta, Wilfried. *Who Rules Iran? The Structure of Power in the Islamic Republic.* Washington, D.C. 2000.
Frye, Richard N. *The Golden Age of Persia. The Arabs in the East.* London 1975, 2nd ed. 1977.
Halm, Heinz. *Die Schia.* Darmstadt 1988.
Halm, Heinz. *Der schiitische Islam. Von der Religion zur Revolution.* Munich 1994.
Halm, Heinz. *Der Islam.* Munich 1999, 4th ed. 2002.
Hooglund, Eric, ed. *Twenty Years of Islamic Revolution: Political and Social Transition in Iran since 1979.* Contemporary Issues in the Middle East. Syracuse, NY, 2002.
Iran. Natur – Bevölkerung – Geschichte – Kultur – Staat – Wirtschaft. Ed. Ulrich Gehrke and Harald Mehner. 2nd ed. Tübingen/Basel, 1976.

Keddie, Nikki R. (in collaboration with Yann Richard). *Roots of Revolution. An Interpretive History of Modern Iran.* New Haven/London 1981.
Keddie, Nikki R. *Qajar Iran and the Rise of Reza Khan, 1796– 1925.* Costa Mesa 1999.
Lambton, Ann K. *Landlord and Peasant in Persia. A Study of Land Tenure and Land Revenue Administration.* London/New York/Toronto 1953.
Lambton, Ann K. *Continuity and Change in Medieval Persia. Aspects of Administration, Economic and Social History, 11th–14th Century.* London 1988.
Lockhart, L. *Nadir Shah. A Critical Study Based Mainly Upon Contemporary Sources.* London 1938.
Löschner, Harald. *Die dogmatischen Grundlagen des schi'itischen Rechts.* Erlangen/Nürnberg 1971.
Manz, Beatrice F. *The Rise and Rule of Tamerlane.* Cambridge 1989.
Matthee, Rudolph P. *The Politics of Trade in Safavid Iran. Silk for Silver, 1600 –1730.* Cambridge 1999.
Migeod, Heinz-Georg. *Die persische Gesellschaft unter Nâsiru'd-Dîn âh (1848-1896).* Berlin 1990.
The Mongol Empire and Its Legacy. Ed. Reuven Amitai-Preiss and David O. Morgan. Leiden/Boston/Köln 1999.
Morgan, David O. *Medieval Persia 1040 –1797.* London/New York 1988.
Richard, Yann. *Der verborgene Imam. Die Geschichte des Schiismus im Iran.* Berlin 1983.
Röhrborn, Klaus-Michael. *Provinzen und Zentralgewalt Persiens im 16. und 17. Jahrhundert.* Berlin 1966.
Roschanzamir, Mehdi. *Die Zand-Dynastie.* Hamburg 1970.
Rubin, Michael. *Into the Shadows: Radical Vigilantes in Khatami's Iran.* Policy Papers 56. Washington D.C., 2001.
Savory, Roger. *Iran under the Safavids.* Cambridge 1980.
Smith, Peter. *The Babi and Baha'i Religions: From Messianic Shi'ism to a World Religion.* Cambridge 1987.
Spuler, Bertold: *Die Mongolen in Iran. Politik, Verwaltung und Kultur der Ilchanzeit 1220 –1350.* 4th ed. Leiden, 1985.
Spuler, Bertold. *Iran in früh-islamischer Zeit. Politik, Kultur, Verwaltung und öffentliches Leben zwischen der arabischen und der seldschukischen Eroberung 633–1055.* Wiesbaden 1952.
Taheri, Amir. *The Spirit of Allah: Khomeini and the Islamic Revolution.* London 1985.

www.ingramcontent.com/pod-product-compliance
Lightning Source LLC
Chambersburg PA
CBHW020941230426
43666CB00005B/113